SEATTLE
AC

D0484790

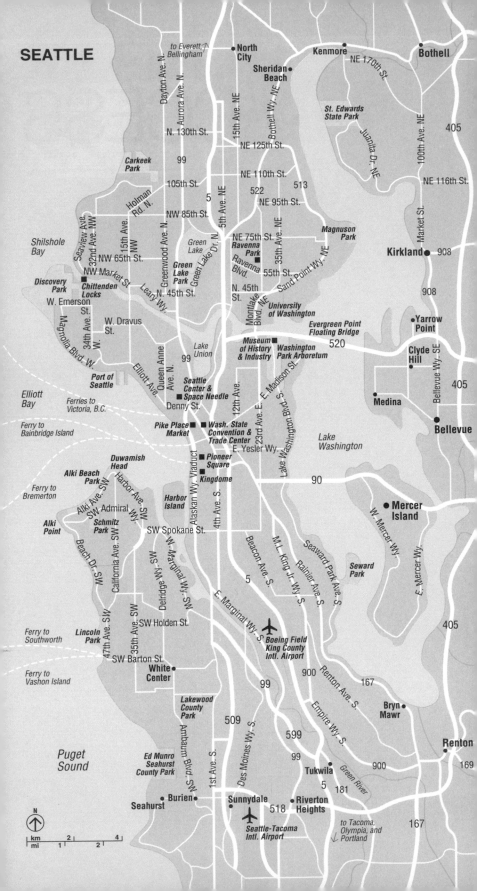

Orientation

In November 1851, when city founder Arthur Denny and his party of 23 anchored in a rainstorm off what is now **West Seattle**, they dubbed their new home *New York-Alki*, Chinook for "New York By-and-By." This bit of wishful thinking came to seem prophetic more than a century later when, in 1989, the city's skyline had grown so tall and dense that height-restrictive building codes had to be instituted. Fueled by the national media and wallet-waving tourists, both of whom "discovered" the city during the 1980s, the area's population grew by 18 percent (twice the national average) during that decade. Attracted by low unemployment and exponential growth in the high-tech industries, its reputation for cleanliness and safety, and an innovative and enthusiastic arts community, people from as far away as Vietnam and as nearby as Los Angeles flocked to Seattle. The newcomers couldn't shut the entry gates behind them fast enough to safeguard what they'd found, but the influx could not be stemmed. Housing prices shot up, and residents started to fret that air pollution, not just fog or rain clouds, was obscuring the city's noble vistas.

And the panoramas are noble indeed, filled with breathtaking beauty. There are the sharp peaks of the **Cascade** and **Olympic Mountains** embracing the city from the east and west, neighboring **Puget Sound** aswim with giant octopuses and killer whales, sparkling downtown towers of white terracotta, all seen through the drizzle of winter . . . and spring . . . and fall . . . and sometimes summer. In *Another Roadside Attraction,* Tom Robbins, a resident of nearby La Conner, Washington, describes the Puget Sound basin as having "a blurry beauty (as if the Creator started to erase it but had second thoughts)." And though Seattle hates to be called mellow, life among its 518,000 or so residents remains relatively calm; after all, it's mostly ferries—rather than more expeditious bridges—that carry commuters across the water to the city.

Visitors, too, should take their time enjoying the city. Not the mythological Seattle of rain-washed skies and leaping salmon, but the real city, which is so much more interesting. Without doubt, the city's most popular attraction is the lively almost-90-year-old **Pike Place Market**, where there's far more color than just that of the carrots, crabs, and chrysanthemums for sale by the more than 600 merchants. **Pioneer Square**, with cobblestone streets and 19th-century brick buildings, was the city's original downtown (before it was decimated in the Great Fire of 1889) and is now home to many art galleries and boutiques. North and west, through the **Business District**'s high-rise office buildings, is the **Seattle Center**, a futuristic remnant of the 1962 World's Fair, complete with the **Space Needle** and **Alweg Monorail**. Architecture buffs might want to wander the streets of **Capitol Hill** or **Queen Anne**, and bibliophiles may head for the **University District**'s many bookstores and cafes. Hikers and cyclists can meander the city's many areas of green—there are nearly 5,000 acres of parks spread from one end of Seattle to the other. The watersports' enthusiast can also find lots of activities—from windsurfing on **Green Lake** to sailing from **Shilshole Marina** in **Ballard**. And, finally, back to West Seattle, where it all began, where the **High Point**, literally the highest point in the city, affords skyline views of the self-proclaimed "Emerald City" in its splendid setting of mountains and sea.

M. BLUM

Space Needle

How To Read This Guide

SEATTLEACCESS® is arranged by neighborhood so you can see at a glance where you are and what is around you. The numbers next to the entries in the following chapters correspond to the numbers on the maps. The text is color-coded according to the kind of place described:

Restaurants/Clubs: Red   **Hotels:** Blue

Shops/ 🌳 Outdoors: Green **Sights/Culture:** Black

Rating the Restaurants and Hotels

The restaurant star ratings take into account the quality, service, atmosphere, and uniqueness of the restaurant. An expensive restaurant doesn't necessarily ensure an enjoyable evening; however, a small, relatively unknown spot could have good food, professional service, and a lovely atmosphere. Therefore, on a purely subjective basis, stars are used to judge the overall dining value (see the star ratings below). Keep in mind that chefs and owners often change, which sometimes drastically affects the quality of a restaurant. The ratings in this guidebook are based on information available at press time.

The price ratings, as categorized below, apply to restaurants and hotels. These figures describe general price-range relationships among other restaurants and hotels in the area. The restaurant price ratings are based on the average cost of an entrée for one person, excluding tax and tip. Hotel price ratings reflect the base price of a standard room for two people for one night during the peak season.

Restaurants

★	Good	
★★	Very Good	
★★★	Excellent	
★★★★	An Extraordinary Experience	
$	The Price Is Right	(less than $10)
$$	Reasonable	($10-$25)
$$$	Expensive	($25-$35)
$$$$	Big Bucks	($35 and up)

Hotels

$	The Price Is Right	(less than $80)
$$	Reasonable	($80-$120)
$$$	Expensive	($120-$180)
$$$$	Big Bucks	($180 and up)

Map Key

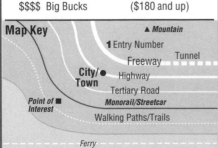

▲ Mountain
1 Entry Number
Freeway   Tunnel
City/ ● Highway
Town
Tertiary Road
Point of ■   Monorail/Streetcar
Interest
Walking Paths/Trails
Ferry

Area code 206 unless otherwise noted.

Getting to Seattle

Airport

Seattle-Tacoma International Airport (SEA)

This sprawling airport—also known as "Sea-Tac"—sits 13 miles south of Seattle. The layout is simple: a main terminal with four concourses, and two satellite terminals. An efficient subway connects the main terminal with the satellites; be sure to allow an extra 15 minutes to reach the outlying gates.

Airport Emergencies	433.5385
Business Service Center	242.6977
Currency Exchange	243.1231
Customs	553.4676
Ground Transportation	431.5904
Immigration	553.5956
Information	431.4444
Interpreters	433.5367
Lost and Found	433.5312
Parking	431.4444
Police	433.5400
Traveler's Aid	461.3888

Airlines

Air Canada	800/776.3000
Alaska Airlines	800/426.0333
American Airlines	800/433.7300
America West	800/235.9292
British Airways	800/247.9297
Continental Airlines	800/525.0280
Delta Air Lines	800/221.1212
Northwest Airlines	800/225.2525
TWA	800/447.9400
United Airlines	800/241.6522

Getting to and from the Airport

By Car

The airport is about a half-hour drive from downtown, except during peak traffic periods (between 3PM and 6PM on most days) when the trip can take up to an hour.

To get to downtown Seattle from **Sea-Tac,** take Freeway 518 east to connect with Interstate 5 north; for the **Eastside** take Freeway 518, which becomes Interstate 405. There are well-marked exits all along the way.

To get to the airport from downtown, head south on Interstate 5, or take Interstate 405 south (becoming Freeway 518) from the east. Long-term and short-term parking lots are within easy walking distance of the main terminal.

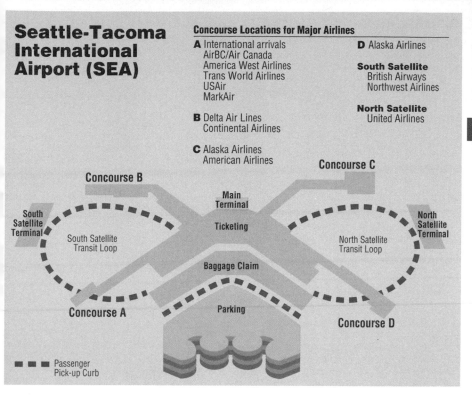

Seattle-Tacoma International Airport (SEA)

Concourse Locations for Major Airlines

A International arrivals
AirBC/Air Canada
America West Airlines
Trans World Airlines
USAir
MarkAir

B Delta Air Lines
Continental Airlines

C Alaska Airlines
American Airlines

D Alaska Airlines

South Satellite
British Airways
Northwest Airlines

North Satellite
United Airlines

Concourse B

Concourse C

Main Terminal

Ticketing

South Satellite Terminal

South Satellite Transit Loop

North Satellite Terminal

North Satellite Transit Loop

Baggage Claim

Concourse A

Parking

Concourse D

■ ■ ■ Passenger Pick-up Curb

By Bus and Shuttle

Gray Line Airport Express (626.6088) buses leave every 15 minutes from 5AM to midnight and drop off passengers at 11 downtown hotels. Return trips to the airport run daily from 5AM to 11:30PM; departure times depend on the stop. The trip takes about about 50 minutes. One-way adult fare is $7; round-trip is $12. Reservations are not necessary.

Metro Transit's (553.3000) *No. 194* bus runs to the airport, a half-hour trip that leaves from the downtown **Metro Bus Tunnel** (Pine St, between Third and Fourth Aves) about every 30 minutes. The *No. 174* bus, departing from **Second Avenue** downtown, also goes out to the airport every half-hour (a 45-minute excursion).

Shuttle Express (622.1424, 800/487.7433) operates 24-hour, door-to-door service for $16 (one way) to Seattle, $21 to the east side of **Lake Washington.** Note: Two people traveling together cost only a few dollars more than one. Reservations are essential when traveling to the airport, but are not required on the way into town. One warning: the company's policy is to get you to the airport *at least* an hour in advance of your flight.

Car Rental

Alamo	433.0182, 800/327.9633
Avis	433.5231, 800/331.1212
Budget	682.2277, 800/527.0700
Dollar	433.6777, 800/421.6868
Enterprise	243.4257, 800/325.8007
General	433.6777, 800/327.7607
Hertz	439.9199, 800/654.3131
National	433.5501, 800/227.7368
Sears	224.7888, 800/527.0770
Thrifty	246.7565, 800/367.2277

By Limousine

Those who prefer private car service can make arrangements with **Carey Limousine** (762.3517, 800/526.0554) or **Washington Limousine** (523.8000).

By Taxi

There are usually taxis waiting at the airport for passengers; if not, pick up one of the "hot line" phones outside the baggage claim area. Fare to downtown Seattle is about $25 one way, excluding tip.

Bus Station

The terminal for **Greyhound** (628.5526, 800/231.2222) buses is at 811 Stewart Street, between Eighth and Ninth Avenues.

Train Station

Long-distance train service is provided by **Amtrak** (382.4120, 800/872.7245); there are daily arrivals and departures from **King Street Station** at Third Avenue South and South Jackson Street.

Getting around Seattle

Bicycles

Most of Seattle and the suburbs are laced with bicycle routes, clearly marked with the universal two-wheel bike trail symbol. Cyclists have several scenic recreational options; chief among them are **Myrtle Edwards Park** (see page 84) and the **Burke-Gilman Trail** (see page 168). Bikes can be rented from **Gregg's Greenlake Cycle** (7007 Woodlawn Ave NE, at Second Ave NE, 523.1822); information about bicycle routes can be obtained from **Gregg's** or **REI** sporting goods' emporium (1525 11th Ave E, at E Pine St, 323.8333).

Buses

Negotiating the streets of Seattle aboard **Metro Transit** buses is easy, but long trips may require transfers and taking a lengthy detour through downtown. Service is free in the commercial core (bounded by the **Waterfront** on the west, I-5 on the east, **Jackson Street** to the south, and **Battery Street** to the north) from 6AM to 7PM daily. But beyond that, a two-zone system charges 85¢ within the city ($1.10 at peak times, Monday through Friday from 6AM to 9AM and 3PM to 6PM) and $1.10 if you travel beyond the city limits ($1.60 at peak times). Heading out of downtown, pay when you get off; going in, pay when you board. Drivers don't carry change, so have the correct amount in hand or overpay in dollar bills.

Bus stops (identifiable by their yellow-and-white signs) are usually posted with current timetables, but schedules are also available aboard the buses and at most public locations around town, including libraries and shopping malls. The buses are generally clean, comfortable, and on time. About 70 percent are wheelchair accessible, and some even sport exterior bicycle mounts (you'll see them on the fronts of buses; the drivers usually like to hook your bike up for you). Drivers can be quite garrulous, launching into tour monologues as they pilot through the city or, during particularly bad winter slowdowns, engaging their passengers in a chorus or two of "Let It Snow."

An L-shaped bus tunnel, designed to shave a whopping five minutes off the time necessary to travel through the congested downtown traffic, was completed beneath the commercial core in 1990. There are a total of five entrances between the **Washington State Convention & Trade Center** and the **International District.** Call **Metro Transit**'s help line (553.3000) for trip-planning information 24 hours a day.

Driving

Residents of Seattle voted back in the late 1960s to pump money into more freeways, rather than into mass transit—a big mistake. Today, even the most reserved Seattleites have begun to honk their car horns downtown, as the cumulative swell of bicycle couriers, buses, cabs, and pedestrians forces motorists to play dodge between red lights. Beware especially of the human crush at **Pike Place Market,** where pedestrians always enjoy the right-of-way.

Even some outlying routes, such as **45th Street** between **Wallingford** and the University District, **Broadway** on Capitol Hill, and **Lake City Way** rounding Lake Washington's upper reaches, crawl on weekday afternoons. And it's a wonder there haven't been riots in front of the **Fremont Bridge,** which opens to allow boats passage through the Lake Washington Ship Canal while overheating cars are forced to wait.

Freeway traffic snarls here don't yet rival LA, but they're close: the average commuter takes about 30 minutes to drive into downtown, and even that sounds zippy to some folks living east of Lake Washington. The average speed during rush hours is 22 mph, and peak-period delays are only expected to worsen. The two floating bridges that cross Lake Washington are particularly congested. Express lanes relieve some of the pressure north of downtown along I-5; and there are High-Occupancy Vehicle lanes (for cars carrying more than two or three people) on both I-5 and westbound on the 520 Freeway. Highway 99, or Aurora Avenue, remains a decent alternative to I-5. In general, however, you're better off avoiding freeways and highways in Seattle from 6AM to 9AM and 3PM to 6PM.

Ferries

Perhaps the most memorable sound in Seattle is the moan of ferry horns on a fog-cloaked evening. The **Washington State Ferry System** is the nation's largest, carrying some 18 million passengers a year over nine routes. The busiest run on weekdays is between **Bainbridge Island** and downtown Seattle, a 25-minute commuter chug. On weekends, and especially during the summer, the **Edmonds-Kingston Ferry** is shoehorned full of tourists, and it's not uncommon to wait three hours for car space on ferries from **Anacortes** (about 90 minutes north of Seattle) bound for **Victoria, British Columbia.**

Walk-ons stand a better chance than drivers of catching their boat of choice. Most passengers pay a round-trip fare up front, and costs vary according to distance. Food and beverages on the boats are mediocre at best, so you may want to pack something to snack on. Credit cards are not accepted, and travelers headed for Canada must have a passport or other proper identification. Schedules change from winter to summer; call 464.6400 or 800/843.3779 for current departure times and rates.

Monorail

Built for the 1962 World's Fair, the **Alweg Monorail** (its official moniker) runs only a 90-second, 1.2-mile route from downtown's **Westlake Center** to the old World's Fair grounds, now the **Seattle Center.** It's great for children, who love the train's smooth and uninterrupted ride. Adults pay 80¢ one way, $1.60 round-trip; kids ages 5 to 12 go for 60¢ ($1.20 round-trip), and children under 5 ride free. Seniors and riders with disabilities pay 25¢ one way, 50¢ round-trip. Trains depart every 15 minutes from 9AM to midnight during the summer; in winter they run until 9PM on weeknights and until midnight on Friday and Saturday. Call 684.7200 for more information.

Parking

There are numerous covered garages and open-air lots throughout the city. Facilities like the **Kingdome** and **Husky Stadium** have their own lots, as do most downtown hotels. Centrally located garages charge up to $8 per day; less expensive ones are located on the fringes of downtown—along **Alaskan Way** on the Waterfront, in the International District, and near **First** and **Bell Streets.** Free parking options in the city are relegated to the rim areas—at the southern end of the Waterfront near **Jackson Street,** for instance, or on **Elliott Avenue** bordering **Myrtle Edwards Park.** Closer to downtown, most meters offer only a half-hour's time, and many others (marked in yellow) are off-limits except to delivery vehicles. Beware of parking infractions: An overtime parking ticket costs about $20; for parking in a truck-loading zone the charge is a little higher; and parking illegally in a handicapped-only spot results in a $50 ticket.

Taxis

There are about 2,300 cabs in King County, and they're a fairly cheap means of transport, but they're controlled by dispatchers and almost impossible to hail from the street. They usually can be picked up at the bigger downtown hotels (especially the **Four Seasons Olympic Hotel** and the **Westin**), as well as at the **King Street** train station. Otherwise, call; one will arrive in anywhere from 10 to 30 minutes. Companies include: **Broadway Cab** (622.4800), **Checker Deluxe Cab** (622.1234), **Farwest Taxi** (329.7700), and **Yellow Cab** (622.6500). **STITA** (246.9999) is a cooperative cab enterprise offering transportation between downtown and the airport.

Tours

The city's most popular tour is **Underground Seattle** (682.4646), an hour-long excursion literally beneath the streets of Pioneer Square. When this district was rebuilt after the Great Fire of 1889, the decision was made to raise this land higher above water level to improve drainage and expand buildable acreage. To allow for this regrading, structures adopted double sets of entrances—one at the original ground level and another one story up, where sidewalks eventually would be laid. This all seemed fine but, as it turned out, the streets were raised long before the sidewalks could be elevated to meet them. Victorian ladies and gents, therefore, had to scale tall ladders just to cross from one side of the street to the other. Strolling in the neighborhood at night was a particular hazard, given the shortage of streetlamps. Engineers finally made the roads and the sidewalks even, but they did so without destroying the lower-level pedestrian ways. The remaining "underground city" was condemned in the early 1900s, but for many years after, it was the province of the criminal element. Not until the 1970s did a local historian and author, the late Bill Speidel, win the permits he needed to conduct public tours of those all-but-forgotten corridors. Docents today have a somewhat corny spiel, and the mustiness below ground can be daunting, but for history buffs this trip is worth it.

Tours leave from **Doc Maynard's Public House** (610 First Ave, between James and Cherry Sts) and last about 1.5 hours; they're available from late morning until mid-afternoon most days of the year; reservations are recommended.

Chinatown Discovery Tours (236.0657) escorts visitors through Seattle's International District, taking in such attractions as a fortune-cookie factory and an herb dispensary, and breaking for a dim sum lunch. **City Hunt** (625.0607) organizes interactive tours of the city that are a cross between treasure hunts and self-guided walking tours in which clues are provided to guide visitors from site to site. In addition to a tour providing an overview of downtown Seattle, there's an art hunt, a bicycle tour, and a progressive-dinner restaurant experience. **Gray Line** (626.5208) offers a variety of sight-seeing excursions, including runs along Seattle's waterways and, in the summer, out to **Mount Rainier,** and deep into "Twin Peaks" country (**Snoqualmie Falls** and the tiny town of **North Bend**). **Argosy** (623.1445) schedules cruises through the **Hiram Chittenden Locks** and around **Lake Washington** and historic **Elliott Bay.** And the Seattle Architectural Foundation and the local chapter of the American Institute of Architects cosponsor **Viewpoints Tours** (448.0106), a guided series that explores the historic architecture of various neighborhoods; it's available from May through November.

Brochures for most tour companies can be found at the tourist information booth on the galleria level of the **Washington State Convention & Trade Center** (800 Convention Pl, at Eighth Ave and Pike St), and at **Sea-Tac International Airport** (lower concourse, baggage claim area).

Trolley

Seattle's real trolleys were stripped from service decades ago, but **Metro Transit** (553.3000) has imported vintage machines from Australia to make the 15-minute trip along the Waterfront from **Pier 70** through Pioneer Square to the International District. The fare is $1.10 Monday through Friday from 3PM to 6PM; 85¢ all other times; children under 5 ride free.

Walking

Long city blocks, some daunting hills, and the polar separation of Seattle's two principal tourist meccas, Pioneer Square and **Pike Place Market,** make downtown an area best taken in small doses—take a bus from one point of interest to another, and then walk around in that immediate area. There's an impressive diversity of architecture and street life in the city, but green spaces are mostly relegated to the neighborhoods, with little open space downtown; it's basically concrete canyons between **Cherry** and **Pike Streets.**

Neighborhoods offer better strolling opportunities, particularly along **Broadway** on Capitol Hill, along **Market Street** in Ballard, and down **University Avenue** in the University District. On the suburban Eastside, only downtown **Kirkland** boasts enough sites within a small area to be walkable.

FYI

Accommodations

In addition to the individual hotel and bed-and-breakfast listings in each chapter, there are general reservations services available that help match visitors' needs to available properties. The **Seattle Hotel Hotline** (800/535.7071) offers one-stop shopping for price and location of city hotels. **A Pacific Reservation Service** (784.0539) lists over 200 bed-and-breakfasts, cottages, condos, and guest houses in Seattle and throughout the Pacific Northwest. Both services are provided free of charge and operate from 9AM to 5PM Monday through Friday.

Climate

The predictions of local meteorologists are often studies in equivocation, along the lines of "partial sunshine, followed by partial low-cloudiness, and maybe turning to showers in the afternoon." Look out your window for an accurate assessment, but remember that the weather you're experiencing may be quite different from what's going on only two miles away. Warm offshore currents, mountains, and cold fronts from the north conspire to give Seattle a changeable but fairly moderate climate. July and August are the warmest months of the year, with relative humidity of 50 percent, and usually no more than an inch or so of rain. Winter is wetter with an average of five inches of rain each month, but the temperature is warm enough to make snow and ice infrequent; when they do hit, however, the city turns into a huge frozen sculpture and traffic stops dead in its tracks.

Months	Average Temperature Range (°F)
December-January	46
March-May	58
June-August	73
September-November	53

Drinking

Washington's legal drinking age is 21. Bars usually stay open until 2AM, and wine and beer are available at most supermarkets and groceries. Hard liquor must be purchased at one of the many state-regulated liquor stores.

Money

Banks are generally open Monday through Friday from 9:30AM to 5PM, and some also open on Saturday mornings. Most of the larger downtown institutions will exchange foreign currency and traveler's checks. Better rates, however, may be available Monday through Friday at **American Express** (600 Stewart St, at Sixth Ave, 441.8622) or at **Thomas Cook Currency Exchange** (906 Third Ave, between Madison and Marion Sts, 623.6203). In a pinch on weekends, **Check Mart** (1206 First Ave, at Seneca St, 622.2274) exchanges money on Saturday from 9AM to 7PM, and Sunday 11AM to 7PM.

Personal Safety

The Seattle police force patrols the streets by motorcycle, car, mountain bike, horse, and on foot, which is reassuring to all but jaywalkers (more than 3,500 jaywalking tickets are issued here annually). Pickpockets are rare, but they do turn up in such crowded areas as **Pike Place Market,** along Broadway on Capitol Hill, and in shopping malls. Panhandlers can be a problem, too, although they are essentially harmless. Seattle isn't known for its violent crime (theft is the principal threat here), but some cabdrivers refuse to venture into the comparatively poor **Central District,** fearing at least robbery or assault. As with any large city, be more careful at night, especially in the downtown area.

Publications

The city's two daily newspapers—the *Seattle Post-Intelligencer* (also called the *"P-I"*) and the *Seattle Times*—have been in the velvet grip of a Joint Operating Agreement since 1983, ending an often vituperative rivalry. Both publish separate papers Monday through Saturday, but only one (*Times*-dominated) Sunday edition. The Hearst-owned morning *P-I* is strong on news and sports, but unimaginative in feature sections. The more successful afternoon *Times* is owned primarily by the local Blethen family (with a minority share held by Knight-Ridder), and is better known for its feature writing. The Eastside's principal paper is the daily *Journal American,* which is loaded with upscale-neighborhood stories.

Seattle Weekly, published on Tuesday, has shed its scrappy "alternative" image over the years, becoming successful and mainstream, but the tabloid continues to attract readers with its arts coverage, essays, and opinionated calendar of events. A free sister publication, *Eastsideweek* (available on Wednesday), covers communities east of Lake Washington with a slightly more irreverent eye. Slick bimonthly *Seattle* magazine covers a scattershot of topics, from politics to gardening and history, while *Pacific Northwest* offers a nine-times-a-year editorial menu of travel, food, and pretty pictures. *The Rocket* (monthly) concentrates on the local pop-music scene, and *Reflex* (also monthly) is an often-quirky tabloid focusing on trends and politics affecting the arts.

Puget Sound Business Journal (weekly) and the *Daily Journal of Commerce* both keep track of local financial transactions, but the *PSBJ* is usually more readable. The monthly *Media Inc.* concentrates on developments in local print, broadcast, and advertising realms, while *Washington CEO* is a monthly magazine of features about the state's financial movers. *Seattle Skanner, The Medium,* and *The Facts* all serve the black community on a weekly basis. The monthly *Seattle's Child* features a wealth of activities and health materials directed at families. Every Friday *Seattle Gay News* reports on subjects of interest to local gays and lesbians. *Seattle Chinese Post* now publishes an English-language edition, *Northwest Asian Weekly.* The *North American Post* (published three times a week) is the Northwest's single Japanese-language paper, and *Hispanic News* is a bilingual weekly.

Up-to-date calendars of events can be found in *Seattle Weekly*, the *Seattle Times'* Friday "Tempo" section, the *Seattle Post-Intelligencer*'s Friday "What's Happening" section, and in *Eastsideweek*.

Radio Stations

AM:

KSEA (adult contemporary) 100
KIRO (talk) 710
KRPM (country) 770
KING (news) 1090

FM:

KCMU (alternative music) 90.3
KING (classical) 98.1
KEZX (jazz) 98.9
KISW (rock) 99.9

Restaurants

Reservations are necessary for most popular restaurants, and it's best to book far in advance for the hottest dining spots such as the **Dahlia Lounge** and **Wild Ginger**. In general, jackets and ties are not required (except at the poshest of places), and most establishments accept credit cards.

Shopping

Galleries and antiques stores abound in the Pioneer Square area. Downtown, **Rainier Tower** and the **Pacific First Centre** offer several upscale shops; **Fifth** and **Sixth Avenues** are also lined with specialty stores. There's **Pike Place Market** for fresh produce, seafood, flowers, and souvenirs. Bargain hunters will want to head for **Fremont**'s resale shops; shopaholics for the **Bellevue Square Mall**.

Smoking

Health-conscious Seattle has a low threshold of tolerance for smokers. Restaurants that don't outright ban lighting up usually have separate smoking sections; many hotels have separate floors for smokers. Bars and taverns tend to be more lenient, but it's the rare place that permits cigars or pipes. Smoking is prohibited in all city-owned buildings.

Street Plan

You can generally tell the location of a place by the directional reference tacked on to the street name: for example, a place in Ballard will have an "NW" somewhere in its address, while an address in the **Seward Park** area will have an "S." Most north-south roads in Seattle are "Avenues" and their compass directions are listed *after* their name or number. East-west thoroughfares are "Streets," and their compass directions appear *before* their name or number. Aberrations are the occasional "Ways," which usually run diagonally to the city grid, and the Interstate 5 highway which slices right through the city.

If you're lost, remember that Seattle is shaped like an hourglass, with downtown smack in the middle. Puget Sound is always west of the city, and Mount Rainier rises up to the east.

Taxes

Washington state sales tax is a hefty 8.2 percent on all purchases except groceries. The hotel tax is 14.2 percent.

Telephones

The area code for Seattle and outlying districts is 206. Local pay-phone calls (including those from Seattle to Bainbridge Island and the Eastside) cost 25¢. Note: Hotels generally charge regally for outgoing calls, so it may be worthwhile to dial from the public phone booths.

Tickets

Two clearinghouses offer tickets to a variety of performing arts and venues. **Ticket/Ticket** sells half-price, cash-only, day-of-show tickets from two locations: **Broadway Market** on Capitol Hill and **Pike Place Market** (they're both open Tuesday through Sunday; call 324.2744 for more information). **TicketMaster** (628.0888) is a computerized ticket and charge service for concerts and sports; there are several cash-only centers around town. Some theaters (including the **Bathhouse Theatre**, the **Empty Space Theater**, and the **New City Theater**) schedule special "pay-as-you-can" performances, and many offer reduced-price preview tickets.

Tipping

A 15-percent tip is standard in restaurants and taxis, and $1 per bag is expected by hotel porters. Concierges anticipate tips based on the quality of their service and a guest's individual largess: $20 for a week's worth of consistently good advice would be a healthy thanks, although some guests prefer to give $1 per service.

Visitors' Information Offices

There are two main visitors' information centers: on the galleria level of the **Washington State Convention & Trade Center** (800 Convention Pl, at Eighth Ave and Pike St, 461.5840), and at **Sea-Tac International Airport** (lower concourse, baggage claim area, 443.5217). Both are open Monday through Friday from 8:30AM to 4PM, and Saturday from 10AM to 5PM.

Seattle is the country's 14th most populous urban area, according to Census Bureau data. New York, Los Angeles, Chicago, Dallas, Houston, Miami, and Atlanta are all larger, but between 1980 and 1990, Seattle rose ahead of Baltimore, St. Louis, and Minneapolis. The Seattle urban area was only the 20th largest in 1970 and the 17th largest in 1980. (Note: The census takers lump Seattle together with Tacoma, Everett, and Bremerton when assessing its population.)

Phone Book

Emergencies

Ambulance/Fire/Police	**911**
AAA of Washington	448.5353
AIDS Hotline	296.4999
Auto Impound	684.5444
Auto Theft	684.8940
Dental	362.3644
Hospital (University of Washington)	548.3300
Locksmith (AAA 24-hour)	325.1515
Medical	622.6900
Pharmacy (open 7AM-11PM)	322.3835
Poison Control	526.2121
Rape Crisis	632.7273

Visitor Information

American Youth Hostels	622.544:
Amtrak	382.4120, 800/872.724:
Better Business Bureau	448.888:
Convention and Visitors Bureau	461.580:
Greyhound Bus	628.5526, 800/231.222:
Handicapped Visitors' Information	362.227:
Metro Transit	553.300:
Time	464.640:
US Customs	553.467:
US Passport Office	553.794:
Washington State Ferries	464.640:
Weather	526.608:

The Main Events

Seattle residents, ever the aspiring extroverts, love to party. Inspiration may come from occasions as noble and mystical as the return of salmon to Northwest spawning grounds or as ignominious as the approach of fall and winter rain showers. Calendars in this area weigh heavily with annual fests, sporting events, and artsy convocations. Some of the most popular year-round celebrations include:

January

Chinese New Year The **International District** comes alive with fairs, dragon-dense parades, and cultural displays. Festivities celebrating the symbolic expulsion of demons used to last a month, but West Coast Chinese have whittled their events down to about a week. Seattle's is held in either January or February, depending on the lunar calendar. Call 623.8171 for more information.

February

Fat Tuesday Pioneer Square jiggles with jazz, rock, and Cajun melodies, plus a waiter/waitress race and a wild (by local standards) parade, as Seattle presents its own spin on Mardi Gras. Events begin Wednesday of the week preceding Fat Tuesday (the day before Ash Wednesday and the beginning of Lent). For details, call 623.1162.

Northwest Flower and Garden Show This veritable Eden of horticulture seems to grow each year, feeding Seattle's much-written-about fondness for gardening. Hundreds of demonstration plots, supply sales booths, statuary displays, and lectures by landscapers and gardening writers round out the schedule. The event takes place at the **Convention & Trade Center;** admission is charged. For information, call 789.5333.

March

St. Patrick's Day Downtown resounds with bagpipe music and the beat of dancing feet as an annual parade follows a special green stripe painted down Fourth Avenue, from City Hall to **Westlake Center.** Call 623.0340 for more about the parade. Meanwhile, the popular four-mile St. Patrick's Day Dash leaves from **T.C. McHugh's** (21 Mercer St) bound for **F.X. McRory's** (419 Occidental Ave S) in Pioneer Square; call 223.3608 or 865.9134 for information about the race.

Whirligig An indoor carnival for preschoolers features puppet performances, music, juggling, and even yo-yo instruction. Rides include a giant slide. The fun takes place at the **Center House** in the **Seattle Center;** call 684.7200.

Mainly Mozart Festival The **Seattle Symphony** schedules three concerts honoring the genius of Wolfgang Amadeus Mozart. Admission is charged and performances take place at the **University of Washington's Meany Theater.** For schedules, call 443.4740.

April

Daffodil Festival The warm-up act for Skagit Valley's Tulip Festival later in the month, this half-century-old tradition includes a parade of flower-bedecked private boats along with some Navy craft and a giant floral parade that marches through four towns—**Tacoma, Puyallup, Sumner,** and **Orting**—all in one day. The mid-April event is free; call 206/627.6176.

Skagit Valley Tulip Festival It is not always eas to gauge precisely when the 1,500 acres of tulip fields north of Seattle will bloom, but it's guaranteed that thousands of Washingtonians will rush to see them when they do. Because **Skagit Valley** roads are regularly jammed with flower lovers during this time the best plan of action is to find a bicycle and ride casually between the fields, perhaps purchasing a few brilliant bunches along the way. Capitalizing on he floral draw, the adjacent town of **Mount Vernon** celebrates tulip season with parades and a street air. And **La Conner** almost explodes at the seams as tourists finish off their visit with a stroll through hat burg's many small shops. Salmon barbecues, pancake suppers, and formal bike tours may also be on the docket. Watch newspapers for the official blooming announcement. The tulip fields are located outside of Mount Vernon, 60 miles north of Seattle on Interstate 5. Call 428.8547 for further details.

May

Opening Day of Yachting Season This is a big deal in a city that claims one boat for every 12 people. On the first Saturday in May there's a ceremonial regatta on **Lake Union**, races to showcase the talents of the **University of Washington** rowing team, and lots of Sunday sailors just trying to steer clear of collisions on **Lake Washington**. Call the **Seattle Yacht Club** at 325.1000 for more about this free event.

Northwest Folklife Festival With booths offering handmade crafts, banjo players, gospel performances, storytelling sessions, and clog-dancing exhibitions, this free four-day hootenanny—said to be the country's largest folk fest—strives to show that Seattle hasn't sold out completely to glitz. Like most major functions at **Seattle Center**, it's dominated by food booths. Attendees are asked to help defray administrative costs by purchasing commemorative event pins. The festival is held every Memorial Day weekend; 684.7200.

Pike Place Market Festival One of the city's most boisterous neighborhood hooplas, this free festival offers live-music stages, plenty of food and drink, clowns, and an activities area set aside specifically for children. It's held every Memorial Day weekend at **Pike Place Market;** for details, call 587.0351.

Poulsbo Viking Fest Break out your horned helmets and help celebrate the Scandinavian heritage of **Puget Sound**'s most deliberately Norwegian village. Expect live music, traditional dancing, and a group of iron-stomached guests engaging in a *lutefisk*-eating contest. The event is free and it's held in **Poulsbo**, on the **Kitsap Peninsula**, 12 miles northwest of the **City of Bainbridge Island** (on **Bainbridge Island**) on Highway 305; call 779.4848 or further information.

Seattle International Film Festival Founded in 1976, this is supposedly the best-attended film festival in North America, showing more than 160 new works from around the world at several Seattle theaters. Screenings run from mid-May through early June. Series tickets go on sale in January. Call 324.9996 for information.

University Street Fair Fed by a colorful cross section of **University of Washington** students and well woven with curious arts and crafts booths, this free two-day street party, begun in 1970, is always worth a look. There are lots of mimes, musicians, and street eats, plus great people watching. It's

usually held the third full weekend in May on **University Way NE.** For more about the fair, call 527.2567.

June

Fire Festival More than a century after the Great Fire of 1889, which completely flattened downtown, the city can commemorate that blaze without pangs of loss. Fire equipment parades along **First Avenue,** live entertainment heats up **Occidental Park,** and historical exhibits teach the dangers of pyromania. Pioneer Square marks the center of activity; call 623.1162.

Fremont Arts and Crafts Fair Fremonsters show up by the thousands for this eclectic neighborhood celebration featuring not only food and crafts booths but live-music stages and plenty of independent performers. It takes place at **North 34th Street,** just north of the Fremont Bridge. For more about the fair, call 548.8376.

Out to Lunch Summer is officially declared when the sounds of midday concerts (from jazz to calypso) begin resounding from downtown's canyonlands. The series is free and usually continues through early September. Call 623.0340 for specific locations.

Seattle International Music Festival The two-week schedule includes master classes and open rehearsals, as well as chamber-music concerts. Violinist Dmitry Sitkovetsky, director of the Finnish music festival Korsholm, directs this series. Performances are held at the **Plymouth Congregational Church** (6th and University Sts) and the **Meydenbauer Center Theater** (11100 NE 6th St, Bellevue). Admission is charged; 233.0993.

Seattle-to-Portland Bicycle Rally (STP) Thousands of cyclists have departed from the **Kingdome** since 1979 on this annual 200-mile pedalthon through the valleys, forests, and farmlands of western Washington on the way to Portland, Oregon. Riders complete this "Tour de Northwest" in one or two days, depending on their exercise history and/or their threshold of masochism (facilities halfway through the course are available to overnighters). Sponsored by the Cascade Bicycle Club, registration is first-come, first-served, with a 10,000-rider limit. For further details, call 522.2453.

July

Bite of Seattle Here's yet another shameless opportunity to eat yourself silly in public, as 50 or more local restaurants serve their specialties from open-air booths. Don't forget the Tums. This food fest takes place at the end of July at the **Seattle Center;** 684.7200

King County Fair Enjoy five days of rodeoing, pig racing, and music headliners at the state's oldest county fair beginning the third Wednesday in July. The **King County Fairgrounds** are in Enumclaw, just 42 miles southeast of Seattle; take Interstate 5 south to the Auburn exit, then Highway 104. For more about this event, call 206/825.7777.

Mercer Island Summer Celebration Booths display arts and crafts, jugglers perform, children are invited to participate in distracting building projects, and Saturday night swings with a live band beside the dance floor. This event takes place the second weekend of July at various venues in the **Mercer Island** central business district; call 236.2545.

Olympic Music Festival The **Philadelphia String Quartet** (confusingly, based in Seattle since 1966) joins other musicians in an 11-weekend series of chamber-music performances, held in a turn-of-the-century barn on the nearby **Olympic Peninsula** from late June through early September. Bring blankets for sitting and keeping warm. Admission is charged and the festival is held in **Quilcene,** on the west side of Puget Sound, 11 miles west of the Hood Canal Bridge on Highway 104; 527.8839.

Pacific Northwest Arts and Crafts Fair Bellevue upstages Seattle with this exhibition of performing arts, crafts displays, and a juried show of visual arts at the **Bellevue Art Museum** in **Bellevue Square** (at NE Eighth St and Bellevue Way NE, Bellevue). It's free and takes place the last weekend of July; 454.4900.

San Juan Island Dixieland Jazz Festival Ferries chugging to **San Juan Island** are especially full when Dixieland lovers swarm toward one of this area's finest summer musical events. The three-day festival showcases bands from around the world; performers have ranged from **Black Dogs** (of Florida) to **Hot Frogs** (of Australia). Shows take place in both the town of **Friday Harbor** and at nearby **Roche Harbor,** with a shuttle bus running between the two. Warning: Lodging reservations can be hard to find in the San Juan Islands during this time (late July), so call *very* early to score a room. Three- or individual-day passes are available. San Juan Island is northwest of Seattle by ferry. Call 378.5509 for more about the festival.

Seafair Before Seattle became a politically correct kind of town, the **Seafair Pirates**—a horde of brawny, hard-drinking guys who dressed up once a year like Blackbeard's minions and kidnapped (at least temporarily) prominent Seattleites—were a colorful aspect of the local summer celebration scene. Now they're often considered kitschy. Some humorless critics even say these buccaneers are too frightening for children. The rest of the festival, at least, maintains the flavor and support it has enjoyed since 1950. Milk carton boat races on **Green Lake,** a torchlight parade, hydroplane races on Lake Washington, and a fly-over by the acrobatic **Blue Angels** are all on the schedule. Just give a wide berth to those dudes with their cutlasses. This event is mostly free and it's held from the third weekend of July through the first Sunday in August at various venues; 728.0123.

August

Evergreen State Fair Animal shows, stock-car races, a chili cook-off, totem-pole carving, and cow-milking contests are all part of this 11-day show-and-tell in the backwoods hamlet of **Monroe,** 30 miles northeast of Seattle. The fair takes place from late August through Labor Day and there is an admission charge; 794.7832.

September

Bumbershoot Seattle's premier entertainment event, playfully taking its name from a British term for umbrella, is a four-day extravaganza of music, art shows, literary readings, and food, food, food. **Seattle Center** fills with crafts booths, fortune tellers, balloon artists, and the riffs of nationally known musicologists. Admission is charged and it's held Labor Day weekend; 684.7200.

The Great Northwest Microbrewery Invitational On the last weekend in September you can sample the breadth of this region's primo craft brews. Admission is charged and the pouring takes place at the **Seattle Center;** 684.7200.

Leavenworth Autumn Leaf Festival The Cascade Mountains village of **Leavenworth,** 150 miles east of Seattle, applauds the color shift of deciduous trees with a schedule of Bavarian music, lots of Germanic foodstuffs, and a parade. New England expats shouldn't miss this free event; it's held the last weekend in September through the first weekend in October. Call 509/548.5807 for more information.

Western Washington Fair Most folks just call this country fest the "Puyallup Fair," as in the slogan "Do the Puyallup" (for out-of-towners, that's pew-*al*-up). For 17 days, children can stuff themselves silly on cotton candy and then try to hold it all down as they bump along on carnival rides. Adults watch rodeos and livestock shows, and listen to well-known country-and-western musicians. The smells of livestock and the grunts of pigs abound. The fair takes place at the **Puyallup Fairgrounds,** 35 miles south of Seattle off Interstate 5. For more information, call 841.5045.

October

St. Demetrios Greek Festival Lovers of bouzouki music and gyro sandwiches take note. This partially covered ethnic tribute to Rain City's 10,000-plus Greek descendants, held at **St. Demetrios Church,** thrives on dancing, heaped plates of Athenian cuisine, wonderfully sticky baklava, and arts-and-crafts exhibits. Long lines form at the food booths, so come early. Admission is charged. The date varies, based on parking availability due to **UW Husky** football games; call 325.4347.

Issaquah Salmon Days This free two-day event, held the first weekend of October, commemorates the annual return of the Northwest's premier sporting fish to its spawning grounds with a parade, salmon bake, hydroplane races on **Sammamish Lake,** and live entertainment. Pony rides and face painting are favorites for children. Events are held all over **Issaquah,** 15 miles east of Seattle on Interstate 90; call 392.0661.

November

KING 5 Winterfest A free five-week holiday jamboree beginning Thanksgiving weekend offers entertainment for children, ice skating, symphony concerts, senior dances, holiday music, and, of course, a jolly old St. Nicholas. Sponsored by local **KING-TV**, it runs through early January at the **Seattle Center**. Call 684.7200.

December

Christmas Ships The Christmas Ships sail over Elliott Bay and Lake Washington, sparkling with colorful lights and adding a festive spirit to Seattle's holiday season. Bonfires are set up on local beaches to watch the crafts' passage. For site information, call 684.4075.

The Messiah This is one of very few American performances of Handel's celebrated work to employ authentic instrumentation. Call early (323.1040)

for reservations, as tickets always sell out. The performances are held from early- to mid-December at **St. Mark's Cathedral**.

The Nutcracker The **Pacific Northwest Ballet's** rendering of this classic fairy tale might be only vaguely recognizable to Russian Tsar Nicholas II, for whom Tchaikovsky first staged his ballet in 1892. Seattle artist Maurice Sendak's set designs help make this performance both more whimsical and more memorable than its competitors. Tickets go on sale in October; 292.2787.

New Year's Eve at the Space Needle As many as 20,000 chilled and damp celebrants huddle on three levels of the **Needle** (on the observation deck, in the **Space Needle Restaurant,** and at the skyline level) to offer toasts and kisses. Local bands hold forth at the tower's base. As midnight approaches, one of the elevators climbs the **Needle,** finally lighting a 12-foot-high set of numbers that heralds the beginning of the new year. Admission is charged; for details, call 443.2100.

Bests

Fred Bassetti
Architect/Bassetti, Norton, Metler, Rekevics

A hundred years ago Bourke Cockran told the young Winston Churchill, "What the people want is the truth. That is the exciting thing. Tell the simple truth." Where do you find the truth in Seattle?

Start at the alley between Second and Third Avenues at Lenora Street and go south two blocks to **Stewart Street.** (Don't do this at night unless you have an unusual taste for adventure.) Note the brick paving and brick-arched windows, old signs and hobo messages, shipping docks, steel-ladder fire escapes, back doors, human-scale spaces, and old pipes and wires. Everything has the ring of truth.

Turn right two blocks to Post Alley, which leads north to shops and restaurants and south to the heart of **Pike Place Market.** Do you want haggis, kippers, fennel honey, fried burdocks, Bolivian shrimp soup, or a hundred varieties of spice? There must be 98 restaurants in the market. I go to the **Athenian Inn** for Greek, Dalmatian, Italian, Portuguese, or American food and a superb harbor view, and to **Campagne** for unvarying quality.

Walk to the offbeat **Waterfront** on the south end of downtown, passing through Seattle's oldest district, **Pioneer Square,** on the way. Our only street with the old buildings on each side is **Occidental Avenue,** between **Main** and **Jackson Streets.** Stop for a world-class *latte* at **Torrefazione Italia.** Go through the lofty **Grand Central Arcade** to First Avenue, north to Washington Street, and one block left to the beginning of the Waterfront. Note the ornate iron pergola at the public boat landing there.

From the end of the boat landing you get an unusual view of Seattle's dramatic skyline. Walk south past shipping container yards and the backs of old brick

buildings. You will come, after a few blocks, to the railroad yards; continue a block or so farther on and, at Massachusetts Street, turn right to the water's edge. I like to sit here on a chunk of broken concrete, munch my sandwich, admire the gigantic orange loading cranes and oceangoing ships nearby, look for floating logs and birds, and let calm take over.

Fishermen's Terminal in Ballard, where hundreds of fishing boats (purse seiners and trollers mainly) moor for the winter. Walk out on the docks to look at the high tech fishing nets and to explore. **Chinook's** restaurant on the main quay is famous for its fish and unique wild blackberry cobbler.

From here go north across the Ballard Bridge and turn right. If you walk or bicycle to **Fremont,** which is about 1.5 miles to the east along the ship canal, you will experience a working waterfront with all manner of industrial activity.

At the north end of the Fremont Bridge, Seattle's most beloved sculpture, *Waiting for the Interurban* by Richard Beyer, invites endless "dressing up" by uninhibited citizens. Another work of genius is *The Black Sun* at **Volunteer Park** by Isamu Noguchi.

Houseboats, almost unique to Seattle, are *real* houses on floats. They line the east and part of the west side of Lake Union and the west side of Portage Bay, across the water from the **University of Washington.** They are becoming gentrified, so look for the unimproved ones that used to sell for $700.

In this general area, at the south end of **Lake Union** (Seattle's in-town lake), is **The Center for Wooden Boats,** a much valued keeper of tradition. Take time to visit the famous old salt-codfish schooner *Wawona* next door.

Bourke Cockran would feel right at home in any of these places.

Pioneer Square/ International District

In the middle of a parched summer in 1889, when Seattle had been an incorporated city for a mere 20 years, its business district—now known as Pioneer Square—started burning beyond control. Thirty central city blocks, a total of 64 acres, were leveled before the Great Fire of 1889 fizzled amid tidelands where the **Kingdome** stadium stands today. Amazingly, not a single person is known to have perished in the blaze.

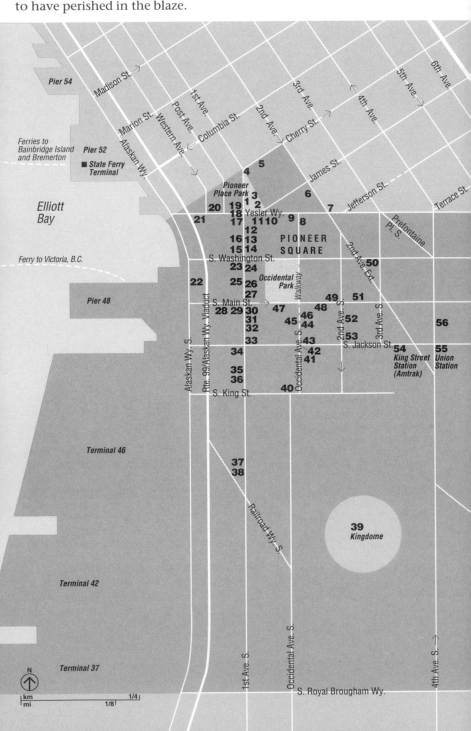

No sooner did the smoke dissipate than civic boosters began to see the calamity as a boon for Seattle, a second chance to become a showplace and commercial capital. The fledgling city immediately began to rebuild—this time instituting regulations requiring that all new downtown buildings be constructed of brick, stone, and iron. And the structures were constructed on higher ground.

Ever since claims had first been staked on **Elliott Bay** in 1852, city engineers used dredging and landfill to both expand Seattle's commercial acreage and to lift it above water level. After the fire, this strategy was adopted for Pioneer Square as well; and much of it was filled in with excess earth graded down from the hills, burying the first stories of many buildings and creating what is now known as **Underground Seattle.**

Thanks in large measure to James J. Hill, who designated Seattle as the western terminus for his **Great Northern Railroad**, the town was back in business less than two years later—more populous and optimistic than ever. Then came the beginning of the Alaskan Gold Rush in 1897, which transformed Seattle into a wealthy embarkation point. Pioneer Square celebrated a commercial heyday until after the turn of the century.

In about 1900, the city began to develop northward and Pioneer Square was left with honky-tonk taverns, bawdy houses, and transient hotels. Opium dens and, during Prohibition, speakeasies, sprang up in the shadowy tunnels created by regrading. During the Depression the area became totally decrepit, and by 1966 the proposal was made to level it to make room for more parking lots and new offices.

Architects and preservationists were incensed. So was well-known local newspaper columnist Emmett Watson. "I swear, my friends," Watson lamented in print, "progress is going to be the death of this city yet!" But Pioneer Square escaped death once again. Banks initiated incentive loan programs to revive the neighborhood, and businesses moved in to restore its sturdy buildings. Today, approximately 88 acres of offices, restaurants, art galleries, and specialty stores populate what was the city's first historic district.

The International District (or "I.D.," as locals say), bordering Pioneer Square on the east and encompassing the city's Chinese and Japanese enclaves, has a similarly troubled but far different heritage. Seattle's original **Chinatown** was actually centered at **Second Avenue** and **Washington Street,** smack in what was then the middle of the city. Its inhabitants had come to Puget Sound to work on railroads and in lumber mills or mines. Later, they developed successful cigar-making and dry-goods businesses, but by the mid-1880s, as unemployment rose in the Northwest, white laborers came to resent the Chinese and their "cheap labor." In February 1886 mobs of Sinophobes (including, it's said, many police officers) invaded Chinatown and herded almost all of the city's 350 to 400 Chinese residents to steamships bound for San Francisco. Martial law was declared to halt the expulsion, but at least half of Seattle's Chinese population left anyway, fearful of the consequences should they remain. Only well after the Great Fire of 1889 did the Chinese begin returning to Seattle, and by then new Japanese immigrants had filled up much of the labor vacuum.

Chinatown relocated to the blocks around **King** and **Jackson Streets** in the early 1900s. Meanwhile, the Japanese immigrants had settled in an area just north of there, which they called *Nihonmachi*. By 1910 *Nihonmachi* housed more than 6,000 Japanese residents. But World War II took a toll on both Asian communities. Many Japanese were interned in camps all over the West Low-income housing subsequently invaded the south end of downtown and condemnation proceedings were brought against a number of older structures. But in the 1970s, a concerted effort went into revitalizing the I.D., and much of it has since been renovated. Families started to move back in, the **Kingdome** stadium was opened nearby, parks were laid out, and new businesses—especially the Asian restaurants—now attract visitors as well as residents from all parts of town to sample dim sum or sushi.

Pioneer Square

1 Pioneer Place Park The spiritual hub of Pioneer Square was once a disregarded and clumsy intersection called Yesler's Corner. Only after the fire of 1889 did it become a landmark. This cobblestoned triangle is home to many panhandlers and pigeons, but it's also a good spot for people watching or studying the surrounding architecture.

A red cedar totem pole has stood on this spot since 1899. The original, carved by Tlingit Indians, was chopped down and taken as a "souvenir" from Alaska's Tongass Island by an excursion party from Seattle. After an arsonist damaged the monolith in 1938, it was shipped back to its home, where local carvers (apparently unperturbed by Seattle's filching of the original) crafted the current replica. A drinking fountain and bust of Chief Sealth designed by James A. Wehn and installed in 1909 are also here. A cast-iron-and-glass pergola was erected at the park's southern tip in 1909 (and rehabilitated in 1970) to serve as a shelter for pedestrians waiting to board passing trolleys. The pergola also marked the entrance to Seattle's first public rest room (opened in 1909)—a lavish underground hideaway of Alaskan marble and skylights that offered shoe shines and a newspaper stand until plumbing problems forced its closure in 1939. The facility still exists, but it's accessible now only through a manhole. So far the city has refused efforts to reopen the rest room. ♦ First Ave (between Yesler Way and Cherry St)

2 Pioneer Building Two years after this structure was completed in 1892, the American Institute of Architects labeled it "the finest building west of Chicago." Commissioned by Seattle pioneer and entrepreneur Henry Yesler (whose first home sat on the same property), and designed by Massachusetts emigrant **Elmer Fisher,** the building is a paradigm of this neighborhood architecture. (Fisher would go on to create some 50 other buildings in and around Pioneer Square, lending it a homogenous but hardly disagreeable look.) Its style is Romanesque Revival, as developed and refined by such visionary architects as **Henry Hobson Richardson** and **Louis Sullivan.** A rusticated stone base and Roman archway give way to progressively different window treatments in the upper stories. The structure was originally endowed with a pyramid-topped central tower, but that was taken down (along with other towers and cornices in the district) as a precautionary measure after an earthquake rumbled up from Olympia to clobber Seattle in 1949. Although the building houses private offices, you can stop in the lobby and take a peek at the Italian red-marble interior and atrium. ♦ 606 First Ave (at James St)

2 Doc Maynard's Public House ★$ This restored pub is high on atmosphere (check out the magnificent carved bar), and on a sunny day, its outdoor tables invite you to take a seat and wet your whistle. The menu is pedestrian, running to sandwiches and bar munchies, but the pub does offer a lively repertoire of rock and R&B bands on Friday and Saturday nights. It's also the jumping-off point to tours of **Underground Seattle,** a long-buried maze of corridors that were once the sidewalks and first floors of Pioneer Square. (See page 7 for tour details.) ♦ American ♦ Cover F-Sa. Daily 9AM-4PM, 8PM-2AM. 610 First Ave (between James and Cherry Sts). 682.4649

3 Romio's Pizza ★★$ Seattle is certainly not short on pizza joints, but few can beat the crust on the pies created in this pizzeria and four other branches around town (in Magnolia, Greenwood, Eastlake, and Belltown). Ingredients are liberally apportioned and the crusts are thick and chewy. The GASP (a wonderful concoction of garlic, artichoke hearts, sun-dried tomatoes and pesto) is the house specialty. For more tender palates, there's the soothing Zorba, which is like a flat, open gyro sandwich, with beef, onion, feta cheese, green olives, and homemade *tzatziki* (yogurt, herb, and cucumber sauce). Of course, they deliver. ♦ Pizza/Takeout ♦ Daily. 616 First Ave (between James and Cherry Sts). 621.8500. Also at: 3242 Eastlake Ave E (at Fuhrman Ave E). 322.4453; 2001 W Dravus St (between Thorndyke and Gilman Aves W). 284.5420; 8523 Greenwood Ave N (near N 85th St). 782.9005; 917 Howell St (at Ninth Ave). 622.6878

3 Old Timer's Cafe $ The wood-and-brass decor are Pioneer Square clichés, and the boxcar narrowness of this tavern ensures it will seem crowded, even when there are only a few people inside. The draw is the nightly performances by local blues and jazz musicians. The food is of a Southern bent, including gumbo, barbecue ribs, catfish, and mustard greens. ♦ Southern ♦ Cover. Daily lunch and dinner; music until 2AM. 620 First Ave (between James and Cherry Sts). 623.9800

Restaurants/Clubs: Red   Hotels: Blue
Shops/ 🌳 Outdoors: Green   Sights/Culture: Black

Art by the Foot

Strolling through Pioneer Square is especially popular on the first Thursday of every month, when most of the area's art galleries, plus many of its specialty clothing stores and crafts shops, stay open late to show off their new displays. It's a chance to cover a lot of ground without the interference of businesspeople crowding the streets. Some art lovers miss the old days when galleries poured wine for "First Thursday" visitors, but at least there are enough restaurants and taverns in Pioneer Square that you won't be without a place to sit beside friends and discuss the nuances of your evening's art grazing.

First Thursday's actual hours vary—they begin around 5:30PM and last until at least 8PM. Start at any gallery in Pioneer Square. There's no central number for First Thursday information, but contact one of the more prominent galleries, such as **Linda Farris Gallery** (623.1110) or **Foster/White Gallery** (622.2833), if you have questions.

---

4 Lowman Building The only French Renaissance Eclectic–style tower at Pioneer Place, this building (finished in 1900) is quite a standout from the parade of Romanesque piles. The principal designer was **August Heide,** an import from back east who worked primarily in the nearby town of Everett. ♦ 105 Cherry St (at First Ave)

5 Seattle Mystery Bookshop Proprietor Bill Farley carries an abundance of new and used works, paperback and hardcover, including some detective and spy novels that just don't seem to turn up elsewhere in town. There are special sections for Sherlock Holmes and for Puget Sound crime novelists (such as Earl Emerson, J.A. Jance, Robert Ferrigno, and Aaron Elkins). Mailings alert regular patrons to signings by well-known authors. ♦ Daily. 117 Cherry St (between First and Second Aves). 587.5737

6 Second & James Parking Garage In an earlier era, one of the city's first and finest hotels occupied this triangular block, now home to a parking garage shaped like a ship's prow. The **Occidental Hotel** opened in the 1860s with 30 rooms. But in 1865, as the Civil War was ending, an entrepreneur named John Collins arrived in Seattle, unstrapped $3,000 in gold dust from his waist, and purchased a one-third interest in the ivory-hued hostelry. Collins would go on to write Seattle's first charter, serve on its first city council, develop coal fields on the east side of Lake Washington, and start the Seattle Gas Light Company, as well as serve a term as mayor. His hotel was no less ambitious.

While Collins was sitting in the first Washington Legislature (1883-84), he had the hotel completely rebuilt in ostentatious style, complete with an elevator, hyperbolically proclaiming it the "leading hotel in the Northwest." Guest capacity was expanded to 400. But then came the Great Fire of 1889. Collins tried to save his hotel by buying up the surrounding clapboard structures and blowing them to smithereens, but the transactions couldn't be made fast enough, and the hotel went up with most of the rest of old Seattle. Collins went on to build a third incarnation of the hostelry, which he later renamed the **Seattle Hotel;** it stood on this site until the early 1960s. ♦ Second Ave (between Yesler Way and James St)

7 Smith Tower When it opened on 4 July 1914, this was the tallest building (pictured below) outside of Manhattan—42 floors, 522 feet—and for 48 years thereafter, it remained the highest west of the Mississippi River. (The record was broken officially in 1969 by the **Seattle-First National Bank Tower,** now the **1001 Fourth Avenue Building,** at 50 stories or 609 feet.) Bankrolled by Lyman C. Smith, the armaments entrepreneur turned typewriter baron, the building was also Seattle's first fireproof steel structure, decorated with terra-cotta facing and cornices.

Smith Tower

M. BLUM

Smith was an upstate New Yorker. Visiting Seattle in 1909 to do some real-estate speculation, he saw it as ripe ground on which to demonstrate the depth of his success, and thereby commissioned the firm of **Gaggin & Gaggin** to build a skyscraper that would anchor downtown Seattle once and for all near its starting place. (A forlorn hope: commercial construction moved farther and farther north, fashionably away from the "old city.") Smith also wanted a building that wouldn't be exceeded in height during his lifetime. That wish came true in a twisted way: he died before this building was completed.

His "two-stepped" legacy, perhaps inspired by New York City's magnificent Woolworth Building, remains Seattle's best-loved, if not loftiest, construction. An observation deck on the 35th floor provides a marvelous panorama of downtown; and on the same floor can be found the teak-ceilinged **Chinese Room,** which Smith conceived especially for his daughter's marriage and where weddings are still held. The West Coast's only manually operated elevators (complete with original-style levers) are also to be found in this building. And don't miss the enchanting carved Indian heads above the first-floor elevator doors. ♦ 506 Second Ave (at Yesler Way)

Within Smith Tower:

G&G Cigar Store No, this pungent place was not named, as many have supposed, after **Gaggin & Gaggin,** the firm that designed the tower. In fact, the tobacco shop was established elsewhere in 1895 and relocated here only after its completion. Its moniker comes from the initials of former owners Gifford and Good. The cigar selection is rather limited; but with a wooden Indian in the window and aging paraphernalia throughout, it rates high in the historical gem category. ♦ M-F. 623.6721

8 Interurban Building (Smith Tower Annex) The exceptional brick masonry, stone carving, and terra-cotta trim make this oft-overlooked office building another excellent example of Pioneer Square's Romanesque–Victorian style. Fenestration carefully orchestrated from floor to floor gives rhythm and a fine scale to the architecture. The corner entrance is ornamented with a lion's head. Not surprisingly, the architect who designed this 1890 building, **John Parkinson,** was an **Elmer Fisher** contemporary, who later employed **Fisher** as a designer in Los Angeles. Until 1920, this was the **Interurban Railway Depot.** And during World War II, Boeing had its headquarters here. ♦ 102-108 Occidental Ave S (at Yesler Way).

The longest and steepest escalator west of the Mississippi is in the Seattle bus tunnel's Pioneer Square Station at Yesler Way and Third Avenue.

9 Madame & Co. This is one of the classier vintage-clothing outlets in town; you'll be lucky to find anything here made after Amelia Earhart disappeared. The pieces are in fine condition, including some 19th-century apparel kept out of harm's way in the back, and there's usually a good pick of antique wedding dresses. ♦ Tu-Sa. 117 Yesler Way (at Occidental Ave S). 621.1728

10 Merchant's Cafe ★$ Originally a wooden drugstore occupied this spot, and upstairs was a gallery displaying work by E.M. Sammis, Seattle's first resident photographer. Then, in the late 1890s, it became a tavern where Klondike gold miners swilled five-cent beers or patronized the high-class brothel upstairs. More wild and uproarious tales and outright whoppers have been swapped in this joint than beer has been spilled on its wooden floors.

The city's oldest tavern, it is also one of its most democratic: down-and-outers occupy bar stools right next to newcomers, but somehow every discussion winds around to "the way Seattle used to be." There's often good live blues music in the evenings, and on summer days black-clad university students gather at sidewalk tables to smoke, eat burgers and other pub grub, and generally cool out. With its wonderful decorative glass and sputtering neon sign out front, this long-time establishment is a genuine spot of Seattle history and style. ♦ American ♦ Daily lunch and dinner. 109 Yesler Way (between Occidental and First Aves S). 624.1515

11 Rocky Mountain Chocolate Factory You've never seen so many candy-coated apples in one place. Just walking by this store is probably fattening, but oh, the smells! ♦ Daily. 105 Yesler Way (between Occidental and First Aves S). 682.2392

12 Cow Chip Cookies Only the very hungry or metabolically advantaged snackers will be able to tackle one of the gooey, mammoth munchies served at this chain outlet. Scientific researchers studying the effects of sugar overload are also welcome. ♦ M-Sa. 102 First Ave S (between Yesler Way and S Washington St). 292.9808

13 Greetings Trend Shop If you've been in the market for a salmon snout to strap over your nose, try this kooky shop. Other diverting kitsch includes wild-looking earrings, coffee cups bearing cartoons by Seattle native Gary Larson, and T-shirts bearing obnoxious messages. ♦ Daily. 106 First Ave S (between Yesler Way and S Washington St) 624.7713

14 Delmar Building (State Hotel) Pioneer Square preservationists managed to save some of the city's classic neon signs and painted billboards. One of the most endearing still hangs from the former **State Hotel,** an excellent brick-and-terra-cotta pile that went up in 1890 and was once a popular stop for gold-seekers coming back from Alaska and lumberers rolling into Seattle on a bender. "Rooms 75 Cents," it reads. Penny-pinchers will be disappointed to learn that the hotel went out of business in 1962. ♦ 114-116 First Ave S (between Yesler Way and S Washington St)

Within the Delmar Building:

The New Orleans Creole Restaurant ★$ Internationally recognized jazz bands are generally showcased here on weekends, but this restaurant-cum-honky-tonk is hardly quiet during the remainder of the week. Monday nights feature Dixieland bands, Tuesday is Cajun night, and Wednesday is designated for contemporary jazz. Ragtime, zydeco, and R&B artists all make periodic showings. The food is good but not especially memorable. Gumbo and crawfish are distinctive picks, but the catfish can be oily. An adjoining dark-wood bar is the only place in town where mint juleps ("The South's revenge for losing the war," as one wit put it) are regularly featured on the drinks roster. ♦ Cajun/Creole ♦ Cover F-Sa. Daily lunch and dinner. 622.2563

15 Maynard Building One of the more sophisticated structures in the area, this building illustrates the wide range of possibilities within the Romanesque Revival style. Compared to the bombast of **Elmer Fisher**'s **Pioneer Building,** this structure, designed in the **Richardson** Romanesque style by **Albert Wickersham** in 1892, is a whisper of refined detail.

The exterior's handsome sandstone is from Bellingham Bay, to the north of Seattle, and the gray brick was shipped by rail from St. Louis. Window designs in the upper stories show an expressiveness similar to **Louis Sullivan**'s. In the lobby, the frame of an elevator shaft flaunts a brilliant bouquet of cast iron, and the staircase shows exquisite wood detailing. For years, the building was a banking center; since its 1975 rehabilitation, however, it has been occupied by many different businesses. ♦ 117 First Ave S (between Yesler Way and S Washington St)

Within the Maynard Building:

Flora & Fauna Books Had Charles Darwin discovered this cloistered basement establishment, he might never have left. The packed stacks are filled with new, used, and rare natural history and life sciences books: approximately 25,000 titles in all. ♦ M-Sa. 121 First Ave S (between Yesler Way and S Washington St). 623.4727

16 Colour Box This spirited club specializes in alternative rock and industrial dance. Just the names of some of the groups appearing here (from **Liquid American** to **Running with Scissors**) are enough to draw you in. Before the shows, the bar runs beer specials the way some establishments have dinner specials. ♦ Cover. Daily 3PM-2AM. 113 First Ave S (between Yesler Way and S Washington St). 340.4101

17 Yesler Building During a flag-waving tour of the Northwest in 1891, President Benjamin Harrison speechified from the balcony of this small, granite-based structure, which stands where Henry Yesler once had a dance hall. Erected in 1890, this **Elmer Fisher** creation was damaged during the 1949 quake, and later repaired. It now houses private offices. ♦ 95 Yesler Way (at First Ave S)

17 WE Hats Remember trying on all the old hats boxed away in your grandparents' attic? You'll recapture that feeling here, where walls are adorned with wacky and delightful chapeaus for men and women, and salespeople don't care if you try on 68 different styles. A well-made fedora or a duckbill cap might just be what you've always needed. Many of the works on sale are made in the shop upstairs. Special orders are accepted. ♦ Daily; F-Sa until midnight. 105 First Ave S (at Yesler Way). 623.3409

18 Yesler Way Arriving in Seattle in April 1852, pioneer Henry Yesler was enthusiastically embraced by the town's few inhabitants when he announced his desire to build a sawmill in what is now West Seattle. The enterprise was deemed too important to be located so far away, and Yesler was given this ribbon of property running from the waterfront up to his claim of 320 forested acres.

First called Mill Street, the narrow strip of land eventually assumed the nickname Skid Road, for the skids used to transport the logs downhill from Yesler's property to the sawmill. Then, in the early 20th century, it acquired another nickname: the Deadline, or simply the Line. "Bawdy houses and low theaters were expected to stay south of the Line," explains Murray Morgan in his enthusiastic history *Skid Road*. But the nickname Skid Road predominated. After World War II, when businesses all but abandoned Pioneer Square, the whole quarter came to be known as Skid Road. So did other down-at-heel urban areas throughout the country, although it was paraphrased into *skid row*. Today it's home to various commercial establishments. ♦ Between Alaskan Way and Interstate 5

19 Mutual Life Building Additions can often detract from an architect's vision, but in this case they seem to have enhanced the look of this grand box, which sits where Seattle's first "restaurant"—Henry Yesler's cookhouse— once did business. Most critics agree that the basement and first floor were designed by **Elmer Fisher** and finished around 1892. Upper stories, completed in 1897, are slightly contrasting creations from the partnership of **Robertson and Blackwell.** Another 30-foot hip was added to the west side in 1904, and a 1983 renovation cleaned up the old elevator cars, gave the exterior a swabbing of postmodern hues, and modernized the lobby. ♦ 605 First Ave (at Yesler Way)

Within the Mutual Life Building:

Flying Shuttle The front windows of this shop are filled with lots of handwoven clothing and offbeat jewelry—great for browsing from the sidewalk. Or tempt yourself further: Go in and try on some of the stylish pieces. ♦ Daily. 607 First Ave (at Yesler Way). 343.9762

Magic Mouse This must be where all stuffed animals pray they'll wind up, and hundreds of them do, especially teddy bears. The store's high-quality selection also includes wooden train sets, art supplies, award-winning children's books, and more than enough bathtub gizmos to occupy the kids. ♦ Daily. 603 First Ave (at Yesler Way). 682.8097

20 Trattoria Mitchelli ★★$ Owner Dany Mitchell defies Seattle's reputation for rolling up its sidewalks before 10PM. Late-movie crowds, Pioneer Square's after-theater clientele, and a jolly assortment of famished insomniacs end up at this festive, noisy joint at all hours of the night. Crave a heaping plate of ravioli in butter and garlic at 2AM? A tasty Italian breakfast frittata at 3AM? Step this way, your table's waiting. Plentifully apportioned lunches and early dinners are also served, but people watching before "The Tonight Show" lacks the eatery's usual color. The service is often tardy, but who notices after midnight? ♦ Italian ♦ Daily breakfast, lunch, and dinner until 4AM. 84 Yesler Way (between First and Western Aves). 623.3885

Restaurants/Clubs: Red	Hotels: Blue
Shops/ 🌳 Outdoors: Green	Sights/Culture: Blac

21 Al Boccalino ★★★$$$ Gone is Luigi DeNunzio, the former co-owner and effervescent front man who, for so long, made it a pleasure just to walk through this restaurant's door (he walked out that same portal in 1992 to create **La Buca,** on Cherry Street). Chef Tim Roth continues, however, to use the robust recipes that DeNunzio brought over from his Italian hometown. The *gamberoni agli spinaci* (prawns with garlic and spinach) is especially tasty. Intimate rooms and brick walls make this an ideal setting for romance. ♦ Italian ♦ M-F lunch and dinner; Sa-Su dinner. Reservations recommended. 1 Yesler Way (at the Alaskan Way Viaduct). 622.7688

22 OK Hotel Cafe/Gallery For a déclassé joint hutched away on the noisy back side of this block, in the dread shadow of the Alaskan Way viaduct, this place has scored a lot of good press. It went through a cafe-of-the-moment phase in the late 1980s. Paintings by local artists were hung on the walls, and an adjoining gallery still features underground cartoons and the like.

But what really made the cafe's rep were its live performances, which were open to all ages. Acoustic singers and/or songwriters, free-jazz improvisers, storytellers, and poets—all of them took spins across the stage. Hard-core punk bands, however, were the most popular. They played seven nights a week for more than two years to crowds of "moshers"—dancers jumping in wild pogo-stick fashion. The scene was electric, to say the least. In 1992 a mosher suffered a mild concussion, and safety became an issue. The club has stopped booking punk bands, but continues to schedule other types— presumably more sedate—of music acts. The cafe serves light fare, and has a beer-and-wine license. ♦ Cover; admission to gallery. Gallery: daily; Cafe: M-Th 7AM-midnight; F-Sa until 4AM; Su until 3AM. 212 Alaskan Way S (between S Washington and S Main Sts). 621.7903

23 J&M Cafe ★$ Pioneer Square's most popular saloon has the longest lines, and no amount of fast-talking will get you past the Gibraltar-sized door sentries. The hamburgers and nachos are worth every cent you fork out for them; but the beer selection is skimpy, and the ambient noise level inside almost requires you to use sign language to communicate. The cafe prospers on its hip rep and the fact that it does have one of the snazziest wooden bars this side of San Francisco. The building and tavern date back to 1900. ♦ American ♦ Daily lunch and dinner. 201 First Ave S (between S Washington and S Main Sts). 624.1670

24 Northwest Gallery of Fine Woodworking For people who thrill to the feel of soft smooth wood, this is a heaven on earth. The gallery showcases local woodcraft and does so in a simple, well-lighted, inviting space without hype or pressuring sales-people. Imagine how the elegant chairs, desks, dressers, and assorted boxes might look in your home. Just don't gander at the price tags. ♦ Daily. 202 First Ave S (between S Washington and S Main Sts). 625.0542

24 Sound Winds/Air Arts Tiny and whimsical, this shop only *looks* like it sells kites. Actually, it specializes in a bright collection of wind socks and banners. ♦ Daily. 206 First Ave S (between S Washington and S Main Sts). 622.4386

25 Central Tavern and Cafe What kind of place would tout itself as Seattle's only second-class tavern? It's got to have a sense of humor, and this joint—dating back to 1889 and looking not quite every year of its age— has that. It also has live music seven nights a week starting at 9PM; mostly rock, blues, and R&B. ♦ Cover. Daily 11AM-2AM. 207 First Ave S (between S Washington and S Main Sts). 622.0209

25 Larry's Greenfront This is one of Seattle's best blues clubs, but claustrophobes beware! When one of the regular bands gets its riffs kicking on a Friday or Saturday night, your personal space is destined to be violated— constantly. Table service is legendarily slow, but getting your own beer on a crowded band night is no easier. ♦ Cover. Daily 7AM-2AM. 209 First Ave S (between S Washington and S Main Sts). 624.7665

26 FireWorks Gallery Local artists get to show and sell at this popular shop. Playful bowls and lighthearted jewelry are the specialties, but there are also more serious pieces of furniture for sale. Many a hard-to-shop-for giftee has received a present from this store's unusual stock. ♦ Daily. 210 First Ave S (between S Washington and S Main Sts). 682.8707. Also at: Westlake Center (at Fourth Ave and Pine St). 682.6462

Early Indian names for the area we now call Seattle included the far less mellifluous *Duwamps* and *Mulckmukum.* And Pioneer Square was called *Djidjilaletch,* after the Duwamish Indian winter village once located there.

27 Grand Central Arcade What a long, strange trip it's been for this site. In the 1870s arms magnate Phil Remington acquired it and several other nearby blocks on speculation. He was subsequently bought out by his entrepreneurial son-in-law, Watson C. Squire, who in 1879 opened the three-story **Squire's Opera House**—Seattle's first *real* theater—on the property. President Rutherford B. Hayes, visiting the West Coast in 1880 (which no sitting president had done before), was given a warm reception at the theater, but he had to shake some 2,000 hands before being released for the evening.

Two years later Squire remodeled the top two floors into the **Brunswick Hotel.** Of course, the Great Fire of 1889 burned it down (an estimated $9-million loss), but Squire was one of the first business leaders in town to announce his intentions to rebuild. In 1890 the new **Squire-Latimer Building** was completed on the same site. The facility supplied central heating and lighting to many other establishments in the district and reportedly made a profit doing so. Yet when the Alaskan Gold Rush took off in 1897, Squire again decided that a hotel would be even more of a moneymaker; he called the new venture the **Grand Central.**

Meanwhile, Squire had become a politician. When Seattle's anti-Chinese riots broke out in 1886, it was Washington Territorial *Governor* Squire who declared martial law. After Washington earned statehood in 1889, Squire was one of its first US senators. The hotel was ultimately less successful. It declined with the rest of the old city and, during the Depression, became a flophouse. Only after 1970, when the Pioneer Square National Historic District was founded, did the hotel again receive attention. It was one of the Square's first major restoration projects, and now bustles with two levels of mall shops. ◆ Daily. 214 First Ave S (at S Main St). 623.7417

Within the Grand Central Arcade:

David Ishii Bookseller Would that everyone could adopt the laid-back demeanor of proprietor David Ishii. At just about any time of the business day, it seems, you can walk by his antiquarian bookstore and see him slouched in a chair, reading his own dusty merchandise. Ishii's two passions and specialties are fly fishing and baseball, so if you share his interests you're likely to find just the obscure volume you're seeking in this small, cluttered shop. Books about other subjects are stocked capriciously. ◆ Daily. First floor. 622.4719

Millstream This place takes it to the max in promoting the natural attributes of Seattle and the Pacific Northwest: There are walls of ferry and whale pictures, salmon sculptures, and a trickling fountain just to establish the proper peaceful mood. Even jaded natives have been known to fall under the shop's spell. ◆ Daily. First floor. 233.9719

Grand Central Baking Co The bakery on one side of **Grand Central**'s chandelier-festooned main foyer is famous for its rustic breads and cinnamon rolls. Across the way, an affiliated deli does its best work with hearty soups and well-endowed salads (the sandwiches can be somewhat lackluster). Seating is available in the foyer. ◆ Daily. First floor. 622.3644

The Paper Cat On the lookout for greeting cards, comical postcards (yuppies take a clobbering in these racks), or rubber stamps? This is a good place to check out. Not all the merchandise follows the cat theme, but there's enough to give this shop "purrsonality." ◆ Daily. First floor. 623.3636

Megan Mary Olander Florist Fresh blooms abound, but it's even more interesting to see how many delicate and beautiful arrangements have been made of dried flowers. Lots of money could be spent here, but the sales staff is also very good at working within minuscule budgets. ◆ M-Sa. First floor. 623.6660

The Blacksmith Shop An ideal anachronism for an area steeped in history, this establishment rings all day long with the pounding of metal upon metal. Owner Mike Linn has been in this business for 20 years, making custom furniture, candlesticks, hooks and brackets, and similar pieces. A sign out front, however, makes it clear that this blacksmith "does not do horseshoes." Visitors can watch Linn work through a glass wall that separates his work area from the retail side of the shop. ◆ Tu-Sa. Basement. 623.4085

28 Ragazzi Upscale womenswear custom-made by Seattle designers beckons the clothes hound. ◆ Tu-Sa. 85 S Main St (between First Ave S and Alaskan Way S). 682.6977

Pillars of the Community

That tourists regard Seattle as home to so many totem poles is an odd quirk of taste and history. Native Americans of the Seattle area, after all, did not create this detailed form of columnar art, but Seattleites took a shine to it way back in the 19th century. Ever since, totem poles have been imported, duplicated locally, or stolen for their aesthetic attributes rather than for their regional relevance. Poles scattered around town are generally the work of the Tlingit people of southeastern Alaska, the Haida of the Queen Charlotte Islands, or the Kwakiutl and Tsimshian Indians of southwestern British Columbia. They symbolize this city's longstanding reputation as the Gateway to the North.

Totem poles originated as memorials, grave posts, and architectural supports. Their designs traditionally included creatures of nature transformed into specific mythological figures—Raven, Frog, Coyote, and others—each with its own temperament, style, and power. The representations were stacked on a totem pole in ways that retold bits of Native American history or legends, with the top figure identifying the clan whose story was being told.

The 50-foot-tall western red cedar pole in **Pioneer Place Park** is Seattle's best-known totem. The original monolith, a Tlingit pole stolen by a Seattle expeditionary party during the 19th century, stood in that park from 1899 until it was damaged by dry rot and arson in 1938. What exists today is a replica, also carved by Tlingit. This totem symbolizes not one but three myths, the predominant legend involving the cunning Raven (a figure depicted at the top of the totem at right), who stole the sun and the moon from Raven-at-the-Head-of-Nass and brought them to the world. (When you're looking at this pole, notice how the figure at the top still holds the moon in its beak.) In addition, this totem tells how intermarriages between Raven and Frog clanspeople, who have been transformed into humans, are complicated when their offspring are shaped like frogs. The obelisk also recalls a sea voyage taken by Mink and Raven in the belly of Killer Whale. During the trip, the two passengers feast on their host's body until they reach its heart, at which point Killer Whale dies and washes ashore. The adventure leaves Raven with a sleek and oily sheen, while Mink has become dirty from rolling in rotten wood to clean himself.

In **Pioneer Square**'s peaceful **Occidental Park** is a totem called *Sun and Raven,* a 32-foot pole carved by artist Duane Pasco for the 1974 Spokane World's Fair. Three other Pasco pieces—*Man Riding on Tail of Whale, Tsonoqua* (a mythical giant of the deep forest), and *Bear*—are also in the park. And at **Seattle Center,** near the **Center House**'s southwest corner, you can see a 30-foot Pasco pole with four main figures: Hawk, Bear (holding a salmon), Raven, and Killer Whale.

The 35-foot-tall carved cedar pole at the intersection of **Alaska Way South** and **South Washington Street** was commissioned by the Port of Seattle to commemorate links between Seattle and Alaska. This 1975 piece, created at the Alaska Indian Arts Center in Haines, Alaska, includes several symbols of the 49th state. Eagle, representing the main Tlingit tribe, sits at the top; below him is Brown Bear holding a coin, symbolizing Alaska's great size and wealth, and Killer Whale, representing tenacity and strength; and at the pole's base is the figure "Strong Boy," which stands for the state's youth and vigor.

The more traditional of the two poles in **Victor Steinbrueck Park,** at the north end of **Pike Place Market,** does not depict a legend but includes mythical figures inspired by Haida Indian designs, all of which stand for qualities of strength and abundance. The other, a nontraditional unadorned totem pole, was apparently inspired by a pole found near Ketchikan, Alaska, that features Abraham Lincoln; Seattle's version is topped by two eight-foot-high figures of a farming couple standing back to back. These pieces were designed by both Quinault Indian artist Martin Oliver and Seattleite James Bender.

A 1937 example of the art, carved originally for a fish cannery in Waterfall, Alaska, by a Haida Indian, can be seen just east of the **Montlake Bridge** on **East Shelby Street.** After many years of greeting fishers returning to Alaska, this pole was carved and stored in a Seattle warehouse until it could be purchased and reassembled by philanthropic locals. The 40-foot-tall obelisk tells about a very old woman whose brother, a Haida chief, considered her worthless. When the chief moved his people, he ordered that his sibling be left behind without food or fire. She, however, called upon the spirits for help, and her prayers were answered by an eagle that brought her food each day. When a bear tried to steal the raptor's gifts, the woman again appealed to the spirits, who sent someone to kill the thieving bruin.

Two other fine examples of totem art are located north of Seattle in Vancouver Island's **Stanley Park.** Charles James carved the turn-of-the-century house posts, both of which depict Thunderbird at the top. They were originally designed to serve as architectural supports for communal homes.

M. BLUM

29 Bread of Life Mission Victorian in style, with projecting bays but flat fenestrated detailing, this building housed Seattle's first store, founded in 1890 by pioneer David "Doc" Swinton Maynard, a Clevelander who'd come west hoping to cash in on the fish trade to gold-seekers in California. The building is now one of several help centers for elderly and disadvantaged residents of the Pioneer Square neighborhood. ◆ 301 First Ave S (at S Main St)

30 Earl D. Layman Street Clock Time doesn't stand still, and neither has this fine pedestal timepiece. It used to decorate the sidewalk at the corner of Fourth Avenue and Pike Street, in front of **Young's Credit Jewelers,** but it was moved in 1984 and dedicated to the city's first historic preservation officer (who held office from 1973 to 1982). ◆ First Ave S and S Main St

30 The Elliott Bay Book Company Opened in 1973 in what used to be the **Globe Hotel** (and before that was the site of Seattle's first hospital), this is the city's second-largest bookstore; its name is known to bibliophiles across the country. (**University Bookstore,** off the tourist-beaten-path in the University District, is the largest.) The store enjoys a great deal of intellectual cachet, thanks in part to its very popular series of readings by well-known authors. It even publishes its own quarterly paper, *Book Notes,* full of staff reviews.

History, current affairs, cooking, poetry, fiction, and mystery—all are well represented here. Travel books have their very own level; works for children occupy a separate and substantial chamber. Staffers are knowledgeable and wonderfully responsive. If there's anything to quibble about, it's shortages in the architectural history and nature-lit departments. Author readings and/or signings are held several times a week, always at 7:30PM. The readings are free, but seats are limited. ◆ M-Sa until 11PM, Su until 6PM. 101 S Main St (at First Ave S). 624.6600

Inside the Elliott Bay Book Company:

Elliott Bay Cafe ★★$ Could anything be more civil than buying a new book and then trotting downstairs to read it in this brick-and-book-lined retreat? The food runs the gamut, from sandwiches to rather overpriced (or is it just undersized?) desserts; beer and wine are available, as are steaming cups of coffee, just the right brace for a dive into the latest Gore Vidal doorstop. ◆ American ◆ Daily breakfast, lunch, and dinner. 682.6664

31 Bowie & Company, Inc., Booksellers The only way this newish shop (illustrated at right) could survive next door to **Elliott Bay Book Company** is by attracting a completely different

audience; and that's what it does, with its shelves of first editions and cases of incunabula. Prices range from under $10 to several thousand dollars. Old maps and postcards are also available, as are mail-order catalogs. ◆ Daily. 314 First Ave S (between S Main and S Jackson Sts). 624.4100

31 Grand Central Mercantile If you're the kind of cook who loves a well-equipped kitchen, then plan to visit this store. Test your connoisseur's skill: Try to figure out the purposes of the many esoteric gadgets that line the walls. ◆ Daily. 316 First Ave S (between S Main and S Jackson Sts). 623.8894

32 The Wood Shop Keepers of this shop like to play with their own toys, which is always a good sign. At least one salesperson has been seen delighting young customers with a dog hand puppet. Shelves of teddy bears and other sturdy toys charm even adults. The goods come from around the world. Check out the Russian stacking dolls (painted like Boris Yeltsin, Mikhail Gorbachev, and other previous Soviet and Russian rulers) if they're still available. ◆ Daily. 320 First Ave S (between S Main and S Jackson Sts). 624.1763

33 Bud's Jazz Records Don't be afraid to open the metal gate and descend the narrow staircase from Jackson Street—there's nobody down here, but there are a lot of ghosts. Well, in a manner of speaking, anyway. Chicago emigré and jazz aficionado Bud Young has created what must be the largest selection of jazz CDs, tapes, and records this side of the Windy City, some 150,000 titles.

Whole afternoons could be spent in the cavelike and cluttered atmosphere, flipping through racks of works by John Lee Hooker, Dizzy Gillespie, Stanley Turrentine, Robert Johnson, Lightnin' Hopkins, and an eclectic lineup of other musicians who created the basis of contemporary jazz. Music searches are accepted and jazz trivia questions are happily fielded by employees. ◆ Daily. 102 S Jackson St (at First Ave S). 628.0445

34 Pacific Marine Schwabacher Building
An honest-to-goodness cornerstone of Seattle's development, this was the city's original hardware store. The exquisite brick structure from 1905, by **Leonard Mendel** and English-born architect **Charles Bebb** (who later established a partnership with renowned Seattle designer **Carl Gould**), only punctuates the store's success and stature in the community. Notice especially the terra-cotta frieze around the front door, at the southwest corner of First Avenue South and South Jackson Street. Details like this used to be commonplace, decoration to dress up relatively plain-faced commercial buildings. ◆ 401 First Ave S (at S Jackson St)

35 Il Terrazo Carmine ★★★$$$ There's so much deliberate sophistication here you can cut it with a knife . . . if you aren't already using that particular utensil to slice off pieces of the marvelous venison medaillons. The veal *piccata* has a large number of local fans, but anyone would happily survive with the savory ravioli. Floor-to-ceiling drapes block out the sun and prying eyes, but on pleasant summer days, the patio out back is available (the nearby Alaskan Way Viaduct, however, often casts too much noise this way to allow for intimate conversation). ◆ Italian ◆ M-F lunch and dinner; Sa-Su dinner. Reservations recommended. 411 First Ave S (between S Jackson and S King Sts). 467.7797

36 A La Francaise One of the best French bakeries in town, this shop has an intimate atmosphere—despite its position on the edge of industrial Seattle—and loaves of French bread that may not make it home untasted. (A few small tables are available for those who can't wait.) ◆ Daily. 415 First Ave S (between S Jackson and S King Sts). 624.0322. Also at: 2609 NE University Village Mall (at 25th Ave NE and NE 45th St). 524.9300

37 Franglor's ★★$ Although this Creole restaurant couldn't exactly be called spacious, nor would anyone label its countertop or dark-recessed, plastic-covered tables elegant, the food here is sublime. It draws a crowd of expatriate southerners and others (like Mayor Norm Rice) who long for spicy servings of jambalaya, catfish, and short ribs in gravy. The sausage-filled gumbo is a bit on the thin side, but still excellent. And a jukebox rocks with Cajun and country tunes.

Hot days are a problem, since there's no air-conditioning and fans just don't do the trick. Beware of game nights at the nearby **Kingdome** sports arena, when parking congestion may cause you to leave your car closer to the real New Orleans than to this little bit of New Orleans in Seattle. ◆ Cajun/Creole ◆ Tu-W lunch; Th-Sa lunch and dinner. 547 First Ave S (between S King St and Railroad Way S). 682.1578

38 Triangle Hotel Building C. **Alfred Breitung** was born in Austria and trained as an architect in Europe before he arrived in Seattle in 1900. Like many other young designers, **Breitung** was attracted to Puget Sound's turn-of-the-century prosperity and the reputations of such people as **Elmer Fisher.** His name is now familiar because of several large constructions in Seattle, including the **Good Shepherd Center** in Wallingford. This hotel was certainly one of his more unusual commissions. When it was completed in 1907 the building housed an eight-room hotel on the second floor, said to be the West Coast's smallest such hostelry. Today it is full of offices. ◆ 551 First Ave S (at Railroad Way S)

39 Kingdome Newcomers are overwhelmed by some of this stadium's statistics: it claims the largest single-span concrete roof on the planet, seven acres in size, with no posts to interfere with spectator viewing; the top of the dome is 250 feet from the floor; and the concrete used in its construction weighs some 105,600 tons. But such grandeur is not without problems. In 1994 the stadium was closed for four months for repairs after a few tiles fell from the ceiling; all tiles have since been removed.

Almost from the moment this round building opened in 1976, Seattleites have criticized it. "Ugly" is one of the nicer epithets used. Many liken it to a huge orange-juice squeezer. One newspaper columnist suggested that its roof be painted beige, its exterior walls be horizontally banded with green, cream, brown, and beige hues, and the city rent it to **McDonald's** as a huge advertisement for Big Macs. Many other residents wish the city would rip off the roof or replace it with something retractable, so that sunshine might fall on the **Seattle Mariners'** baseball games. (The city so far contends that a movable roof assembly is "cost-prohibitive.") The stadium's seating capacity varies depending upon the type of event: for **Seahawks'** football games, it seats 64,800; for **Mariners'** baseball games, 59,600; and for concerts, about 80,000. No matter what event goes on inside, the "'Dome" creates traffic problems when cars spill from its huge parking lots onto the tree-lined streets of Pioneer Square. Tours of the 650-foot-diameter stadium take at least an hour (reservations aren't necessary; just call ahead for times and show up at Gate D). ◆ Tours M-Sa mid-Apr–mid-Sept. S King St (at Second Ave S). 296.3663, tickets 296.3111

Restaurants/Clubs: Red	**Hotels:** Blue
Shops/ 🌳 Outdoors: Green	**Sights/Culture:** Black

Local Heroes

By ample justification and sometimes by the slimmest opportunity, people like to associate their hometown with one-time inhabitants who've gone on to fame and, perhaps, fortune. Seattle has an ample gallery of favorite sons and daughters.

Red-headed funnywoman **Lynda Barry** was born in 1956 in Seattle's south end. Her first cartoons were published by the **University of Washington**'s *Daily* in 1976, which led to publication in the now-defunct *Seattle Sun, Esquire,* and New York City's *Village Voice.*

Herman Brix, a star football player and trackman at the University of Washington, took off for California, changed his name to **Bruce Bennett**, and became one of the first in a long string of Hollywood Tarzans.

Gregory "Pappy" Boyington, whose exploits as a World War II flying ace were heralded in the TV series "Baa Baa Black Sheep," was born in Idaho in 1912 but graduated from the **University of Washington.**

Efficiency expert and entrepreneur **James Emmet Casey** (and three partners) founded the American Messenger Service in a tiny basement in Pioneer Square in 1907. Casey's creation grew to become today's United Parcel Service. The original Seattle office location (at the corner of Second Avenue and South Main Street) is marked by a pleasant waterfall garden.

Miss West Seattle of 1954 was aspiring actress Diane Friesen, who later changed her name to **Dyan Cannon.**

Barney Clark, the first person to receive a permanently implanted artificial heart, was a retired dentist from Des Moines, Washington, just south of Seattle. He lived on the device for a remarkable 112 days.

Kurt Cobain, founder and lead singer of the band **Nirvana,** made his home and his name in Seattle. He died here in 1994.

Novelist **Pete Dexter** (*Paris Trout, Brotherly Love*) lives on **Whidbey Island.**

Howard Duff was born in nearby Bremerton in 1917 but was reared in Seattle. He attended **Roosevelt High School** and worked as a window trimmer at **The Bon Marché** department store in the 1930s before heading off to Hollywood.

Frances Farmer, born in Seattle in 1914, graduated from **West Seattle High School** in 1931. Farmer was "discovered" by a Hollywood producer and went on to star with Tyrone Power, Cary Grant, and Walter Brennan, before she was committed to **Western State Hospital** in Steilacoom. After getting religion, Farmer was released and worked for several years as a maid in Seattle's **Olympic Hotel.** She made her TV comeback in 1957.

Mark Helprin, famous for his collection *Ellis Island and Other Stories,* and more recently for his novel *A Soldier of the Great War,* makes his home in Seattle.

Software entrepreneur **Bill Gates,** the boss and brains at computer giant Microsoft, was born in

Seattle in 1955. He attended preppy **Lakeside Schoo** where fellow students thought him a bit absent-minded.

Guitarist **Jimi Hendrix** was born in **Seattle General Hospital** in 1942 and reared in the **Central District.** Starmaker Chas Chandler, of the rock group **The Animals,** first heard Hendrix in 1966. He took Hendri to London and launched a music career that burned brightly but briefly: Hendrix died from a drug overdose in 1970. He's buried at **Evergreen Memorial Cemetery** in Renton, just east of Seattle.

Poet **Richard Hugo** may be most famous for the year he taught and wrote in Montana, but he was born in 1923 in White Center, just south of Seattle, and died of leukemia in Seattle in 1982.

The late choreographer and ballet-company founder **Robert Joffrey** was born Abdullah Jaffa Anver Bey Kahn in Seattle in 1930.

Charles Johnson, author of the National Book Award–winning *Middle Passage,* lives and works in Seattle.

Born in Seattle in 1910, **Ted Jones** was a Boeing Company employee (he hung wings on B-17s) befor he launched the modern hydroplane in 1950.

Elizabeth Julesberg, the woman responsible for the "Dick and Jane" childhood readers, lived in Seattle f many years and died here in 1985.

Cartoonist **Hank Ketcham,** creator of "Dennis the Menace," was born in Seattle in 1920. The comic strip's first newspaper appearance was in 1951.

Gary Larson, whose "The Far Side" cartoons are syndicated in more than 700 newspapers, was born here in 1950 and continues to live and work in the city

Stripper and burlesque queen **Gypsy Rose Lee** (née Rose Louise Hovick) was born in Seattle in 1914.

Martial artist **Bruce Lee,** most familiar from his movies (including *Enter the Dragon*) and his role as Kato on the old "Green Hornet" TV series, lived for four years in Seattle and attended the **University of Washington.** He died in Hong Kong in 1973, but he i buried in **Lake View Cemetery** on Seattle's **Capitol Hil**

Betty MacDonald, who captured Washington farm life as never before in her novel *The Egg and I* (and later in the old "Ma and Pa Kettle" films, inspired by the book), moved to Seattle in 1917 and died here in 1958.

The talented and controversial choreographer **Mark Morris** was born in Seattle in 1956 and attended Mount Baker's **Franklin High School.**

Peg Phillips, who plays the beloved Ruth-Ann on TV's "Northern Exposure," is a current Seattle resident.

Reclusive novelist **Thomas Pynchon** worked as a technical writer at Boeing from 2 February 1960 unt 13 September 1962.

Tom Robbins, author of *Jitterbug Perfume, Even Cowgirls Get the Blues,* and other novels, lives in La Conner, a slow-paced town to the northwest.

Eccentric poet **Theodore Roethke** taught at the **University of Washington** from 1947 until his death in 1963.

Anna Roosevelt, daughter of Franklin and Eleanor, was married to John Boettinger, publisher of the *Seattle Post-Intelligencer* in the late 1930s. Eleanor Roosevelt was a frequent guest at the Boettinger's Magnolia Bluff home, and FDR twice visited the Puget Sound area during World War II.

Seattle native **Alice B. Toklas**—cook, author, and companion of writer Gertrude Stein—graduated from the **University of Washington** at the turn of the century with a degree in music.

Essayist and novelist **E.B. White** landed in Seattle in 1922, long before he penned *Charlotte's Web*. He arrived from Manhattan in a Model T he'd dubbed "Hotspur" and settled quickly into a job as the first full-time columnist for the *Seattle Times,* writing a sometimes-humorous anecdotal "Personal Column." Nine months later the Seattle daily fired him, saying it was "no reflection on [his] ability."

40 F.X. McRory's Steak, Chop and Oyster House ★$$ Talk about a split personality. On one hand, this spot wants to be a high-class establishment, serving grilled meats, succulent bivalves, and substantial dinner salads that earn critical raves. On the other hand, it dearly loves being a party place, full of rambunctious college kids and young professionals who drop by after night games at the 'Dome. The latter identity better matches the food, which, while tasty, is not awe-inspiring. And don't wait for a table in the dining room. Eat in the atmospheric high-ceilinged bar, with its full-mirrored wall of liquor bottles and its Leroy Neiman art. There's a good selection of Northwest microbrews and an outdoor seating area for bright afternoons. ♦ American ♦ Daily lunch and dinner. 419 Occidental Ave S (at S King St). 623.4800

41 Great Winds Kite Shop It's like a bigger-than-life kaleidoscope here, with kites, wind socks, and kite-flying accoutrements available in almost as many brilliant colors as styles. ♦ Daily. 402 Occidental Ave S (between S Jackson and S King Sts). 624.6886

42 Occidental Avenue At the turn of the century, railcars clanked and wobbled down Occidental Avenue, bound from Seattle for Tacoma. Exclusive parlor cars for spendthrift passengers willing to shell out 85 cents, rather than the regular fare of 60 cents, brought up the rear. First Avenue (then known as Front Street) was Seattle's oldest thoroughfare, but aged photographs show commercial Occidental Avenue being just as busy during Pioneer Square's post-fire renaissance. Both streets eventually fell on hard times, but after the district earned national landmark status, Occidental Avenue's revitalization was a top priority. Cobblestones were retained, two blocks were closed to cars, and plane trees were planted from Jackson Street to Yesler Way to lend the new mall, called **Occidental Park,** a leisurely Parisian boulevard atmosphere.

Today, food and art vendors gather here on weekends, and starry-eyed couples are often seen strolling the stones, hand in hand. There's a handsome, old-fashioned shelter at the corner of Occidental Avenue and Main Street where you can hitch a ride on a streetcar running from the Waterfront up to the International District. And a shady plaza between Main and Washington Streets contains totem poles and a horse trough that can be converted to a drinking fountain simply by cupping your hand over it. Sadly, many tourists and even more Seattleites avoid this plaza, fearful of its ubiquitous panhandlers; and the mall's northernmost block, between Washington Street and Yesler Way, has never quite overcome the shabbiness of pre-1970 Pioneer Square. ♦ Occidental Ave S (between S Jackson and S Main Sts)

43 Pacific Northwest Brewing Company ★$$ Seattle is a pub-lover's town, but this joint—with its shiny brass beer tanks and high ambient noise levels—is not the norm. It's a sleek and upscale place; not surprisingly, it was created by a New Yorker. Bratwurst steamed in ale, the fish cakes, and a spicy gumbo are the choice dishes. Crowds are biggest at lunch and after **Kingdome** events. ♦ American ♦ Daily lunch and dinner. 322 Occidental Ave S (at S Jackson St). 621.7002

44 Torrefazione Italia ★$ Quiet, filled with cozy small tables and books on Italian art, and serving potent coffee in colorful earthenware cups, this is one of the most pleasant places in town to wait for a friend. ♦ Coffeehouse ♦ Daily. 320 Occidental Ave S (between S Jackson and S Main Sts). 624.5773

45 Davidson Galleries A changing selection of works by local and international artists is on display, along with a special collection of 19th- and early 20th-century American paintings. ♦ Daily June-Aug; M-Sa Sept-May. 313 Occidental Ave S (between S Jackson and S Main Sts). 624.7684

45 Foster/White Gallery Established Northwest talents, such as Morris Graves and Mark Tobey, are represented here. Some Pilchuck glasswork is also on display. ♦ Daily. 311½ Occidental Ave S (between S Jackson and S Main Sts). 622.2833

46 The Sunday Funnies What looks like a children's store is really for adults who love comics and want cups decorated with Garfield and T-shirts that bear the nostalgic likeness of Popeye. Most of the material is Disney-inspired. ♦ Daily. 312 Occidental Ave S (between S Main and S Jackson Sts). 621.8265

47 Klondike Gold Rush National Historical Park On 17 July 1897 the steamship *Portland* arrived almost empty in Seattle. But after word spread that it was carrying two tons of gold found in Alaska, a full complement of passengers signed up for the return voyage—men who thought they could make a profit from Alaska's biggest gold rush, and women "of questionable virtue" who knew they could mine the pockets of any men who actually struck it rich.

This gold rush couldn't have come at a more propitious time for Seattle. Like the rest of the nation, the town was still trying to overcome the hard times that followed the infamous Panic of 1893, so it took full advantage of its position as a principal embarkation point for prospectors (or sourdoughs, as they were called then). Hotels sprang up almost overnight to accommodate the thousands of men funneling through Puget Sound on their way north, and a number of mining schools also opened. Local outfitters, capitalizing on a Canadian law that required gold seekers to bring along a year's worth of goods, grew rich from the hundreds of dollars each would-be miner had to spend on such provisions. The chamber of commerce even hired a hucksterish former editor of the *Seattle Post-Intelligencer,* Erastus Brainerd, to cement commercial links between this city and the Klondike. Magazines such as *Frank Leslie's Popular Monthly* bought right into Brainerd's game. "The eyes of the civilized world today are turned upon two points—namely the gold fields of Alaska and the City of Seattle," *Leslie's* wrote. A government assay office was established on Seattle's Ninth Avenue in 1898. During its first four years of business, it ran more than $174 million over its scales.

The **Klondike Gold Rush National Historical Park** is a highfalutin name for what is really a colorful storefront museum (the *real* park is actually divided between Alaska and the Yukon). Through old photographs, walking tours of Pioneer Square, and films, the museum does basically what Erastus Brainerd did so well a century ago: proves that Seattle was indeed "the gateway to the Klondike." ♦ Free. Daily. 117 S Main St (between First and Second Aves S). 553.7220

48 Artworks Gallery You'll love the eclectic selection of colorful design subjects here, everything from painted tablecloths to handmade paper and bright ceramic chicken sculptures. ♦ M-Sa. 155 S Main St (between Occidental and Second Aves S). 625.0932

49 Waterfall Garden Filled with crashing waterfalls and benches perfect for lunch breaks, this corner plot is a soothing escape from the business world. Yet its very existence is rooted in business, specifically the United Parcel Service. UPS grew from a packaging and delivery enterprise that opened in a basement under this spot in 1907. The company's principal founder, James Emmett Casey, was a Nevada boy who delivered his first parcel on behalf of a Seattle department store in 1899. ♦ Second Ave S and S Main St

50 Washington Court Building What the historian Bill Speidel called "the most glorious and sumptuously furnished palace of sin in the city" once operated from this unpretentious, four-story brick Victorian. The madam was Lou Graham, a strong-willed businesswoman who took this site in about 1888, rebuilt it after the Great Fire, and for another dozen years entertained well-to-do gents and their scions. So successful was her business, writes historian Paul Dorpat, that "Graham and her ladies. . . helped keep the city solvent through the hard times of the mid-1890s." The building is now rented mostly by lawyers. ♦ 221 S Washington St (at Third Ave S)

51 Comedy Underground National acts, as well as local Seinfeld-wannabes, show up at this joint tucked below **Swannies** bar and restaurant. Monday and Tuesday are "open-mike" nights for amateurs, and other stand-up comics entertain Wednesday through Saturday. ♦ Cover. ♦ Shows M-Th 8PM; F-Sa 8PM, 11PM. Reservations recommended. 222 S Main St (between Second and Third Aves S). 622.0209

52 Cafe Huê ★★$ Created by a Vietnamese husband-and-wife team, Huê's (pronounced *way*) cuisine reflects that country's colonial past. Vietnamese dishes display definite French touches, such as escargots seasoned with ginger. And the spring rolls and soups are not to be missed (try the filling crab soup). Chef Kieutuy Nguyen was trained in Saigon by a French baker, so it's no wonder that desserts here (including the wonderful Parisian éclairs amandines, and traditional napoleons) are so plentiful and rich. Everything is presented with artistry. Service is fast and efficient, and there's no high-turnover mentality here. Despite its proximity to the **Kingdome,** this spot doesn't usually suffer from overcrowding on game nights. ♦ Vietnamese/French ♦ M-Sa lunch and dinner; Su dinner. 312 Second Ave S (between S Main and S Jackson Sts). 625.9833

53 Linda Farris Gallery Fairly inconspicuous on its corner, this gallery is known to artists throughout Seattle and beyond. During her more than 25 years in the business, Linda Farris has established a reputation for displaying some of Seattle's vanguard talent, as well as mounting major shows of work by such nationally known artists as Warhol and Rauschenberg. The gallery's selection is more cutting-edge than middle-of-the-road. ♦ Daily. 320 Second Ave S (at S Jackson St). 623.1110

54 King Street Station Still operating as a railroad depot, this Neo-Classical station (pictured above) was built in 1906 for James J. Hill's **Great Northern Railroad.** In 1910, 62 passenger trains pulled up on the tracks adjacent to this depot every day, disgorging 3,500 passengers. Now, only a handful of **Amtrak** trains arrive here daily. Minnesota architects **Reed and Stem,** who designed the building, created New York City's Grand Central Station in 1913. The brick exterior has hardly changed since day one, but the interior has been sadly modernized. Notice the clock tower; it was modeled after the Piazza San Marco campanile in Venice, Italy. ♦ Third Ave S and S Jackson St

International District

55 Union Station In 1911 Eastern railroad scion Edward Henry Harriman opened this barrel-vaulted stopping point for his **Union Pacific Railroad** above the tidelands of Jackson Street. The last passenger train pulled away from here 60 years later. Ever since, the depot (designed by San Francisco architect **D.J. Patterson**) has been used for antiques shows and a range of catered events. In the 1970s a proposal was made to revitalize it as a "multiuse transportation center," but that didn't fly any better than a later idea to integrate it into a new City Hall complex. The southernmost entry to Seattle's downtown bus tunnel is located next door. ♦ Fourth Ave S and S Jackson St. 622.3214

56 Chau's Chinese Restaurant ★$ The standard Cantonese dishes are okay, but this place really earns its nickel in its seafood. Try the steamed oysters in garlic sauce or the Dungeness crab, and don't be shy about ordering Seattle's favorite bivalve, geoduck. It's not available everywhere you go, nor is it always so well prepared as it is here. ♦ Cantonese ♦ M-F lunch and dinner; Sa-Su dinner. 310 Fourth Ave S (between S Main and S Jackson Sts). 621.0006

57 Nippon Kan Theater A reminder of Seattle's historic Japantown, opened in 1909 as the **Astor Hotel** and later a performance hall for Kabuki theater, this redbrick building was renovated in 1981 and is now best known for its Japanese Performing Arts Series, which runs from October through May. ♦ Box office daily. 628 S Washington St (just east of Sixth Ave S). 467.6807

58 Maneki ★$ It looks rather shabby outside, notched into the ground floor of what used to be the **Northern Pacific Hotel** (built for rail passengers in 1914 by Seattle architect **John Graham Sr.** who later designed downtown's stately **Dexter Horton Building**), but this edifice boasts what may well be Seattle's first sushi bar. The selections are fresh and tasty. ♦ Japanese ♦ Tu-Su dinner. 304 Sixth Ave S (at S Main St). 622.2631

59 Danny Woo International District Community Garden On one side, facing south, these one-and-a-half acres provide an excellent panorama of the old south end, from **Smith Tower** past **Union Station.** On the opposite side, however, at the top of the slope, Interstate 5 charges by in a smelly roar. Luckily, it's possible at most points in this garden to enjoy the former without enduring the latter. Established in 1975 and expanded five years later, the site contains about 120 individual growing areas, each managed by an elderly resident of Chinatown. But passersby are invited to climb the garden's graveled paths, sniff the fragrance of the many fruit trees, and admire a giant stone lantern at the hilltop, given to Seattle by the Japanese city of Kobe during the 1976 US bicentennial. Benches are available for afternoon reading. A few transients hang about, but they're less obtrusive than in Pioneer Square. ♦ Above Sixth Ave S and S Main St (at Maynard Ave S)

60 Wing Luke Museum Wing Luke was Seattle's first Chinese-American city council representative, elected in 1962, and the first Asian-American elected to public office in the continental United States. He died in a plane crash in 1965, but his interest in meshing the Asian-American experience into Northwest history lives on in this small cultural center, which is full of old photographs, antiques, and Chinese artifacts. ♦ Admission; free Thursday. Tu-Su; Th until 7PM. 407 Seventh Ave S (between S Jackson and S King Sts). 623.5124

61 Linyen ★★$$ The lemon chicken draws much of the clientele to this efficient, well-windowed location in the heart of Chinatown. And the specials, which may include clams in black-bean sauce, pot stickers, and spicy chicken entrées, are likewise delicious. The regular Cantonese menu, however, is not nearly so enthralling. ♦ Chinese ♦ Daily lunch and dinner. Reservations recommended. 424 Seventh Ave S (at S King St). 622.8181

Seattle may have outgrown Pioneer Square (the original center of the city) long ago, but the handsome Pioneer Building, on First Avenue between Yesler Way and Cherry Street, is still the datum point from which all city elevations are measured.

62 Phnom Penh Noodle House ★$
It takes some thought to really appreciate this restaurant, since its menu boils down to seven variations of rice-noodle soup. But each bowl has distinctive characteristics that appeal especially to the local Cambodian population, some of whom will almost certainly be waiting in line for a table ahead of you. ◆ Cambodian ◆ Daily lunch and dinner. 414 Maynard Ave S (between S Jackson and S King Sts). 682.5690.

63 Han II ★★$ There's nothing like barbecued meats prepared at tableside, and this upscale Korean restaurant puts on a good show for the eyes, as well as the palate. Try the short ribs, arranged in a sizzling heap in the middle of your table, or the spicy octopus—the portions are generous. Chicken, pork, and beef are served with a side of pungent *kimchi* (pickled cabbage), a couple of tempura prawns, salad, and rice. ◆ Korean ◆ Daily lunch and dinner. Reservations recommended. 409 Maynard Ave S (between S Jackson and S King Sts). 587.0464

64 Hing Hay Park With its trees and maybe a little rare sunshine, this little park is one of the nicest places to relax in the I.D. The colorful, traditional Chinese pavilion is a gift from the people of Taipei, Taiwan, and the huge dragon mural that decorated the back of the old **Bush Hotel** was designed by John Woo. ◆ Maynard Ave S and S King St

65 Uwajimaya Here is a big, efficient, and clean supermarket, where you can even buy live fish that's ready to be sliced and served as sushi. This store (illustrated above) may be the largest Japanese emporium on the West Coast; it's certainly the hub of Seattle's Japanese community. Founded in 1928 by Fujimatsu Moriguchi, the business moved into this huge location in 1970 but is still owned by the Moriguchi family. It's a great cultural experience, even if you don't purchase any of the innumerable fresh vegetables, porcelain pieces, or appliances on sale. A variety of Asian cooking classes is also offered. ◆ Daily until 8PM. 519 Sixth Ave S (between S King and S Weller Sts). 624.6248

66 Adams/Freedman Building Elaborate facades, with cast-stone canopies at the entrances and an intriguing hierarchical arrangement of windows, make this one of the neighborhood's more elegant structures. Raised in 1910 as a hotel, it's been rehabbed with apartments and commercial space.

◆ 515 Maynard Ave S (between S King and S Weller Sts)

Within the Adams/Freedman Building:

Choy Herbs A native of Hong Kong, Kai Chi Choy has been in this country since 1974, dispensing herbal medicine in a state where such a specialty is neither generally recognized by physicians nor licensed. Choy's diagnoses include taking a patient's pulse, looking at his or her tongue, and carefully examining the face and eyes for signs of internal disorders. (The eyes, it seems, are more than windows on the soul; according to Choy, they reveal kidney or liver problems.) ◆ M-Sa 2PM-5PM. 624.8341

67 Honey Court Seafood Restaurant ★$$
Octogenarian Luk Sing Hing used a term of endearment for her late husband as the name for this much-written-about restaurant. Surely he would have approved of the 160-plus menu items here. Cantonese and Hong Kong styles are integrated to produce inexpensive curries of chicken or beef with rice, as well as the favored plates of barbecued pork over vermicelli noodles with scallions and slivered ginger. ◆ Chinese ◆ Daily lunch and dinner. 516 Maynard Ave S (between S King and S Weller Sts). 292.8828

68 International District Children's Park
If your offspring need a break from foot-touring, give them some time out at this quiet corner with its long curving slide and a bronze dragon sculpture designed by Seattle artist George Tsutakawa. ◆ Seventh Ave S and S Lane St

Bests

David Koch
Producer/Director/Cabaret Owner, Cabaret De Paris

Sunny Spring Days—Shopping in the **Pike Place Market** and ending with an early dinner at **Place Pigalle**. Great views of Puget Sound.

Lunch on the patio of **Serafina's Restaurant** (Eastlake). Secluded, great place to talk over a glass of Pinot Grigio.

Dinner at **Dahlia Lounge**—The most ingenious and delicious combinations of entrées.

Rainy Afternoons—Martinis by the fireplace in the **Sorrento Hotel** lobby.

Walk in **Lincoln Park** (West Seattle). End by driving to **Alki Beach** for fish-and-chips and people watching.

Ferry ride to **Bainbridge Island**—Suntan on the deck of the ferry.

Christmas shopping downtown—Spoil yourself with a suite at the **Alexis Hotel** and dinner at the **Painted Table Restaurant.**

Mocha *latte* at any street corner, store, or freeway entrance.

Walt Crowley
Writer/Retired Activist/Guy on the Left of "Point-Counterpoint" debates on KIRO-TV News

If you're a tourist based in a downtown hotel, here's model day: Start with breakfast in **Pike Place Market** (at the **Athenian Inn, Lowell's,** or **Cafe Sport**) and wander around watching the farmers and craftspeople as they open their stalls for business. Descend the **Hillclimb Corridor** to visit the **Seattle Aquarium,** then walk or ride the streetcar south along the **Waterfront** to **Pioneer Square** to browse and shop. You could lunch there or hop back on the streetcar to the **International District** for more exotic fare.

After lunch, take the bus tunnel from downtown north to University Street. Hop off and walk half a block over to the **Seattle Art Museum,** where you'll probably spend the rest of the day.

My favorite way to blow an afternoon includes lunch at the **Athenian Inn** or **Emmett Watson's Oyster Bar** (one of **Pike Place Market**'s coziest crannies), or a quick curry beef *hum baos* from **Mee Sum Pastries,** a pint or two of Harp at **Kell's,** and a browse at **MisterE Books, Read All About It** newsstand, the **Old Seattle Paperworks,** or all of the above.

Now preserved as an unofficial cultural landmark, the **Blue Moon Tavern** has hosted radicals, poets, novelists, beatniks, hippies, academics, crackpots, and the occasional normal person since 1934.

The **Two Bells Tavern**—Patricia Ryan and her crew cook the best hamburgers in town (served with the most delicious potato salad), and Rolan Bert Garner has turned this tiny tavern's walls into one of Seattle's most interesting art galleries.

The **Virginia Inn**—Under the sensitive management of Patrice Demonbynes, old-timers and newcomers mingle here without friction or displacement.

America's original "Skid Road," now **Yesler Way** in **Pioneer Square,** is still a little raw around the edges, especially after dark—although this doesn't discourage the culture crowd from making the rounds of the area's many art galleries when they turn over their shows on the first Thursday of each month. Take the funky but informative **Underground Seattle** tour. The Central Tavern is my sentimental favorite for a beer, and it's a popular music venue at night. The nearby **Elliott Bay Book Company** has a literate staff, a huge selection of books, and a basement cafeteria where evening readings draw large audiences.

The **Seattle Aquarium,** a jewel on the waterfront, features an underwater dome often inhabited by members of the world's largest species of octopus.

Consistently rated one of the nation's ten best, Seattle's Woodland Park Zoo is a world leader in creating naturalistic habitats for it specimens. It now boasts two troops of lowland gorillas who are feeding like, well, gorillas.

Green Lake offers a pleasant two-mile-plus walk, jog, or skate around its perimeter. The adjacent

Bathhouse Theatre is home to one of Seattle's best acting companies.

Historic Theatres—The Chinese-style **Fifth Avenue Theater** is the best preserved and features Broadway shows; the **Paramount** is the largest and grandest and hosts major pop acts. The **Moore** is the oldest (built in 1908) and boasts the best acoustics for everything from grunge bands to chamber music. The **Coliseum** (the first theater in America designed expressly to show movies) is protected as a historic landmark but will soon house a retail store. The **Eagles Auditorium** was the hub of Seattle's rock scene in the 1960s, but its future is unclear.

The **Museum of Flight**—Aerophiles must visit Boeing's original "Red Barn" factory. Scores of vintage aircraft such as a Boeing Model 80 trimotor biplane, one of the few flyable B-17s left, and a retired Lockheed SR-71 "Blackbird" are housed in a modern gallery or parked on the tarmac.

The **Space Needle**—This futuristic lingam has stood the test of time and taste since it was built for the 1962 World's Fair—despite the unfortunate addition of a banquet hall at the 100-foot level that makes the thing look like it dropped its drawers down around its ankles.

Timothy Egan
Seattle Correspondent, *The New York Times*/Author

Oyster-bar hopping, starting in **Pioneer Square** and ending up at the **Brooklyn Cafe and Oyster Bar Lounge**—the best place to sample Northwest beers.

Elliott Bay Book Company in **Pioneer Square,** where the walls resonate with well-selected words and strong coffee.

Hammering Man, the huge iron moving sculpture in front of the **Seattle Art Museum;** it's destined to take its place with the celebrated **Space Needle** as a quirky Seattle icon.

The first snow on the **Olympic Mountains,** across Puget Sound from Seattle, which usually shows up in early November after several weeks of rain. A magical appearance.

The **Virginia Inn,** near **Pike Place Market,** for good art and ale.

Husky Stadium, any Saturday in the fall, preferably when a team from California is the victim *du jour.*

Gary Levy
Owner, City Fish Company

Pike Place Market.

Having a sandwich at the **Three Girls Bakery.**

Lunching at **Cutter's Bayhouse.**

Watching the salmon run at the **Hiram M. Chittendon Locks** in August and September.

Snoqualmie Falls in the spring—a really spectacular runoff.

Restaurants/Clubs: Red   **Hotels:** Blue
Shops/ 🌳 **Outdoors:** Green   **Sights/Culture:** Black

Business District

"Downtown" Seattle is a geographical ambiguity. Technically, the center of town is at University Street and Fourth Avenue. But the city's true heart is split between **Pike Place Market** and **Pioneer Square**. What lies between the two sites is a high-tide area bounded on the south by **Yesler Way**, on the north by **Virginia Street**, on the west by **Second Avenue**, and on the east by **Interstate 5**. Seattle's financial, shopping, and entertainment operations moved here after the Great Fire of 1889 destroyed the original city center. Downtown's post-fire move north can be tracked through the age and character of its architecture. The area first developed along Second Avenue, dropping enough banks in its wake to create the closest thing Seattle had to a real financial district. A building boom during World War I brought many of the magnificent terra-cotta structures that still stand on Second and **Third Avenues** (for more about these buildings, see "Terra-cotta Town" on page 40). After development of the boxy, modern **Seattle-First National Bank Tower** (now called **1001 Fourth Avenue Plaza**) in 1969, a great fence of high-rises ascended north along **Fourth Avenue**, and the area declared itself Seattle's new financial district.

Walt Crowley, a local TV commentator and longtime civic activist, pointed out some years ago that Seattle "is really a confederacy of neighborhoods. People don't identify so much with downtown as they do with the specific area in which they live. In Portland, Oregon, downtown is everybody's neighborhood. But in Seattle, everybody's neighborhood is their downtown."

Seattleites venture downtown to work, of course. And they come here to shop for special presents and to show out-of-town visitors the sights. But efforts to keep the business core thriving 24 hours a day by transforming old hotels or commercial buildings into condominiums have seen only limited success.

Explore the central Business District on a weekday, when street musicians perform, espresso carts steam, and people watching is at its best. Weekend activities gravitate to the Waterfront and Pioneer Square, with some spillover into **Westlake Center**, while "downtown" goes into siesta mode until Monday morning.

1 Old Public Safety Building Young Seattle took a long time to erect a City Hall to match its optimism and ambition. (For that matter, the city still lacks such a centerpiece, tolerating instead that glass-walled Kennedy-era monstrosity on Fourth Avenue known as the **Municipal Building**.) But in the early days of the 20th century, local burghers hired architect **Clayton Wilson** to erect a new administration building on this triangular block. Comparisons with New York City's Flatiron Building are inevitable, but **Wilson** did better than copy. His five-story structure with a penthouse, faced with brick and sandstone and boasting a curved copper roofline, was properly formal without being pretentious. City government moved in immediately, but only seven years later it had to relocate again to larger digs in the **King County Courthouse** on Third Avenue. **Wilson**'s structure subsequently housed a hospital, a jail, and a police station. Still later, after abuse as a parking garage and as an unofficial sanctuary for the homeless, it was converted back into office space. ♦ 400 Yesler Way (at Fourth Ave)

2 City Hall Park Seattle's City Hall, a rickety hodgepodge of wooden additions derisively nicknamed "Katzenjammer Castle," stood on this tiny treed triangle until 1909. When that was leveled, Mayor George Dilling established this historic but now rather seedy site as the city's first downtown park, originally known as **Court House Park**. ♦ Jefferson St and Yesler Way

3 King County Courthouse From the 1890s until 1916 the county's center of legal activity was several blocks east of this intersection at Third Avenue and James Street. Where **Harborview Hospital** now perches atop its bluff, an old "cruel castle" of a courthouse then loomed, its imposing pillared mass lifting to a dome visible from all over town. Lawyers found the building inconveniently placed; they were often heard panting invectives as they sprinted uphill to reach their litigation, giving rise to the nickname of Profanity Hill. The current courthouse was designed by **A. Warren Gould,** another of early Seattle's prolific designers. His concept broke away from the old notion of a monumental temple of justice

calling instead for a 22-story, H-shaped skyscraper with a pyramid-topped tower in the center. Only six stories were erected initially, with another five added in 1930 under the direction of **Henry Bittman** and **John L. McCauley.** The planned tower and additional floors were never built. ◆ Third Ave and James St

4 521 Cafe $ Midday during a workweek, this spot looks like an annex to the **King County Courthouse** across the street. Judges, lawyers, cops, and more than a few quavering defendants are staples of the clientele, supplemented by other city employees and a few down-on-their-luck types looking decidedly uncomfortable amidst all the designer suits. Burgers (best with grilled onions) are the signature fare at this home-cooking joint. But sometimes it's a hard choice between the burgers and the meat-loaf special. The milk shakes are sublime. Try to grab one of the two tables in the windows up front—they're the best spots for people watching. ◆ American ◆ M-F breakfast and lunch. 521 Third Ave (between James and Jefferson Sts) 623.2233

5 Ruby Montana's Pinto Pony Who would have thought that the kitschware of the 1950s and 1960s would someday become so chic? Lava lamps, pink flamingos, ant farms, and Elvis can all be found here. The array of retro-cultural effluvia salvaged from the Jazz Age to the Information Age is amazing. Just across the street, the **Pinto Pony II** (602 Second Ave, 621.9426) features vintage furniture. ◆ Daily. 603 Second Ave (between James and Cherry Sts). 621.7669

6 Greg Kucera Gallery It's a small space, but this gallery has a big reputation. Exhibits range from the works of nationally known artists—photographs by William Wegman, paintings by Jennifer Bartlett or Terry Winters, prints by Motherwell or Frankenthaler, sculpture by Deborah Butterfield—to the work of such local artists as Alden Mason. The exhibits are always thought-provoking, and sometimes controversial. ◆ Tu-Su. 608 Second Ave (between James and Cherry Sts). 624.0770

7 Alaska Building Opened in 1904, this 14-story structure (designed by the St. Louis firm of **Eames & Young**) was the first in Seattle to employ steel-frame construction. That technology, developed in Chicago office towers as early as the 1880s, allowed exterior masonry to be ornamental rather than strictly load-bearing. Thus, buildings could be made bigger and taller without becoming as heavy as the Romanesque piles of Pioneer Square. The penthouse here was once home to the Alaska Club, a social circle for Last Frontier emigrants, many of whom came south after the 1897 gold rush. Today the building houses municipal offices. ◆ 618 Second Ave (between James and Cherry Sts)

8 Bakeman's Restaurant ★$ Tucked beneath the historic **Hoge Building** (see illustration above), famous for a pride of lion heads along its cornice, is a no-frills lunchtime fave among office workers. Sandwiches (especially the turkey and meat-loaf varieties) are thick enough to defy easy gripping, and the soups are renowned. ◆ American ◆ M-F breakfast and lunch; bar M-F until 7:30PM. 122 Cherry St (between First and Second Aves). 622.3375

9 Cherry Street Parking Garage While it isn't usually on the city tour, this arch-windowed structure was showman John Cort's **Grand Opera House,** the "finest theater in the city" when it opened in 1900. Where cars now puff and park, Seattleites used to gather along two huge balconies to take in turn-of-the-century culture. (Note what looks like the vestige of a grand entrance.) ◆ Third Ave and Cherry St

10 Arctic Building The tusks of the 25 terra-cotta walrus heads (see the illustration on page 41) that stud the handsome facade here are not the same ones that garnered public attention in 1917, when the prestigious old Arctic Club first opened this classically decorated building. It seems the originals were removed during the 1950s, owing to public fear that they'd break off and spear passing pedestrians with their tusks. Not unti the early 1980s, when a loving restoratio of this **A. Warren Gould** edifice took place, did the walruses get their tusks back, this time cast of a special epoxy. Unfortunately, the life-size polar bear that formerly crowned the building's Third Avenue entrance was not replaced. Inside, the restored **Dome Room,** a gold-leafed space once used as a restaurant for club members and now rented for special events, is worth a peek. ◆ 700 Third Ave (at Cherry St)

Restaurants/Clubs: Red   **Hotels:** Blue
Shops/ ☂ Outdoors: Green   **Sights/Culture:** Blac

11 Chamber of Commerce Building An Italian Romanesque basilica notched into the hustle of contemporary downtown? Leave it to the local chamber of commerce to plumb ostentatious associations. This 1924 design was allegedly inspired by a trip to Europe that the principal architect, **Harlan Thomas,** took to view 12th-century Lombardy churches. The chamber moved out of its faux cathedral years ago and the structure is now occupied in large part by the architectural group **TRA,** which rehabilitated the building in 1970 and is the direct descendant of **Schack, Young & Myers,** the firm that assisted **Thomas** in the structure's conception. A sculptural frieze called *Primitive & Modern Industries* by Morgan Padelford extends to either side of the main entrance and refers to aspects of Northwest history. ◆ 219 Columbia St (between Second and Third Aves)

12 McCormick's Fish House and Bar ★★$$$ This restaurant tends to attract an older, conservative, and loyal clientele. Younger drop-ins usually come from City Hall or one of the other government beehives nearby and wind up in the convivial bar. The offerings are pretty reliable and the quality consistent—the menu features simple preparations of seafood, with selections changed daily. Service is almost always efficient. ◆ Seafood ◆ M-F lunch and dinner; Sa-Su dinner. Reservations recommended. 722 Fourth Ave (at Columbia St). 682.3900

13 Columbia Seafirst Center Seattleites love to hate this 76-story cloud-ripper (pictured at right) that is so out of scale with the rest of downtown. You can't help but notice this exclamation point of steel and glass; built in 1985, it's the tallest building in town.

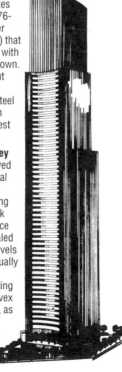

Chester L. Lindsey Architects achieved an unusual vertical and monumental sense by sheathing the center in black glass; a lighter face would have revealed individual floor levels and thus perceptually diminished the building. Alternating concave and convex exterior surfaces, as well as the skyscraper's stairstepped arrangement, create more complex light patterns than would be possible on a straight-sided tower. Stay away from the lower-level shopping floors—they're dingy, overchromed, and generally suburban-ugly. An observation deck on the 73rd floor, however, provides a broad panorama of the city. ◆ Fee. Observation deck M-F. Columbia St (between Fourth and Fifth Aves). 386.5151

14 First United Methodist Church Interstate 5 severed this church from First Hill, to the east, the neighborhood it had served for most of this century. Now it stands out as a handsomely domed anachronism amid the field of central city skyscrapers. Designed by **James Schack** and **Daniel R. Huntington** (the latter served as city architect for many years), this 1907 building combines Roman and Palladian Renaissance qualities, a departure from the Gothic cathedral designs then so popular in America. In addition to its usual religious activities, the church also serves as a lecture hall on occasion. ◆ 811 Fifth Ave (between Columbia and Marion Sts). 626.7278

15 Rainier Club The architect **Kirtland Cutter** is not as well known here as in his adopted hometown of Spokane, Washington (where he designed, for instance, the eclectic old Davenport Hotel). Yet this building, opened in 1904, is indeed one of the most startling and handsome juxtapositions to the skyscrapers of Seattle's central business district. **Cutter** modeled this males-only club after English men's clubs, with rustic brickwork and curvilinear gables drawn from Jacobean, or late English Renaissance, style. (A separate guest entrance for women was tucked away on the Marion Street facade.) In 1929 the prestigious partnership of **Charles Bebb** and **Carl Gould** added 54 feet to the south end of the building, all in character with the original design. The club was created as a haven for the city's meritocracy, a place for them to gather and chat over cigars and brandy. Today it's still private, though the membership is no longer restricted to males. From the outside, little has changed: many Seattleites don't even know what goes on inside these brick walls, for there's no sign outside announcing the building's use. ◆ 810 Fourth Ave (between Columbia and Marion Sts)

In the first two decades of the 20th century, cast-iron street clocks enjoyed unusual popularity in Seattle as an advertising tool for store owners, who would display the names of their shops on the clocks. Out of 24 street clocks that once stood on the downtown sidewalks, half of them remain. That's more street clocks than in any other city in the country (New York boasts a measly eight).

Metropolitan Grill

16 Metropolitan Grill ★★★$$$$ Proving that not all Seattleites are worried about their fat and cholesterol intakes, this restaurant turns out thick mesquite-grilled steaks accompanied by baked potatoes or pasta. The clam chowder makes a good starter, and the onion rings, burgers, and the Hawaiian mahimahi are all tasty, too. An adjacent big-windowed bar is comfortable until 5PM, when financial district habitués start streaming in. "The Met" is popular with Japanese businesspeople, who can request a special translated menu. ♦ American ♦ M-F lunch and dinner; Sa-Su dinner. Reservations recommended. 818 Second Ave (at Marion St). 624.3287

17 1001 Fourth Avenue Plaza
When this modernist bronze monolith (pictured at right) was completed in 1969, professional journals hailed it as among the most technologically advanced buildings of its time. The late **Don Winkelmann,** a partner in the **NBBJ Group** who was responsible for the design, rhapsodized for the *Seattle Times:* "You see a jet move across the horizon above this building and [the] two are compatible. It all fits with rockets to the moon." Many Seattleites took a dimmer view of the 50-story corporate headquarters for Seattle-First National Bank. One popular derisive comment was that the building was the box that the **Space Needle** came in. Others criticized it as a dark birthmark on the predominantly white terra-cotta hand of Seattle, and they didn't like the fact that it so overwhelmed the beloved **Smith Tower,** only 42 stories tall. But time has quieted the cavil, as did a 1986 revitalization that added small shops and a glass-enclosed **Wintergarden,** making the building more people friendly. English sculptor Henry Moore's bronze *Three-Piece Sculpture: Vertebrae* is the most prominent feature of the plaza. ♦ 1001 Fourth Ave (at Madison St)

18 Seattle Public Library This plain-visaged International Style building from 1959 replaced one of the most imposing of the 10 libraries in the Seattle area paid for by iron-and-steel-magnate Andrew Carnegie. (Only one other of the bunch faced the wrecking ball; eight more are still scattered in various neighborhoods, from Auburn to Fremont and Ballard.) The city's earliest library collection was housed in Henry Yesler's mansion at Third Avenue and James Street (now the site of the **King County Courthouse**); but when that burned down in 1901, taking 25,000 volumes with it, the editor of the *Seattle Post-Intelligencer* convinced Carnegie to build the city a *real* book repository. The answer to that wish opened in 1906, a big muscle of gray Tenino sandstone columns and giant arched windows, designed by Chicago architect **P.J. Weber,** that might have pleased even Emperor Nero. Cramping and construction problems finally doomed the Carnegie building.

The rooftop cafe above the present library is a good idea, but it can be noisy up there and other buildings block the view toward Puget Sound. At press time, discussions were underway to build a new library near the **Seattle Art Museum.** ♦ M-Th 9AM-9PM, F-Sa 9AM-6PM, Su 1-5PM Sept-May; M-Sa June-Aug. 1000 Fourth Ave (at Madison St). 386.4636.

19 Stouffer Madison Hotel $$$ Despite its proximity to the Interstate 5 gully, this hotel manages to project a sense of quiet. Maybe it's the regal color scheme, or the muted lighting, or the marble and rich wood that decorates the 554 guest rooms. Perhaps it's the peaceful views from both sides (Elliott Bay on the west, the Cascade Mountains on the east). Luxury addicts can book rooms on the **Club Floors** (25th and 26th), which offer special check-in services, a complimentary continental breakfast, and even a library. A 40 foot-long rooftop pool and Jacuzzi will work out the jet-lag kinks. Indoor parking (for a fee) and free in-town transportation are also available. And there's a soothing piano bar right off the lobby. ♦ 515 Madison St (at Sixth Ave). 583.0300, 800/468.3571; fax 622.8635

Within the Stouffer Madison Hotel:

Prego ★★★$$$ With views of the bay and the mountains from its 28th-floor location, this is a choice romantic spot and one of the city's better restaurants. It's known for its combinations of Northern Italian dishes and seafood. Try the black linguine with sautéed Maine lobster, shrimp, and scallops. ♦ Italian ♦ M-F lunch and dinner; Sa-Su dinner. 583.0300

The "bubble" anchoring the flagpole at the top of Smith Tower was once a giant light directing ships into Elliott Bay.

20 Hotel Vintage Park $$$ Well-known San Francisco hotelier Bill Kimpton has given the formerly disheveled **Kennedy Hotel** a brand new lobby, some elegant furnishings, and a too-quaint-for-words Washington wine theme (the 129 guest rooms are named in honor of wineries and vineyards throughout the state). It's all part of Kimpton's usual "discount luxury" package. Rooms are decorated in splashy textiles but subtle colors, and if they offer some unnecessary accoutrements (direct-dial phones in the bathroom?), their general comfort, as well as the hotel's convenience to downtown, is undeniable.

As at other Kimpton properties on the West Coast, complimentary local wines are poured each afternoon in the fireplaced lobby. Ask for a room high up or on Spring Street, as Fifth Avenue is a funnel for rush-hour traffic. On-site parking and 24-hour room service are available. ◆ 1100 Fifth Ave (at Spring St). 624.8000, 800/624.4433; fax 623.0568

Within the Hotel Vintage Park:

Tulio Ristorante ★★★$$ In the midst of high-rise downtown, patrons here enjoy the pleasant conviviality of an Italian neighborhood gathering spot. Chef Walter Pisano directs a kitchen staff which cures its own meats, makes its own bread and pasta, and even stretches its own mozzarella. The smoked-salmon ravioli is a delicate mating of Northwest and Mediterranean cuisines, but many regulars favor the roasted chicken stuffed with carmelized garlic and sage, and served with a lemon risotto. ◆ Italian ◆ Daily breakfast, lunch, and dinner. 624.5500

21 Pacific Plaza Hotel $ An older property (built in 1929, refurbished in 1989), this is a pleasant surprise in the middle of "Big-Bucks Hotel Land." The 159 rooms aren't luxurious, and they're often too small for families, but the hotel's central location (only five blocks from **Westlake Center**) is real hard to beat at the price. The rate includes a complimentary continental breakfast. The hotel's restaurant also serves lunch and dinner. ◆ 400 Spring St (at Fourth Ave). 623.3900, 800/426.1165; fax 623.2059

22 Holiday Inn Crowne Plaza $$ What it lacks in architectural character, this 415-room hotel tries to compensate for in its services. Upper-level rooms, dressed up in appealing reddish hues, have access to a special lounge and their own concierge, and receive free newspapers. Guests staying on some of the lower floors, unfortunately, find less distinctive accommodations. There's a cafe that serves breakfast, lunch, and dinner.

The lobby is comfortable and the staff helpful, but in a downtown full of historic establishments, this hotel just isn't all that interesting. ◆ Sixth Ave and Seneca St. 464.1980, 800/521.2762; fax 340.1617

23 Freeway Park How better to defy noisy freeway canyons than to cover them with something as peaceful as this five-acre park? Developed in 1976 under the direction of Lawrence Halprin, this $13.8-million greensward on a large overpass atop Interstate 5 features small ponds, flower beds, an engagingly irregular array of stairs leading from level to level, and a concrete abstraction of a waterfall that audibly separates the park from its hectic surroundings. Relax with a good book and imagine the blood pressures escalating on the freeway below you. ◆ Sixth Ave and Seneca St

24 Financial Center The designer of this 1972 rough-concrete tower, with its appealing, punch-cardlike fenestration, was the same man—**Don Winkelmann**—who did the dark **Seattle-First National Bank Tower** (now called the **1001 Fourth Avenue Plaza**) three years before. In the 1970s the architect was sometimes called "Mr. Fourth Avenue" because of the towers he was lining up along that thoroughfare. Despite his influence on the Seattle cityscape, **Winkelmann** appreciated the city's old architecture as much as he did his own. So taken was he with the nearby **Seattle Tower,** for instance, that he insisted his new financial center not block any of its views. His solution, unfortunately, was to lay down a fairly lifeless plaza to one side of the center. ◆ 1215 Fourth Ave (between Seneca and University Sts)

25 Seattle Tower Being surrounded by more contemporary skyscrapers only enhances the nobility of this 26-story Art Deco tower (pictured at right), completed in 1929. Faced with earth- and rock-colored gradations of brickwork—darker at the bottom, becoming lighter as the building ascends—the tower was intended to remind viewers of Northwest mountains. Principal designer **Joseph Wilson** tapered the structure upwards to emphasize its verticality and made the most of setbacks to bring light to a

M. BLUM

maximum of offices. At one time, those setbacks were filled with more than 200 floodlights, which simulated an aurora borealis across the building face. The Third Avenue lobby continues the mountain theme, achieving a cavernlike ambience with its dark marble walls and gilt ceiling. Look for such interior details as Indian headdresses, stylized evergreens, and abstract Chinese characters. ♦ 1218 Third Ave (between Seneca and University Sts)

26 **Washington Mutual Tower** For a while, this tapered, 55-story eye-grabber was wildly popular in Seattle. The much-ballyhooed New York firm of **Kohn Pederson Fox** had bundled it up with historical references: a cruciform floor plan, for instance, harking back to Greek cross churches of the Renaissance, and a stepped-back profile that reminded critics of the Empire State Building. No one seemed to care that it barely related to the surrounding architecture and presented nothing better than a cliff face at sidewalk level. With an exterior of pink Brazilian granite, its playful pyramidal top (inspiring jokes about this being Seattle's largest pencil), and a lobby resplendent in mahogany, the 1988 structure seemed a significant and relieving departure from decades of almost featureless glass boxes. ♦ 1201 Third Ave (at Seneca and University Sts)

27 **Brooklyn Cafe and Oyster Bar Lounge** ★$$$ When land was being cleared to erect the **Washington Mutual Tower,** this splendidly refitted brick building that houses this dining spot somehow survived the wrecking ball. The interior finishings are quite handsome—lots of wood and shiny metal, plenty of big booths, and chic cafe tables surrounded by stools. But the menu—given to steaks and seafood—isn't innovative or consistent enough to make this a regular stop. Appetizers tend to be either too small or too expensive, or both, and service can be slow. ♦ Steak/Seafood ♦ Daily lunch and dinner. Reservations recommended. Valet parking. 1212 Second Ave (between Seneca and University Sts). 224.7000

28 **Cobb Building** This august imposition of brick and terra-cotta, completed in 1910, is the last survivor of a once-grand midtown scheme. In 1861 Seattle pioneers Arthur and Mary Denny and Charles and Mary Terry dedicated this corner, along with the surrounding 10-acre knoll (all at that time on the outskirts of town), as the site of a territorial university. Thirty years later, school regents determined that their original clapboard-and-cupola institution was no longer sufficient, and moved the burgeoning **University of Washington** to its present site at the north end of Lake Union. The city then proposed to develop this knoll as a park. But **UW** had other ideas: Regents signed a 50-year

agreement with the Metropolitan Building Company to improve the acreage for commercial use.

The New York architectural firm of **Howells & Stokes** was engaged, and a comprehensive program was developed to raise uniform, 11-story facades along both sides of Fourth Avenue, with a central plaza and residential apartments on Fifth Avenue. Both this building and the **White-Henry-Stuart Building,** on an opposite corner of Fourth Avenue and University Street, were completed before the plan began to unravel. Later neighboring structures, such as the **Olympic Hotel** (now the **Four Seasons Olympic Hotel**) and the **Skinner Building,** were compatible with the architectural plan but deviated from its uniformity. In the 1960s a contrasting design scheme took control of the tract, and the **White-Henry-Stuart Building** was razed to make room for the popsicle-ish **Rainier Tower.** But the **Cobb** (believed to have been the first medical-dental office building on the West Coast) remains, and it is still very impressive. Note the Beaux Arts–inspired ornamentation, particularly the Indian heads attributed to sculptor Victor G. Schneider. ♦ 1305 Fourth Ave (at University St)

29 **Seattle Pendleton** If consumption of woolen goods has tapered off over the past 2 years owing to the increased use of synthetic materials, it has only made Oregon's Pendleton Woolen Mills more determined to promote its durable line of jackets, sweaters, scarves, and accessories beyond the Beaver State. Hard as it is to believe, this entire business evolved from the lowly Pendleton blanket, first crafted in eastern Oregon by Thomas Kay, an Englishman who'd studied in the textile mills of Philadelphia and came out west in 1863 to "borrow" native blanket designs for his own products. ♦ M-Sa. 1313 Fourth Ave (between University and Union Sts). 682.4430. Also at: Bellevue Square Mall (NE Eighth St, between 100th Ave NE and Bellevue Way NE), Bellevue. 453.9040

30 **Security Pacific Tower (Rainier Tower)** First-time visitors are often caught staring up at this striking white high-rise, alternately wondering how it balances on its 12-story pedestal and whether it might topple down upon them. Not to worry. The principal designer, **Minoru Yamasaki,** knew what he was doing. Born in Seattle, the architect gifted his hometown not only with this building, but another landmark: the **Pacific Science Center** complex at **Seattle Center.** His reputation spread beyond Puget Sound, for he designed the Century Plaza Towers in Los Angeles, the World Trade Center in New York, and corporate offices worldwide. In all his work, **Yamasaki** once said, he strove to offer "delight, serenity, and surprise." He certainly succeeded here in this upside-down pencil of

a skyscraper. Two levels of shops, collectively known as **Rainier Square,** anchor the pedestal. ♦ 1200 Fourth Ave (between University and Union Sts)

Within Rainier Square at the Security Pacific Tower:

Jeffrey Michael Supporting the menswear gospel according to *GQ,* this store carries lots of fine suits and stylish sports attire for the aspiring world conqueror. ♦ Daily. Lower level. 625.9891

Biagio Pricey but excellent leather accessories for the status-conscious shopper can be found at this emporium, where the smells alone are worth a stop. ♦ M-Sa. Lower level. 623.3842

Littler Oxford-cloth suits, Jaegar clothes for women, and other dress-up accessories draw affluent shoppers with distinctly untrendy tastes. ♦ M-Sa. Lower level. 223.1331

Cabaret De Paris For an evening of musical comedy, book a table at this cozy cabaret which makes its home within the **Crepe De Paris** restaurant. The company produces six to eight shows a year, from humorous shows like *Waiter, There's a Fly in my Latte* to Gershwin reviews. ♦ Cover. Reservations required. Shows Th-Sa 8PM. Second level. 623.4111

FOUR SEASONS HOTEL

31 Four Seasons Olympic Hotel $$$$
Seattle newspapers printed special photo sections touting this hotel's virtues when it opened in 1924. Men and women showed up in fancy cars and fancier dress, anxious to celebrate their city's newfound sophistication. The hotel's designers—**George B. Post, Carl Gould,** and **Charles Bebb**—had created an Italian palazzo, with a base of rusticated stone, a terra-cotta face, and such details as Roman arches and dentils. It was a landmark by which Seattle could judge its general prosperity.

After half a century, though, the declining hotel only narrowly escaped demolition. Sale to the Four Seasons chain and a 1982 rehabilitation by **NBBJ** brought grandeur back to both the interior and the exterior. Public rooms, including the cavernous lobby, now showcase lots of marble, thick carpeting, comfortable armchairs, and giant potted plants. A balcony around the lobby features some delightful historical photos of the hotel. The 450 guest rooms are somewhat less ostentatious, but they're still large and attractively appointed with 1920s reproduction furniture. Valet parking, 24-hour room service, and complimentary shoe shines all add to that pampered feeling.

Laura Ashley has a stylish outpost inside the hotel, peddling its demure line of dresses, blouses, nighties, and signature-print home decorations. **Shuckers,** a clubby oyster bar on the Fourth Avenue side, is excellent for winding down after work. The refurbishment added the large-windowed **Garden Court,** above the University Street entrance, where you can enjoy a light lunch or high tea, or dance to swing bands on carefree weekend evenings. ♦ 411 University St (between Fourth and Fifth Aves). 621.1700, 800/223.8772; fax 682.9633

Within the Four Seasons Olympic Hotel:

The Georgian Room ★★★$$$$ With its chandeliers and tall windows, this restaurant looks like a ballroom in a French manor house. Into this classically elegant space chef Kerry Sear has introduced an unexpected menu catering to diners who are health conscious yet still want sophisticated presentation. Originally an artist, he often draws his meals before preparing them in the kitchen. There is, for example, a dazzling five-course vegetarian chef's menu which *Bon Appetit* has called "brilliant." Popular entrées include a chewy vegetable mushroom steak made from portobello mushrooms, and an elaborate cornmeal, squash, and truffle torte. While Sear is a vegetarian, diners can also find plenty of fresh seafood, fowl, and meat dishes here as well. For about $20 extra, the sommelier will select wines complementary to each course, adding further to the delights of your meal. ♦ Continental/Vegetarian ♦ M-F breakfast, lunch, and dinner; Sa breakfast and dinner; Su dinner. Reservations recommended. 621.7889

Longtime Seattleites seem surprisingly undaunted by the precipitation here. Many don't carry umbrellas on wet days, and chances are they don't even *own* one, preferring for some reason to make mad dashes from the car to the office and back. And is it wishful thinking or downright denial that leads locals to buy more sunglasses per capita than residents of any other city in the United States? Probably neither. More likely they stash their old pairs away during rainstorms and, after a while, forget where they put them.

Restaurants/Clubs: Red **Hotels:** Blue
Shops/ 🌳 Outdoors: Green **Sights/Culture:** Black

Terra-cotta Town

Granted it was a raging fire that destroyed early Seattle in 1889, but this very same fire also had a lot to do with how the city's architecture developed over the following five decades. Just trace the growth northward from **Pioneer Square.** Starting at **Smith Tower,** the handsome but weighty Romanesque Revival style of brick and stone gives way to paler, more gracefully ornamented terra-cotta towers that were believed (correctly) to be more structurally sound than their precursors. These buildings were also a kind of insurance policy for Seattle: terra-cotta, it had been proved, was more fire-resistant than many other building materials. Perhaps more significant, however, is that for most of this century these towers would characterize Seattle as a great white city on the water.

Terra-cotta became an accepted building material for Chicago's large-scale projects shortly after that city suffered its own skyline-devastating blaze in 1871. The enriched clay eventually became the facing of choice among early American skyscraper builders, including such architects as **Louis Sullivan** and **Daniel Burnham,** who discovered they could use it to create higher and slimmer towers. They achieved this by assembling steel skeletons to bear most of a building's weight, and then sheathing the structure with a lighter skin of terra-cotta (which weighs about 70 pounds per cubic foot, compared to 170 pounds for granite).

It could also be modeled easily into an infinite variety of shapes before it was hardened by firing—a bottom-line plus during a period when the expense of traditional ornamental stonework was on the rise. As architect **Frank Lloyd Wright** later remarked, terra-cotta "takes the impression of human imagination. . . . It is in the architect's hand what wax is in the sculptor's hand." The material allowed designers to more fully express themselves in the sort of Beaux Arts embellishments popular during the early 20th century. Gargoyles, cartouches, French nymphs, or a ribbon of walrus heads could all be produced cheaply and quickly and in numerous shades to enhance a structure.

Of course, the Northwest's damp climate forced special requirements on terra-cotta manufacturing. More porous versions might have been fine for California, but here the clay renderings had to be highly glazed, a fact that contributed greatly not only to their waterproofing but also to their general longevity. (The Capitol Theater in Yakima, Washington, for instance, was hit by a fire some years back that destroyed the interior but left the distinguished terra-cotta facade standing.)

One of the earliest architects erecting terra-cotta–sheathed edifices in Seattle was **Charles H. Bebb,** an Englishman who'd worked in Chicago with **Louis Sullivan**'s firm. In about 1890 he moved to Seattle to serve as an engineer for an early terra-cotta company owned, at least in part, by pioneer Arthur Denny. **Bebb** formed his own architectural practice in 1898, subsequently linking up with **Leonard L. Mendel** and the talented New Yorker **Carl F. Gould** to create some of Seattle's most significant terra-cotta structures. They were joined in their taste for terra-cotta by local architects **John Graham Sr., Henry Bittman, A. Warren Gould,** and theater designer **B. Marcus Priteca,** an experimental stylist who created molds for classical ornamental motifs that became catalog items and eventually detailed buildings all down the West Coast.

Not until 1930 did the demand for terra-cotta suffer a decline, brought on by the Depression, escalating production costs, and changes in architectural taste. By then, however, Seattle—as well as Portland, Oregon, and San Francisco—all displayed a rich diversity of terra-cotta works. Unfortunately, some of the finest examples have been victims of the wrecking ball (including the old **Rhodes Building** and the **Orpheum Theater,** both once in downtown Seattle), but others are still standing and are definitely worth seeing. A few of the more interesting examples are listed below.

Alaska Building (1904; Eames & Young) Downtown's first steel-girdered high-rise. 618 Second Ave (between James and Cherry Sts)

Arctic Building (1917; A. Warren Gould) This ivory-colored terra-cotta structure has ". . . confectioner's touches of aquamarine and rose," as one architectural guide puts it. The walrus heads lining the edifice (see page 41) speak well of the artistic possibilities in this clay construction. 700 Third Ave (between Columbia and Cherry Sts)

Coliseum Theater (1916; B. Marcus Priteca) For all its decline over the last two decades, this is still one of downtown's most beautifully detailed buildings. 1506 Fifth Ave (at Pike St)

Corona Hotel (1903; Bebb & Gould) This structure's stylistic debt goes to **Louis Sullivan,** who inspired its woven floral ornamentation of unglazed terra-cotta. 608 Second Ave (at James St)

Dexter Horton Building (1922; John Graham Sr.) Like the **Arctic Building** before it, this tower is ivory-hued—a nationally popular color at the time. But it's more sternly businesslike in conception, with giant Doric columns of granite on the north side that express the original height of its lobby. 710 Second Ave (at Cherry St)

Fischer Studio Building (1912, Bebb & Mendel; 1914, Bebb & Gould) In 1914 **Bebb** and his new partner **Gould** added five stories onto the original three of this structure, and integrated the facade into a continuous whole. The seventh and eighth floors, blank on the exterior except for some Venetian-inspired detail, were built to house a Renaissance Revival–style music hall. 1519 Third Ave (between Pike and Pine Sts)

Four Seasons Olympic Hotel (1929; George B. Post) Designed by an important New York architect, with **Bebb & Gould** administering the construction, this brick-clad building has terra-cotta ornaments. 411 University St (between Fourth and Fifth Aves)

Medical-Dental Building (1925; Kreutzer & Albertson, John Graham Sr.) **Graham** designed this as a physical and spiritual extension of his 1919 **Frederick & Nelson** department store. But while the drama of the former **F & N** is apparent at all heights, most of the building's interest doesn't begin until the 14th floor, where Venetian filigrees and a series of setback penthouses and towers are located. 505 Olive Way (between Fourth and Fifth Sts)

Sailors Union of the Pacific (1954; T. Bohannon and K. Better) This is a particularly late and simplistic example of terra-cotta design. 2505 First Ave (at Wall St)

Seafirst Bank (1908; J.J. Baillargeon) A former department store, this building has a great arched entrance, lion heads decorating the lower corners, and fine shell-patterned window frames adorning the ground level. 1100 Second Ave (at Spring St)

Securities Building (1912; John Graham Sr.) This structure is a Greco-Roman design, executed in terra-cotta. Pay special attention to the ornamentation, including playful green cartouches, along Third Avenue. 1904 Third Ave (between Virginia and Stewart Sts)

Smith Tower (1912; Gaggin & Gaggin) The light weight of terra-cotta allowed this early skyscraper to be built taller than was previously possible. 506 Second Ave (at Yesler Way)

Terminal Sales Building (1923; Henry Bittman) This building has tan brick and terra-cotta facing, with English Gothic ornament that stands out pleasantly against its Art Deco profile. 1934 First Ave (at Virginia St)

Woolworth Building (circa 1935; Harold B. Hamhill) Built using Woolworth's standard design, this Moderne-style structure was the only new terra-cotta building constructed in downtown Seattle during the 1930s and 1940s. 301 Pike St (at Third Ave)

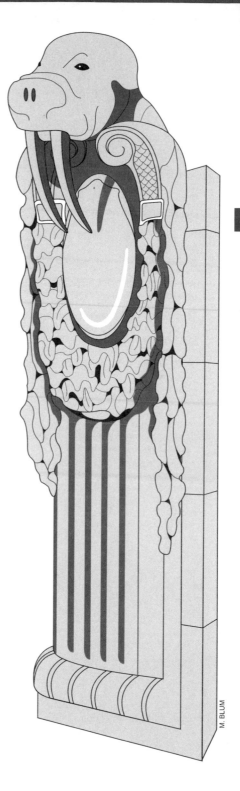

The Arctic Building's walrus heads (like the one pictured here) had their tusks removed more than 30 years ago for fear they'd fall off and mortally wound passersby. During a 1980s restoration, however, the walruses got their tusks back.

M. BLUM

32 Skinner Building What does this blocklong, tile-roofed Mediterranean palazzo from 1926 have to do with the monumental Old Faithful Inn in Yellowstone National Park and the Canyon Hotel at the Grand Canyon? They were all designed by **Robert C. Reamer.** Born in Ohio in 1873, **Reamer** started with an architectural firm in Detroit and moved from there to Cleveland, Chicago, San Diego, and Wyoming. He came to Seattle during World War I to become chief architect for the Metropolitan Building Company. Considered at one time to be a supreme practitioner of his art—a Richardsonian in his architectural aesthetics and a romantic by inclination—**Reamer** has all but disappeared from Seattle history books. Yet his buildings (this structure as well as the **Meany Tower Hotel** in the University District, the **Seattle Times Building** on John Street, and the **1411 Fourth Avenue Building** downtown) are some of the most intriguing around. ♦ 1326 Fifth Ave (between University and Union Sts)

Within the Skinner Building:

Fifth Avenue Theater The **Skinner**'s tame Wilkeson sandstone exterior hides Seattle's loveliest performance space, said to be patterned after the imperial throne room in Beijing's Forbidden City. Gustav Liljestrom, a Norwegian artist trained in China, was responsible for the interior of this former vaudeville house, which features a coiled dragon painted on the ceiling. The theater was restored in 1980 and now hosts touring Broadway shows. Don't miss a chance to venture inside. ♦ Box office M-F. 625.1900

33 Fox's Gem Shop This is a sophisticated and refined environment that's all glittering stones, a finely tailored clientele, and steep prices. There's lots of sterling silver jewelry and a boutique selection of Tiffany products. ♦ M-Sa. 1341 Fifth Ave (between University and Union Sts). 623.2528

34 Eddie Bauer, Inc. Eddie Bauer was born to Russian immigrant parents on Orcas Island, northwest of Seattle, in 1900. Always enchanted with fishing and hunting, it seemed natural that he would move into sporting-goods sales for a career and then be wildly successful at it. He finally opened his own store in Seattle in 1922, attracting customers with his demanding policies about quality and his interest in improving what was already on the market. It was the latter that led him to invent the down jacket.

While fishing on Washington's Olympic Peninsula in 1934, Bauer almost froze to death because he didn't bring along an appropriate jacket. He started thinking about how to make both warmer and lighter outerwear and remembered a tale his uncle had told about surviving the Russo-Japanese War of 1904 by wearing goose-down quilted undergarments. Bauer took some of the down he was already importing from China for use in flyties and shuttlecocks, quilted a few jackets for himself, and when friends declared them a hit, patented both the jackets and their manufacturing process. There are now about 200 stores across the country that bear his name.

Although bought out some years ago by **Spiegel Inc.,** the company still sells the well-known goose-down fashions, as well as sleeping bags, backpacking equipment, knives, sunglasses, and some of the coziest wool socks available anywhere. The store is known for offering hefty price reductions on the Bauer line. ♦ Daily; F until 8PM. Fifth Ave and Union St. 622.2766

35 Seattle Hilton $$ It's rather confusing that this hotel's lobby sits on the ninth floor rather than at ground level (to make way for a parking garage). But that may be the only unusual bit in this cookie-cutter member of the Hilton chain. Furnishings are tasteful, but hardly memorable, and color schemes in the 237 rooms are benign, reflecting the aesthetics of a 1980s redo. A view restaurant, the **Top of the Hilton,** specializes in local seafood and attracts a mostly business clientele to its lounge. (As with most view restaurants, the prices are as high as the elevation.) Very convenient for conventioneers, an underground passage even connects the hotel to the **Washington State Convention & Trade Center** and to **Rainier Square.** ♦ 1301 Sixth Ave (at University St). 624.0500, 800/542.7700; fax 682.9029

36 Eagles Auditorium When completed in 1925, architect **Henry Bittman**'s Renaissance Revival–style home for the Fraternal Order of Eagles was among the country's most distinguished fraternal buildings. Underused and running to shabbiness for years, the block remained a fine example of Seattle's ornate terra-cotta facades. After other historic buildings in the area fell to the wrecking ball, public sentiment supported the plans of **A Contemporary Theatre (ACT)** to relocate here from its Lower Queen Anne digs. At press time, **ACT** had received approval for design modifications for the theater, and had plans to move in 1996. ♦ 1416 Seventh Ave (at Union St); ACT 285.5110

Restaurants/Clubs: Red	**Hotels:** Blue
Shops/ 🌳 Outdoors: Green	**Sights/Culture:** Bla

37 Washington State Convention & Trade Center Too chunky, gray, and cold to be appealing, this 370,000-square-foot convention center can at least accommodate the sort of large-scale get-togethers that Seattle couldn't easily host before. Reception rooms are designed for groups numbering 50 to 4,000 people. Indoor parking is available for some 900 cars. There's a **Visitors' Center** on the galleria level that provides the usual tourist information. ♦ Visitors' Center M-F. 800 Convention Place (at Eighth Ave and Pike St). Convention Center 447.5000, Visitors' Center 461.5840

38 Seattle Sheraton Hotel and Towers
$$$$ This modern hotel is a convenient retreat for businesspeople attending events at the **Washington State Convention & Trade Center,** just up Pike Street from here. An expansive lobby is decorated with Dale Chihuly glass art. Meeting rooms are plentiful. Most of the 840 guest rooms are cramped by comparison, lacking in all but the most essential components. Four VIP floors (31-34) offer more elaborate rooms and a separate concierge. A health club and pool on the 35th floor are open to all overnight guests.

Banners, a casual, well-lighted restaurant off the lobby, offers a sumptuous buffet luncheon. **Gooey's** (named, they say, after that bizarre long-necked mollusk, the geoduck) is a rather small disco with a decent bar. Parking is available for a fee. ♦ 1400 Sixth Ave (at Union St). 621.9000, 800/325.3535; fax 621.8441

Within the Seattle Sheraton Hotel and Towers:

Fuller's ★★★★$$$ Named for Dr. Richard Fuller, founder of the **Seattle Art Museum,** this restaurant is a showplace for some of the city's best cuisine *and* best contemporary art (paintings by Morris Graves and Mark Tobey, and glasswork by Dale Chihuly). Chef Monique Barbeau pairs Northwest ingredients with Asian-inspired reductions and marinades, eschewing fat-laden cream and butter sauces; the results are light and flavorful. Consider for starters the sautéed salmon on cornmeal pancakes with a tomato jam, or a salad of wilted spinach and smoked duck in a honey-sesame dressing. Similarly inspired entrées include a carmelized, pan-seared cod served with jasmine rice and greens. Barbeau was named Best Chef of the Pacific Northwest in the 1994 James Beard Awards. ♦ Northwestern ♦ M-F lunch and dinner; Sa dinner. Reservations recommended. 447.5544

39 Banana Republic The exotic explorer theme may be pushed a bit too heavily (are you really happier buying clothes beneath a palm tree?), but this San Francisco–based company certainly knows how to make casual clothes that last. And they're not all in khaki or green. ♦ Daily. 508 Union St (between Fifth and Sixth Aves). 622.2303

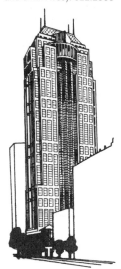

40 Pacific First Centre Although it's a hefty hunk of California glitz and post-Postmodernist doodads staked into downtown Seattle, this building (illustrated above) draws Seattleites with its nationally known retailers. The smaller shops here are also worth a browse. ♦ 1420 Fifth Ave (between Union and Pike Sts)

Within Pacific First Centre:

Ann Taylor In the same way that **Brooks Brothers** purveys timeless fashions for men, so this fine chain courts the women's trade. It's conservative and expensive, but reliable. ♦ Daily. First floor. 623.4818

Design Concern With high-design office supplies and tableware, Japanese clocks, and a broad selection of obscure gadgets, this is a great place to browse and shop for gifts. ♦ Daily. Second floor. 623.4444

Boxer Bay When you weren't looking, men's Skivvies became fashion statements, and here is one store that stepped in to make the most of that trend. In addition to silk drawers and Hugh Hefneresque lounge attire, the store also sells comfy cotton robes and, somewhat incongruously, ties. ♦ Daily. Second floor. 625.9418

PALOMINO

Palomino ★★★$$$ Leave your jeans and T-shirts in the closet. Like owner Rich Komen's other restaurants (**Cutter's Bayhouse** in **Pike Place Market, Triples** on

Lake Union, and **Palisade** in Magnolia), this gleaming, highly stylized spot draws a beautiful crowd of designer-suited gents and women in fancy dresses. Dale Chihuly glass-works sparkle under the directional lights.

The unwalled kitchen and open oven produce excellent king salmon, garlic chicken, and pork loin. Pizzas are thin-crusted and, sadly, also thinly covered. The bar fills up quickly with an after-work crowd, but the people watching is even better here than in the dining area. There's a decent selection of microbrews on tap; have the knowledgeable bartenders help you try some new varieties. ♦ Mediterranean ♦ M-Sa lunch and dinner; Su dinner. Reservations recommended. Third floor. 623.1300

41 Brooks Brothers "BB" has had to make some changes in the last few years to maintain its commercial position, but this corner store (the clothier's only outpost north of San Francisco) doesn't seem to have lost a smidgen of traditional demeanor. A wealth of inventory, including some elegant womens-wear, is presented in a refined manner; the salespeople are helpful but not intrusive, and the guys working the men's suits department might have learned their manners from valets to the Duke of Windsor. It's worth waiting until June and right after Christmas for the annual sales. ♦ M-Sa. 1401 Fourth Ave (at Union St). 624.4400

42 1411 Fourth Avenue Building Textural details spun from Celtic motifs and Art Deco flourishes enliven the facade and lobby of this **Robert C. Reamer** office tower (pictured above), which opened in 1929. The stone facing represented a move away from the brick and terra-cotta that were so common to other structures in the neighborhood. Note the elegant entrance sign created by Lloyd Lovegren (who went on during the 1940s to design the Lacey V. Morrow Bridge across Lake Washington). ♦ Between Union and Pike Sts

Within the 1411 Fourth Avenue Building:

JoAnn's Cookies A must-try here are the chocolate-chip dippers: great disks made all the more dangerous to weight-conscious adults by their half-coatings of chocolate. ♦ M-F from 6:30AM. 623.8853

43 Fourth and Pike Building Also known as the "Liggett Building," this 1926 rise of cream-colored terra-cotta was one of the last commercial high-rises built before the Great Depression brought downtown construction to a screeching halt. The impressive lobby here somehow survived relatively intact, while other downtown buildings were having theirs regretfully "modernized." ♦ 1424 Fourth Ave (at Pike St)

Within the Fourth and Pike Building:

Dashasa Studio Jeweler Daniel Shames has a fondness for intensely colored opaque stones and he crafts them into gorgeous pendants and rings. Pieces are hand-assembled to order and fairly affordable ($500 to $2,500), considering the labor involved. ♦ M-Sa; Su by appointment. Suite 807. 623.0519

Seattle Pen

Seattle Pen This intimate shop sells only writing instruments—new models and exquisitely kept older specimens. Repairs and engravings are available, too. ♦ M-F; Sa until 1PM. Suite 527. 682.2640

44 Sharper Image Across from the **Westlake Center** in the Century Square Building is a browser's delight and a gadgeteer's dream. This catalog-come-alive is full of high-tech sound equipment, full-body massage tables, adult toys, and fancy watches. ♦ Daily. 1501 Fourth Ave (at Pike St). 343.9125

44 Mangeamo ★★★$$$ This Southern Italian restaurant opened in late 1993 with Chef Diane Santucci (formerly of Benjamin's in Portland, Oregon) at the helm. With its small bar and booths for diners, and accented with contemporary art, the place has a relaxed, clubby feel to it. Begin with the *asagio* ("tastings") option: a small combination platter of three appetizers of your choosing—be sure to include the *crema de aglio con peperoni* (garlic custard with a puree of spicy roasted peppers) among them. Seasonal entrée selections may include a scallop-saffron pasta, grilled seafood salad, and braised veal shanks with aromatic vegetables. Santucci encourages patrons to dine in traditional Italian fashion, relaxing and sampling several courses; the kitchen will gladly split orders. ♦ M-F lunch and dinner; Sa dinner. Reservations recommended. 1501 Fourth Ave (at Pike St), Third floor. 622.8955

45 Coliseum Theater Believe it or not, this Italian Renaissance relic from 1916— somewhat the worse for wear now—was the first theater in the world designed specifically to show motion pictures. The owner was Joe Gottstein, an ambitious 23-year-old Seattle native who also built the popular **Longacres** horse track (regrettably torn down in 1992). Gottstein believed the public would flock to the movies if it could enjoy them amidst some class and comfort. So he commissioned **B. Marcus Priteca,** personal architect to vaudeville magnate Alexander Pantages, to create an opulent film palace. The resulting 1,700-seat theater, with its terra-cotta facade detailed with grotesque masks, festoons of fruit, and bullock's heads, was a huge success.

But the passage of time and subsequent sales took their toll on this confection. A tremendous dome that once filled the space above the marquee was taken down, and a jarring neon sign was mounted in its place. Other theaters that opened in downtown drew away business. For years, the theater languished in virtual disuse. At press time, the Banana Republic chain had purchased the landmark and had plans to renovate and reopen the theater as its flagship store. ♦ 1506 Fifth Ave (at Pike St)

46 Nordstrom The department-store chain may have spread nationwide, but Seattleites still consider this locally owned store very much theirs and the Nordy's label a symbol of cachet. The store is famous for its policy of cossetting customers. This is one place where returns are no big deal—in fact, unscrupulous people reportedly return things that they didn't even buy here and the merchandise is accepted without complaint. Salespeople are attentive without being cloying, and they're knowledgeable about current fashion trends. A personal-shopper service accommodates people who haven't the time or the inclination to browse through all the racks themselves.

Because it grew out of shoe-store roots, the footwear department here is one of its largest. Women's clothes take up several floors and a series of departments, each with a character (and often age bracket) of its own. Men enjoy a large casuals section, a broad selection of ties, and suits for any occasion. Gifts and some gourmet foods can be found in the **Boardwalk** department. Several annual sales are much anticipated: the store's anniversary (July), and the two semiannual sales for women (June and November) and men (June and January). ♦ Daily. Fifth Ave and Pine St. 628.2111

47 WestCoast Roosevelt Hotel $ When this 20-floor hotel (then the tallest in town) originally threw open its doors in 1930, the *Seattle Daily Times* could hardly contain its enthusiasm. The building's entryway received particular attention: "The ornately furnished lobby was virtually a tower of flowers as guests and well-wishers trooped into it last evening. Visitors were given the freedom of the house and were enabled to inspect the lounge, decorated in French Moderne style and furnished in highly polished ebony and hardwood, and saunter up a winding staircase past the orchestra balcony to the mezzanine." Unfortunately, that lobby—with its strip skylight and several levels—was lost during a 1987 renovation. The present low-ceilinged space, though appointed pleasantly with light gray decor and glass blocks, was at one time the **Rough Rider Lounge,** sporting a disco dance floor where a baby grand piano now rests.

Designed by architect **John Graham Sr.,** the hotel used to be a warren of 234 small rooms. The floors have since been redivided to allow for only 150 larger accommodations, each decorated with subtle and comfortable furnishings. Superior-class rooms also boast Jacuzzis. The 19th floor (with a skylight enclosing the outdoor landing on that floor) is a town house for one of the building's owners. The top level has a single deluxe guest room, with what is perhaps the structure's best view of the city. ♦ 1531 Seventh Ave (at Pine St). 621.1200, 800/426.0670; fax 233.0335

Within the WestCoast Roosevelt Hotel:

Von's Grand City Cafe ★★$ Occupying the hotel's old main lobby space, this clubby restaurant serves an assortment of sandwiches, fish, and steaks. But it's best known for dispensing quality martinis—and lots of them. ♦ American ♦ Daily breakfast, lunch, and dinner. 619 Pine St (at Seventh Ave). 621.8667

48 Paramount Theater This theater and its smaller sister space in Portland, Oregon, were modeled after the Paramount in New York City. Again, **B. Marcus Priteca** was the architect, but here, 13 years after construction of the **Coliseum,** he played a more reserved hand. Its monumental proportions—from the high-rise brick facade to the tall arched windows out front and roofline decorations— were all meant to emphasize the theatricality and fantasy of screen and stage drama. Where vaudeville performers used to trod the boards, the spotlights now fall mostly on rock musicians.

A group of deep-pocketed investors, headed by former Microsoft marketing exec and arts-management consultant Ida Cole, purchased the theater in early 1993, announcing that they would renovate and add to the theater, as well as replace low-income housing units in the upper stories with commercial spaces. As *Seattle Weekly* put it, "The effort will restore the Paramount as one of the grandest large theaters on the West Coast." At press time no action had yet been taken. ♦ Box office opens one hour prior to show time. Cash only. 901 Pine St (at Ninth Ave). 682.1414; TicketMaster 628.0880

49 WestCoast Camlin Hotel $ Money to finish this brick-and-terra-cotta tower in 1926 was actually embezzled by a pair of hyper-ambitious bankers, Adolph Linden and Edmund Campbell, who were subsequently prosecuted and sent to Walla Walla State Penitentiary in eastern Washington. The architect was **Carl J. Linde** of Portland, Oregon, a onetime brewery designer from Wisconsin who had worked under noted Oregon architect **A.E. Doyle.** Most of **Linde**'s efforts were concentrated on the hotel's Ninth Avenue facade. The basic style was Gothic, complete with lions' heads and other decorative gargoyles. Interestingly, the 11-story structure is only *half* a hotel. A second, 14-story establishment, to have been built just north of the existing hotel (where a parking lot now stands), never made it past the drawing board.

This hotel was isolated to the northeast of downtown when it opened in 1926, but it has since been engulfed by the expanding city. A $2-million restoration in 1985 brought in double-paned windows, so that noise (even from the **Paramount Theater** across the street) isn't a problem in the 136 large guest rooms, each of which is decorated in various shades of beige, with exposed pipe fixtures in the bathrooms and overstuffed chairs. Just try to avoid the gloomier cabanas. ♦ 1619 Ninth Ave (between Pine St and Olive Way). 682.0100, 800/426.0670; fax 682.7415

Within the WestCoast Camlin Hotel:

The Cloud Room ★$$ This restaurant turns out acceptable meals (particularly pasta dishes), but the real attraction of the 11th floor is one of the city's most enjoyable and delightfully kitschy piano bars. ♦ Continental ♦ M-F breakfast, lunch, and dinner; Sa-Su breakfast and dinner. Lounge M-F 11AM-1:30AM; Sa-Su 5:30PM-1:30AM. 682.0100

50 Westlake Center Downtown's $250-million version of a suburban shopping mall is oversanitized, overlighted at night, and offers little in the way of a downtown park—a component that its creators, the Maryland-based **Rouse Company,** promised their center would go out of its way to provide. Overall, the glitzy mall feels little connected to the architectural and social character of Seattle's nexus. And it seems aggressively unconnected to the town's history, even though it stands at what has long been an important hub, which, until 1931, held a glorious flatiron building called the **Hotel Plaza.** Yet, because Seattle has no real civic center, this complex has succeeded in becoming a focus of activity. The third floor's carnival of food counters is awash during weekday lunchtimes with workers from the surrounding office hives. A rather stark public plaza out front stays lively with T-shirt vendors, street musicians, hellfire-and-brimstone preachers, and a fountain that you can actually walk through. And it doesn't hurt business any that the monorail from **Seattle Center** has its endpoint here, or that one of the downtown transit tunnel's five stations sits beneath the center. ♦ Fourth Ave and Pine St

Within Westlake Center:

Alweg Monorail This is the beginning (or end) of the 1.2-mile overhead journey to **Seattle Center.** Trains depart every 15 minutes, and the 90-second trip is over before you know it. Still, how many other places have monorails? ♦ Fee. Daily. Third floor. 441.6038

Jessica McClintock Boutique Characters from a Barbara Cartland novel might shop at this store, which is filled with lots of frills and puffs of lace and flouncy skirts. ♦ Daily; M-F until 8PM. Lower floor. 467.1048

Crabtree & Evelyn The shelves are filled with dozens of different soaps, and jar after ja of bath scents, potpourri, sachets, and room fresheners. Combine a few of these tension-relieving nostrums with a good book and a glass of wine and you could poach in the tub for hours. ♦ Daily; M-F until 8PM. First floor. 682.6776

FireWorks Gallery This downtown branch of the Pioneer Square store is even more devoted to artsy souvenirs and jewelry. ♦ Daily; M-F until 9PM. First floor. 682.6462. Also at: 210 First Ave S (between S Washington and S Main Sts). 682.8707

Williams-Sonoma The French porcelain, chrome gadgets, glassware, and cookbooks look so good in this pristine location that it's a shame to mess them up in your own kitchen. But this is a great place for people who care a much about how their kitchenware works as how it looks. Beware of crowds here at Christmastime. ♦ Daily; M-F until 8PM. First floor. 624.1422

Brentano's Efficiently run and impressively well stocked, this is one of downtown's best bookstores. Look for large selections of general fiction, mystery, science fiction, self-help books, travel, and history. The children's department could be beefed up some, but the magazine racks are amply stocked: if there were any more titles, Seattleites would never return to work from their lunch hours. ◆ Daily; M-F until 8PM. Second floor. 467.9626

Purdy's Chocolates Ice-cream bars dipped in a coating of cocoa and hazelnut brittle that drive tastebuds loco, rich Easter rabbits all tied up with string—these are (no doubt) a few of your favorite things. ◆ Daily; M-F until 8PM. Second floor. 682.8571

Victoria's Secret Sift through a variety of tasteful lingerie, suggestive nighties, sports bras, come-hither scents, and comfortable bathrobes, all at reasonable prices. ◆ Daily; M-F until 8PM. Second floor. 623.6035

BOSTON
SOX

Boston Sox For those who appreciate wildly designed stockings and socks, this is a shoppers' paradise. Great place for Christmas stocking stuffers. ◆ Daily; M-F until 8PM. Second floor. 625.1663

The Disney Store Everything here, from *Lion King* lunchboxes to *Sleeping Beauty* pajamas, is movie tie-ins, but at least it's cheaper than a trip to Disneyland. ◆ Daily; M-F until 8PM. Second floor. 622.3323

51 Metro Bus Tunnel It's not exactly the London Underground, but Seattle's 1.3-mile transit tube isn't a gloomy bat cave, either. Buses passing through here are converted temporarily from diesel to electric power. On a cold or rainy day, shoppers appreciate the interior walkways (just above the bus platform level) that connect **Westlake Center** with **Nordstrom** and **The Bon Marché.**

About $3 million was spent by **Metro** on public art for the five bus stations. At the **Westlake** stop, check out the multicolored terra-cotta tiles that carry leaf and vine patterns. (The **Pioneer Square Station** features large clocks made from masonry remnants and a mural that captures aspects of Seattle history in tile. Origami designs spark up the **International District** bus terminal.) ◆ Ticket window: M-F 5AM-7PM; Sa 10AM-6PM. Pine St (between Third and Fourth Aves). 553.3000

52 The Bon Marché Upholding the tradition of department stores, "the Bon" wants to be everything to everybody. Clothes, cosmetics, china, shoe repair, furniture, candy, liquor—they're all here. Merchandise is well selected and stocked, and prices are often more moderate than at similar stores in town. ◆ Daily; M-F until 8PM. Third Ave and Pine St. 344.2121

53 Key Bank Tower (Olympic Tower) This 1929 Art Deco specimen features a polygonal crown and restored terra-cotta facing. It was the creation of local architect **Henry Bittman.** ◆ Third Ave and Pine St

54 A.E. Doyle Building Built as a department store in 1915, this unobtrusive terra-cotta edifice, designed in the Venetian Renaissance palazzo style, was remodeled in 1973 and now carries the name of its original architect, a prominent figure in early 20th-century Portland, Oregon. ◆ Second Ave and Pine St

Within the A.E. Doyle Building:

M. Coy Books More selective than comprehensive in his selection of books, proprietor Michael Coy is usually on top of the latest best-sellers and new regional publications. General fiction is well represented, and there's a mind-engaging array of nonfiction available, but the range within any particular genre (particularly mystery and science fiction) is fairly narrow. Fortunately, employees are helpful and ready to take special orders. A small coffee shop in the back contributes a relaxed and contemplative atmosphere. ◆ Daily. 117 Pine St (at Second Ave). 623.5354

55 Mayflower Park Hotel $$ The 173 rooms here are furnished in antiques, but they're sometimes small—that's the trade-off for accommodations right in the heart of the downtown shopping district. Just be sure to ask for a room high up in this handsome 1927 tower (illustrated above), where you'll see a slice of the city past surrounding building walls. An antiques-filled lobby provides access to a commodious, high-ceilinged bar and to the neighboring **Westlake Center. Clippers,** just off the lobby, serves three meals daily, but it is best for breakfast and lunch, when its big windows let in plenty of natural light. ◆ 405 Olive Way (at Fourth Ave). 623.8700, 800/426.5100; fax 382.6997

Sippin' Suds

Although Seattle's first brewery opened in the early 1860s at Fourth Avenue and Yesler Way, it was the microbrewery boom of the 1980s that earned this town its reputation among beer lovers. As local people and visitors became more interested in both food and drink, they discovered that a whole world of flavorful brews existed beyond the familiar domestic labels.

Ethnic restaurants had a lot to do with the influx of European beers, matching the stoutness and flavor of those products to their diverse menus. So, too, did Jack McAuliffe, who'd become acquainted with Scottish ales while he was stationed with the US Navy in Britain and returned to the States to open the New Albion Brewing Company in Sonoma, California. Though New Albion was financially tapped out by 1983, it inspired beer lovers up and down the West Coast to try their hands at the microbrewery biz.

In 1982 veteran brewmeister Bert Grant started producing a dense and pungent Scottish ale at his Yakima Brewing & Malting Company, southeast of Seattle, in Yakima. At about the same time, the Redhook Ale Brewery began churning forth a fruity, Belgian-style ale at its plant in the **Ballard** neighborhood. Since then, Redhook has moved into headquarters in **Fremont,** introduced its more successful Ballard Bitter and other complex brews, and happily refined its original Redhook Ale. It is now the city's largest boutique beer maker, defying the traditional definition of a "microbrewery" as one producing fewer than 10,000 barrels a year. Other competitors have followed enthusiastically, from Hale's Ales (with breweries in Kirkland and Spokane, Washington) to Maritime Pacific Brewing Company of Seattle and Roslyn Brewing Company in nearby Roslyn, a town that serves as the set for the make-believe Cicely, Alaska, of "Northern Exposure" fame.

It is the rare Seattle bar or tavern today that doesn't boast at least a few full-bodied microbrews on tap. You can also find a number of brewpubs, where beer is produced right on the premises. Brewpubs offer a wonderful opportunity to sample such unusual concoctions as ales spiced with oregano, barley wines, a variety of wheat beers, and seasonal produced extra-dense porters crafted to help your body ward off winter chills. A few Seattle-area brewpubs worth bellying up to:

Big Time Brewery ♦ 4133 University Way NE (between NE 41st and NE 42nd Sts), University District, 545.4509.

Maritime Pacific Brewery Company ♦ 1514 NW Leary Way (at 15th Ave NW), Ballard, 782.6181.

Pacific Northwest Brewing Company ♦ 322 Occidental Ave S (at S Jackson St), Pioneer Square, 621.7002.

Pike Place Brewery ♦ 1432 Western Avenue (near Hillclimb Corridor), Pike Place Market, 622.3373.

Trolleyman Pub, at Redhook Ale Brewery ♦ 3400 Phinney Avenue N (at N 34th St), Fremont, 548.80●

Although Hale's Ales doesn't have its own brewpub is located right next to and dispenses its beers directly through the Eastside's pleasant **Kirkland Roaster & Ale House** (111 Central Way NE, betwee First and Lake Sts, Kirkland, 827.4400).

If you haven't a friend or acquaintance to help you navigate the maze of microbrewery offerings availa here, consult Bart Becker's spirited book, *Seattle Brews: The Insider's Guide to Neighborhood Alehouses, Brewpubs, and Bars* (1992, Alaska Northwes

56 Times Square Building It was no coincidence that this flatiron structure and the irregular intersection to its immediate west came to be known as Times Square. First off, the building housed the *Seattle Times* newspaper from 1916 until 1931. Second, the intersection bears a strong resemblance to Manhattan's Times Square. Constructed of terra-cotta and granite, with fine Beaux Arts detailing (note the elegant eagles decorating the roofline), it was one of the earliest downtown works by architect **Carl Gould.** A graduate of the Ecole des Beaux Arts in Paris who apprenticed with the famous New York City firm of **McKim, Mead & White** before heading west for his health, the architect would eventually give Seattle a series of landmarks, including the original **Seattle Art Museum** on Capitol Hill and the **Suzzallo Library** at the **University of Washington.** ♦ Bounded by Stewart St and Olive Way, and Fourth and Fifth Aves

57 WestCoast Vance Hotel $ Built in 1926 by the Vance Lumber Company as a stopov● for visiting lumber brokers and other dealmakers, this hotel was pretty seedy whe the WestCoast chain decided to spend $7 million in 1990 on its restoration. The exteri was never meant to be breathtaking, but it does include fine terra-cotta detailing near street level and a nicely polished dark lobby The 165 rooms tend to be smaller than norr but still pleasant, with the best views of the **Space Needle** from above the fifth floor on the north side. ♦ 620 Stewart St (at Seventh Ave). 441.4200, 800/663.1144; fax 441.861

Within the WestCoast Vance Hotel:

Salute in Città ★$$ Although far less romantic than the funky original **Salute,** wh● is north of the University District, this tratto● makes the cut for its excellent and inexpens designer pizzas. They're on the small side, b are ideal nighttime bar fare. ♦ Italian ♦ Daily breakfast, lunch, and dinner. 728.1611. Als● at: 3410 NE 55th St (at 35th Ave NE). 527.8600

Restaurants/Clubs: Red	**Hotels:** Blue	
Shops/ 🌳 Outdoors: Green	**Sights/Culture:** Black	

58 Westin Hotel $$$ You can't miss this place: it's the one with the round twin pillars of guest rooms that look like corncobs. The circular design allows for a maximum number of the 865 rooms, all equipped with balconies. (The best vistas are from above the 20th floor.) Guests enjoy spacious and well-lighted accommodations but contrastingly plain furnishings. Room rates include a complimentary breakfast. The convention facilities are plentiful and spread over several levels. There's a large swimming pool and supervised exercise room and three lounges. ♦ 1900 Fifth Ave (at Stewart St). 728.1000, 800/228.3000; fax 728.2259

Within the Westin Hotel:

The Palm Court ★★$$$ There's not much of a view (just out to concrete-filled Times Square), nor is this restaurant overwhelmed by greenery, as its name suggests, but the entrées here have proved to be excellent (the crab cakes and smoked salmon chowder deserve culinary-museum positions). Evening selections include a piquant braised lamb shank with mushrooms, and roast chicken on a mattress of white beans. Desserts, particularly the chocolate variations, are extra, extra, extra rich. A nice touch: the menu includes wine suggestions with each dish. ♦ Continental ♦ Daily lunch and dinner. Reservations recommended. 728.1000

Nikko ★★★$$$$ It is fitting that a showman and sushi chef such as Tokyo-trained Toyama should be performing on the corner where one of the city's gaudiest theaters, the **Orpheum**, stood for 40 years. But you don't need tickets to watch Toyama's act, just the willingness to let this fine chef take some command of your meal and prepare whatever's freshest—from tuna to fish liver or squid gut. ♦ Japanese ♦ M-F lunch and dinner; Sa-Su dinner. 322.4641

59 Dahlia Lounge ★★★★$$$ Owner/chef Tom Douglas's creation is a colorful place, with bright red walls and rice-paper fish lamps that "swim" above the dining tables. His inventive menu features Northwestern ingredients prepared with Pacific Rim accents. To start, try the shrimp, lobster, and shiitake mushroom pot stickers with a sauce of sake and chili oil. Douglas's crab cakes are legendary in Seattle and are one of the most popular entrées here; a close second is the grilled salmon with ginger-sake butter. Be sure to go all the way and order dessert: the only dilemma is whether to have pear tart with caramel sauce or strawberry rhubarb crisp. All the dishes are consistently fresh and always delicious. The waitstaff are friendly and helpful; don't hesitate to ask for their advice. ♦ Northwestern ♦ M-F lunch and dinner; Sa-Su dinner. Reservations recommended. 1904 Fourth Ave (between Stewart and Virginia Sts). 682.4142

60 Annex Theatre This interesting fringe theater is operated by ambitious, thoughtful twentysomethings. The experimental offerings can run to the dreadful, but there is almost always a spark to them. If you're looking for a sure bet, stop in for the late-night Friday improvs (11PM). ♦ Box office daily 6:45PM-8PM. 1916 Fourth Ave (between Stewart and Virginia Sts). 728.0933

61 Moore Theater and Hotel For many years pioneer Arthur Denny had reserved six acres here in hopes that Seattle might one day capture the Washington state capitol building (which was eventually built in Olympia). But in 1888 he went ahead and filled the site with a first-class hotel—something the city desperately needed after the Great Fire of 1889. The national depression of 1893 stalled construction of this multitowered edifice, and it was finally completed a decade later by Seattle superdeveloper James A. Moore. (President Teddy Roosevelt was the first guest at the new hotel when it opened in 1903.) Almost immediately, Moore had bigger dreams for this area. He wanted to enlarge his hotel and to erect the most artistic and beautiful theater in the West.

Sure enough, the hotel and an adjoining playhouse (both designed by prolific Seattle architect **E.W. Houghton**) went up in 1908. But in the meantime the hotel was razed to make possible the regrading of Denny Hill. James Moore fell on hard times not many years later and so did his theater. Its vaguely Egyptian Revival–style interior is still intact, but the likes of Marie Dressler and John Barrymore no longer perform here. Now the hall is used only sporadically, mostly for concerts. ♦ Box office hours vary, call ahead. 1932 Second Ave (at Virginia St). 443.1744

King Street Station provided the final scene in a particularly bizarre double murder in 1906. The first casualty was one Franz Edmond Creffield, unabashed debaucher and leader of a pseudo-religious cult in Oregon (the Bride of Christ Church), whose followers—almost all women—made a practice of rolling on floors and baying at the moon. On 7 May 1906, during a visit to Seattle, Creffield was shot in the head on the corner of First Avenue and Cherry Street. The killer was George Mitchell, brother of one of Creffield's flock, Esther Mitchell. Shortly after her brother's release from jail, Esther said good-bye to him at the King Street Station. As George turned to leave, Esther drew a gun and executed him in the same way he had Creffield. She was committed to an insane asylum for three years.

The 39 inches of rain that Seattle receives in a year is in fact less than what falls on New York or Boston or Atlanta. Miami actually puts up with a whopping 60 inches annually.

Pike Place Market/ Waterfront

The market is a kinetic profusion of people, energy, and individual enterprise. Flowers for sale. Pottery. Pastries. Scarves. Cigars. Seascapes. T-shirts. Teacups. Fish peddlers toss huge flounder above the heads of awed customers. A ragtag band coaxes a lively rendition of Jimmy Buffett's "Pencil-Thin Mustache" from time-distressed instruments. A hawker at the **Read All About It** newsstand shouts, *"P-I! Seattle Post-Intelligencer! Seattle Times! New Yo-o-o-rk Times! LA Times! We've got the Times!"* Shoppers jockey with automobiles along the two-and-a-half block stretch of **Pike Place**, with drivers almost invariably losing out. As many as 40,000 people visit this bazaar daily.

There's no guarantee you'll find the freshest produce here, but for urban color, **Pike Place Market**—the oldest continuously operating farmer's market in the country—is unbeatable. *New York Times* correspondent Timothy Egan called it the "Marrakech of the Northwest." Artist Mark Tobey, who haunted the market frequently, beginning in the 1920s, once described it as "a refuge, an oasis, a most human growth, the heart and soul of Seattle."

The market began in 1907, when food wholesalers formed a "Produce Row" along **Western Avenue.** Farmers who couldn't take the time off to sell their crops relied on wholesalers to do the job for them. But local growers suspected (quite rightly, in many cases) that these intermediaries were cheating them of a fair price for their goods and, at the same time, gouging customers with excessive fees. The city's response was to establish a *true* farmer's market. The location was based primarily on convenience (aggressive

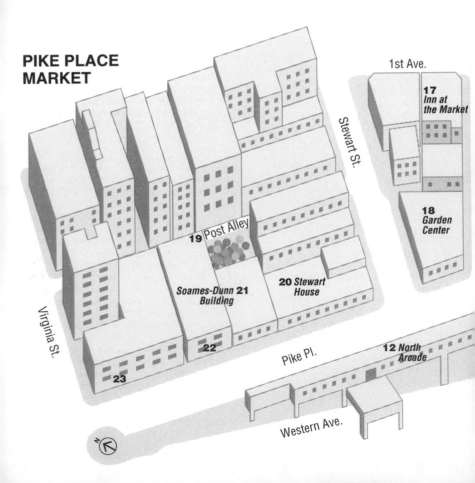

PIKE PLACE MARKET

1st Ave.

Stewart St.

17 Inn at the Market

18 Garden Center

19 Post Alley

20 Stewart House

Soames-Dunn **21** Building

22

23

Virginia St.

Pike Pl.

12 North Arcade

Western Ave.

N

regrading had recently leveled the land at **Pike Street**'s western end, and newly planked **Western Avenue** connected it with the Waterfront). On opening day, 17 August 1907, fewer than a dozen wagons showed up (and one of those, driven by a Japanese farmer, was ransacked), but thousands of Seattleites came eager to buy. The next week, 70 wagons took positions on the Pike Place curb. Fishmongers soon infiltrated the neighborhood, as did other small businesses. Stall sizes had to be reduced to fit everybody in and canopies were built to keep commerce chugging along through the Seattle rains. Several proposals called for **Pike Place Market** to grow into a grandiose commercial complex spilling down from its bluff on **Elliott Bay** into a railroad and marine terminal on the Waterfront. But residents voted to keep the market small and personable: exuberant with Italians, Japanese, and Sephardic Jews hawking their goods; replete with local characters like Horseradish Jerry, who ground roots into relish, or the old-timers who droned tall tales of the Klondike Gold Rush. Within 10 years the market had become Seattle's funky equivalent of a community square.

The 1929 Depression exacted its toll on **Pike Place Market**. So did World War II's internment of Japanese farmers; the decline of **First Avenue**, from a worker's mall to a strip of peep shows and honky-tonks; and the insurgence of supermarkets. By 1963, with the market and indeed all of Seattle in wan condition, planners encouraged the city to bulldoze the market in favor of a parking and high-rise development. Only a concerted effort by preservationists, politicians, local architects (among them the persistent **Victor Steinbrueck**, who had designed the **Space Needle**), and eventually voters saved the heart and soul of Seattle. A seven-acre Market Historical District was established in 1974.

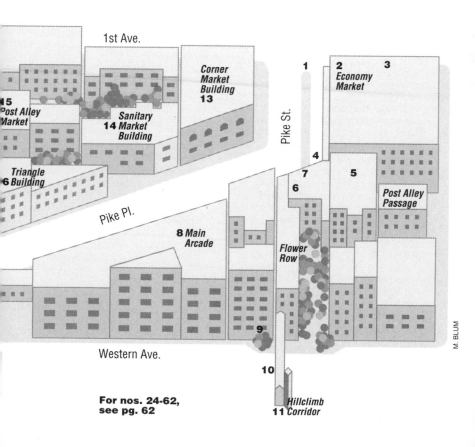

1st Ave.

1   2 Economy Market   3

Corner Market Building 13

15 Post Alley Market

Sanitary 14 Market Building

Pike St.

4

7   5

6

Triangle 16 Building

Post Alley Passage

Pike Pl.

8 Main Arcade

Flower Row

9

Western Ave.

10

For nos. 24-62, see pg. 62

Hillclimb 11 Corridor

M. BLUM

Regular guided tours will give you an overview of the market, but the best way to get a feel for it is to wander about its well-preserved edifices, exploring the alleys, stairways, and ramps where the many buildings have been strung together throughout the years. However, it would take years to fully appreciate all the attractions and rhythms of the place; in fact, even most natives know it only in passing. **Pike Place Market** (which is also referred to as the "Public Market") is open daily from early May through December, and Monday through Saturday the rest of the year. Individual shop hours vary, as do the seasonal schedules of businesses not contained completely within market buildings.

Since **Pike Place Market** achieved historic status, every one of its buildings has been renovated or reconstructed. Unfortunately, less attention has been paid to Seattle's Waterfront. This was once the center of local commerce, a strip alive with the shouts of merchants and the jibs of the **Mosquito Fleet**, an early ferry service. But several decades ago the Waterfront was severed from the rest of downtown by the **Alaskan Way Viaduct** and—except for the estimable **Seattle Aquarium** and the too small **Waterfront Park**—has since been all but completely given over to fast-food joints and kitschy emporiums. Hope for its revitalization is now centered on the **Bell Street Pier**, an 11-acre span of urban shoreline that is being developed as a maritime and trade facility that is scheduled to open in the summer of 1996.

Pike Place Market

1 **Market Information Booth** Market maps and other visitor info are happily dispensed here. This is the starting point for tours of the neighborhood. ♦ Daily. First Ave and Pike St. 682.7453

2 **Economy Market** Promoter and investor **Frank Goodwin** was an eccentric who played heavily with penny stocks, put together an early steam-powered automobile, and practiced a strict vegetarian diet. He bought heavily into Pike Place real estate and was the man who finally brought the market in out of the rain in 1907, when he constructed the **Main Arcade**.

An amateur architect, **Goodwin** designed and built a multistory expansion of the market down Pike Place bluff to Western Avenue. In 1916 he obtained a lease on the **Bartell Building** (completed in 1900) at the corner of First Avenue and Pike Street, transforming it into today's **Economy Market.** Look for his design work in this building's Doric columns and the plaster garlands of fruit and flowers. Preservation architect **George Bartholick** headed a rehabilitation of the market in 1978. The angled ramps in the atrium used to be trod by horses, which were checked through here on their way to the main market. ♦ Pike St and First Ave

Within the Economy Market:

Read All About It One of the two best-stocked newsstands in this city (the other contender is **Bulldog News** in the University District), the inventory here reflects a walloping diversity of American and international periodicals. Expect everything from *Popular Mechanics* to *Sassy*. Looking for the *International Herald Tribune* or the *Nome Nugget?* They're here, too. ♦ Daily. 7AM-7PM. Main floor. 624.0140

Stamp Happy Children of all ages could spend hours here testing out the available and often comic rubber stamps, but buyers are also welcome. ♦ Daily. Main floor. 682.8575

Daily Dozen Doughnuts Snag a baker's dozen sack of miniature doughnuts—plain, covered with powdered sugar, or cinnamon. Then hope nobody witnesses your abject gluttony. ♦ M-Sa. Main floor. 467.7769

DeLaurenti's Specialty Foods Exotic Mediterranean canned goods, meats, and wines are shoehorned into a space barely big enough to contain them all. Though the history of this shop is commonly traced back to owners Pete and Mamie DeLaurenti in the 1940s, Mamie's very Italian mother, Angelina Mustelo, had opened a small store in the market's lower level in 1928. ♦ M-Sa. Main floor. 622.0141. Also at: 317 Bellevue Way N (between NE Second and NE Fourth Sts), Bellevue. 454.7155

The Great Wind-Up Follow the noise of barking dogs, growling dragons, and hopping bunnies to this toy-filled corner shop. While children gather ideas for Christmas, adults will enjoy a tableful of windup kangaroos, chattering teeth, and mince-stepping eyeballs. ♦ Daily. Atrium. 621.9370

Restaurants/Clubs: Red	**Hotels:** Blue
Shops/ ♥ Outdoors: Green	**Sights/Culture:** Bla

Sasquatch Whether descended from prehistoric primates or born from human imagination, Sasquatch (or Bigfoot, if you prefer) has become the Northwest's signature monster. Its appearances hark back to the tribal mythology of virtually every native people from coastal British Columbia to northern California. The name Sasquatch comes from *sas-kets,* a term used by Salish-speaking tribes of southwestern British Columbia to describe the hairy, humanlike giants they said lived in the Fraser River Valley and communicated via whistles and shrill screams. More than 2,500 Sasquatch sightings have been recorded since the 1960s, most of them in Washington. This brooding sculpture was carved by artist Richard Beyer. ♦ Atrium

Tenzing Momo Any moment you expect the Dalai Lama to come sailing through the door of this herbal apothecary to buy a stick of incense or some bulk herbs. You can pick up fluid extracts, Chinese nostrums, ear-wax candles, or books on witchcraft. The store's name, translated from Tibetan, means "illustrious dumpling." This is holy ground for worshipers in the temple of natural health. ♦ M-Sa. Atrium. 623.9837

3 Liberty Malt Supply Company/Pike Place Brewery This shop has sold fresh hops, malted barley, and home-brewing supplies since 1921. Beer-making classes are offered several times a year, covering basics as well as fermentation, bottling, and stylistic variations. Nearby, the **Pike Place Brewery** has been producing fine-quality beers, carried by some of the best taverns in town, since 1989. Brewery tours are available daily; call for times. ♦ Daily. Liberty Malt Supply Company: 1419 First Ave (between Pike and Union Sts). 622.1880; Pike Place Brewery: 1432 Western Ave (near the Hillclimb Corridor). 622.3373

4 Lower Post Alley This was once a major commercial route connecting the market with Western Avenue's Produce Row, the Waterfront, and Pioneer Square. Guttering beneath the main market sign and clock, the alley is now pretty much ignored, yet it is supposedly the only completely restored cobblestone street in the Northwest. The glass-walled bridge above the alley's entrance off First Avenue was known historically as the Bridge of Sighs. Apparently, from here south, the alley used to be lined with bars, and sailors would stop in at each of them for a nip before shipping out of town. It's said that from the bridge women would watch their men amble slowly away and, presumably, sigh. ♦ Between Pike and Union Sts

Along Lower Post Alley:

Il Bistro ★★$$$ Trimmed in dark woods and set off by arches, this quiet dining spot is like a European cave or wine cellar. People come here after work to decompress, sipping wine or whiskey in the jazz-filled bar, or chatting over dinner in the restaurant's more secluded reaches. Italian dishes got this place off the ground, and, while a variety of seafood plates have been introduced with varying degrees of success, pasta is still instrumental in keeping it popular. Both the tortellini with garlic, pine nuts, and tomatoes and the linguine *carretiera* (with seasonal mushrooms, hot pepper flakes, tomato, cream, and vodka) will satisfy your appetite. The cioppino is also a standout. ♦ Italian ♦ M-Sa lunch and dinner; Su dinner; bar until 2AM. 93A Pike St. 682.3049

5 LaSalle Hotel This bay-windowed building beside the **Public Market** sign was the first bordello north of Yesler Way and survived to become the last of this city's big-time bawdy houses. Erected in 1909 as the **Outlook Hotel,** prior to World War II it was owned by a Japanese family who catered to frugal workers and the elderly. After the 1942 internment of Japanese residents, the hotel was taken over by Nellie Curtis (née Zella Nightengale), who had run orderly disorderly houses across Canada before moving to Seattle in 1931. Small and birdlike, with a warm laugh, she drove Cadillacs, kept her money stuffed in drawers rather than banks, wore ermine shawls, and collected hats with the same superfluousness with which Imelda Marcos would later gather shoes. As Alice Shorett and Murray Morgan recall in their jolly history, *Pike Place Market: People, Politics, and Produce,* the hotel even had "enough rooms so that some could be used for legitimate hotel purposes, thus providing a cover for more profitable activities."

Shortly after business got under way here, some of Nellie's "girls" went down to the Waterfront to meet incoming ships and hand out business cards: "LaSalle Hotel—Friends Easily Made." That night hundreds of libidinous wharf rats and sailors tried to anchor in one of the hotel's 57 berths, attracting attention not only from the local military but from reform Mayor William Devin, who ordered a prostitution crackdown. But Nellie's fortunes went undisturbed.

It was only in 1949, after her nephew botched a temporary management of the place and Seattle had been shaken by its first major earthquake, that Nellie decided to sell the hotel. The buyers were a Japanese-American couple, George and Sodeko Ikeda, who had trouble convincing some of Nellie's old clients that there were no longer any "working girls" in the hostelry. The Ikedas subsequently sued Nellie for overstating profits to be made from the property. Not only did Nellie lose $7,500 in court, but she finally attracted the attention of the Internal Revenue Service. The hotel was rehabilitated in 1977 and now contains commercial space as well as low-income housing. ♦ Lower Post Alley (off First Ave, between Pike and Union Sts)

6 Market Clock Rising from the elbow that connects the **Economy Market** to the **Main Arcade,** this timepiece and the **Public Market** sign that surrounds it are supposed to be the oldest examples of public neon in Seattle, dating back to the 1920s or 1930s. The clock is a favorite among visiting photographers, and on New Year's Eve, crowds of happily tipsy Seattleites gather below it to celebrate at the stroke of midnight. ♦ Pike Pl and Pike St

7 Rachel, the Market Pig This overgrown piggy bank is the Market Foundation's friendliest fund-raiser. More than $35,000 has been dropped into her belly since she took up her position below the **Market Clock** in 1986. ♦ Pike Pl and Pike St

8 Main Arcade Frank Goodwin's first market building, dating from 1907, reflects a simpler architectural style than he applied to his reworking of the **Economy Market.** About 50 percent of the market's fish and produce stalls are located here, with many others just across the street. Take a look at the engraved floor tiles covering the arcade's main level, laid out as part of a fund-raising project in the mid-1980s. Seattleites paid $35 apiece to have their names imprinted on these tiles; Ronald and Nancy Reagan are also represented here, although they didn't pay anything for the privilege. Two floors (making up what used to be called the **Labyrinth**) descend from street level in this building and are known simply as "First Floor Down Under" and "Second Floor Down Under." ♦ Pike Pl (between Pine and Pike Sts)

Within the Main Arcade:

The Athenian Inn ★$ Opened in 1909 as a Greek bakery/luncheonette, and later operated as a bar (it received one of Seattle's earliest liquor licenses, in 1933), this is among the market's most democratic restaurants. Fishers hunker up to the bar counter while designer-suited sales reps wait in line for tables with views of Puget Sound. The menu hits all the local standards—from grilled oysters to fat burgers—with the breakfast fave being red-flannel hash. (The breakfast menu is available all day long.) The bar has 16 beers on tap but stocks more than 300 brews. ♦ American/Greek ♦ M-Sa breakfast, lunch, and dinner until 6:30PM. Main floor. 624.7166

City Fish This busy stall was started by the city in 1918 to offer Seattleites fresh and reasonably priced fish. Newspaper reports of overcharging had led Mayor Hiram Gill to make his health commissioner responsible for setting up a market space stocked with dirt-cheap hatchery fish. Prices began at one-third to one-quarter of what was being charged elsewhere for fish. For four years, this operation was profitable, but as sales waned, the city sold out. David Levy, one of the first Sephardic Jews to arrive in Seattle, bought the stall in 1926 and quickly earned the nickname "Good Weight Dave" for keeping his thumb off the scale. The business, still in Levy family hands, continues to sell high-quality fish and also offers overnight shipping to any location in the continental US. Look for the well-preserved **City Fish Market** sign on Pike Place. ♦ Daily from 7:30AM. Main floor. 682.9329

Lowell's Restaurant $ Substantive, though not surprising, meals (try the fried oysters and the Monte Cristo or Reuben sandwiches) are served at this classic cafeteria and restaurant. It was opened as a coffee shop in 1908 by brothers Edward and William Manning, veterans of the New England coffee and tea trade, who did something early on that much later would become a Seattle signature: They started selling roasted coffee beans in bulk. The Mannings eventually expanded their business down the West Coast, moving their headquarters to San Francisco in the 1920s and finally selling their Pike Place enterprise in 1957. Reid Lowell, a former manager for the Mannings, owned and operated the place for many years until he passed it along to his insurance agent, Bill Chatalas, in 1981. ♦ American/Seafood ♦ Daily breakfast, lunch, and dinner until 5PM. Main floor. 622.2036

Market Spice Olfactory overload! More than a hundred flavors of tea, bulk coffee beans, and giant jars of seasonings can be found here, as can tea-brewing paraphernalia and boxes of fine sweets. Head first to the free-tea dispenser, just beside the cashier's counter and usually filled with the popular house blend (developed by the wife of a pharmacist in the 1970s). Then roam the aisles with an open mind . . . and an open nose. Mail orders accepted. ♦ Daily. Main floor. 622.6340

Maximilien-in-the-Market ★★$$$
You've got to admire the ego of a restaurant that showcases a review written in French. Are you just to *assume* that the report is favorable, or should you simply allow yourself to be seduced by the old-fashioned charm and exceptional Puget Sound views here? Owned by Francois and Julia Kissel, this restaurant is proud of its "Frenchness," but that doesn't translate to hautiness; in fact, the staff is pleasant and attentive. Entrées include boneless chicken baked with apples and sausage in cider, fresh salmon and mussels, as well as the more pedestrian (but well prepared) fish-and-chips. The bar is a fine redoubt from winter chills. ◆ French ◆ M-Sa breakfast, lunch, and dinner; Su brunch and dinner. Reservations recommended. Main floor. 682.7270

Pike Place Fish In 1947 the Seattle City Council forbade singing by market vendors. But wait until you hear the bellowing hawkers here, whose voices positively explode from beneath the **Market Clock.** Crowds gather to observe the iced beds of crab and to gape as fishmongers hurl salmon over tourists' heads for weighing behind the counter. Founded in 1930, the store ships fresh fish anywhere in the US. ◆ Daily from 6:30AM. Main floor. 682.7181, 800/542.7732; fax 682.4629

Place Pigalle ★★$$ Time was when this was essentially a bar, frequented by men (many were patrons of the **LaSalle Hotel** bordello) who drank with their hats on. Now it's one of the most pleasant dining spaces in the market—the floor is covered in alternating black-and-white tiles, and the outlook on Puget Sound is wondrously unobstructed. The menu includes whatever is seasonally fresh, leaning heavily toward such seafood as Dungeness crab, hazelnut-covered red snapper, and salmon in a brandy and Bing-cherry sauce. Pork medaillons in a saffron-almond sauce, and an open-faced chicken sandwich with chipotle pepper aioli are other worthy choices. The only disappointment is the oyster stew, which, while rich and flavorful, can be skimpy with the bivalves. A porch is available for outdoor dining in the summer.
◆ Continental/Northwestern ◆ M-Sa lunch and dinner. Reservations recommended. Down the staircase behind Pike Place Fish. 624.1756

Golden Age Collectables This crowded corner store carries the city's largest selection of comics, everything from standards such as

Spiderman, Legends of the Dark Knight, and the *Green Arrow* (the last now drawn by local talent Mike Grell and set in Seattle), to *Aliens, Swamp Thing, Bikini Confidential,* and some of the more obscure titles from the Dark Horse publishing house of Portland, Oregon. There's a wide array of vintage comics, too, plus science-fiction novels, models, sports cards, and binders full of classic, movie-star publicity stills. Special orders are taken. ◆ Daily. First Floor Down Under. 622.9799

Market Magic Shop Common thrills here are the impromptu performances by owners Darryl Beckmann and Sheila Lyon, who always seem willing to open their bags of tricks. With professional paraphernalia and joke props, replicas of old Houdini posters, and juggling clubs, this is an ideal spot to conjure up an afternoon's escape—mental, if not physical. ◆ Daily. First Floor Down Under. 624.4271

Old Seattle Paperworks With the feel of a richly cluttered attic, this is a narrow storehouse of old postcards for sale, classic black-and-whites from Seattle's early years, and piles of dusty *National Geographic* magazines like the ones your grandparents have held onto for half a century. ◆ Daily. First Floor Down Under. 623.2870

MisterE B♥♥ks

MisterE Books This store is tiny but caters nicely to both best-seller addicts and readers who collect first-edition mysteries, science fiction, and Westerns. Racks of old records take up one end of the space. ◆ Daily. First Floor Down Under. 622.5182

Grandma's Attic One of several collectibles outlets on the arcade's lowest level, this one is filled with delicate, feminine vintage outfits and knickknacks. ◆ Daily. Second Floor Down Under. 682.9281

Yesterdaze Intriguingly cluttered with well-kept old hats, ties, and jewelry but especially known for its period military clothing, this shop is a perfect stop for collectors. ◆ M-Sa. Second Floor Down Under. No phone

9 Seattle Parrot Market and Reptile House Just follow the squawking to this "birdhouse." Almost every conceivable breed of parrot can be found here. The most exotic resident is the female electus parrot from the Solomon Islands and New Guinea, famous for her stunning coat of fine, deep red feathers. ◆ Daily. 1500 Western Ave (near the Hillclimb Corridor). 467.6133

San Francisco may have left *its* heart in Seattle: it's estimated that 30 to 40 tons of Telegraph Hill were taken on as ships' ballast and then dumped into Elliott Bay for landfill.

KASALA

10 Kasala A glass-walled corner location provides a cheery showplace for contemporary and high-style (but surprisingly comfortable) furniture for office and home. There are lots of high-tech floor lamps and other European accessories. Salespeople are readily available but usually leave you alone to browse. ◆ Daily. 1505 Western Ave (near the Hillclimb Corridor). 623.7795. Also at: 1014 116th Ave NE (between NE 12th St and Bel-Red Rd), Bellevue. 453.2823

11 Hillclimb Corridor In the market's early days, a wooden pedestrian overpass (built in 1912) connected Pike Place with Waterfront piers, an essential link. Many sellers at the market arrived by boat, often on craft belonging to the old **Mosquito Fleet,** an armada of 70 small steamers that hustled people and products to 350 ports on Puget Sound. In 1973, after the market gained historical status, those rickety steps were replaced with these landscaped stairs (designed by **Calvin/Gorasht and Sanders**) down to the Waterfront and the **Seattle Aquarium**. The incline is steep (some refer to it as Cardiac Gulch), yet the **Hillclimb** has proved a magnet for both shops and shoppers. ◆ Between Western Ave and Alaskan Way

On the Hillclimb Corridor:

El Puerco Lloron ★$ It looks like a cafeteria decorated by cheesy Tijuana trinket collectors, but the handmade tortillas, tamales, and exceptional *chiles rellenos* more than make up for the decorative deficiencies. Beware of the salsas: it's always best to taste first before pouring them over your meal. ◆ Mexican ◆ Daily lunch and dinner. 624.0541

Procopio Treat yourself to a delicious homemade gelato sans artificial anything. Appropriately enough for this city, flavors include cappuccino and mocha. ◆ M-Th until 10PM; F-Sa until midnight. 622.4280

Chicken and Egg Northwestern style is showcased here: canopied beds, well-stuffed sofas, and rush-woven bench seats, all showing the knots and unique bulges of the Douglas fir trees from which they were shaped. Logs used to make this furniture are peeled to their cambium layers and then cured in late summer sunshine until they achieve a

palomino gleam. Knots are sanded and hand-rubbed with beeswax. The warmly natural, unmanicured results fit surprisingly well into even the most modern settings. Profits from sales go to funding child-abuse prevention efforts and school programs through the Children's Trust Foundation and Cities in Schools. And don't worry that forests are being devastated; the firs used are culled only from overgrown stands. Also available are decorative accoutrements (dried flowers, small sculptures) and interior-design books supporting the natural look. ◆ Daily. 1426 Alaskan Way. 623.6144

12 North Arcade This has become one of the slowest moving pedestrian areas in the market, as everybody stops to look at the tables piled with handknit sweaters, homemade jellies and jams, and arrangements of dried flowers. On warm days merchants even stretch out north along the sidewalk, selling some of the more interesting T-shirts available here, as well as jewelry and pottery. ◆ Pike Pl (between Pine and Virginia Sts)

13 Corner Market Building One of the things about **Pike Place Market** that most fascinates architects is that so little of the development here can be ascribed to professional designers. An exception is this formal structure built in 1912, and conceived by **Harlan Thomas,** designer of the **Sorrento Hotel** and **Harborview Hospital,** both on First Hill, and the Byzantine **Chamber of Commerce Building** downtown on Columbia Street.

A three-story brick structure, this building is best recognized by its graceful arched top-level windows. The first tenant was **Three Girls Bakery,** which now operates in the **Sanitary Market Building.** Also housed here was the Northwest's first homegrown grocery chain: Herman Eba moved from the **Main Arcade** stall he'd occupied since 1910 to the **Corner Market** in 1929, and six years later adopted the business name **Tradewell,** a label that later became familiar to supermarket shoppers around the region. This was the first market landmark to be rehabilitated (1975). ◆ Pike Pl and Pike St

Within the Corner Market Building:

The Crumpet Shop ★$ A welcome alternative to the preponderance of coffeehouses in Seattle, this cozy tearoom prepares its own spongy crumpets, which are great topped with raspberry jam, marmalade, or even ricotta cheese. This is a wonderful choice for a unique and inexpensive breakfast; lox or ham on crumpets are available at lunch, as are more conventional sandwiches. The space can be loaded with take-out patrons early on weekday mornings, but it's a comforting crowdedness—really. ◆ Teahouse/Takeout ◆ Daily breakfast, lunch, and afternoon tea. First floor. 682.1598

Left Bank Books It takes a while to acquaint yourself with the categorization (books written by men, for instance, are philosophically as well as physically divided from books by women), and the array of new and used volumes tends to be more funky than complete. But there's an endearing, antiquarian nature to this place, buttressed by a lack of computerization and pack-rat mentality. The bent is toward liberal, sometimes revolutionary works. ♦ Daily. First floor. 622.0195

Cafe Counter Intelligence ★$
You've got to appreciate the decor in this long narrow joint, where the artwork along one wall may be a series of dinner plates decorated with desperado mug shots and where the countertop is a mosaic of tiny tiles spelling out the shop's moniker. Noshes include toasted crumpets, seasonal fruits, sandwiches, and special soups. But the true culinary stars here are the coffee (in a dizzying array of permutations) and the milk shakes (especially the peppermint and the Dutch chocolate varieties). ♦ Coffeehouse ♦ Daily. Second floor. 622.6979

CHEZ SHEA

Chez Shea ★★★★$$$$ This restaurant is especially romantic late at night, when candlelight is the principal illumination, torch songs are the featured entertainment, and the half-moon windows allow a softened perspective on the market below and the ferries gliding over Puget Sound.

A dinner here might open with a savory phyllo tart decked in tomato and grated onion, followed by a sweet and moist corn pudding. Melt-on-the-tongue scallops sit in a crisp potato-string nest, and tender duck is served on a bed of *stroganoff*. The mixed greens pale by comparison, but they may be followed by the remarkably smooth French silk (chocolate) pie. The wine list represents both top West Coast and European vintages. Recently opened, **Shea's Lounge** (get it?) serves libations and a lighter menu.
♦ Continental/Northwestern ♦ Tu-Su dinner; lounge until 2 AM. Reservations required. Second floor. 467.9990

Pike Place Bar & Grill ★$ Sandee and Gordy Brock's joint is a market standard, not flashy but satisfying. Newcomers usually wind up at the restaurant end, filling themselves with sandwiches (thumbs up, especially for the French dip) or pleasing pasta and fish

specials. Seattleites gravitate to the noisier bar, where the same menu is available but you can also find the best views of the market. Piano players keep the bar's resident instrument well exercised. ♦ American ♦ M, Su lunch; Tu-Sa lunch and dinner. Second floor. 624.1365

14 Sanitary Market Building The name derives from the fact that this was the first building in the market that didn't allow horses inside. It was four stories tall when erected in 1910, but the upper floors (which originally held garment shops) were destroyed by a fire 31 years later, one of several conflagrations to sweep through the market since its inception. City architect **Daniel R. Huntington** redesigned it in 1942 as a two-story edifice with rooftop parking. The building was rehabilitated again in 1981 by **Bassetti/Norton/Metler**.
♦ Pike Pl (between Pine and Pike Sts)

Within the Sanitary Market Building:

Jack's Fish Spot $ Behind the fresh shellfish tanks (the only ones in the market) is a walk-up seafood bar. Try the cioppino or the fish-and-chips before you depart with your purchases. ♦ Seafood ♦ Restaurant: daily lunch; fish market: daily from 7:30AM. Lower floor. 467.0514

Rasa Malaysia ★$ This is the first in a popular chain of restaurants where the emphasis is on noodles, usually sautéed with very fresh veggies, peanut or another mildly spicy sauce, and a variety of fish, shrimp, or meat. Try a fruit smoothie or some of the fresh and not overly sweet lemonade.
♦ Malaysian/Takeout ♦ Daily lunch and dinner until 6PM. Lower floor. 624.8388. Also at: Broadway Market (401 Broadway E), 328.8882; 7208 E Green Lake Dr N (near NE 72nd St), 523.8888

Three Girls Bakery ★$ Its roots are in the **Corner Market Building,** where it opened in 1912, but this bakery is now an institution at its current location. You can tell by the crowded lunch counter and the line weaving from its take-out window down the sidewalk. In addition to the baked goods, a delicious assortment of soups and sandwiches are featured; the corned beef and the ham are savvy buys. ♦ Deli/Bakery ♦ M-Sa breakfast and lunch. Lower floor. 622.1045

Ace Loan This pawnshop is packed with wristwatches, cameras, and other hocked possessions. ♦ M-Sa. Upper floor. 682.5424

"Seattle is a moisturizing pad disguised as a city."
Jerry Seinfeld, comedian

Restaurants/Clubs: Red   **Hotels:** Blue
Shops/ ♠ **Outdoors:** Green   **Sights/Culture:** Black

15 Post Alley Market Designed in 1983 by **Bassetti/Norton/Metler,** this building is strictly functional (unlike some of the other nearby structures). Shops at the bottom give way to offices up top. ◆ Post Alley (between Pike and Pine Sts)

Within the Post Alley Market:

Made in Washington Locally made jams, coffee cups that sport rigid whale-tail handles, and similar souvenirs are sold here. ◆ Daily. 467.0788

SBC ★$ It's the rare Seattleite who would remember this, but Jim Stewart began selling roasted coffee in 1970, when he had an ice-cream parlor called the **Wet Whisker** in Coupeville on Whidbey Island. He opened his first city location with his brother, Dave, in 1971 at Pier 70 on the Waterfront. Ten years later, the **Stewart Brothers Coffee** shop began business in Bellevue Square. By 1989, when the name changed to **SBC Coffee** (defined archly as "Seattle's Best Coffee"), Jim Stewart had several locations on both sides of Lake Washington, including a snazzy glass-walled stop in the **Westlake Center.**

This contemporary corner shop in **Pike Place Market** was designed by architects **Olson/Walker.** On warm days the alleyside wall opens and patrons spread onto sidewalks. Both bulk coffee beans and cups of espresso variations are available. ◆ Coffeehouse ◆ Daily from 7AM. 467.7700

Sisters ★$ During summer months the glass front opens to the elements so patrons sitting along the counter can eavesdrop on alley strollers. And year-round, this is a bright and warm-hearted establishment, specializing in grilled European sandwiches on focaccia. The Corsica (Black Forest ham, artichoke hearts, fontina cheese, and tomato) and the Gesundheit (sun-dried tomato, cream cheese, avocado, and alfalfa sprouts) are no-fail faves. Black-bean chili and borscht are good winter warmers. Breakfasts of waffles and German rolls with selected deli meats and cheeses are served all day. ◆ European deli ◆ Daily breakfast, lunch, and dinner until 5PM. 623.6723

16 Triangle Building When it was constructed in 1908 as home to the South Park Poultry Company, shoppers used to browse here among the stripped chickens that hung from the ceiling. The structure was rehabilitated in 1977 by architect **Fred Bassetti,** along with the adjoining **Silver Oakum Building** to the north. ◆ Pike Pl and Pine St

Within the Triangle Building:

Cinnamon Works The signature cinnamon rolls here may be filling, but the chocolate-chocolate-chip cookies are some customers' secret weakness. ◆ Daily from 7AM. First floor. 583.0085

Mr. D's Greek Deli Fast food, Aegean style, with *spanakopita* (spinach and feta cheese wrapped in phyllo), juicy gyro sandwiches, and Greek pastries to go. There are a few tables in the back where you can chow down. ◆ Greek Deli/Takeout ◆ Daily. First floor. 622.4881

Mee Sum Pastries The service can be a bit surly, but it's a small price to pay for the fine Chinese pot stickers and *hum baos* (meat- or vegetable-filled doughy buns) here. ◆ Daily. First floor. 682.6780

Copacabana Cafe ★$ This restaurant was opened in 1963 by Ramon Pelaez, a writer, a former owner of Bolivia's largest radio station, and a political activist (Franklin Roosevelt once thanked him for leading Bolivian opposition to the Nazis). In 1953 Pelaez was jailed by the new leftist government and forced to disperse his holdings. He later spent 10 years in Chile before coming to Seattle to open a restaurant in the market, though he barely knew how to cook.

Ramon Pelaez died in 1979, but his daughter and son-in-law continue to run the city's only Bolivian restaurant, using many Pelaez family recipes. Look up one level as you stride the bricks of Pike Place and you're likely to spot the crowded, two-tables-wide deck that surrounds this place—a favorite summer dining option. Service here can be abysmal; don't be surprised if your beer order is forgotten or if you're given your check before receiving your lunch. But the food is worth missing a meeting or two. Best choices from the regular menu are the filling paella and the *pescado a la Española*, a delicate halibut steak in a sauce of onions and tomatoes. Order the shrimp nachos (with a side of beer) as an appetizer. ◆ Bolivian ◆ Daily lunch and dinner. Second floor. 622.6359

17 Inn at the Market $$ What finer location for a Seattle hotel than smack dab in the midst of its famous market district? And in most aspects, this 65-room hotel, wrapped about a surprisingly peaceful courtyard, will live up to your expectations. There's a well-respected restaurant located right downstairs, a large deck overlooking the market and Elliott Bay, blessedly little chance that you'll be surrounded by conventioneers (thanks to a shortage of facilities in the hotel for their use), separate floors for nonsmokers, and a warm, European personality that shouldn't be undervalued.

Rooms are good sized, and they're decorated with sculptures and flowers. Though the hotel doesn't have a kitchen, the restaurant provides room service. The downside is that the same thing that makes the market a wonderful place to be—the bustle and the attendant noise—can also detract from the intimacy and comfort. Rooms on the west side have the best views, but there's disruptive noise for most of each day; those on the east, or First Avenue, side suffer traffic clatter. This is a hotel for lovers of the urban experience. ♦ 86 Pine St (at First Ave). 443.3600; fax 448.0631

Within the Inn at the Market:

Campagne ★★$$$ Romantically appointed, with Oriental rugs and a satisfying view of Elliott Bay, this restaurant's Provençal menu enchants its patrons with such dishes as salmon in a cognac-and-champagne butter sauce, lamb salad, and herb chicken filled with goat cheese. When complaints surface, they usually have to do with brusque service. ♦ French ♦ Daily dinner; lighter fare served until midnight; bar daily until 2AM. Reservations recommended. Jacket required. 728.2800

Dilettante Chocolates Formulas for making this shop's sweet temptations were passed down from Julius Rudolph Franzen, who created pastries for Emperor Franz Josef of Austria and was master candy maker to Nicholas II, the last czar of Russia. Just before both his former bosses were assassinated, Franzen immigrated to the US, where he educated his American brother-in-law, Earl Davenport, in the chocolatier's art. Now, Davenport's grandson produces some of the most tempting truffles, butter creams, and dragées (nuts or dried fruits dredged through dipping chocolate) you'll ever try. ♦ Daily. 728.9144. Also at: 416 Broadway E (at E Republican St). 329.6463

DeGraff Books This bookshop is cozy, with helpful salespeople and a good assortment of contemporary fiction, especially mysteries. ♦ Daily. 441.0688

n the Market for a Good Time?

hink of **Pike Place Market** as a separate village within a city, one that claims its own rules of conduct, its wn traditions, its own unique style and pace. You really need a kindly old uncle or aunt to show you the opes, but barring that option, here are a few tips for getting the most out of Seattle's spiritual nexus.

Show up here early in the morning (between 7AM and 8AM) to see the farmers and craftspeople setting up their colorful stalls. If your goal is to find the best choice of fresh foodstuffs, come between 8AM and 11AM, before lunchers descend upon the market. And if you're hoping to score last-minute discounts on the day's still-unsold edibles, arrive at about 4:30PM.

Vendors new to the market don't have enough seniority to earn display space on weekends, so they tend to bring their novel works to the market Monday through Friday. You'll find more familiar, longtime craftspeople here on weekends.

Just as it is impolite in foreign countries to bargain for goods and then choose not to buy them, it also is considered gauche in the market to listen to street musicians for any length of time without contributing at least a few coins to their buckets or violin cases.

Despite ongoing discussions about making **Pike Place** a car-free zone, the market just wouldn't be the same without the constant jockeying of humans and autos here. If you're happy to move at slug speed, stay on the crowded sidewalks. Otherwise, step right onto the brick-covered street and walk with the cars. Just keep a wary eye out for drivers wheeling in and out of the angled parking spaces.

- The odds of finding a parking spot around **Pike Place** are poor at best. Try, instead, the 550-space **Market Garage** just west of the **North Arcade,** off Western Avenue, which allows free parking with shopping validations from many market merchants. On-street parking is easiest to find heading north of the market, between Bell Street and Denny Way. Avoid parking lots along First Avenue, as they tend to be overpriced.

- Do not depend on market merchants to choose your produce. The best way to get the quality you pay for is to paw lightly over the foodstuffs yourself—no matter how much sellers try to discourage this practice.

- Two sets of public rest rooms are available in the market. One is at the south end of the **Main Arcade,** downstairs from **Pike Place Fish.** The other can be found at the **Main Arcade**'s north end, by descending the ramp adjacent to **City Fish.**

- One-hour tours of the market are scheduled on Saturday mornings, at either 9AM or 10:30AM, depending on the availability of guides. They set out from the **Market Information Booth,** at the corner of First Avenue and Pike Street. The charge is $5 per person and reservations are required. Call 682.7453 for weekly schedules and to sign up for an informative walk.

18 Garden Center Originally an egg market, this building became the place for flowers and plants in 1946. ♦ Pike Pl (between Stewart and Pine Sts)

Within the Garden Center:

Seattle Garden Center Potted plants decorate the sidewalk outside, and indoors are planters, tools, birdhouses, and more seed packets than most people would think to use in a lifetime. Polish up that green thumb. ♦ Daily. 448.0431

Sur La Table Shirley Collins's hillside lodestone for butchers, bakers, and candy-stick makers represents the height of kitchen chic. Even amateurs can appreciate the shiny and varied wealth of gadgets, dishware, picnic baskets, and kitchenware here. The staff is knowledgeable, and there's a wide assortment of pricey cookbooks to further expand your culinary expertise. Just watch out for weekends and lunch hours, when the cramped aisles seem to become all feet and elbows. ♦ Daily. 448.2244, 800/243.0852

19 Upper Post Alley Horse-drawn hearses once clattered down this uneven brick path to deposit corpses in the basement crematorium of the Butterworth Mortuary, now home to **Kell's Restaurant & Pub** (see below). This is still the only section of Post Alley open to vehicular traffic. ♦ Between Stewart and Virginia Sts

Along Upper Post Alley:

The Glass Eye Gallery Mount St. Helens' volcanic eruption in 1980 proved a big boon to some of the Northwest's novelty glass makers. The co-owners of this shop, Rob Adamson and Dale Leman, caught on early to the possibilities (they're still riding the trend) and incorporated the peak's ashen and slightly iridescent detritus into their hand-blown glass pieces. Look here for dishware, blown-glass fruit, and shapely vases. ♦ Daily. 441.3221

The Perennial Tea Room For all the coffee talk in Seattle, there is the occasional tearoom, and this is one to remember. It features an assortment of lovely teapots, from what you'd expect in the parlor of a proper

English home to outrageous and funky. The shop also is well-stocked with biscuits, a variety of teas, tea cozies, and all manner of things to accessorize your afternoon sip. ♦ Daily. 448.4054

Kell's Restaurant & Pub ★$$ You're likely to miss this hidden-away pub. But don't. It's everything a pub should be: aged and full of smoke-darkened woods and sporting prints, this is a place where patrons aren't afraid to argue and maybe fight for their politics. Guinness is available on tap, or dip into a pint of one of the Northwest's assertive brews. The menu complements the Irish ambience with homemade stews and meat pies. And live Irish music is featured Wednesday through Saturday nights. In summer a small outdoor dining area is cordoned off in the alley. ♦ Irish ♦ Cover F-Sa nights. Daily lunch and dinner. Bar open daily until 2AM. 728.1916

The Pink Door ★★$$ Although some summer visitors know this place solely for its alfresco dining, this high-ceilinged trattoria serving inexpensive Italian fare is romantic year-round—at night candles illuminate the surroundings. Service can be forgetful and sometimes you have to wield sharp elbows to find lunchtime seating, but such dishes as fettuccine with clam sauce and lasagna are hard to beat. ♦ Italian ♦ Tu-Sa lunch, afternoon antipasto, and dinner; bar Tu-Th until 11:30PM; F-Sa until 1:30AM. 443.3241

20 Stewart House A workingperson's hotel, built in stages between 1902 and 1911, this place closed in the 1970s for failure to meet city housing codes. A 1982 renovation by **Ibsen Nelsen & Associates** rehabilitated the original wooden structure and included a four-story brick-faced addition. Studios for senior citizens and people with disabilities are located above the street-level shops. ♦ Stewart St and Pike Pl

Within the Stewart House:

Cucina Fresca Stop by for exceptional pasta salads, entrées to warm in the oven or consume picnic-style, and other Italian deli take-out goodies. ♦ Daily. 448.4758

Le Panier Warm, fragrant French breads are the main attraction, but once you're inside, the pastries are no less an enticement. This is no place to be worried about your waistline. ♦ M-Sa from 7AM. 441.3669

Market Tobacco Patch In maverick style, owner Bill Coulson defies political correctness to maintain Seattle's premier pipe and cigar emporium. Pipe tobacco is available in a splendid variety, and Coulson keeps 60 to 80 types of cigars in stock. But the real treat here (for smokers, at least) is stepping inside the climate-controlled cigar humidor and inhaling deeply. ♦ Daily. 728.7291

21 Soames-Dunn Building Two adjoining structures from 1918—one held Dunn's Seeds, the other the headquarters of Soames Paper Company, which peddled paper bags to market merchants—were combined to make this building. A 1976 rehabilitation was accomplished by architect **Arne Bystrom.**
♦ Pike Pl (between Stewart and Virginia Sts)

Within the Soames-Dunn Building:

Emmett Watson's Oyster Bar ★$
Watson is a former semipro baseball player, now the city's curmudgeonly veteran columnist (with the *Seattle Times,* after an early stint slinging ink for the competing *Post-Intelligencer*). He was the journalist who first discovered and notified the world that Ernest Hemingway's 1961 death in Ketcham, Idaho, was a suicide. In more recent years he's led the so-called Lesser Seattle movement, endorsing slow or no growth for the city and railing against the local influx of Californians.

This oft-crowded restaurant named in Watson's honor has earned institution status for its consistently fresh and varied selection of oysters. Salmon soup and hearty helpings of fish-and-chips can also be had, if you'd rather not slurp from the shell. Wash your food down with something from the ample beer roster. One warning: niched beside a courtyard at the back of the **Soames-Dunn Building,** the restaurant can be hard to find. Rather like Watson's column in the *Times.*
♦ Seafood ♦ Daily lunch and dinner. 448.7721

The Soap Box Indulge your inner child with the bath oils and the rubber duckies that are sold here. ♦ Daily. 441.5680

The Souk Foods and spices from the Middle East, Pakistan, India, and Africa stock these shelves. ♦ Daily. 441.1666

Starbucks ★$ Judging from the old Turkish proverb, "Coffee should be black as Hell, strong as death, and sweet as love," the ancient Turks would be shocked to witness the local fate of their heady brew. The ol' black magic has all but disappeared from the coffee in the Seattle area, where ordering a cup of regular, "unmilked," unadorned java will fetch you the same kind of bug-eyed stares offered to asylum escapees. The caffeine craze in Seattle can mostly be attributed to this chain, which grew to ubiquity (not only in Seattle, but throughout the country) after this storefront opened in 1971. It's always

crowded on weekends, when classical violinists regularly perform just outside the front door. ♦ Coffeehouse ♦ M-Sa from 7:30AM; Su from 8:30AM. 448.8762

22 Louie's on the Pike While most market shops specialize, here is a general-interest grocery store—*the* place to shop if you're looking for something so pedestrian as a bottled soft drink or an ice-cream bar. There's also a decent deli counter inside. ♦ Daily. 1926 Pike Pl (between Stewart and Virginia Sts). 443.1035

23 Pike & Western Wine Merchants This shop stocks a wide range of wines; the selection of French and German vintages is especially well chosen. ♦ Daily. 1934 Pike Pl (between Stewart and Virginia Sts). 441.1307

24 Victor Steinbrueck Park It's fitting that such a lively spot (designed in 1982 by both **Steinbrueck** and **Richard Haag**) should be dedicated to an architect who sought to maintain the vibrancy of **Pike Place Market.** This grassy viewpoint bustles on warm days with businesspeople lunching, tourists pondering the passage of ferries on the Sound, and the usual Seattle complement of panhandlers. A pair of Northwest Indian totem poles designed by Quinault tribe member Marvin Oliver were carved with the assistance of James Bender. The bad news is that right below the park rushes the interminably noisy Alaskan Way Viaduct. ♦ Western Ave (between Virginia and Lenora Sts)

25 Cutter's Bayhouse ★$$ People either love this place or they would sooner swear off *lattes* for life than dine here again. The problem isn't the food; like other stylish formula establishments owned by Restaurants Unlimited (**Triples** on Lake Union, **Palisade** in Magnolia, **Palomino** downtown), this one shows skill in the kitchen. So what if the menu is all over the map—a little Chinese, some Cajun, a dash of Italian just to keep things cooking—as long as the pasta, seafood, and the garlicky focaccia remain impressive. The bar is somewhat overlighted, but nonetheless handles the crucial business of mixing and pouring cocktails with aplomb. No, the trouble here lies with the clientele: lots of competitive yuppie comers, lots of fatless body fanatics from the nearby **Seattle Club,** and everybody checking out everybody else's other's vital stats. ♦ International ♦ Daily lunch and dinner; bar (serving light meals) daily until 1:30AM. 2001 Western Ave (between Virginia and Lenora Sts). 448.4884

Restaurants/Clubs: Red   Hotels: Blue
Shops/ 🌳 Outdoors: Green   Sights/Culture: Black

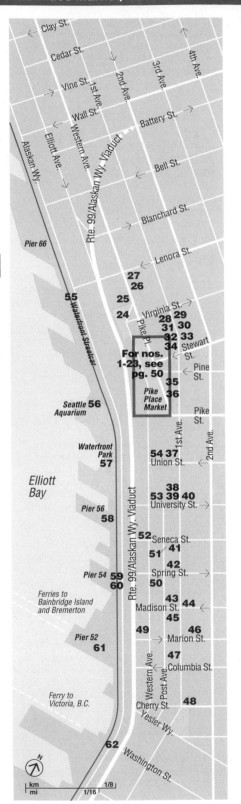

26 The Seattle Club On the edge of the **Pike Place Market,** this 2,400-member health club features all the usual exercise equipment and free weights, as well a pool, indoor track, basketball, racquetball, and squash courts, and aerobics classes. A number of downtown hotels offer their guests temporary club memberships here. ◆ Daily. 2020 Western Ave (between Virginia and Lenora Sts). 443.1111

PHŒNIX RISING GALLERY

27 Phoenix Rising Gallery Simultaneously playful, pricey, and *very* crowded with merchandise, this shop is decorated with table after table of contemporary glassworks, jewelry, business gifts, and home accessories. ◆ Daily. 2030 Western Ave (at Lenora St). 728.2332

28 The Virginia Inn A favorite hangout for newspaper and magazine types, the "V.I." (originally the **Virginia Bar**) has anchored this corner of First Avenue and Virginia Street since about 1908. Unlike many similar pubs, it never closed during Prohibition but was converted temporarily into a card- and lunchroom. Knife-scarred wooden booths hug a corner near the door, leaving the remaining floor space to a maze of little round tables and a long elegant bar that can barely be seen through the mass of revelers on weekdays after 5PM. The choice of craft beers and wines, while not extensive, is select. There's not much in the way of pub grub, although the platter of smoked salmon and bread provides a reasonable light lunch. Art on the brick walls changes frequently. The rest rooms are worth a peek: *True Detective* motif in the men's john, and lip prints next door for women. ◆ Daily until 2AM. 1937 First Ave (at Virginia St). 728.1937

28 The Kaleenka ★$$ Seattleites may be most familiar with this Russian restaurant because of the popular food stands it sets up at such city fairs as Bumbershoot and the Northwest Folklife Festival, from which it purveys hot, hearty piroshkis (meat and cheese wrapped in soft baked dough). But the sit-down menu here is far more extensive and no less satisfying; it includes a terrific multivegetable borscht, chicken Kiev, and *galubtzi* (cabbage leaves filled with beef, pork, and rice and then baked in a sour cream and tomato sauce). ◆ Russian ◆ M-Sa lunch and dinner. 1933 First Ave (between Virginia and Stewart Sts). 728.1278

29 Peter Miller Books Specializing in architecture and design books (new as well as out-of-print titles), with such nifty accessories as build-it-yourself paper replicas of the **Space Needle,** this bookstore is a great place to while away an hour. There's a mail-order catalog, too. ◆ Daily. 1930 First Ave (between Virginia and Stewart Sts). 441.4114

30 Labuznik ★★★$$$ Owner Peter Cipra defies current wisdom that says restaurants must continually change in order to remain interesting. For two decades, this has been a comforting holdout of traditional Central European cuisine (Cipra, himself, is from the former Czechoslovakia). The dinner-only menu is built around roast pork, veal chops, and rack of lamb, with side dishes of sweet-and-sour red cabbage, sauerkraut, and dumplings. The fish soup is usually remarkable. ◆ Central European ◆ Tu-Sa dinner. Reservations recommended. 1924 First Ave (between Virginia and Stewart Sts). 441.8899

31 Uno This is the second stylish clothing boutique owned by Donald Fletcher and his wife, Roni Vincent-Fletcher (who runs the women's store, **Duo,** just north on First Avenue in Belltown). Donald has a fondness for distinctive attire that may show up best in this store's layout of fine-print ties and the racks of comfortable suits. The staff is friendly and willing to hunt down special colors or styles of garments. ◆ Daily. 1927 First Ave (between Virginia and Stewart Sts). 728.9420. Also at: 2209 First Ave (between Blanchard and Bell Sts). 448.7011

31 Pensione Nichols $ Prices at Lindsey Nichols's bed-and-breakfast establishment are extremely reasonable for the location—just a block off Pike Place and convenient to a superfluity of restaurants and shops. It's easy to miss the entrance: it's just a single doorway off the sidewalk, letting onto a cliff of stairs. The *pensione* occupies two floors up the stairs; check in at the desk on the third floor. The eight guest rooms and two suites are brightly painted, cozy, and overlook either First Avenue or Elliott Bay; the latter are slightly quieter, but the former seem more intimate. A large third-floor sitting room embraces views of Elliott Bay and is replete with soft couches for reading or clandestine romancing. Guests (save for those in the suites) must share bath and rest-room facilities, but they are quite comfortable and well maintained. A continental breakfast is included in the room rate.

While the establishment has collected national raves, local attention has been far more stingy. Overshadowing it has been the nearby **Inn at the Market,** a higher-priced and more expensively retailed hostelry. Also weighing against it may be the fact that the *pensione* occupies two floors directly above a porno-movie house. Whatever the reason, the slight is unfortunate, for Nichols manages a secret uptown gem. ◆ 1923 First Ave (between Virginia and Stewart Sts). 441.7125

31 Cafe Sophie ★★$$ If the stone gargoyles, decorative angels, and cathedral ceilings inside give you an oddly sepulchral feeling, it's not without cause: the gaudy (and reportedly haunted) dining room was originally the chapel of a three-story funeral parlor built by undertaker Edgar Ray Butterworth. Architect **John Graham Sr.** designed the stone-footed, Victorian-Romanesque building—his first commercial structure in Seattle—in 1903, before venturing on to create such landmarks as downtown's **Bon Marché** and **Frederick & Nelson** stores, as well as the **Seattle Yacht Club** in Montlake. Owners/chefs Scott and Sue Craig's European menu features a seared swordfish salad, garlic linguine, succulent lamb chops, to name a few. Desserts are rich and wonderful. ◆ International ◆ Tu-Sa lunch and dinner. 1921 First Ave (between Virginia and Stewart Sts). 441.6139

Locals refer to Mount Rainier as "The Mountain," even though the city seems surrounded by noteworthy peaks. If someone says "The Mountain is out today," it doesn't mean that 14,410-foot-high Rainier has escaped its earthly tether, but that the frequent embrace of clouds has given way enough to see it.

32 du jour ★★$ The lowercase moniker should not suggest lower-class cuisine. Indeed, this cafeteria-style eatery serves dishes suitable for a "downtown businessperson's lunch," as one employee describes it. Included are thick, delicious sandwiches, hearty soups, and a spread of tempting salads. (Try the chicken-pecan salad if it's available.) This is also a great find for lovers of morning baked goods. A dining area at the rear, aggressively white in its decor, provides agreeable views of Puget Sound. Takeout is also available. ♦ Cafeteria ♦ M-F breakfast, lunch, and dinner until 6PM; Sa until 5PM. 1919 First Ave (between Virginia and Stewart Sts). 441.3354

33 Fast Forward Owners Jason Harler and Harry Green focus on works created by local designers of jewelry, eye-catching shirts, and dresses that can be tucked into a bag no larger than your fist. A small art gallery in the back (look for the steer skull with neon horns hanging over the doorway) schedules periodic shows. ♦ Daily. 1918 First Ave (between Virginia and Stewart Sts). 728.8050

34 Zebra Club This unisex store carries sporty and lightweight street attire for those who favor the ultracasual look. Ubiquitous video equipment heightens the youth-oriented tone. An espresso cart out front is particularly popular. ♦ Daily. 1901 First Ave (at Stewart St). 448.7452

35 Local Brilliance There's playfulness in owner/designer Renata Tatman's affordable assortment of locally created womenswear and accessories. Note especially the fluid works of Sara Campbell, whose designs in contemporary fabrics take their inspiration from styles of the 1920s through the 1940s. ♦ Daily. 1535 First Ave (between Pine and Pike Sts). 343.5864

35 Ragin' Cajun ★★$$ This tiny eatery with four booths, a couple of tables, and counter service opened in 1993. The chef/owner is Danny Delcambre, who learned traditional Cajun cooking from his mother and later interned with Paul Prudhomme. Try the blackened catfish or the red beans and rice with andouille sausage—they're all top-notch. The restaurant serves beer and wine and offers outdoor seating in the summer. Delcambre is deaf and blind, and believes he is the only similarly disabled restaurateur in the country. ♦ Cajun ♦ Tu-Sa lunch and dinner. 1523 First Ave (between Pine and Pike Sts). 624.2598

36 Retro Viva Everything old is new again, as they say. Vintage jewelry, jazzy bras, men's shirts, and hats that barely escaped the pages of early fashion mags—this shop is full of attire (at fair prices) for the funky fashion plate. ♦ Daily. 1511 First Ave (between Pike and Pine Sts). 624.2529. Also at: 4515 University Way NE (at NE 45th St). 632.8886; 215 Broadway E (between E Thomas and John Sts). 328.7451

37 South Arcade This tower, a jarring, neon-highlighted contrast to the sedate **Pike Place Market,** was designed in 1985 by **Olson/Walker.** ♦ 1411 First Ave (at Union St)

Within the South Arcade:

Shorey Books Antiquarian and used books are jumbled on shelves on two floors and in many stuck-away warrens. Trying to find exactly what you're looking for can be frustrating, especially when the tomes are shelved two-deep. But chances are that something unexpected will attract your eye along the way. ♦ Daily. 624.0221

World Class Chili ★$ Arguments about what chili is and what it isn't could (and do) fill whole cookbooks. Joe Canavan, who collected recipes for years before he opened this small place, has decided to give purists and bean lovers something to sink their spoons into. Here the Texas-style bowl, dense with beef and chilies, leads the herd. Other versions mix beef and pork with ingredients like chocolate and cinnamon, substitute chicken for red meat, or throw out the meat altogether in favor of lentils and veggies (sacrilege!). ♦ Chili ♦ M-Sa lunch and dinner until 6PM. 623.3678

38 Center on Contemporary Art (COCA) The Northwest's only alternative space for local, national, and international artists, this organization thrives on "risk-oriented" programs with controversial exhibits. A recent show, "Cult Rapture," featured art and propaganda from survivalists, fundamentalists, UFO contactors, right- and left-wing terrorists, and SWAT teams, among others. ♦ Tu-Sa. 1309 First Ave (between Union and University Sts.) 682.4568

39 Inside Owner Pia Rochon has filled this former **COCA** annex with an artist's trove: colorful glass pieces; wild screens; picture frames; wreaths crafted of bent sticks and dried flowers; and antique furnishings, from beds to end tables. Drapes take the place of walls and create an exotic tone. Local designers are featured. ♦ Tu-Su. 1305 First Ave (at University St). 623.5646

Restaurants/Clubs: Red   **Hotels:** Blue
Shops/ 🌿 Outdoors: Green   **Sights/Culture:** Black

The Word Out West

Seattle is a bibliophile's kind of town. Nationally, the average per-household expenditure for books is $50 a year. Here, it's about double that. Meanwhile, Seattle public libraries loan out more volumes per capita than any other system in the country. Noteworthy authors—from Norman Mailer to Terry McMillan, Carlos Fuentes, Philip Roth, Jill Eisenstadt, and Robert B. Parker—cycle through town for readings or book signings, and the **Seattle Arts and Lectures Series** schedules about half a dozen famous writers annually for lectures and special events (call 621.2230 for schedules and registration). And a number of nationally recognized authors—including Mark Helprin, Jonathan Raban, and Pete Dexter—have relocated to Puget Sound country.

Is Seattle's bookwormish tendency attributable to high standards in local education? Or can it be traced simply to the number of inclement days that send waterlogged residents inside to the comfort of their reading lamps? Whatever the reason, the publishing industry has benefited. Counting the number of bookstores per person, Seattle ranks seventh in the nation (San Francisco tops the list).

A number of useful guidebooks and historical studies have evolved with Seattle's increasing popularity. The city has also become a popular setting for detective novels. However, there is still nothing that can be pointed to as the quintessential Seattle Novel—nothing that acutely captures the spirit and essence of the city. The local literati wait. For the time being, however, here are some must-reads on the city of Seattle.

Nonfiction

Bertha Knight Landes of Seattle: Big City Mayor, by Sandra Haarsagen (1994, University of Oklahoma Press). A biography of Seattle's—and America's—first woman mayor, elected in the 1920s.

The Good Rain: Across Time and Terrain in the Pacific Northwest, by Timothy Egan (1990, Alfred A. Knopf). Prepare to enjoy an eminently readable and not-too-egregiously romanticized take on the Northwest's beauty and blemishes by *The New York Times*'s local bureau chief.

Impressions of Imagination: Terra-Cotta Seattle, edited by Lydia S. Aldredge (1986, Allied Arts of Seattle). Spend a few hours flipping through this handsome, essay-filled encomium to Seattle's days as a white city on the Sound. It offers a wonderful architectural history.

Living By Water: Essays on Life, Land & Spirit, by Brenda Peterson (1991, Alaska Northwest). This book examines the sometimes soothing, sometimes antagonistic relationship between Northwesterners and their moisture-laden environment.

Meet Me at the Center, by Don Duncan (1992, Seattle Center Foundation). An entertaining former *Seattle Times* writer looks back at the 1962 World's Fair and forward to the future of the site that has become the **Seattle Center.**

Out Here, by Andrew Ward (1991, Penguin). A Bainbridge Islander and lighthearted commentator with National Public Radio draws his sights on beggars, road-kill dogs, and other local exotica.

Seattle in the Twentieth Century, Volumes I and II, by Richard C. Berner (1991, 1992; Charles Press). If you want to find out the city's population in any year from 1900 to 1940 or brush up on political machinations in early Seattle, these are the pages to start scanning. Volume I, "From Boomtown, Urban Turbulence, to Restoration," covers 1900 to 1920; Volume 2, "From Boom to Bust," dissects 1921 to 1940.

Seattle Emergency Espresso, by Heather Doran Barbieri (1992, Alaska Northwest). A handy drinking companion in a town that cares beans about coffee, this guide designates the best and most convenient neighborhood java stops, plus the meaning of such local terminology as the "double tall skinny billiard ball" (a tall *latte* made with one percent or nonfat milk, without foamed milk on top).

Seattle Now and Then, Volumes I through III, by Paul Dorpat (1984-89, Tartu). Dorpat's work has terrific historical photos and a generosity of clever anecdotes, but there's sometimes just enough information about the city's past to make you regret there isn't more.

Skid Road, by Murray Morgan (1978, Comstock). Morgan's book is an irreverent, insightful, often embarrassingly candid parsing of Seattle history. No one who wants to know about this area's past should be without this book.

Fiction

Fish Story, by Richard Hoyt (1985, Viking). Private eye John Denson, connoisseur of screw-top wine and raw cauliflower, gets mixed up in a Native American fishing rights case that leads to the disappearance of a federal judge and the grisly discovery of various human body parts in **Pioneer Place Park.**

Picture Postcard, by Fredrick D. Huebner (1990, Random House). Lawyer Matt Riordan's efforts to locate a famous but long-missing Northwest painter take him back 50 years to a fateful house-boat party on **Portage Bay** and embroil him with more than a sufficient share of dangerous characters.

40 Seattle Art Museum (SAM) Asked to explain the intent behind his firm's design of the new downtown **Seattle Art Museum** (pictured below), Philadelphia architect **Robert Venturi** said he wanted to create a "current urban art museum that is popular yet esoteric, closed but open, monumental yet inviting, an accommodating setting for the art, but a work of art itself." In other words, a little bit of everything: a sophisticated but unimposing juxtaposition of convex and concave curves, all faced in fluted limestone and terra-cotta ornament.

The main entrance on First Avenue is enlivened by sculptor Jonathan Borofsky's *Hammering Man* (illustrated at right), a black, 48-foot-tall mechanical piece that took a spill during its installation and had to be repaired before final placement.

Working within zoning requirements that dictated view corridors to Puget Sound, **Venturi,** his partner **Denise Scott Brown,** and their associates created a waterfall of an outdoor staircase along the south wall that's almost mirrored by a processional stair inside, leading from the lobby to second-floor galleries and punctuated by sculptures of Chinese military guardians, camels, and rams. Brightly hued arches hang majestically over those inside stairs. It's a bit disappointing, however, after this elaborate staircase, to deal with the narrow twisting flights of stairs and elevators that continue the escalation within the building. The loftlike galleries are pleasant, if spare, and broad, curving hallways are well lighted from view windows at either end.

The second-floor exhibition space hosts special shows. Native-American, African, Chinese, and Near Eastern treasures occupy the third floor. The fourth level contains a history of European and American works, including pieces by such Northwest artists as Morris Graves, Jacob Lawrence, and Kenneth Callahan. A cafe providing refreshments (open the same hours as the museum) is located on the mezzanine level.

The museum's extensive Asian collection was moved to the renovated **Old Seattle Art Museum** in **Volunteer Park,** a broad-shouldered 1933 Art Deco creation from architect **Carl Gould.** Renamed the **Seattle Asian Art Museum,** it opened to the public in the summer of 1994 (see "Capitol Hill to Seward Park" chapter) and also houses a study center. ◆ Admission; free for children 12 and under, members, and the first Tuesday of each month; discount for senior citizens and students. Tu-Su; Th until 9PM. 100 University St (at First Ave). 654.3100

41 Grand Pacific Hotel Displaying a stone and arched face that would have been more familiar in Pioneer Square than this far north on First Avenue, this building (known upon opening in 1898 as the **First Avenue Hotel**) was at no time a luxury inn. Its tenants were miners, sailors, and businessmen of modest means, in the early years many of them blowing through town on their way to the gold fields of the Klondike. But the structure, with its Romanesque stone footing, arched windows along the third floor, and fine detailing over most of its brick upper facade, doesn't lack class or style. Now restored, it's been joined internally to the neighboring **Colonial Hotel,** and divided into residential units. ◆ 1115-1117 First Ave (between Seneca and Spring Sts)

42 Watermark Tower This sculpted 20-story edifice (designed by **Bumgardner Architects** in 1983) bursts upward from the preserved terra-cotta facade of the 1915 **Colman Building** (conceived by **Carl Gould** and **Charles Bebb**). Pay special attention to the dynamic entry arch on Spring Street. ♦ First Ave and Spring St

Within Watermark Tower:

McCormick & Schmick's ★★$$$
Waiters in black bow ties add a touch of class to this restaurant that specializes in seafood and grilled meats. The lamb chops don't disappoint, nor do the salmon dishes. Enjoy a preprandial cocktail in the comfortable, dark-wood barroom. The Irish coffees served here are better than most. ♦ Seafood ♦ M-F lunch and dinner; Sa-Su dinner. Reservations recommended. 1103 First Ave (at Spring St). 623.5500

43 Alexis Hotel $$ Designed in 1901 by architect **Max Umbrecht**, this former **Globe Hotel** was rehabilitated in 1982 as part of a large-scale, privately funded project that also fixed up several nearby edifices. It's now one of the most intimate hotels (only 54 rooms) in town, convenient to **Pike Place Market**, the **Seattle Art Museum**, and Pioneer Square.

Trapped between the revolting Alaskan Way Viaduct and noisy First Avenue, there are no views to speak of here, but a handful of balconied rooms face an interior courtyard and thus provide the most peace and quiet. Suites are outfitted with Jacuzzis, wood-burning fireplaces, and marble fixtures. Complimentary services include shoe shines, sherry in your room, continental breakfast, and a morning newspaper. Short-term memberships are available to the popular **Seattle Club**, an athletic facility near the market. "Discount luxury" hotel operator Bill Kimpton, who also owns the **Hotel Vintage Park** in the business district, is now at the helm. Parking around here can be a problem. ♦ 1007 First Ave (at Madison St). 624.4844, 800/426.7033; fax 621.9009

Within the Alexis Hotel:

The Bookstore Bar This is actually a better taproom than it was a bookstore. With its shelves full of literature, the place still maintains a bit of the feeling of its previous incarnation. The atmosphere is conducive to political discussions and after-work jousts with colleagues. Appetizers from the **Painted Table** restaurant are available as bar snacks,

and there are microbrews on tap. ♦ M-Th until midnight, F-Su until 2AM. 624.4844

The Painted Table ★★★$$$ After a stint at **Place Pigalle** and as the co-chef at the **Cafe Alexis** when it occupied this space, chef Emily Moore now exhibits her skill and creativity here. Her special shine is with such dishes as crab cakes, salad with goat cheese and carmelized walnuts, risotto with wild mushrooms, and most of the salmon entrées. And her chocolate desserts are sublime. Don't be surprised if Moore stops by your table to see how things are going; she's friendly and down-to-earth. The space is large and hung with rotating art exhibits, some more pleasant than others. ♦ Northwestern ♦ M-F breakfast, lunch, and dinner; Sa-Su breakfast and dinner. Reservations recommended. 624.3646

Cajun Corner ★$ Dark-wood appointments, including a handsome vintage bar, suggest a comfort and Old World camaraderie that aren't backed up by the service (slow and careless) or the clientele (sparse and mostly male). The menu is a bevy of bayou standbys: a decent but not outstanding gumbo; a shirt-splashing array of catfish, mussels, and rock shrimp in Creole rum sauce; a fine rendition of red beans and rice; and several sandwiches. ♦ Cajun ♦ M-Sa lunch and dinner. 90 Madison St (at Post Alley). 682.5019

The Legacy The collection of historic baskets, masks, and carvings from Northwest Indians and Eskimos here is rounded out with some newer native merchandise. ♦ M-Sa. 624.6350

44 Warshal's Sporting Goods An anachronism on increasingly chic First Avenue, this store has occupied the same post–Great Fire edifice for half a century. In addition to its broad selection of hunting, fishing, and other sports equipment, there are also photography and darkroom supplies. Look for frequent specials. ♦ M-Sa. 1000 First Ave (at Madison St). 624.7300

45 Old Federal Office Building Looking very much like a snowcapped mountain range, what with its brick facing topped by terra-cotta detailing, this memorable stepped-back Art Deco structure was one of the few projects raised in downtown during the Depression. The architect was **James A. Wetmore.** ♦ 909 First Ave (between Madison and Marion Sts)

Pier 54, now the Waterfront home of Ye Olde Curiosity Shop, is remembered by old-timers as the place where, in 1940, Two-Ton Tony Galento, a 350-pound boxer, climbed into a tank of seawater to wrestle a 75-pound octopus. Brokered by the late Seattle restaurateur Ivar Haglund, the bout ended in a draw.

46 Henry M. Jackson Federal Office Building With its hipped and tiled roof, and a fenestration of interlocking prefab concrete segments, this tower (designed by **Fred Bassetti,** along with **John Graham & Company**) gives off a Mediterranean palazzo feel. The lobby appeals with its wood finishes, but the star of this building is its outdoor cascading hillside stairs, which include remnants of **Elmer Fisher**'s 1889 Victorian **Burke Building,** torn down to make room for this 1974 tower.

Before it was the **Burke,** this site held what was once this city's most ostentatious landmark: the **Frye Opera House,** mansard-roofed atop brick walls, featuring 1,400 seats and a stage punctured with seven trapdoors. The 1889 fire began at this intersection, in a woodworker's basement.

Sculptor Isamu Noguchi contributed an abstract grouping of pink granite blocks, called *Landscape of Time,* to the Second Avenue plaza. ◆ Bounded by First and Second Aves, and Madison and Marion Sts

47 Colman Building Scottish immigrant James M. Colman's namesake structure had trouble getting off the ground in more ways than one. A mechanic and a steam-mill operator, Colman first acquired this property by running a ship aground here long enough to earn legal title; he planned simply to build over the hull. But his original, very ornate design (conceived by architect **Stephen Meany** before the Great Fire of 1889) was stunted by Colman's business caution after the blaze. He went ahead with only the concept's first two stories, waiting to see what demand there was for more office and commercial space in the rapidly rebuilding city. Not until about 1904 did architect **August Tidemand** completely revamp these two floors in brownstone style; he then added four more austere brick stories above those to form the basic edifice you see today. In 1930 Seattle architect **Arthur B. Loveless** performed another remodeling that incorporated several Art Deco elements into the glazed street canopy and lobby. ◆ 811 First Ave (between Columbia and Marion Sts)

48 Metsker Maps Joseph Conrad captured the appeal of maps in *Heart of Darkness,* when Marlowe explained: "Now, when I was a little chap, I had a passion for maps. I would look for hours at South America, or Africa, or Australia, and lose myself in all the glories of exploration." Marlowe might have begun many a voyage at this shop, which sells hundreds of maps as well as guidebooks and assorted travel paraphernalia to satisfy the hunger of wanderlust. ◆ M-Sa. 702 First Ave (at Cherry St). 623.8747

48 La Buca ★★$$ Another Italian restaurant—just what Seattle needs, right? But with a couple of familiar powerhouses behind it (Luigi DeNunzio, formerly of **Al Boccalino** in Pioneer Square, and Raffaele Calise, who helped create the popular **Salute** restaurants), this dining spot has survived the glut. Stuck below street level (the name means "The Hole") in an orange-walled space once occupied by the now defunct **Skid Road Theater,** the restaurant specializes in Southern Italian cuisine.

There's lots of whole-wheat pasta, calamari, and chicken and veal. Favorite dishes include the *risotto di mare* (*arborio* rice bobbing with prawns, mussels, and clams, all accented with saffron) and the tenderloin of pork sautéed and served with red-pepper sauce and olives. The kitchen also turns out some savory fish specials, particularly halibut. Forget the grilled and marinated prawns, though. And two cautions: main-course portions are small and the ambient noise level can be high. ◆ Southern Italian ◆ M-Sa lunch and dinner; Su dinner. Reservations recommended. 102 Cherry St (at First Ave). 343.9517

49 Western Coffee Shop ★$ So narrow you couldn't get a horse through here, Niko and Jeanie Rondos's charmingly campy coffee shop is an omnium-gatherum of little plastic cowboys, spurs, and black-and-whites from Old West days. A counter up front (the best place to be) gives way to a handful of booths in back. The cooking technology here seems to have progressed little since "Bonanza" days, but the omelettes, corned-beef hash, and chunky hash browns served here are all good. For lunch do not, by any means, pass up the thick meat-loaf sandwiches. Creamy espresso milk shakes come with the metal shaker full of whatever wouldn't fit in your glass. It's crowded on weekends but worth the wait. ◆ Coffee Shop ◆ Daily breakfast and lunch until 3PM. 911½ Western Ave (between Marion and Madison Sts). 682.5001

50 Italia ★★$ This high-ceilinged space is many things to many people. It's part cafeteria (with glorious pasta salads), part art gallery, and part sit-down restaurant, with occasional

---

Restaurants/Clubs: Red   **Hotels:** Blue
Shops/ 🍴 **Outdoors:** Green   **Sights/Culture:** Black

adventures as a lecture hall (art talks are given the second Thursday of every month).

The kitchen turns out superb cheese-filled tortellini with brown butter and sage, king salmon with roasted-fennel salsa, and great lunchtime pizzas covered in wild mushrooms, caramelized onions, and spinach, or with chicken, basil, tomatoes, and scallions. The fragrantly herbed focaccia and a couple of Northwest beers could easily satisfy for a light dinner. ♦ Italian ♦ M-Sa breakfast, lunch, and dinner. Reservations recommended. 1010 Western Ave (between Madison and Spring Sts). 623.1917

51 Tlaquepaque ★$$ Its obscure position (in an alley beneath an exit ramp from Highway 99) seems to have had little negative effect on this boisterous restaurant and cantina. Other places may open up in the neighborhood, yet this one still draws the crowds. The combo dinner platters (with mesquite chicken, *chile con queso,* roast-pork *carnitas,* and a refreshing mango salsa) are prepared for two to five diners, and they are the best bargain as well as an ideal way to sample the kitchen's depth. The bar provides the liveliest environment, where the house specialty is— of course—margaritas (the blended ones are the best). There's a Happy Hour all day Sunday. ♦ Mexican ♦ Daily lunch and dinner. Reservations recommended. 1122 Post Ave (at Seneca St). 467.8226

52 Current The high-style moderne furniture that turns up in these expansive showrooms is unquestionably elegant. There are pieces for every room in the house, with a special focus on sconce lighting. The prices, unfortunately, can be quite steep. ♦ Daily. 1201 Western Ave (at Seneca St). 622.2433

53 Seattle Bagel Bakery Lines are long on weekends, as at-home brunchers slip in for supplies of pumpernickel, onion, or salt bagels. Even topped with lox or cream cheese, the chewy dough dominates the taste buds. This is one of Seattle's top bagelries. ♦ Daily from 7:30AM. 1302 Western Ave (at University St). 624.2187

54 Wild Ginger ★★★$$$ The satay bar here was the first of its kind in the nation and continues to be a main event. You can just hang out, enjoying the grilled chunks of chicken, beef, prawns, or veggies on skewers that are served with a zingy peanut or soy and black-vinegar sauce, or take a place in the dining room and order them as appetizers. The fragrant Wandering Sage soup is another house specialty. The seafood, particularly the scallops, is delicious, as are the beef curry and a sweetly flavored duck. Specials are influenced by cooking from around the Pacific Rim and are based on what's seasonally fresh. ♦ Asian ♦ M-Sa lunch and dinner; Su dinner; satay bar until 2AM. 1400 Western Ave (at Union St). 623.4450

Child's Play

After the requisite trip on the **monorail,** what's a parent to do on those rainy Seattle days? Here are ten tips for keeping the kids entertained:

1. Visit the **Tropical Rain Forest** at the **Woodland Park Zoo** and check out the poison-dart frogs.

2. Prick up your ears for Saturday morning story time at **Elliott Bay Books.**

3. Rent a paddleboat and churn up the waters of **Green Lake.**

4. Climb into a space capsule at the **Pacific Science Center.**

5. Walk under the sea at the **Seattle Aquarium.**

6. Attend a performance of the **Seattle Children's Theater.**

7. Take a guided nature walk with the park rangers at **Discovery Park.**

8. Build a miniature sailboat at the **Center for Wooden Boats.**

9. Shop for shrunken heads (and peek at Sylvester the Mummy) at **Ye Olde Curiosity Shop.**

10. Tour the city scavenger-hunt style with **City Hunt**

There's Something Fishy Here

Turn over a rock at **Golden Gardens** park on **Shilshole Bay** and you have a good chance of encountering *Pachygrapsus crassipes,* the lined shore crab. You may only have a minute to extend greetings, however, before this inch-long green creature scurries off sideways in search of a new hideout. Don't bother giving chase. Plenty of other charming, if equally reclusive, animals can be found along this sandy stretch of land.

Puget Sound is inhabited by several thousand marine species. Most are small-bodied invertebrates (oysters, clams, urchins, crabs, anemones, and squids), but some are certifiable giants, thriving on this briny soup's ample food supply and fairly mild oceanic climate. Less than a hundred feet off the **Golden Gardens** shore, for instance, lurks *Octopus dofleini,* the world's largest octopus, a mottled red Schwarzenegger of a cephalopod with an arm span extending 25 feet. A bit farther out, on the Sound's silty bottom, rests the 10-pound geoduck (pronounced *goo*-ee-duck), a mega-mollusk that qualifies as the world's largest burrowing clam.

Like the secretive shore crab *Pachygrapsus,* many local invertebrates are beach dwellers, occupying cozy niches in what scientists call the intertidal zone—that thin strip of earth bathed by ocean tides. To survive under such transitional conditions, many animals have radically changed their looks and behaviors. For example, the small colonial sea anemone, *Anthopleura,* resembles a plant more than an animal, while the limpet (a tiny, rock-hugging cousin of the snail) could very easily pass for a smooth stone.

On the rocky beaches (such as in **Mukilteo,** 20 miles north of Seattle), fish and invertebrates hide in the cracks and crevices between boulders or among the kelp and other seaweeds that grow abundantly at the water's edge. Sandy shores (like those at **Golden Gardens** or the city of **Edmonds,** another short excursion north of Seattle) are usually featureless plains that merge into eelgrass beds—underwater meadows that offer food and shelter to anything that lives on or near the bottom. Both beach types make fine destinations for intertidal explorers.

To get better acquainted with this curious, often colorful, community of the sea, visit the **Seattle Aquarium** (Pier 59 on the Waterfront, 386.4320), where you'll meet all local beach dwellers face-to-face. Afterward pick up a good field guide to intertidal life, either Gloria Snively's *Exploring Seashore Life in British Columbia, Washington, and Oregon* (1978, The Writing Works) or *Seashore Life of the Northern Pacific Coast* by Eugene Kozloff (1983, University of Washington Press). And finally, procure a local tide table, available from larger bookstores in the city. Tidepooling requires taking advantage of two brief windows of opportunity, periods of approximately four to six hours each day, when the tides ebb and the intertidal zone is most accessible to exploration. Exactly how long and how wide these windows swing varies daily. But in the summer the lowest tides generally occur around midday. As winter approaches they fall between 9PM and midnight, making tidepooling a more difficult enterprise but no less rewarding as long as you have a flashlight in hand.

Don't presume, however, that only cold-blooded creatures will be joining you at the beach. A vast array of waterfowl and shorebirds also visit Seattle's coastline. Several of these, including the diminutive Bonaparte's gull, travel thousands of miles from central Alaska just to winter in the Emerald City. Others, such as the western and glaucous-winged gull, prefer the year-round comfort of urban beaches, piers, and marinas over life on the road. Regardless of their summer plans, all arrive at the local seashores with one thing in mind: the seafood smorgasbord that's uncovered with every outgoing tide.

Binoculars might help you espy some warm-blooded mammals—particularly harbor seals and California sea lions. Still farther from shore swim the area's sleek black-and-white killer whales (like the one pictured above), highly intelligent and surprisingly swift hunters of salmon, cod, halibut, and hake. Killer whales (or orcas) are actually more closely related to dolphins than to whales, and they spend their entire lives in extended family groupings called pods. (For an excellent background on these mammals, read Sasquatch Books' 1990 *Field Guide to the Orca* by David G. Gordon and Chuck Flaherty.)

Waterfront

55 Waterfront Streetcar Seattle's original trolleys were stripped from service decades ago, but, for nostalgia's sake, **Metro Transit** imported these vintage machines from Australia to make the clattering 15- to 20-minute run from Pier 70 through Pioneer Square to the International District. ♦ 85¢ off-peak; $1.10 M-F 3PM to 6PM; children under 5 free. Daily. Off Alaskan Way (from Pier 70 to the International District) 553.3000

56 Seattle Aquarium Designed by **Fred Bassetti and Company** in 1977, this Waterfront institution attracts visitors with its more-than-generous complement of tanks holding marine exotica, its "discovery lab" where children can pet starfish and peer through microscopes, and the playful clans of seals and sea otters that occupy its upper reaches. (Look for feeding-time notices: it's the best time to watch these jesters.) Farther inside, visitors walk under a 4,000-gallon glassed-in pool where sharks and myriad other Puget Sound creatures swim. One of the newest exhibits opened in 1993: a six-foot-long water monitor lizard in a naturalistic environment. The lizard, a native of Malaysia, is a descendant of dinosaurs. Expect to spend at least two to three hours at the aquarium. ♦ Admission; children age 2 and under free; discount for senior citizens, disabled persons, children ages 3 to 5, King County residents, and groups of 10 or more. Daily. Pier 59 (off Alaskan Way). 386.4320

57 Waterfront Park A soothing "boardwalk" hugging Elliott Bay, the elevated walkways here give visitors a better perspective on the city and the Sound. It's a good place for picnics, offering a superfluity of fish, hot dogs, and ice-cream parlors nearby. Long gone is adjacent Pier 58, where the first cargo of tea from the Orient arrived in 1896 and where the steamer *Portland* anchored in 1897 with the first news that gold had been discovered in the Klondike; a plaque here recalls the beginning of Alaska's gold rush. The minipark was designed in 1974 by the **Bumgardner Partnership.** ♦ Pier 57 (off Alaskan Way)

58 Elliott's Oyster House & Seafood Restaurant ★★$$$ Water views, fast service, and some of the best oysters in town are served here. ♦ Seafood ♦ M-Sa lunch and dinner. Pier 56 (off Alaskan Way). 623.4340

The Economy Market Atrium at Pike Place Market was home to Fagan's Grist Mill in the 1920s. It was there that the first version of dry pancake mix was sold commercially. Patents were later bought by the now-prosperous Albers company for $200.

59 Ye Olde Curiosity Shop A mecca for tourist-trinket junkies, founded in 1899, this carnival-flavored shop sells rubber slugs, Seattle T-shirts, Russian nesting dolls, seashells, scrimshaw, and shrunken heads—they're all here, alongside such Barnum-esque oddities as a bottled pig with eight legs, three eyes, three mouths, and a pair of tails. Most popular is Sylvester the Desert Mystery: a mummified murder victim found in the Arizona sandflats in 1895 with a bullet through his stomach and with mustache and fingernails still intact. ♦ Daily; Th-Sa until 9PM. Pier 54 (off Alaskan Way). 682.5844

60 Ivar's Acres of Clams and Fish Bar ★$ Ivar Haglund, who died several years back, was Seattle's quintessential promoter. He's remembered for his corny commercial slogan (Keep Clam), his guitar playing and storytelling, and the carp wind sock that he ran up the flagpole on **Smith Tower** when he owned that building, beginning in 1976. This full-service restaurant offers a variety of seafood; best choices are usually the clam nectar and the cod-and-chips. The outdoor seating can hardly be beat for Seattle charm. A sentimental statue of Ivar feeding gulls holds pride of place nearby. ♦ Seafood ♦ Daily lunch and dinner. Pier 54 (off Alaskan Way). 624.6852.

61 Colman Dock Elliott Bay's worst docking collision occurred here in April 1912, when the ocean liner *Alameda* charged right into this pier, toppling its previously elegant clock tower into the drink. The *Alameda* suffered barely a scratch. The clock from the tower was retrieved after the collision, and restored; you can see it inside. It wasn't the first time this dock was rebuilt, nor would it be the last. The original wharf went up by order of Scottish immigrant James Colman in 1882. The current modern incarnation is its sixth and least interesting form, dating only to 1966. **Washington State Ferries** leave from here many times daily, bound for Bainbridge and Vashon Islands (call 464.6400 for ferry schedules). ♦ Pier 52 (off Alaskan Way)

62 Washington Street Public Boat Landing Built in 1920 from a design by city architect **Daniel R. Huntington,** this iron-and-steel pergola—much less ornate than the older Pioneer Place pergola only two blocks to the east—was intended to house Seattle's harbor master and be the entry point for visiting seamen. Now rehabilitated, it is more a curiosity than anything else, being located near Pier 48 but away from other Waterfront landmarks. Watch for it on the **Waterfront Streetcar** ride. ♦ Alaskan Way (at Washington St)

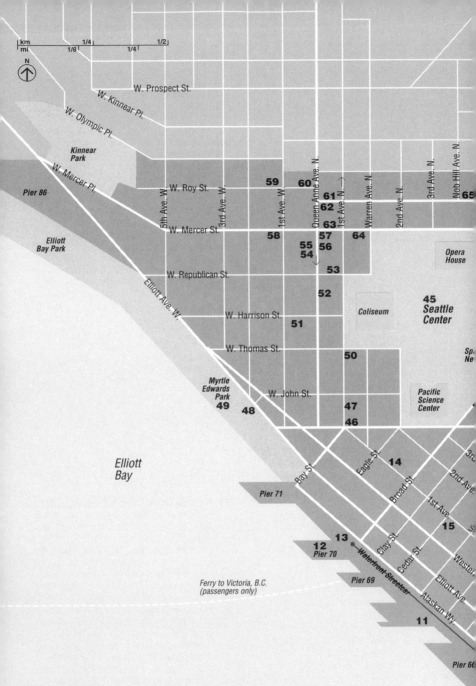

Belltown/Seattle Center

No matter what you call it—Belltown or the **Denny Regrade District**—this area just north of downtown is Seattle's boulevard of forgotten dreams, at least those of an urban-development nature. During the late 19th century, one of Seattle's first settlers, William Bell, hoped to create a commercial center here, but he died before his plans could amount to much. Between 1906 and 1911 city engineer Reginald H. Thomson ordered that 3,000-foot-high **Denny Hill**, which loomed up from the corner of Second Avenue and Virginia Street, be sluiced into **Elliott Bay**. The regrading was supposed to

inspire business development by making the neighborhood flatter and thus easier to traverse. The notion, however, fell upon deaf ears.

In 1911 engineer Virgil Bogue unveiled a plan that would have made the intersection of **Fourth Avenue** and **Blanchard Street** the nexus of a new and improved downtown Seattle. Bogue proposed the construction of a civic center that would stretch from this intersection all the way to **Lake Union.** It would feature boulevards, federal buildings, a courthouse, library, art museum, 15-story memorial tower, and subway, all of which would transform dowdy Seattle into a major metropolitan center. Bogue was an urban visionary and, like most visionaries, his ideas were rejected.

It wasn't until 1962, with construction of the Century 21 Exposition and the landmark **Space Needle**, that Belltown made the leap into the future. This World's Fair was "The Jetsons" incarnate, a spectacle that *Life* magazine called "out of this world." Attorney General Robert Kennedy, actors John Wayne and Danny Kaye, Prince Philip of England, and even Lassie showed up to take a gander. Elvis Presley arrived amid a wail of shrieking teenagers to shoot a mediocre movie called *It Happened at the World's Fair.*

The fairgrounds have now become the **Seattle Center**, the closest thing the city has to a community center. Thousands of people crowd in here year after year for events such as the Northwest Folklife Festival and Bumbershoot. Parents bring their children to visit the museums; teens hang out with friends at the amusement park, gobble pizza in **Center House**, and attend dances and karaoke competitions; and the **Space Needle** remains a popular upscale dating destination. Sporting events, ranging from national-league basketball (the **Seattle SuperSonics**) to high-school football, take place in the **Coliseum** the **Arena**, and at **High School Memorial Stadium.** Several stages deliver theater and musical productions, and there's a proposal in the works to create the world's first museum dedicated to the memory and music of local guitar wizard Jimi Hendrix.

Belltown still inspires dreams, but now they're more of the bohemian and artistic sort. Secondhand shops, bookstores, art galleries, and coffeehouses have sprung up in buildings vacated long ago by more conventional businesses, and Belltown has become a focus of Seattle's dance-club scene, attracting a wide roster of rock bands. Restaurants, which once eschewed the neighborhood as just too far from the city's critical office mass, have begun to move in. And while drug dealing and some violence encourage caution at dusk, the growth of this arty fringe area has not been stemmed.

1 Gravity Bar ★$ This chic establishment has literally moved up in the world, from a slope just above **Pike Place Market** to more spacious quarters in the Terminal Sales Building. But the move seems not to have affected the laid-back attitude here or the menu. Healthy vibes positively emanate from the place, what with all the pine nuts, sun-dried tomatoes, tuna, and brown rice being dished up. Even chili gets a politically correct spin here, resulting in something like a black-bean soup served with corn bread. Only the daring or truly reckless order the signature wheat-grass juice, which is rather like mowing a lawn with your gums. Stick to the carrot-based libations or the hot apple, lemon, and ginger drink instead. Founded in 1986 by local ceramic artist Laurrien Gilman, this healthy eatery has an atmosphere and a clientele that are distinctly artsy. ◆ Vegetarian ◆ M-F lunch and dinner; Sa-Su brunch and dinner. 113 Virginia St (between First and Second Aves). 448.8826. Also at: Broadway Market (415 Broadway E). 325.7186

2 Vogue Variety is the key word that keeps this dance club happening. On any given night the dark interior and silver walls become the background for a different theme—reggae, gothic, industrial rock, and fetish music that sometimes extends to the dancers' outfits, makeup, and jewelry. ◆ Cover. Daily until 2AM. 2018 First Ave (between Virginia and Lenora Sts). 443.0673

3 Jet City Vintage Take a neon-illumined trip down memory lane, complete with tables full of ceramic ashtrays and chrome toasters, walls covered in old movie posters and Marilyn Monroe images, and a smattering of bubblegum and pinball machines. This shop makes for terrific browsing and offers reasonable prices. ◆ Daily. 2200 First Ave (between Blanchard and Bell Sts). 728.7118

4 Queen City Grill ★★$$ A rich mahogany bar, several small booths, and burnt sienna walls all combine to create a chic yet casual atmosphere. Credit for the success of this stylish grill goes to co-owners Peter Lamb (also responsible for **Il Bistro** in **Pike Place Market**) and Steven Good, as well as to chef Paul Michael, who does marvelously simple but wonderful things with grilled fish or meats and garlic. Now, if the portions would only grow to match the owners' ambitions. ◆ American ◆ M-F lunch and dinner; Sa-Su dinner. 2201 First Ave (between Blanchard and Bell Sts). 443.0975

5 Duo This womenswear shop features clothes that are dressy and a bit daring. Refreshingly, shoppers don't have to drop a month's salary on an outfit here. Walking through the breezeway, you'll encounter **Uno**, its menswear mate. Both shops are owned by a husband and wife, Donald Fletcher and Roni Vincent-Fletcher. ◆ Daily. 2209 First Ave (between Blanchard and Bell Sts). 448.7011. Also at: 1927 First Ave (between Virginia and Stewart Sts). 728.9420

6 Casa-U-Betcha ★★$ A gift from Portland, Oregon, where the first **Casa** opened to raves in the mid-1980s, this ultrahip "tacoria" has two things going for it: the blue margaritas (stupid looking but quite tasty), which help you forget that the food here bears only a passing resemblance to anything served south of the border. But patrons don't come here for traditional dishes; they come because, despite naysayers, it's a happening place full of people sidling up to the bar and crowding into the too-loud dining room with their beautiful *compadres*. The food is filling and, usually, *muy bueno*. ◆ Southwestern/Mexican ◆ Tu-Su lunch and dinner; bar daily until 2AM. 2212 First Ave (between Blanchard and Bell Sts). 441.1026

7 Odd Fellows Hall/Austin A. Bell Building The connected brick structures you see here, plus the **Hull Building** kitty-corner across First Avenue, are about all that remain of an ambitious 19th-century scheme to develop Belltown as a commercial hot spot. The architect was **Elmer Fisher,** who put his stamp all over Pioneer Square, but the plan was the brainchild of pioneer William Bell and his son, Austin Americus Bell.

In 1883 William Bell erected the impressive four-story, mansard-roofed **Bell Hotel** (subsequently renamed the **Bellevue Hotel**) at the corner of Battery Street and what's now First Avenue. Four years later Bell died from a "softening of the brain" that had brought on fits and confusion. His son came north from his home in California to attend the funeral and claim his inheritance. In 1888, while architect **Fisher** was working on a new hall for the Odd Fellows fraternal group two doors south of the hotel, Austin commissioned him to design a compatible apartment building that would fit between the hall and the hotel. This was to be Austin's first big mark on Seattle and, though he'd suffered from periodic depression, he seemed enlivened by the project. But in the spring of 1889, after a hearty breakfast and a stroll to his office, he wrote a shaky note to his wife and shot himself in the head. He was 35, the same age his father had been when he carved out the clearing that would become Belltown. His wife, Eva, completed Austin's handsome structure and named it in his honor.

The **Bellevue Hotel** has long since vanished, and the **Odd Fellows Hall** is now the **2320 First Avenue Building,** its upper stories warrened with offices. But the **Austin A. Bell Building** has been boarded up, a disheveled ghost of a tormented man's dream. ◆ 2320 First Ave (between Bell and Battery Sts)

8 Lampreia ★★★$$$ This sleek and spare restaurant, which opened in 1993, seems even more elegant amidst its gritty Belltown surroundings. Chef Scott Carsberg marries highly seasoned Italian oils and sauces with fresh Northwest produce to create such appetizers as *pizzelle* (crisp little waffles) with thin slices of marinated tuna and pesto. Entrées are similarly inspired: think cannelloni stuffed with Dungeness crab or braised saddle of rabbit wrapped in pancetta. Dessert lovers will not want to pass up the chocolate *feuitillue* (thin alternating layers of chocolate and praline). ◆ Italian ◆ Tu-Sa dinner. Reservations recommended. 2400 First Ave (at Battery St). 443.3301

9 Down Under The music at this sizable weekend-only club is a blend of Top-40/MTV mainstays with a touch of hip hop. As always, much depends on the DJ. It's worth a stop, but don't make it the focus of the evening. ◆ Cover. F-Sa until 4AM. 2407 First Ave (between Battery and Wall Sts). 728.4053

Restaurants/Clubs: Red   **Hotels:** Blue
Shops/ 🌳 Outdoors: Green   **Sights/Culture:** Black

10 Cyclops ★★$$ If "funky" is not your style, don't come within a mile of this place, cluttered inside and out with heaps and piles of kitschy detritus. Its walls glow purple, green, and yellow from a perverse series of paintings and torrents of seemingly bizarre music wash out of the sound system (klezmer is a common choice). But some surprisingly good fare is on the menu: Italian, Russian, French, vegetarian—the proprietors aren't afraid to experiment and are incapable of botching anything. Their credo is: "We *Never* Serve French Fries." The help can be a little surly, but the food is worth the abuse, and the hours accommodate night owls. ♦ International ♦ M-F lunch and dinner; Sa-Su brunch and dinner; F-Sa open until 4 AM. 2416 Western Ave (at Wall St). 441.1677

11 Edgewater Inn $$ Rooms here literally hang out west over Puget Sound, affording marvelous scenery during the day and fresh salt air at night. At one time this hotel rented fishing poles to guests who wished to wet a line from their rooms (the **Beatles** were supposed to have indulged in this sport during an early visit here). But too many people made a mess while cleaning their catches, so the service was discontinued several years ago when the hotel was remodeled to give a mountain-lodge ambience. Waterside rooms are the quietest, but city-view rooms are fine as well and cheaper. Parking is free, and there's a good restaurant with a piano lounge, **Ernie's Bar & Grill.** ♦ Pier 67 (at Alaskan Way and Wall St). 728.7000; fax 441.4119

12 Pier 70 The **Ainsworth & Dunn Wharf** has stood at the north end of the Waterfront for nearly a hundred years—a marvelous building, with wide-plank flooring, rough-hewn log walls, and cavernous open spaces. (A history of this fine structure is mounted just inside the entrance.) It now houses a variety of curio, candy, and T-shirt shops for tourists. ♦ Off Alaskan Way (at Broad St)

Within Pier 70:

Panos ★★$$ Back in the 1980s, when it sat high atop Queen Anne Hill, this restaurant was a mecca for lovers of Greek cuisine. Many foodies mourned owner Panayotes Marinos's decision to close shop and depart for Europe. But he returned, and his restaurant re-creation—in a bright new Waterfront location— happily lives up to all of its past glories.

The rich moussaka is the primo menu pick, but the *keftedes* (spaghetti with meatballs a *mizithra* cheese) and *spanakopita* (spinach pie) are not to be missed either. And the lig fried squid rings may be the best in Seattle. The *aginares politikes,* a sort of soup with artichoke hearts, potato chunks, and carrot an olive oil, lemon, and dill sauce, is too ric and not sufficiently complex. Overall the service is responsive, but the bouzouki mus tends to blare, and both the wine and beer l could be expanded and improved. ♦ Greek ♦ M-F lunch and dinner; Sa-Su dinner. Reservations recommended. 2815 Alaskan Way (at Broad St). 441.5073

13 Waterfront Streetcar Seattle's original trolleys were stripped from service decades ago, but, for nostalgia's sake, **Metro Transi** imported these vintage machines from Australia to make the clattering 15- to 20-minute run from Pier 70 through Pioneer Square to the International District. ♦ 85¢ c peak; $1.10 M-F 3PM to 6PM; children und 5 free. Daily. Pier 70 (off Alaskan Way and Broad St). 553.3000

14 Take It From Us ★★$ Try the riesling chicken and mushrooms, the shepherd's p or the corn chowder at this bright but dinky cafeteria-style eatery. Grazers will want to sample from the appetizer bar. Owned by David and Sandra Brand, this place does a lunch and take-out trade (you can fax in yo order). It's rather out of the way but worth discovering. ♦ American/Takeout ♦ M-F breakfast, lunch, and dinner. 2904 First Av (between Eagle and Broad Sts). 448.3442; 448.8827

15 A-Jay's ★★$ Attention early risers: See out this incredibly popular breakfast spot (beware of crowds, especially on Sundays serving fluffy buttermilk pancakes in stack four, with real maple syrup on the side, an generously stuffed omelettes. The hash bro consist of great blocks of potato accented onion. And in a city where it's near imposs to find old-fashioned black coffee, this din brews a pleasing cup. Early bird specials a available until 10AM, and the breakfast me is available until 3PM. Lunch dishes aren't such standouts, running to sandwiches an juicy burgers, but the service is always cheerful and the atmosphere unpretentiou ♦ American ♦ Tu-Sa breakfast, lunch, and dinner; M, Su breakfast and lunch. 2619 Fi Ave (between Cedar and Vine Sts). 441.15

Wet Side Story

An agglomeration of funky marinas, fishing boats, and scruffy light industry, **Lake Union** is Seattle's hardest- and longest-working waterway. Oh, sure, a few bits of upscale urban fluff have been thrown in for good measure: gentrified, kite-happy **Gasworks Park** at the north, for instance, and a sleek row of seafood restaurants on the south side. And on the boards is an ambitious and expensive plan to transform some 400 acres of land at the lower end of Lake Union into a parklike "urban village" called **Seattle Commons,** with docks and pavilions jutting out onto the waters. But basically, nothing has changed and Lake Union remains inextricably linked to Seattle's blue-collar marine origins.

After the **Lake Washington Ship Canal** opened in 1917 to allow boat traffic access from **Puget Sound,** five- and six-masted schooners, barkentines, and other sailing craft would slip into these fresh waters for a winter's rest and cleaning. Ship moorages still dot these shores, and every summer the lake is strewn with fluttering sails, but nothing typifies Lake Union better than its houseboat community. There aren't many houseboat neighborhoods left in America, and even Seattle's has been decimated—from a peak of about a thousand units in the 1930s to maybe 450 today.

These houseboats used to be cheap, jerry-built abodes for feisty stevedores, lumberjacks, and Wobblies, with a few bohemian types—artists, students, leftist political organizers—filling out the population. It was a community awash with colorful characters such as the white-bearded Robert Patten, who moved to Seattle in 1900 at the age of 90 and settled on a Lake Union houseboat, wore a hat shaped like an umbrella every day of his life (no matter the weather), and was last heard from when he left here to start a new life in California at the formidable age of 99.

"Floating homes" ("houseboats" is considered by some an unflattering term) are no longer the province of impoverished workers or romantic artists, however. In the 1940s you could buy a houseboat for $1,000, and old-timers recall bitter protest meetings when monthly moorage fees went from $15 to $17. But a massive cleanup of Lake Union in the 1960s, combined with increasing property values, led to a reappraisal; these days, floating homes have gone upscale. Many of them are architect-designed multistory wonders that can cost as much as (or more than) a brand-new home on solid ground, with high moorage fees tacked on top of that.

Many people think of these residences as antiquated, and efforts have been made over the years to eliminate them from the lake frontage. But there's still something special, something eminently freeing, about these gently bobbing domiciles that can't be experienced in a land-bound home. It's a romance captured well by newspaper journalist H.E. Jamison, who in the 1930s wrote about life on Lake Union for the now-defunct *Seattle Star:*

"Come on folks, and sit with me on the front porch of my houseboat. . . . And let's heave a sigh for *les misérables* who live in a city of hills and lakes and salt water and yet have nothing better on which to feast their eyes when they return from their day's labors than the uninteresting walls of neighboring buildings. . . .

"It is night; to our left, and a little astern of us, a row of houseboats edges the shore. Each has at least one lighted window that stains the water a soft and shimmering yellow.

"A swell from [a stubby tug] rocks the house ever so gently—a slight shiver that suggests life. There's a gurgling and slapping of waves under the porch. . . . Somewhere a mooring chain creaks and groans. The lights reflected in the now disturbed water dance fantastically.

"Lights and shadows, shadows and lights, peace and contentment. An anodyne for frazzled nerves, a refuge from a troubled world—a moment of inertia in the movement of life. A reprieve, if you please, from the grim sentence that hangs over everyone's head."

16 Cafe Septième ★★$$
Welcome to Belltown Central, a cozy cafe with excellent salads and sandwiches, hot entrées, desserts, and espresso, espresso, and more espresso.
The fine coffees are served in handsome pottery bowls—*very* European. The cafe is fine for reading but even better for visiting with friends. Check out the wealth of magazines and newspapers scattered around. ◆ Coffeehouse ◆ Daily; M-Sa until midnight. 2331 Second Ave (between Battery and Bell Sts). 448.1506

17 Rendezvous The primary battleground for the hearts and minds of Belltown, the bar here is worth a look, but in general steer clear of it unless you're into knocking back triple scotches. Instead, head straight to the **Jewelbox Theater** in back, surprisingly elegant (done up in what might be termed Cheesy Art Deco) and seductively comfortable. Entertainment includes an offbeat, highly imaginative, always interesting film series (Japanese monster flicks, jazz films, hippie movies, etc.) and a wildly uneven menu of live music. ◆ Cover. W, F-Sa 9PM-2AM. 2320 Second Ave (between Battery and Bell Sts). 441.5823

18 2-11 Billiard Club Once upon a time this fine old establishment (with roots back to 1936) was located downtown. But, to Belltown's eternal benefit, the club was forced to move north during construction of the Metro Bus Tunnel. Its regular clientele moved with it; they're the ones decorating the bar with their personal billiards equipment. Don't be intimidated—pool-playing expertise is not required. The tables are adequate, although the cue sticks are less so. The club's best feature is its laid-back atmosphere, conducive to hours of chasing the balls across a field of green felt. ◆ Daily. 2304 Second Ave (between Battery and Bell Sts). 443.1211

19 Mama's Mexican Kitchen ★$ Every inch of wall space here is a witty adventure, overdecorated with Mexicana. Is there a stick of furniture in the place that matches any other? Probably not. Food comes in huge portions, with lots of taco and burrito plates and rice and beans on the side—a carbo-loader's fantasy. Little on the menu will blow you away, though. Come here on a warm summer's night when you get a table outside and eat basket upon basket of the saltless tortilla chips, washing it all down with Corona beer. ◆ Mexican ◆ Daily lunch and dinner. 2234 Second Ave (at Bell St). 728.6262

20 Dingo Gallery Aficionados of World's Fair–era kitsch will find plenty artfully displayed here in about 10 rooms. The prices are not bad, but the real fun is soaking up the owner's impressive aesthetic in mounting and arranging each separate room. ◆ Tu-Sa 1PM-6PM. 2222½ Second Ave (between Bell and Blanchard Sts). 443.6935

20 Signature Bound The stock of this tiny bookstore is skimpy but well-chosen, running toward bohemian tastes of the 1980s and 1990s—selected classics, a smattering of science fiction, banned and obscure material, feminist tracts, poetry, and self-published 'zines. Both new and used books are sold. ◆ M-Sa. 2222 Second Ave (between Bell and Blanchard Sts). 441.3306

20 Crocodile Cafe During the day this cafe is an only moderately successful diner. But at night it turns into one of Seattle's most adventurous and intriguing rock clubs, booking cutting-edge acts from the city and around the country. Kitsch art crams every cranny and literally drips off both the ceiling and walls, even in the rest rooms. One of the more creative displays is the salad-fork mélange in the men's room. ◆ Cover. Tu-F 7AM-2AM; Sa 8AM-2AM; Su 9AM-3PM. 2200 Second Ave (at Blanchard St). 448.2114, music information 441.5611

21 Vonnie's, A Garden Cafe ★$ This delightful garden-court bistro is surrounded by brick walls and centered on a gurgling fountain—a wonderful spot for Sunday brunch. Pasta and sandwiches may be the finest picks from the regular menu. The rotating roster of specials includes omelettes and tender seafood. ◆ Continental/American ◆ Tu-W lunch; Th-Sa lunch and dinner; Su brunch. 120 Blanchard St (between First and Second Aves). 441.1045

22 Bethel Temple Erected around 1915, this elegantly appointed terra-cotta edifice, designed by famed theater architect **B. Marcus Priteca**, originally housed the ritzy **Crystal Swimming Pool**. Where the corner of this structure now drops back to glass doorways and a lighted sign at Second Avenue and Blanchard Street, a huge metal dome used to rise over a pillared base. Model T's would drive up and drop youngsters here for an afternoon dip. The only hint of this building's early purpose may be the stylized green dolphins that decorate its roofline. It's now a Pentecostal church. ◆ 2033 Second Ave (at Lenora St).

23 Bushell's Auctions Owner Mary Bushell deals mostly in estate sellouts and private offerings, and some of the goods are real finds. There are lots of household items, including dishware and bedroom sets. ◆ Call ahead for dates and details for preview and auctions. 2006 Second Ave (between Lenora and Virginia Sts). 448.5833

24 Caffè D'Arte ★$ One of the better finds for Seattle caffiends, this establishment anchors the most exposed corner of what used to be the nine-story **Calhoun Hotel** (constructed in 1918), now an apartment property called the Palladian. ◆ Coffeehouse ◆ M-Sa. 2000 Second Ave (at Virginia St). 728.4901. Also a 125 Stewart Ave S (at Second Ave). 728.446

24 The Poor Italian Cafe ★★$ This *caffè* serves hearty calamari and creamy pasta, including a rich ravioli guaranteed to commit criminal acts against your best dress shirt. Owner Gregory Pesce maintains a friendly, open environment. The wine list gets only a passing grade, but the service is cheery and the bread terrific. ◆ Italian ◆ M-F lunch and dinner; Sa-Su dinner. Virginia St and Second Ave. 441.4313

25 Pacific Galleries Here's an auction house that specializes in liquidating estates. Like all such places, it's a crapshoot—sometimes a gold mine, sometimes mediocre goods. ◆ Call ahead for dates and details. 2121 Third Ave (between Lenora and Blanchard Sts). 441.9990

26 Fourth and Blanchard Building Affectionately known by locals as the "Darth Vader Building" for its resemblance to the *Star Wars* villain, this dark, 440-foot-tall glass monolith was designed by the same folks who brought you the **Columbia Seafirst Tower** downtown (**Chester L. Lindsey Architects**). It's all astonishing surfaces, with dramatic angles at the top that make it eerily reminiscent of New York architect **Philip Johnson**'s Pennzoil Place in Houston. ◆ 2101 Fourth Ave (between Lenora and Blanchard Sts).

Restaurants/Clubs: Red   **Hotels:** Blue
Shops/ 🌳 Outdoors: Green   **Sights/Culture:** Bla

rounds for Celebration

eattle "caffiends" are as notorious for their love of ood coffee—consuming an estimated 929,000 cups f the stuff each day—as are the British for their love f tea. The city's caffeine culture percolates with 200- lus licensed espresso carts and at least as many offee bars and cafes. More than a dozen coffee asters are headquartered here, including **Starbucks** redited with starting the craze back in the 1970s, hen it opened this area's first roasting company), d two others praised by the national media, **orrefazione Italia** and **Caffé D'Arte.** Drive-up spresso windows beckon from all over the city, and dewalk stands are appended to everything from ardware stores to insurance companies. A local agazine, *Cafe Olé,* is dedicated to the coffee-loving e, and there's even an "espresso dentist" in **eenwood,** where patients waiting to have their teeth amined can sip *caffè lattes.* Other towns have their wn unifying symbols; Seattle's is the ubiquitous offee cup.

ewing the perfect Seattle espresso involves a rtain amount of know-how. Technically, it can be ade with any bean or roast, but residents of this ty—who've become shamelessly snobbish about offee over the last several years—favor high-quality ans, usually locally roasted. (At least 25 percent of e coffee gulped here is brewed from specialty ends, a much higher figure than the national norm.) d the espresso can't be made in diner-size volume. well-trained Seattle *barista* (that's Italian for spresso puller) will use impeccable technique to epare only a cup or two at a time: water is heated d forced under pressure through finely ground (but t powdery) coffee, well tamped, in a stovetop or untertop espresso maker. The combination of water d pressure extracts the celluloids and oils that give e beverage its characteristic aroma, body, and flavor.

st getting a cup of coffee in Seattle may demand the me sort of care. The typical connoisseur uses so any espresso variations that you have to be precise hen placing an order. Fess up to any lack of know- dge; *baristas* are usually patient and helpful, and eir assistance could mean the difference between a easant blend and a straight shot of sludge ending up your cup. Note also that locals have created their wn espresso-speak, names for beverages that you obably won't hear elsewhere. Among the more usual: "Thunder Thighs" (a double-tall mocha ade with whole milk and topped with extra whipped

cream) and the "Yankee Dog with White Hat on a Leash" (an "Americano"—which is basically a watered-down espresso—with foam, to go). The fave, however, is still the *caffè latte,* one or more shots of espresso with steamed milk, for $2 or less. The drink has become so popular, in fact, that *Seattle Times* columnist Jean Godden now calls Seattle "LatteLand." Yuk.

Here are some of the best caffeine-driven hangouts where you can test your ordering prowess:

B&O Espresso ♦ 204 Belmont Ave E (at E Olive St), Capitol Hill, 322.5028; and Broadway Market (401 Broadway E), Capitol Hill, 328.3290

Cafe Allegro ♦ 4214 University Way NE (at NE 42nd St), University District, 633.3030

Cafe Septième ♦ 2331 Second Ave (between Battery and Bell Sts), Belltown, 448.1506

Caffé D'Arte ♦ 2000 Second Ave (at Virginia St), Belltown, 728.4901; and 125 Stewart St (at Second Ave), Business District, 728.4468

Gravity Bar ♦ Broadway Market (415 Broadway E), Capitol Hill, 325.7186; and 113 Virginia St (between First and Second Aves), Belltown, 448.8826

SBC ♦ Pike Place Market (Post Alley Market), 467.7700; and Westlake Center (Fourth Ave and Pine St), Business District, 682.7182

Starbucks ♦ Pike Place Market (Soames-Dunn Bldg), 448.8762; 10214 NE Eighth St (between 102nd Ave NE and Bellevue Way), Bellevue, 454.0191; 2350 Carillon Point (at NE Lake Washington Blvd), Kirkland, 827.2130; 3320 W McGraw St (at 34th Ave W), Magnolia, 298.3390; 2201 Queen Anne Ave N (at W Boston St), Queen Anne, 285.3711; 2210 N 45th St (between Bagley and Meridian Aves N), Wallingford, 548.9507; 4101 SW Admiralty Way (at 41st Ave), West Seattle. 937.5010.

Torrefazione Italia
♦ 320 Occidental Avenue S (between S King and S Main Sts), Pioneer Square. 624.5773

27 Warwick Hotel $$$ Rather large to be considered intimate and too small to feel so corporate, this hotel is an odd beast, the eternal second choice. The 229 rooms are comfortable and large, with balconies that offer decent downtown views. There's a pool in the health club, albeit a shallow one, and the piano lounge provides entertainment nightly. Front-desk personnel are friendly and efficient. A 24-hour courtesy van will whisk you to downtown engagements. Room rates, however, even the reduced corporate tariffs,

are steep for accommodations so far from the heart of the city. The **Liaison** restaurant serves breakfast, lunch, and dinner.
♦ 401 Lenora St (at Fourth Ave). 443.4300; fax 448.1662

Seattle is the only city in the Pacific Northwest that fields major league teams in all three primary spectator sports: the Seahawks football, SuperSonics basketball, and Mariners baseball teams.

28 Alweg Monorail Walking along Fifth Avenue just north of Pine Street after dark, when the ghostly monorail flashes by overhead, is one of Seattle's finest urban experiences. The monorail is really quiet, all alight with peering faces. The slingshot-shaped concrete supports make for a fine Hitchcock scenario, with generous geometric lines and shadows. Locals who've pushed for the monorail's removal—so a clear view of the **Space Needle** can be opened along Fifth Avenue—don't appreciate the drama of this silver-skinned dinosaur. Film director Alan Rudolph did, however, and he made plentiful use of it in his 1985 film *Trouble in Mind.* Be on your guard, especially at night: this stretch of Fifth Avenue is not heavily populated.
♦ Fifth Ave (between Pine St and the Seattle Center)

29 Dimitriou's Jazz Alley Longtime jazz producer John Dimitriou owns this club, a genuine treasure for blues and jazz fans alike. Some of the most significant names in the genre have graced the room: Harry Connick Jr. used to play here before he was famous, and Diane Shuur has been a regular performer throughout the years. Expect to see such entertainers as Charles Brown, Ray Brown, Maynard Ferguson, and Betty Carter, seven days a week, every week. The food is nothing special, but the room is excellent, with comfortable seating. If you're a music fan, don't miss this place. ♦ Cover. Tu-Su. Reservations recommended. Sixth Ave and Lenora St. 441.9729

30 Sixth Avenue Inn $ One step above a motel (some rooms even have brass beds, and room service is available), this 166-room hostelry is reasonably priced and centrally located, fairly convenient to both the downtown core and the **Seattle Center,** and has a basic restaurant for quick meals. Street noise can be a problem, especially on the Sixth Avenue side. ♦ 2000 Sixth Ave (at Virginia St). 441.8300; fax 441.9903

31 Art/Not Terminal After four initial years operating in a space converted from a **Trailways** bus station (hence the name), this co-op gallery/shop moved into more upscale digs. Shows change each month, though some stay longer. Exhibits draw from the work of about 200 member artists, including sculptors, photographers, and painters. The nonprofit gallery is good to its artists, taking an uncharacteristically small percentage from the sales, and customers can even work out layaway plans with individual artists. New show openings, with live music and refreshments, are scheduled the Saturday immediately following the first Thursday of each month. ♦ Daily. 2045 Westlake Ave N (at Lenora St). 233.0680

32 Elephant Car Wash Sign A tacky fave among locals, this blinking and revolving pink sign won a 1956 design contest held by car-wash owners. It has since proliferated (several replicas now adorn branches from here to Puyallup) and become almost as renowned a symbol of Seattle as the **Space Needle.** *Cosmopolitan* magazine even suggested that single women of the 1990s should be on the look out for this pink pachyderm, as the establishments it decorates tend to be hangouts for eligible yuppie dudes.
♦ 616 Battery St (at Seventh Ave)

33 Group Health Building (P-I Building) The New York firm of **Lockwood-Greene** was responsible for most of the architecture of the three-story block, and the landscaped top level was added in 1978 by Seattle's **Naramore, Bain, Brady & Johanson** (now the **NBBJ Group**). The *Seattle Post-Intelligencer* newspaper moved out of the building in the late 1980s, taking along the giant revolving globe that had capped the rounded tower. The *P-I* now operates from a glass cliff on the Waterfront, while Group Health Cooperative has taken over this structure. ♦ 521 Wall St (at Sixth Ave)

34 Ditto Tavern A Belltown focus for the disgruntled, this tavern attracts those inclined to read, write, and recite poetry. It's charming enough, particularly with the manual typewriters scattered about and the writers busy at them. Poetry readings are held Sundays, beginning at 7PM. The second Monday of every month features prose readings by aspiring novelists. Live alternative rock, with some jazz tossed into the mix, is scheduled most nights, beginning at 10PM.
♦ Cover for live music. Tu-Su until 2AM. 2307 Fifth Ave (between Bell and Battery Sts). 441.3303

35 The Two Bells Tavern ★$ Belltown's great altar of burger worship is almost impossible to get into at lunchtime, when the suits mix with the bohemians in the booths and at the bar. Come for one of the Paul Bunyan–size decks beef covered in fried onions, with a sidecar of chunky potato salad. It's messy but worth the dry-cleaning bill. The lemonade and the salad are also recommended. Small rock groups o solo singer/songwriters appear here on Monday nights, beginning at 10PM. All in all, it's a good place to see and be seen. ♦ American ♦ Daily lunch and dinner; bar daily until 2AM. 2313 Fourth Ave (between Bell and Battery Sts). 441.3050

36 Engine House No. 2 A fire station has occupied the corner of Fourth Avenue and Battery Street since 1890, although the original wooden building—**Engine House No. 4**—sat across Battery Street from where architect **Daniel R. Huntington**'s 1920 brick structure now stands. Unlike **No. 4,** which had to depend on horse-driven fire engines, the new **No. 2** was the talk of the town during the Jazz Age for its "motor-powered apparatus." ♦ Fourth Ave and Battery St

37 Exotique Records The selection at this interesting and offbeat record store runs toward the adventurous. What the stock lacks in range, it makes up in depth: There is plenty to riffle through here, especially independent releases in worlds of acid jazz, underground dance, and alternative music. ♦ Daily. 2400 Third Ave (between Battery and Wall Sts). 448.3452

38 Taki's ★$ Though this restaurant specializes in pizza and pasta, the lasagna is particularly good. Prices are very reasonable, and the room is a nice place to sit and visit—a great lunch spot. ♦ Italian ♦ M-Sa lunch and dinner. 425 Cedar St (between Fourth and Fifth Aves). 448.7750

39 Chief Seattle Fountain This bronze memorial to the city's namesake (who was originally called Chief Noah Sealth, not Seattle, by the way) was the first public artwork commissioned by the City of Seattle. With the Alaska-Yukon-Pacific Expo approaching in 1909, local business leaders prevailed upon the city to set aside a triangle of property where they proposed to commemorate the friendship between the white settlers and Native Americans of Elliott Bay. The symbol of that friendship was to be a life-size rendition of Chief Seattle, the leader of the Duwamish and Suquamish tribes who had negotiated the treaty that gave up title to what's now much of northwestern Washington state. The sculptor was James A. Wehn, who two years later would design the fountain and bust of Chief Seattle at **Pioneer Place Park** and go on to establish the sculpture department at the **University of Washington.**

Disputes over which foundry should cast the work delayed the statue's unveiling, but it was finally put on view in 1912. For many years after that it stood green from advanced oxidation. In 1989 a local cabdriver took it upon himself to rectify the shameful situation and, using some solvents and a lot of elbow grease, completely cleaned Chief Seattle

under cover of night. The first reaction from city officials was that the cabbie had wrecked this historic monument, and a warrant was issued for his arrest. He fled town before it could be determined that his actions had in fact been harmless. It's still a mystery what happened to that taxi driver, but the statue does look rather nice now. ♦ Tilikum Place (between Cedar St and Denny Way)

40 Oz One of Seattle's largest and oldest dance clubs caters to a predominantly twentysomething clientele. The sound runs to retro, industrial dance, and generally alternative music—sometimes provided by DJs, sometimes by live bands. ♦ Cover. W, F until 2AM; Sa until 4AM. ID is required; the dress code—no jeans, T-shirts, or sandals— is strictly enforced. 131 Taylor Ave N (between Denny Way and John St). 448.0888

41 Denny Park Pioneer David Denny donated the land on which this two-block-size oasis of trees was established in 1890. It is the city's oldest park. Previously, it had been **Seattle Cemetery.** (The dear departed are now at Lake View Cemetery on Capitol Hill.) ♦ Denny Way (between Dexter and Ninth Aves N)

42 13 Coins ★$ While other swankier joints have failed, this culinary institution just keeps going and going. What's the secret? Probably a combination of the fact that it stays open 24 hours; has a huge menu of pasta, grilled meats, and fish entrées; and serves a dynamite Caesar salad. The portions are generous and the people watching in the wee small hours is some of the best around. ♦ American ♦ Daily 24 hours. 125 Boren Ave N (between Denny Way and John St). 682.2513

43 Seattle Times Building The city's afternoon newspaper occupies a lesser-known building among those designed by architect **Robert C. Reamer** (who was also responsible for the **Skinner Building** and **1411 Fourth Avenue Building** downtown). Completed in 1930 but added to since, this Moderne-style headquarters is notable for the grillwork at its entrance and the understated sign cut along its facade. ♦ Fairview Ave N and John St

Seattle's *Virginia V,* built in 1922 as part of Puget Sound's Mosquito Fleet and still chartered for celebratory cruises, is the last inland-water, passenger-carrying steamer operating west of the Mississippi.

44 Cafe Lôc ★$ Good, basic, inexpensive Vietnamese fare is served quickly, unpretentiously, and abundantly. There's another outlet in the **Seattle Center,** but for atmosphere and comparative tranquillity, this venue is much preferred. ♦ Vietnamese ♦ Daily lunch and dinner. 407 Broad St (between Denny Way and John St). 441.6883. Also at: Center House, Seattle Center. 728.9292

45 Seattle Center Site of the 1962 Century 21 Exposition, the center is now a motley aggregate of structures dotting 74 acres just north of Belltown (for a map of the center, see page 83). When it was built it evoked a vision of a gleaming, streamlined world to come. Americans saw in the World's Fair a future of upward mobility, a course paved with the mystifying gifts of science—from monorails to paper clothes and commuter helicopters. Now somewhat faded and worn, despite spot renovations over the years, the center stands as a glorious antique of the Kennedy era, with a feeling at once modern, dated, silly, and thrilling.

Plans to completely modernize the center, including a fanciful $335-million Disney expansion scheme from the late 1980s, have so far met with resistance. The **Charlotte Martin Theatre,** however, opened in 1993 as home for the nationally acclaimed **Seattle Children's Theater.** ♦ Bounded by First and Fifth Aves N, and Denny Way and Mercer St. 684.8582

Within the Seattle Center:

Space Needle "Back when we were in school, if you wanted attention, you put up your hand. That is what the Space Needle will do for the [1962 World's] Fair and Seattle." The speaker was Joe Gandy, used-car salesman and president of the Century 21 Expo. His enthusiasm for "the Noodle," as locals say in jest, was not unfounded: In its three-plus decades, the **Space Needle** has become the supreme symbol of Seattle, the city's equivalent to San Francisco's Golden Gate Bridge. If it seems perfectly absurd at first, don't worry, it will grow on you.

This monument was the brainchild of World's Fair organizer Eddie Carlson. He scribbled his idea on a napkin one night, an image that looked like a flying saucer on a tripod. Architects **Victor Steinbrueck** and **John Ridley** gave it a kind of "Amazing Stories" reality. Construction proved to be an enormous project. Consider some of the stats: the foundation is 30 feet deep and weighs 5,850 tons; what you see above ground

weighs 3,700 tons; the legs are anchored by some 74 bolts, the dimensions of which are 4 inches by 32 feet; the tower claims 24 lightning rods and can endure winds of up to 150 miles per hour; and it stands more than 600 feet high. The elevator takes 43 seconds to reach the peak (and is literally a breathtaking experience). The restaurant floor at 500 feet turns a single revolution every hour, thanks to a single-horsepower motor. And the view is magnificent from the **Observation Deck,** particularly on clear days. Check it out. ♦ Fee for the Observation Deck. Daily until midnight. 443.2111

Within the Space Needle:

Space Needle Restaurant ★$$$ It's sad to say, but this casual restaurant and the swankier **Emerald Suite** (★$$$$; 443.2150) don't measure up to their lofty positions on the same floor of the tower. It's understood, of course, that you're paying for the view, and it is a very fine panorama. But the cost is just too steep for the meals served here, which have a reputation for dipping to mediocre and rising only to very good. Both restaurants specialize in Northwestern fare, especially seafood. Diners ride the elevator free of charge. A dress code (no T-shirts, tennis shoes, or jeans) is enforced at the **Emerald Suite.** ♦ Northwestern ♦ M-Sa breakfast, lunch, and dinner; Su brunch and dinner. Reservations recommended. 443.210

Fun Forest Amusement Park Originally called the **Gayway** in World's Fair days, this facility is only so-so, although kids in the middle of their second Sno-Cone and fifth Tilt-a-Whirl ride won't care. For the old-at-heart there's a carousel and classic bumper cars. Call ahead for hours and special offers. ♦ Daily noon-11PM Memorial Day-Labor Day; hours vary widely off-season. Fee for rides. 728.1585

Alweg Monorail The **Seattle Center** marks this train's northern terminus. It travels from here south to **Westlake Center,** departing every 15 minutes. ♦ Fee. Daily. 441.6038

Pacific Science Center It's an interesting stop for adults, but with its hands-on exhibits and full slate of activities and programs (about dinosaurs, for instance, and whales), this place is even better for children. It's a sort of minicampus with six interconnected buildings. Designed for the World's Fair by well-known Seattle-born architect **Minoru Yamasaki,** along with **Naramore, Bain, Brady & Johanson,** it claims a wonderfully tranquil and inviting space outside, full of pools and soaring arches. ("It is as if Venice had just been built," crowed Alistair Cooke when the complex opened.) But the inside all too often feels cramped and constricted. There's a fine planetarium, a laser theater, and an IMAX theater. ♦ Admission. Tu-Su. 443.2880

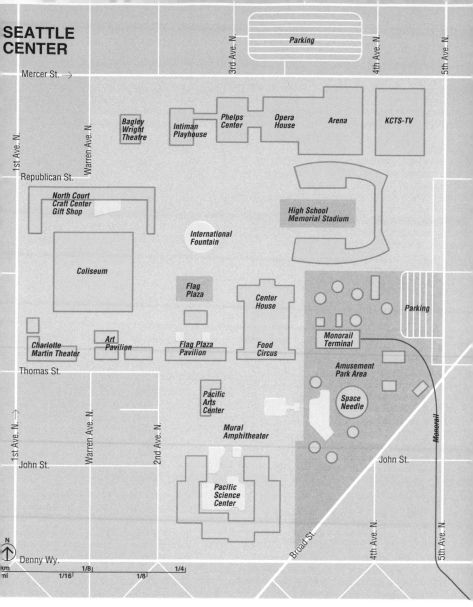

SEATTLE CENTER

Mercer St. →

Parking

3rd Ave. N.

4th Ave. N.

5th Ave. N.

1st Ave. N.

Warren Ave. N.

Republican St.

Bagley Wright Theatre

Intiman Playhouse

Phelps Center

Opera House

Arena

KCTS-TV

North Court Craft Center Gift Shop

International Fountain

High School Memorial Stadium

Coliseum

Flag Plaza

Center House

Parking

Charlotte Martin Theater

Art Pavilion

Flag Plaza Pavilion

Food Circus

Monorail Terminal

Thomas St.

1st Ave. N. →

Warren Ave. N.

2nd Ave. N.

Amusement Park Area

Pacific Arts Center

Space Needle

Mural Amphitheater

John St.

John St.

Monorail

Pacific Science Center

N

Denny Wy.

km
mi   1/16   1/8   1/8   1/4

Broad St.

4th Ave. N.

5th Ave. N.

Pacific Arts Center Presenting work by children and teens (and with a full slate of activities for them as well), this is a surprisingly worthwhile stop for anyone who enjoys prowling art galleries and museums. Really. ◆ Free. Tu-Su. 443.5437

Charlotte Martin Theater Inaugurated in 1994, this $10.4-million project is the first new building to be erected in the **Seattle Center** since 1983. It was designed by **Mahlum & Nordfors McKinley Gordon** to be the home of the popular **Seattle Children's Theatre (SCT).** Artist Garth Edwards's functional art delights the eye even as it serves a structural purpose: characters from smiling cacti to fanciful sea creatures adorn handrails, archways, even heating grills. ◆ Box office: M-Sa. 441.3322

Center House If much of the center reminds you of the 1960s, this structure lurches the aesthetic forward one decade, leaving you with a claustrophobic, closed-in space redolent of 1970s suburban malls. It's full mostly with overpriced fast-fooderies and knickknack shops. However, the **Seattle Children's Museum** (441.1768) is located on the lower level and provides special multicultural programs as well as a permanent **Playcenter,** a supervised play area for the little ones. In 1993, the **Group Theater** (441.1299), which performs multicultural plays, opened on the lower level. ◆ Daily. 684.7200

International Fountain This is perhaps the ugliest water spout you can ever hope to see (John Wayne, looking it over in 1962, drawled, "What's that? An airplane crash?"), and therein lies its charm. A great pit is lined with poured cement and boulders, and a globe at the bottom center randomly spews liquid from 117 nozzles. (At night, this water may be set aglow with colored lights.) Meanwhile, an antiquated sound system valiantly pumps out wheezing strains of classical music. Is there a connection between the music and which nozzle will next let fly? Debate rages on.

Opera House Some of the finest cultural offerings to be found in Seattle cross the stages of this large structure along Mercer Street. This building used to be Seattle's **Civic Auditorium** but was remodeled for the World's Fair by **B. Marcus Priteca** and **James Chiarelli.** It is now home to the **Seattle Opera, Seattle Symphony, Seattle Youth Symphony,** and the **Pacific Northwest Ballet.**

James Fitzgerald's refurbished and graceful *Fountain of the Northwest* stands in front of the **Intiman Playhouse,** home to the theater company of the same name, and the **Bagley Wright Theater** hosts the **Seattle Repertory Theatre.** The quality of productions at these venues ranges widely, but they are all first-rate houses in their own right. ♦ Mercer St (between Warren and Fourth Aves N). Seattle Opera 389.7676; Seattle Symphony 443.4747; Seattle Youth Symphony 362.2300; Pacific Northwest Ballet 441.9411; Intiman Playhouse 626.0782; Bagley Wright Theater 443.2222

Champion Wine Cellars

46 Champion Wine Cellars The selection of wines here is both imported and domestic, and staffers are helpful, knowledgeable, and bewilderingly happy to answer your every oddball query. The store also stocks imported beers, but the choice is much more limited. ♦ M-Sa. 108 Denny Way (at First Ave N). 284.8306

47 Romper Room This funky dance club is unafraid to throw house, rave, industrial, and even good old grunge music into the stew. Live acoustic sets are scheduled on Monday night, and Tuesday is open-mike night. Look for occasional drink specials. There may be too much black-light ambience here for some dancers, but a pool table and art gallery in a side room provide a momentary escape from the fashion parade. ♦ Cover. Su-Th 4PM-2AM; F-Sa 4PM-3AM. 106 First Ave N (between Denny Way and John St). 284.5003

48 P-I Globe At least as tacky as the **Elephant Car Wash**'s pink proboscidean is this revolving neonized world atop the *Seattle Post-Intelligencer*'s offices. It's easily visible from many points on Elliott Bay (including the ferry routes and harbor tours), as well as, suddenly and unexpectedly, from many parts of Belltown, **Seattle Center,** and the Queen Anne neighborhood. Locals have come to rely so much on the regularity of this landmark's spin that when mechanical problems cause a halt, you can almost see the psychological pal it casts. ♦ 101 Elliott Ave W (at W John St)

49 Myrtle Edwards Park Situated on the Waterfront just north of downtown and southwest of the **Seattle Center,** this spot makes for a spectacular city stroll. On nice days catch an unmatched view of the Olympic Mountains, Mount Rainier, the Seattle skyline, and more along the rolling greensward's two-mile-long walkway. On less-nice days (for which a rain slicker is heartily recommended) it offers moody sky and coal-gray churning waters. This is a favorite place for picnickers, in-line skaters, and lunchtime runners. ♦ Alaskan Way (between Bay and W Thomas Sts)

50 Pottery Northwest Most of this building is devoted to studio space for local artisans. A small gallery lets visitors in on what residents are up to, which is often interesting, brightly colored work. Some classes are held here, too. ♦ Tu-Sa. 226 First Ave N (between John and Thomas Sts). 285.4421

51 Kaspar's ★★★$$$ Owner/chef Kaspar Donier, who earned his culinary credentials at the Four Seasons in Vancouver, BC, recently moved his operation from the fifth story of a Belltown office building to this location long inhabited by Le Tastevin. The restaurant's interior is bright and airy with neutral shades of tan, cream, and taupe complemented with lush plants. Some of the dinner attractions include crab-and-salmon hash cakes topped with a mushroom sauce; seasonal asparagus spears in a marinade of olive oil, herbs, and garlic; and duck with a port wine and dried cherry sauce. The before- and after-theater crowd can choose from a good selection of smaller offerings from the bar menu. ♦ Continental ♦ M-Th, Sa dinner; F lunch and dinner. Reservations recommended. 19 W Harrison St (between First Ave W and Queen Anne Ave N). 298.0123

"One of Seattle's oddities is that while residents here own more Birkenstocks per capita than anywhere else—a fact—it's a city of hills and a lousy place to get around in sandals."

Smart Money magazine

Restaurants/Clubs: Red   **Hotels:** Blue
Shops/ 🌳 Outdoors: Green   **Sights/Culture:** Black

52 Espressly Yours Here's one for the books: an espresso shop sharing its space with an auto-body repair joint. Only in Seattle. The coffee is not bad, and the hours are good for weekday early risers. ♦ M-F from 6:30AM. 418 Queen Anne Ave N (between Harrison and Republican Sts). 282.0658

53 Inn at Queen Anne $ Former studio apartments have been converted into 37 suites with small kitchens—nothing fancy, but very functional. Long-term rentals are available as well. It's located within two blocks of the **Seattle Center** and a major grocery store, **QFC**, which is good because there's no restaurant here. ♦ 505 First Ave N (at Republican St). 282.7357; fax 282.7619

54 Uptown Espresso ★$ One of the best cups of espresso available in Seattle (and that's saying a lot) is served with pizazz, baked goods, and cutting-edge attitude. ♦ Coffeehouse ♦ Daily. 525 Queen Anne Ave N (between W Republican and W Mercer Sts). 281.8669

55 Sorry Charlie's $ Food and drink are only the marginal reasons why people come here. The real attraction is a piano bar, where singers and tin ears alike hold forth with enthusiasm. This was the original karaoke-type singing, before technology took over. And as with karaoke, piano sing-alongs always risk painful embarrassment for both listeners and crooners. ♦ American ♦ Daily breakfast, lunch, and dinner. Bars (regular and piano) daily until 2AM. 529 Queen Anne Ave N (between W Republican and W Mercer Sts). 283.3245

56 Park Avenue Records This may be the best used-record store in Seattle (the used-CD selection is good, too). To get exactly what you're looking for, you may have to return more than once, but the browsing is always fun. Whether your taste runs to rock, jazz, country, or show tunes, one new treasure per visit is almost guaranteed. The selection of blues is the store's single failing. ♦ Daily. 532 Queen Anne Ave N (between Republican and Mercer Sts). 284.2390

57 Keystone Corner Cards Baseball and other sports-card aficionados share a deep respect for this place. ♦ M-Sa. 534 Queen Anne Ave N (at Mercer St). 285.9277

57 Titlewave The selection is small at this general-interest used-book store, but it's put together with excellent taste, which means

you might spend less than 15 minutes browsing here but still turn up something you've wanted for a while. Unfortunately, the stock tends to be pricier than you'd expect. ♦ Daily; F until 10:30PM. 7 Mercer St (between Queen Anne and First Aves N). 282.7687

57 T.S. McHugh's Restaurant & Pub ★$$ Owned by formula restaurateur Mick McHugh, this is an American place masquerading as a British pub. There's the required (but faux) time-darkened facade outside and the rich wood appointments inside. There's an Old World conviviality at the bar, where the bartenders chat up the customers and help them expand their knowledge of liquors and local microbrews. Skip the dining room and stay right here at the bar where you can order a hefty sandwich or burger, accompanied by terrific fries, and sample the plentiful stash of beers. ♦ American ♦ Daily lunch and dinner; bar daily until 2AM. 21 Mercer St (between Queen Anne and First Aves N). 282.1910

58 Emerald Diner ★$ A burger joint with attitude for the 1990s (they call it vegetarian-friendly), this place boasts chrome and neon fixtures, shimmering color schemes, design angles so acute you don't want to bump against them, and neo-1950s and 1960s kitsch decor. If you don't want a hamburger, try a nut-burger (they're better). The fries are fine and so are the desserts and breakfasts. There's live entertainment (from Brazilian bands to rock and gospel) on weekends, and Monday is open-mike night for musicians. ♦ American ♦ Cover for live performances. Daily breakfast, lunch, and dinner. 105 W Mercer St (at First Ave W). 284.4618

59 A Contemporary Theatre (ACT) The type of plays fluctuates wildly at this equity house (just to be sure of what you'll get, ask around or see newspaper reviews before attending shows here). Expect primarily recent plays, with an annual holiday production of Dickens's *A Christmas Carol*. The season runs from May through December. ♦ Box office daily noon-6PM. 100 W Roy St (at First Ave W). 285.5110

60 Mediterranean Kitchen ★$ Vampires will want to keep clear of this garlic-heavy Middle Eastern restaurant, but budget diners will praise the ratio of price per pound of food. It's unusual *not* to see patrons exiting here with a carton or more of leftovers, maybe the remains of the superb Farmer's Dish (tart lemon chicken on a hillock of rice) or a helping of lamb shank with couscous, carrots, and potatoes. Dinners come with a bowl of soup (lentil, if you're lucky) and a soothing romaine salad with mint leaves. Owner Kamal Aboul-Hosn, who also runs a Middle Eastern fast-foodery on Capitol Hill (**The Oven** on Broadway), offers several tempting appetizers (the *baba ganooj* and hummus both deserve plaudits), but who other than the most ambitious gourmand can ever spare room for them? ♦ Middle Eastern ♦ Tu-F lunch and dinner; M, Sa-Su dinner. 4 W Roy St (between First Ave W and Queen Anne Ave N). 285.6713.

61 **Orestes'** ★★$ Legends regarding this lumpy white monstrosity abound. It was supposedly built by an aspiring Mexican restaurateur who lived in it as a recluse after his venture failed. Nightclub entrepreneurs later tried unsuccessfully to make a go of it, failed, and then left the building empty for many years. Now a Greek restaurant, the present incarnation does a particularly outstanding job with stuffed grape leaves and tabbouleh, and it's far more pleasant than its exterior promises. ♦ Greek ♦ M-Sa dinner; Su brunch and dinner. 14 Roy St (between Queen Anne and First Aves N). 282.5514

62 **Cinema Espresso** ★$ A fine little corner spot, this coffee shop is decked out in movie memorabilia and peopled by drifting screenwriters and actors just back from or about to go to LA. Usually not crowded, it's a good place to spend an afternoon reading a book. Desserts here are worth a shot. ♦ Coffeehouse ♦ Daily. 600 Queen Anne Ave N (at Roy St). 286.0866

63 **Tower Books** Stuffed to overflowing, this outlet of the national chain is up to snuff in fiction standards, with an especially large selection of sci-fi and mysteries. There's also a large children's literature department and a huge magazine array. Browsers are welcome. ♦ Daily until midnight. 20 Mercer St (at First Ave N). 283.6333. Also at: 10635 NE Eighth St (between 106th and 108th Aves NE), Bellevue. 451.1110

64 **The Famous Pacific Dessert Company** ★★★$ This late-night place makes a great evening finale for sugar lovers. The cafe features exquisite chocolate confections, fruit pies and tarts, espresso, and herbal teas. It's decorated with changing exhibits of local art ranging from mediocre to very good (and whoever does the chalkboards is positively gifted). Warning: This place fills to overflowing after theater performances at **Seattle Center.** ♦ Dessert ♦ Daily until 11PM. 127 Mercer St (between First and Warren Aves N). 284.8100. Also at: 420 E Denny Way (at Olive Way). 328.1950; Crossroads Mall, Bellevue. 649.0306

65 **Bamboo Garden** ★$$ A decidedly odd vegetarian experience, but one not to be missed, this restaurant (aka the "fake-meat palace") lists items on its Hong Kong–style menu according to which meats they simulate. The only thing to avoid is the faux "beef"—trust us on this one. ♦ Vegetarian/Chinese ♦ Daily lunch and dinner. 364 Roy St (between Nob Hill and Fourth Aves N). 282.6616

66 **Bahn Thai** ★★$ Zestful but not overpowering Thai fare is served in an ornately overdecorated setting within a converted house. The curry of the day is usually an excellent choice, as is the chicken satay. Only menu listings with more than two or three stars are hot. ♦ Thai ♦ M-F lunch and dinner; Sa-Su dinner. 409 Roy St (between Fourth and Fifth Aves N). 283.0444

67 **Jillian's Billiard Club** This pool hall, in what was once a Toyota showroom, offers 33 tables and a pedestrian munchies menu, along with beer, wine, champagne, and the ubiquitous espresso drinks. A bar at one end of the club provides a salutary windowed retreat. It's a dress-up joint, not your classic dark pool hall like the **2-11 Billiard Club** (see page 77) in Belltown. Billiards lessons are available. ♦ M-Th, Su until 2AM; F, Sa until 4AM. 731 Westlake Ave N (between Valley and Aloha Sts). 223.0300

68 **Wawona** Harking back to Seattle's maritime heritage is this tri-masted, 468-ton schooner built in 1897. For three decades, beginning in 1914, the ship sailed north to hunt for cod in the Bering Sea. Ironically, those fish that ended their lives on the *Wawona* actually helped extend this ship's own life, preserving the inner hull with their oils. In 1970 it was the first US ship to be declared a national historic site. ♦ Every $1 donation goes toward the ship's upkeep. Daily. Northwest Seaport Dock (near the corner of Westlake Ave N and Valley St, just west of the US Naval Reserve station). 447.9800

Coincidence or karma? The electric guitar was invented in Seattle. Jimi Hendrix was born in Seattle. You be the judge.

Restaurants/Clubs: Red   Hotels: Blue
Shops/ ♣ Outdoors: Green   Sights/Culture: Bla

69 The Center for Wooden Boats

A historical museum and boat-rental dock are rolled into one, with many vintage and replica craft on view. The center also offers classes in sailing, sail repair, boat-building, and other maritime skills. ♦ Admission to museum; rentals range from $8 to $15 per hour. Museum/gift shop: M, W-Su. Boat rentals: daily. 1010 Valley St (at Lake Union). 382.2628

70 Chandler's Crabhouse and Fresh Fish Market ★$

One in a series of glitzy nosheries that round the southern end of Lake Union and attract a libidinally active clientele, this spot does its best with crab (no surprise here) in a multitude of variations. There's also a daily fresh-fish roster and a satisfying Sunday brunch. ♦ Seafood ♦ M-Sa lunch and dinner; Su brunch and dinner. 901 Fairview Ave N (at Lake Union). 223.2722

70 Duke's Chowderhouse and Outrageous Canoe Club ★$

Stuck into the lower corner of the **Chandler's Cove** retail complex, this spot is rather hard to find. But the view of Lake Union can't be beat, even when the sun is bright enough to pierce your retinas, and the deck dining area makes a terrific after-work hangout. (The interior, by contrast, is often too noisy for a pleasant chat.) Fresh seafood is available daily, but the sandwiches and fries fit equally well with the yacht-club atmosphere. ♦ American ♦ Daily lunch and dinner. Bar daily until 2AM. 901 Fairview Ave N (at Lake Union). 382.9963

71 Cucina! Cucina! ★$$

Being seen is the most important thing here—it's a good thing, since it's so noisy no one can hear you anyway—so dress smartly for you will definitely be checked out. This restaurant is big on pasta, focaccia, and designer pizzas (try the smoked-chicken pie), with deck seating out back where you can watch boats and pontoon planes on Lake Union. ♦ Italian ♦ M-Sa lunch and dinner; Su brunch and dinner. Bar daily until 1:30AM. Reservations recommended. 901 Fairview Ave N (at Lake Union). 447.2782. Also at: Bellevue Place (10500 NE Eighth Ave, at 105th Ave NE). 637.1177

The Odd Fellows Hall (now the 2320 First Avenue Building) once played host to comedian W.C. Fields. Novelist Tom Robbins lived in the building in the mid-1980s; he says he was once visited there by Timothy Leary, who declared the place haunted.

72 I Love Sushi ★★$

The beloved menu of the popular sushi palace of the same name in Bellevue is now offered at this outpost. Tuna, eel, and Dungeness crab remain ever-popular selections. Hara-San, one of the master chefs from the original restaurant, wields the knives here. ♦ Japanese ♦ M-Sa lunch and dinner; Su dinner. 1001 Fairview Ave N (at Lake Union). 625.9604. Also at: 11818 NE Eighth St (near 118th Ave NE), Bellevue. 454.5706

73 Kamon on Lake Union ★★$$

In addition to sushi, this restaurant offers an array of American classics, but the sushi is best. The high-design, neon bar employs vigorous, efficient chefs who work well with fresh ingredients. The remainder of the restaurant provides a more pedestrian environment and certainly less entertainment. There's a sister restaurant, **Kamon of Kobe** (644.1970), in Bellevue. ♦ Japanese ♦ M-Sa lunch and dinner; Su dinner. 1177 Fairview Ave N (at Lake Union). 622.4665

74 Lincoln Towing

Another stop in the official "Outrageous, Never to be Sanctioned by the Chamber of Commerce" kitsch tour of the Emerald City features this company's pink, pedestaled pickup truck, accessorized with a gargantuan toe protruding from its roof. Get those cameras ready! ♦ Mercer St and Fairview Ave N. 622.0415

75 St. Spiridon Orthodox Church

The city's first Russian Orthodox church was established in 1898, the same time Americans were rushing through Seattle on their way to gold fields in the old Russian outpost of Alaska. This tiny church, conceived by architect **Ivan Palmov** (who also designed **St. Nicholas Russian Orthodox Church** on Capitol Hill), came along much later—in 1938—yet it contains all of the arresting clichés of Eastern churches. Drivers racing down Interstate 5 are often bewildered to see its white-and-blue onion domes towering to the west. ♦ Yale Ave N (at Harrison St). 624.5341

Bests

Bob Whitt
Insurance Sales, The Whitt Agency

Watching the sun set from **Golden Gardens** park. There's nothing like the Seattle **Waterfront** for great sunsets.

The deck of **Ray's Boathouse** is probably the best place to enjoy Seattle seafood while watching the action on the Waterfront.

Sailing on **Elliott Bay**—getting out on **Puget Sound** is by far one of the best activities the city of Seattle has to offer.

If you have enough time, the **San Juan Islands** offer the best getaway by either private boat, float plane, or state ferry. Destinations such as **Roche Harbor** and **Friday Harbor** share a diverse landscape and represent the best of what the Northwest has to offer.

Capitol Hill to Seward Park

In a city of diverse neighborhoods, those areas lying just east of downtown—along the hilly ridge that separates downtown skyscrapers from placid **Lake Washington**—are by far the most diverse. The wealth of old Seattle is entrenched here, but these streets are also home to penniless refugees, leather-clad punks with Jello-bright hair, and, in August, fans for Seafair's annual hydroplane competition.

The 1990 census identified two dozen distinct racial and/or ethnic groups in this enormous area. While the majority of residents are European-American, an estimated one-third are African-American and almost a quarter are Asian-American. Latinos and Native Americans also appear in significant numbers. Diversity reaches its apex on Capitol Hill, where any given block may be home to young singles, blue-collar Boeing workers, members of the gay and lesbian community, and émigrés from a half-dozen nations. If there is a minority group in this part of town, it might be the white families with children that predominate throughout the rest of the city.

There's no real central focal point here, and indeed the neighborhood boundaries are ill-defined; even City Hall may find itself divided as to whether a given residence is located in, say, **Leschi** or **Madrona**. Outside of boisterous **Broadway** on Capitol Hill and a few neighborhood pubs, a visitor will not find much nightlife on these tree-lined streets. But there are other diversions. **Madison Park** hosts an impressive enclave of stately and well-preserved mansions, surpassed only by **Millionaires' Row** and the **Harvard-Belmont Historic District** on Capitol Hill.

First settled by Italian farmers, the nearby **Central District** became more urban and residential during World War II, as African-Americans from the south arrived to work in Seattle's booming economy. In recent years, much of the neighborhood has fallen into disrepair, and vice and violence have crept in. But there's also a closeness felt by the residents here, people bravely fighting modern urban plagues.

There are a plethora of parks in the area—from the traditionally styled **Volunteer Park** on Capitol Hill to the urban wilderness of **Seward Park** on Lake Washington. The lake draws flocks of citizens to its shores in warm months and is used year-round for fishing and boating. **Washington Park Arboretum** will captivate both the casual stroller and the professional botanist. And these are just the largest greenswards; perhaps a dozen smaller (but no less charming) acreages are tucked away, known to neighborhood residents and waiting to be discovered by the visitor.

Madison Park

1 Nellie Cornish Memorial Sculptures
Artist Parks Anderson's 1989 stylized windmills, jutting up from the waters of Lake Washington at the western end of the Evergreen Point Floating Bridge (Highway 520), were installed in honor of longtime Seattle arts advocate Nellie Cornish, founder of Capitol Hill's **Cornish College of the Arts.** Each tower consists of four steel legs rising from a concrete base and topped with two bronze wind-wheels that rotate in opposite directions. Above these, and not visible except from boats that can get closer than cars to these sculptures, is a tiny bear, balanced whimsically on a golden ball, with another smaller ball perched on its nose. When the Northwest isn't experiencing a drought, fountains shoot eight-foot-tall sprays of water up the legs; they're lighted at night and create an eerie spectacle. ♦ West end of the Evergreen Point Floating Bridge

2 Museum of History and Industry (MOHAI) Opened in 1952, the city's premier repository of the past had a long gestation period. In 1911 historians began efforts to erect a permanent museum, but sufficient funds weren't gathered until the late 1940s. After locating choice property on the current site, however, museum backers faced opposition from the **University of Washington,** which owned the land—or thought it did, anyway. It turned out that a portion of the property was under federal control; museum supporters lobbied for its use and won.

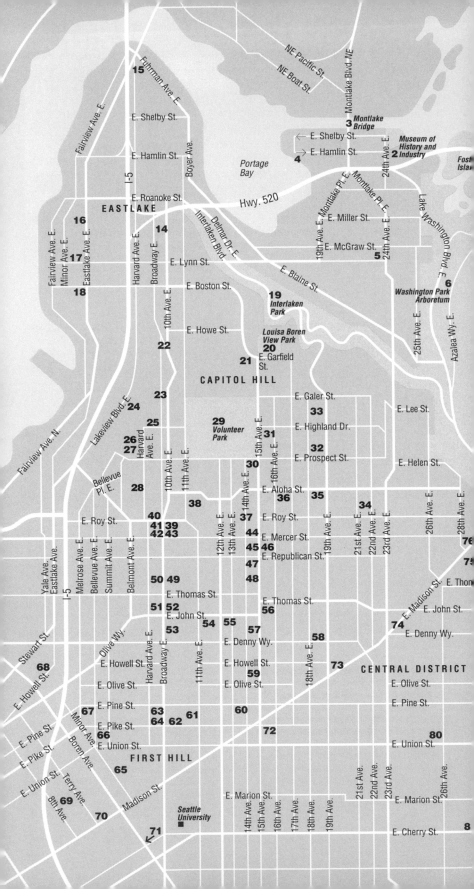

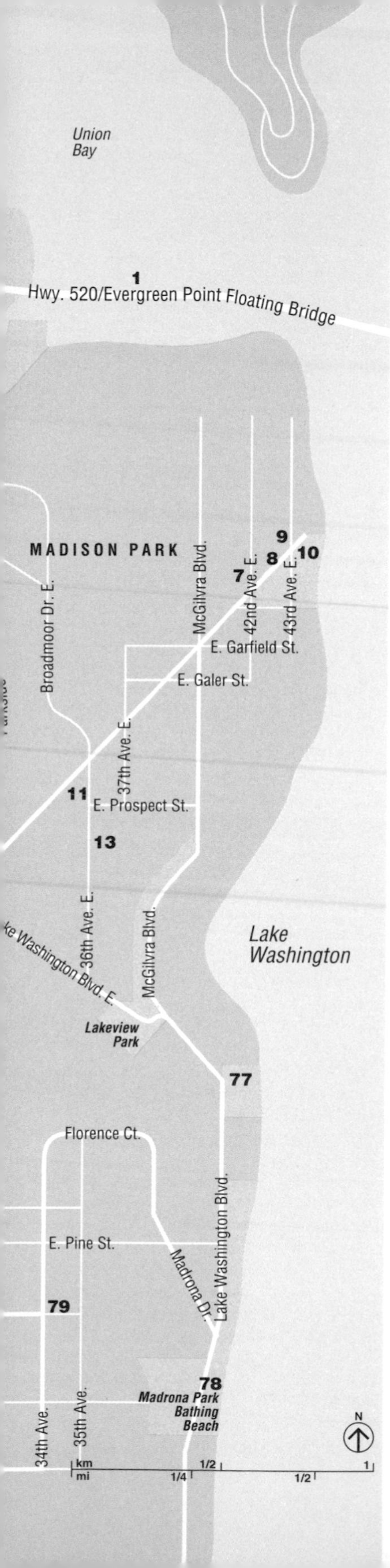

The museum now chronicles the city's heritage with displays of fire engines, a cable car, and numerous artifacts from the lumber, shipping, and fishing industries. Seattle is the birthplace of the Boeing Company, so it's no surprise to find a 1920s Boeing mail plane here. The museum also boasts a rich maritime collection—the model ships and figureheads are popular with children—and one of the state's most extensive arrays of historic photographs from the region. ♦ Admission. Daily. Reservations required to visit the photo archives. 2700 24th Ave E (at E Hamlin St). 324.1125

2 Foster Island Walk At the bottom of MOHAI's parking lot is the start of the largest wetlands trail system left in Seattle. A 20-minute nature walk starts off along wooden plankways and winds through a tangle of tall grasses, marshland exposed after the opening of the Lake Washington Ship Canal lowered the lake by 20 feet. The trail leads to tiny Foster Island, a historic burial ground for the Union Bay Indians, now a pleasant picnic spot. From this point, you may gaze at the regular parade of boats crisscrossing the canal from Lake Washington to Lake Union. It's very soothing here—walk at water's edge past the white water lilies, yellow irises, and cattails and listen to the sounds of song sparrows, red-winged blackbirds, and marsh wrens. Dreamy as it is, your powers of reverie must be able to block out the discordant howl of traffic and the unsightly concrete of nearby Highway 520. No pets or jogging are allowed on this quiet trail, which continues past Foster Island another half-hour to the **Washington Park Arboretum**. ♦ 2700 24th Ave E (enter from the MOHAI parking lot)

3 Montlake Bridge Built in 1925, with distinctive Gothic-inspired towers (visually linking it to the nearby **University of Washington**), this span was designed by the university's architect, **Carl Gould**. At that time, the need for a bridge had only existed for eight years, since the ship canal, finally linking Puget Sound with Seattle's "inland sea," plowed through what had originally been an isthmus. An earlier, more easily crossed canal (about a hundred yards south of the present Montlake Cut, and filled long ago) had been completed in 1884 but was used only for logs and the occasional canoe, as it was too narrow to carry ships.

Completion of the **UW** stadium in 1920 initiated interest in a bridge; in fact, in preparation for the stadium's first football game (**UW** and **Dartmouth**), a graduate manager at the school tied a row of barges together near this point to allow fans easy passage north from the Montlake neighborhood. Three elections later, this bridge was built. A pleasant walkway runs along the south side of the canal and beneath the bridge. ♦ Montlake Blvd NE (off Hwy 520)

Restaurants/Clubs: Red   Hotels: Blue

Shops/ 🌳 Outdoors: Green   **Sights/Culture: Black**

91

4 Seattle Yacht Club A water-oriented city, Seattle has a long list of yacht clubs—some spiffy, some not. This 3,000-member organization is the largest, the oldest (founded in 1892), and the hardest to get into (you must be nominated by a current member). It sponsors Seattle's traditional raft of events revolving around the opening day of yachting season, which is the first Saturday in May. The clubhouse was designed around 1920 by architect **John Graham Sr.** Facilities also include four docks full of well-oiled teak and mahogany. ♦ 325 E Hamlin St (on Portage Bay). 325.1000

5 Cafe Lago ★★$$ The chefs at this cozy bistro pride themselves on their gnocchi, but the real prize here is the antipasti selection. Order the eggplant marinated in garlic and olive oil and the *coppa* ham. Arrive early, reservations are not accepted. ♦ Italian ♦ Tu-Su dinner. No credit cards. 2305 24th Ave E (between E McGraw and E Lynn Sts). 329.8005

5 The Daily Grind ★$ Expansive and well-lighted, this corner cafe is redolent with the scents of fresh baked muffins and a raspberr coffee cake that is out of this world. It's grea for extended planning sessions (nobody eve

Seattle on Celluloid

New York and Los Angeles are both overused (and increasingly expensive) backdrops for films, so directors are branching out, schlepping their cameras and their lights and their dealmakers to Northwest locales. Portland, Oregon, and especially Vancouver, British Columbia, already have been discovered by Hollywood, while Seattle—with enough lovely and quirky settings to turn any artist's eye—is beginning to cash in on the trend. The city has a movie coordinator and is looking forward to the riches that may come from film fame. A few of the better-known theatrical films and television flicks shot in Seattle:

American Heart (1993) tells the story of ex-con and ambivalent father Jeff Bridges, who struggles for survival and dignity on the seamy side of Seattle.

Black Widow (1987) pits determined investigator Debra Winger against murdering seductress Theresa Russell.

Cinderella Liberty (1973) shows a shabby Seattle, a perfect backdrop for the troubled engagement between sailor James Caan and hooker Marsha Mason.

The Fabulous Baker Boys (1989) takes place in a jazzy Seattle, home to two piano-tickling brothers (Jeff and Beau Bridges) and singer Michelle Pfeiffer.

Frances (1983) is a haunting portrayal of Seattle native and film star Frances Farmer (played by Jessica Lange).

The Hand That Rocks the Cradle (1992) tells the story of an embittered childless widow (Rebecca DeMornay) who seeks revenge against the couple who has everything—Annabella Sciorra and Matt McCoy.

Harry and the Hendersons (1987) is a lighthearted Sasquatch fantasy film starring John Lithgow.

House of Games (1987) stars Joe Mantegna as a gambler who fears he'll be murdered over a bad debt and Lindsay Crouse as a psychiatrist who becomes intrigued with his big-stakes world in playwright David Mamet's directorial debut.

Little Buddha (1994) is Bernardo Bertolucci's tale of Buddha past and present, set in contemporary Seattle and timeless Bhutan.

It Happened at the World's Fair (1963) shows Elvis Presley eating dinner at the **Space Needle** and singing on the **monorail.**

McQ (1974) stars John Wayne in a chasefest about Dirty Harry–like cop who lives on a boat in **Fremont**

The Night Strangler (1973) was a TV film that featured Darren McGavin as a rumpled reporter hot on the trail of a murderous member of the "living dead" beneath the streets of **Pioneer Square.**

An Officer and a Gentleman (1982) was shot in Seattle and Port Townsend. Richard Gere plays a loner and aspiring Navy pilot who tries not to fall in love with local factory worker Debra Winger, who in turn refuses to become pregnant to trap Gere into marriage. The second intense relationship in this story is between Gere and a strict sergeant played b Lou Gossett Jr.

The Parallax View (1974) tells the tale of a senator's assassination. Warren Beatty portrays a local reporter in Alan Pakula's Space Needle–hanger.

Say Anything (1989) is a charming coming-of-age story about a straight-A student and closet beauty (Ione Skye) caught in an uncertain world inhabited by an unlikely but supportive swain (John Cusack) and a benevolent but ultimately dishonest father (John Mahoney). Cameron Crowe directed.

Singles (1992) stars Campbell Scott, Bridget Fonda and Matt Dillon. Director Cameron Crowe's disarmingly sweet-spirited tale of twentysomething love is set amidst Seattle's grunge-rock scene.

Sleepless in Seattle (1993) This mega-hit romance written and directed by Nora Ephron, stars Tom Hanks and Meg Ryan.

Trouble in Mind (1985) is a not-quite-futuristic yarn with Kris Kristofferson as an ex-cop and ex-con trying to remake his life in "Rain City," a Seattle of the imagination, in which the old **Seattle Art Museum** building on **Capitol Hill** becomes the mansion of an arch-gangster.

Tugboat Annie (1933) stars Marie Dressler and Wallace Berry. The film was inspired by Norman Reilly Raine's popular "Tugboat Annie" stories of t 1930s, which were in turn inspired by the tale of Thea Foss, who, operating from Tacoma in the late 19th century, began one of the country's largest tugboat empires.

Twin Peaks: Fire Walk with Me (1992) is director David Lynch's prequel to his weird, but popular, TV series.

kicks you out of this place) and very early morning good-byes. ♦ Coffeehouse ♦ M-F 4AM-2PM; Sa-Su 4AM-1PM. 2301 24th Ave E (at E Lynn St). 322.9885

Arboretum

6 Washington Park Arboretum This 200-acre woodland, planned in 1936 and stretching south from Lake Washington's Union Bay, is the city's jewel in a necklace of parks designed by the Olmsted Brothers' landscaping firm of Massachusetts.

The arboretum was a long time in the making. After putting the area aside as parkland in 1904, the city developed Lake Washington Boulevard East (the narrow, curving thoroughfare that cuts through the park) as a scenic entryway to the 1909 Alaska-Yukon-Pacific Exposition, held on the **UW** grounds. But it didn't develop the park until the university agreed to help manage it. The arboretum first featured native plants (despite the Olmsteds' historical antipathy toward Northwest flora), but in the 1940s, it expanded to include species from all over the globe. Today more than 5,500 kinds of trees, shrubs, and flowers flourish on the grounds.

Visitors to the park can find a spot to fit almost any mood: toss a Frisbee across the broad, open meadows; stroll through the ornamental gardens, or enter into the serene, otherworldly atmosphere of the tea garden. A harmonious collaboration of natural elements and human stewardship prevails throughout the park. Many plants have identification tags, but the thickly wooded grounds have none of the fussy feeling familiar from some public gardens. There are several hours' worth of trails to explore. Dogs love to romp in this park, but the city's leash laws should at least be acknowledged, if not followed to the letter. ♦ Bounded by Lake Washington Blvd E and E Madison St, and 25th Ave E and Parkside Dr E

Within the Washington Park Arboretum:

Graham Visitors' Center The park's focal point offers trail maps, botanical pamphlets, and a small gift shop and bookstore. The center schedules two large sales during the year, one of plants (in April) and another of bulbs (in October), when you may see normally serene local gardeners locked in combat for possession of a bewildered baby rhododendron. Just outside the front door, several hiking trails lead to wooded areas. ♦ Daily. Group tours of the park Sunday at 1PM and every second Wednesday of the month at 10AM (except in December). 2300 Arboretum Dr E (off Lake Washington Blvd E). 543.8800

Winter Garden Plants that thrive in the mild Northwest climate and bloom between October and March are displayed here. Witch hazel and viburnum are prominent attractions. In early spring, the tall cornelian cherry shrubs burst forth with their small yellow flowers, set against an underplanting of Lenten roses. ♦ Adjacent to the Visitors' Center. 543.8800

Azalea Way This wide, grassy three-quarter-mile path was the site of a raceway for harness horses in Seattle's pre-auto era, but is now considered too fragile to withstand even joggers—it's for walkers only. Crowds gather along the path on weekends from April through June to see flowering cherry trees, azaleas, and dogwoods. Farther along is the **Rhododendron Glen,** where a pond reflects a riot of colors. ♦ Between Lake Washington Blvd E and Arboretum Dr E

Japanese Tea Garden Designed in the Momoyama style in 1960 by Japanese architect **Juki Iida,** this 3.5-acre garden is a tranquil world of Asian and Northwest plantings, rookeries, bridges, granite lanterns, waterfalls, and glassy pools. Believed to be one of the most authentic outside of Japan, construction of the garden required transporting more than 500 massive granite boulders, each wrapped in bamboo matting to prevent scratching, from high in Washington's Cascade Mountains. The original cypress-and-cedar teahouse, hand-constructed in Japan, was destroyed by fire in 1973, then rebuilt following the original plans. The teahouse offers monthly demonstrations in Chado, the highly ritualized Japanese tea ceremony. ♦ Admission. Daily; closed Dec-Feb. E Lee St (between 24th Ave E and Lake Washington Blvd E) 684.4725, tea ceremony demonstrations 324.1483

7 Madison Park Hardware Yes, there are lots of standard supplies here, plus a frosting of kitchen paraphernalia, toys, and baskets. But the bonus is proprietor Lola McKee, the unofficial mayor and historian of Madison Park, who has become a tenacious advocate for preservation of this community's many charms. ♦ M-Sa. 1837 42nd Ave E (off E Madison St). 322.5331

8 The Red Onion Tavern This is a classic neighborhood joint where the never-rowdy clientele grows younger as the night wears on; by closing time young singles predominate. The pool tables are bumpy, and the pizza is filling but mediocre. However, a fireplace does much to promote lingering conversation. ♦ Daily until 2AM. 4210 E Madison St (between 42nd and 43rd Aves E). 323.1611

"Pill Hill" is a local nickname for First Hill, the home to most of Seattle's major hospitals.

8 Cactus ★★$$ Popular Spanish and Mexican specialties are served here, authentic right down to fish flown in from the Yucatán. But the primo draws are the invitingly displayed and spicy tapas. Try the shrimp served with a sauce of tomatoes and roasted almonds. ◆ Spanish/Mexican ◆ Daily lunch and dinner. Reservations recommended. 4220 E Madison St (at 43rd Ave E). 324.4140

9 Sostanza ★★★$$$ The name translates from Italian to mean substance, and that's exactly what chef Erin Rosella delivers at her intimate, very European restaurant. Rosella is a well-known name around here: her family supplies fresh produce to many Seattle restaurants, and her reputation as a chef was earned at **Saleh al Lago** and First Hill's late lamented **Settebello.**

The salad of romaine hearts with gorgonzola and candied walnuts is a wonderful introduction to the meal, as are two appetizers: the peppered beef tenderloin carpaccio with gorgonzola cream, and a light fry of calamari and prawns. Move on to such dishes as boneless breast of chicken pan-roasted in brown butter, or grilled veal chop stuffed with prosciutto and spinach and served with sautéed wild mushrooms. The wine list is hefty, if rather pricey.

An informal foyer opens onto a busy kitchen and then gives way to a pleasant dining room centered around a raised fireplace. Low lighting helps create a romantic atmosphere, as does the seemingly unhurried service from a knowledgeable staff. In the winter, ask to be seated by the fireplace, and in the summer repair to tables on the front patio. ◆ Italian ◆ Daily lunch and dinner. 1927 43rd Ave E (off E Madison St). 324.9701

10 Madison Park and Beach Not a component in the Olmsted Brothers' greenbelt scheme but linked to it by later planners, this is the northernmost in a continuous string of parks that lines Lake Washington's western banks. There are roped-off swimming areas and lighted tennis courts, and on steamy summer afternoons droves of sunworshipers jam the beach.

In the 1890s the **Madison Street Cable Car Company** ran a line out here to a small amusement park with a 500-seat pavilion, boathouse, ballpark, and racetrack. Boat cruises around the lake began from this spot, and summer vacationers came to mount big canvas tents on specially constructed platforms.

In preparation for the AYP Exposition, $30,000 was spent on improvements to the amusement park, then called **White City,** and a ferry line to Mercer Island and other nascent Eastside communities was added. But it all fell into disuse after the Expo ended. In 1919 the city bought the streetcar line, along with the park and its entertainment facilities. Twenty years later the city initiated a WPA landscaping program to take advantage of new waterfront space created here after the ship canal lowered Lake Washington by 20 feet. ◆ E Madison St (on Lake Washington)

11 Alexander Pantages House Lying south of Madison Street and north of where Lake Washington Boulevard dips down to the lake from the **Washington Park Arboretum** is a wooded and palatial residential canton called Washington Park. Although it only began to develop after the 19th century, the neighborhood has the classic weight of a much older subdivision. One of the most impressive architectural statements made here is the home of impresario Alexander Pantages, who owned vaudeville theaters all over the West. His half-timbered mansion, designed in 1909 by **Wilson & Loveless,** carries overtones of California Mission Revival style. It's a private residence. ◆ 1117 36th Ave E (between E Prospect and E Madison Sts)

12 Lake Washington Boulevard Those landscaping Olmsted Brothers, and their father before them, were great believers in contouring human developments to the land. Their comprehensive plan for Seattle included this scenic and meandering boulevard along the west side of Lake Washington, running south from the AYP Exposition grounds (now the **UW** campus) to **Seward Park.** Today, some parts of this 1910 contoured drive have been bypassed by straighter Lakeside Avenue South (especially the famous curves through **Colman Park,** just south of the Lacey V. Morrow Floating Bridge/I-90). But you can still follow the old route; watch closely for signs. ◆ Between E Calhoun and S Orcas Sts

13 Ames House Architects **Charles Bebb** and **Leonard L. Mendel** designed this stately Colonial Revival manse in 1907. It is now the residence of the **University of Washington's** president. ◆ 808 36th Ave E (between E War and E Valley Sts)

Eastlake

14 Rain City Pub & Grill ★$ Plumbing the moist Northwest scene for every drop it's worth, this newly renovated eatery does its best work with focaccia sandwiches but has also won plaudits for its salads. With hardwood floors, a green-maroon-mustard color scheme, and exhibits by local artists, this restaurant has become more casual with its updated decor. ◆ Northwestern ◆ M-F lunch and dinner; Sa-Su dinner. 2359 10th Ave E (at E Miller St). 322.4401

14 Roanoke Park Place Tavern This is a prime watering hole for the just-over-21-and frisky set down from Capitol Hill. It's lively and good for people watching but definitely *not* the place to go if you're feeling your age.

Burgers and beer are the two essential food groups. ♦ Daily until 2AM. 2409 10th Ave E (near E Miller St). 324.5882

15 Romio's Pizza ★★$ A late entry in the pizzeria chain, this branch is more spacious but less homey than its brethren. It's hard, though, to diss a joint that serves pizza as fabulous as this. ♦ Pizza/Takeout ♦ Daily until 11PM. 3242 Eastlake Ave E (at Fuhrman Ave E). 322.4453. Also at: 2001 W Dravus St (between Thorndyke and Gilman Aves W). 284.5420; 8523 Greenwood Ave N (between N 85th and N 86th Sts). 782.9005; 917 Howell St (at Ninth Ave). 622.6878; 616 First Ave (between James and Cherry Sts). 621.8500

16 Tio's Bakery & Cafe ★$ This place serves omelettes for breakfast and paella and red snapper at dinnertime, but the real reason to come here is for the baked goods—coffee cakes, muffins, cinnamon rolls, and breads. Late-night or early weekday morning visits provide the most peaceful environment; there are huge crowds on Saturday and Sunday mornings. ♦ Spanish/Bakery ♦ Daily breakfast, lunch, and dinner; W-Sa until midnight. 2379 Eastlake Ave E (at E Louisa St). 325.0081

17 Carrot Cafe ★$ It's a popular place and on weekends you may have to cool your heels outside the front door with a newspaper. The vegetarian menu features such dishes as butternut-squash bisque, mushroom omelettes, and sprouts, sprouts, and more sprouts. ♦ Vegetarian ♦ Daily breakfast and lunch. 2305 Eastlake Ave E (at E Lynn St). 324.1442

18 Serafina ★★$$ A few taverns have always been present in Eastlake, plus the odd used-books outlet and some totally forgettable office buildings, but such refined establishments as this place have enhanced the neighborhood's profile in recent years.

Begin with a few small appetizers in the tapas style—the *crostini* with Tuscan olive spread and goat cheese is particularly good. The entrées, including penne with smoked mozzarella in a tomato cream sauce, smoked-chicken salad with chèvre, peas, and a raspberry vinaigrette, and *salsiccia toscana* (sausage braised with caramelized onions and cabbage and served over polenta) are all delicious.

This is a popular place and often crowded; on busy nights the service can be slow. When there aren't a lot of patrons, it can be a

romantic setting, especially with the occasional addition of live piano music. There's a wonderful wood deck out back, where diners at a handful of tables can relax in a tranquil garden setting. ♦ Italian ♦ M-F lunch and dinner; Sa-Su dinner. Reservations recommended. 2043 Eastlake Ave E (at E Boston St). 323.0807

19 Interlaken Park This park is really just a serpentine, tree-lined street with a few shady footpaths frequented by neighborhood residents. It was originally the route of a short-lived bicycle path, built during a Seattle bike craze around the turn of the century. Interlaken Drive now connects the **Washington Park Arboretum** and Lake Washington Boulevard East with Capitol Hill, before heading west into Highway 520 and Interstate 5. ♦ Interlaken Blvd (off Delmar Dr E)

Capitol Hill

20 Louisa Boren View Park Pike Place Market hero **Victor Steinbrueck** designed this small park in 1975. Looking north, it commands views of Portage Bay, the **UW** campus, Lake Washington, and the Cascade Mountains. The park was named after Louisa Boren Denny, the last survivor of the 1851 Alki Point settlers. The large untitled Cor-Ten steel sculpture, composed of 10 interlocking blocks rusted to an even brown color, was created by Portland, Oregon, artist Lee Kelly. ♦ 15th Ave E and E Garfield St

21 Lake View Cemetery Before **Volunteer Park** could begin to grow in the 1890s, the city had to relocate one of its principal graveyards from what is now the park's north end. Regrettably, most of the dead residents had already been moved once before, in 1885, when the city turned its pioneer cemetery into **Denny Park,** south of Lake Union. Two years later Leigh S.J. Hunt, owner and editor of the *Seattle Post-Intelligencer,* convinced the city council that the graves should be moved again, just a few hundred feet north. This final site is now the **Lake View Cemetery,** with perhaps the best views of any graveyard in the city.

People come from as far away as Japan and China to visit the gravesite (near the summit) of kung fu star Bruce Lee, a former Seattleite who died in 1973. And there are some wonderful old tombstones here, dating back to the 1850s. Pioneer David "Doc" Maynard, who perished in 1873, is buried here beneath a tall California redwood and beside one of his two wives, Catherine, whose epitaph reads, "She did what she could." Nearby is a rugged headstone under which Chief Sealth's daughter, Princess Angeline, lies in a canoe-shaped coffin. ♦ 1554 15th Ave E (at E Garfield St). 322.1582

22 John Leary House When completed around 1904, this stone and half-timbered manse was one of the largest and most lavish in the city. The architect was Seattle's **J. Alfred Bodley.** The owner, John Leary, arrived in Seattle in 1869 and founded the West Coast Improvement Company, which was primarily responsible for the development of Ballard. In 1882 Leary became principal owner of the *Seattle Post,* which he soon merged with the competing *Intelligencer* to create what is still the city's morning daily, the *Seattle Post-Intelligencer.* He also opened and operated a coal mine, was partly responsible for supplying Seattle with its first natural gas, and set up a waterworks system that brought in water from Lake Washington for the first time.

Not content with his accomplishments, Leary was elected mayor of Seattle in 1884 and served two terms in office. It seemed John Leary could have anything he wanted. But he died at the age of 68 before he could move into his dream house. The mansion is now home to the Episcopal Diocesan offices. A stained-glass window designed for the house by New York's Tiffany & Company is now at UW's **Burke Museum.** ◆ 1551 10th Ave E (at E Garfield St)

23 St. Mark's Episcopal Cathedral This graceful but somewhat chilly Episcopal temple for the Diocese of Olympia was designed by **Bakewell and Brown,** a noted San Francisco architectural firm. Built between 1926 and 1930 in a Neo-Byzantine style, the church has an interior that one critic described as "an immense masonry box."

The cathedral has a world-renowned, 3,744-pipe Flentrop organ, acquired in 1965, which draws musicians from all over the world to perform in the cathedral's annual recital series. ◆ 1245 10th Ave E (at E Galer St). 323.0300

24 Egan House Wedged into a wooded glen, this triangular oddity may well be the most unusual residence in Seattle. Built in 1958, the house is the work of **Robert Reichert,** a local architect well known for unconventional designs. This building's form, write Sally B. Woodbridge and Roger Montgomery in *A Guide to Architecture in Washington State,* "expresses its interior organization, in which levels, like graduated trays, diminish in size as they rise." It's a private residence. ◆ 1500 Lakeview Blvd E (near E Highland Dr)

25 Sam Hill House Designed by the Washington, DC, architectural firm of **Hornblower & Marshall,** this mansion was built in 1909 for the son-in-law of **Great Northern Railroad** magnate James J. Hill. The five-story fortress is a concrete variation of an 18th-century manor house, resembling in many respects the Petit Trianon at Versailles. Hill supposedly built it in order to be able to properly receive Crown Prince Albert of Belgium, who, despite two planned trips to Seattle, canceled both times. It's still a private residence. ◆ 814 E Highland Dr (between Harvard Ave E and Broadway E)

26 C.J. Smith House This beautiful brick mansion, with lead-glass windows and an elegant low brick wall separating the front yard from the sidewalk, was built in 1907. The design, by Spokane architect **Kirtland K. Cutter** and his frequent partner **Karl Malmgren,** was influenced by the work of English architect **Richard Norman Shaw,** who was much in favor in America at the time. Born in 1854, Charles Jackson Smith, a native of Kentucky, was president of the Dexter Horton National Bank, a forerunner of today's Seafirst Bank. The house remains a private residence. ◆ 1147 Harvard Ave E (between E Highland Dr and E Prospect St)

27 Brownell-Bloedel House Architect **Carl Gould** departed from his usual style by sheathing this 1910 Georgian Revival residence in natural wood shingles. It's a private residence. ◆ 1137 Harvard Ave E (between E Highland Dr and E Prospect St)

28 R.D. Merrill House Built in 1910, this modified Georgian mansion, complete with formal garden and carriage house, is the only West Coast structure designed by famed New York architect **Charles A. Platt,** who is best known for his Freer Gallery in Washington, DC. Merrill was born in Michigan in 1869 to a lumber family from Maine. Continuing in the family tradition, he moved to the Pacific Northwest in 1898 to manage the Washington and British Columbia properties of Merrill and Ring, a leading lumber firm of the era. ◆ 919 Harvard Ave E (between E Prospect and E Roy Sts)

29 Volunteer Park During the 1880s this 43-acre plot was known simply as **City Park.** But in 1901 it was renamed to honor Seattle men who fought in the Spanish-American War of 1898. The same year a 20-million-gallon reservoir was carved from the park's southern flanks, and around 1906 a 75-foot-tall water tower (pictured on page 97) was put up to increase water pressure in the mansions sprouting nearby. The Olmsted Brothers engineered the final refinements. As part of their comprehensive plan, they decided that this should be one of several "neat and smooth" central parks (as opposed to such "wild" outlying greens as **Seward Park**). Second-growth fir trees were felled and replaced by a more ordered regiment of blue spruce, flowering cherry trees, and Port Orford cedar. A carriage concourse was laid, fountains and a giant bandstand were built, and a semicircular concert grove was pruned out of the undergrowth. With only a few exceptions, the park today looks much as it did when the Olmsteds completed their work.

Fine clear-weather views of the **Space Needle,** Puget Sound, and the Olympic Mountains are available from this 445-foot elevation. Climb to the top of the brick-faced water tower (illustrated below)—a tricky ascent, given its steep stairs—for an even better perspective. The park fills with people during summer theater performances and weekend festivals. Two outdoor tennis courts are well maintained but underused. A popular children's playground and wading pool lie in the northeastern corner.

Despite the tranquillity, a few cautions should be exercised here. Behind the concrete bandstand, situated just north of the reservoir, is a public rest room where various criminal activities have occurred despite frequent police patrols; it's best to avoid it after nightfall. It seems quite safe at all other hours, however. ♦ Bounded by E Galer and E Prospect Sts, and 15th and 11th Aves E. 625.8901

Within Volunteer Park:

Conservatory Constructed for $20,000 in 1912, this conservatory was patterned after London's spectacular Crystal Palace exhibition hall. It was a prefab building: Manufactured in New York, the components were shipped to Seattle and put together by parks department employees. Capitol Hill's landed gentry of the time readily embraced the conservatory, calling it the finest structure of its kind west of Chicago and contributing plant specimens to its collection.

During the Depression, however, the conservatory fell upon hard times, its humid environment rotting the Southern swamp cypress frames and rusting some of the iron supports. By the 1970s the greenhouse was beginning to list to one side and visitors weren't allowed on the premises during windy weather because panes of glass tended to pop out of their frames. A $500,000 restoration program in the early 1980s re-created the building's graceful roof and sides using steel, cast iron, and Alaska cedar. During refurbishment, a colorful etched-glass canopy— *Homage in Green*—was installed over the entrance. Created by Richard Spaulding, a former artist-in-residence with the Seattle Arts Commission, *Homage* is enlivened with lilies, passion flowers, and

morning glories, all of which are familiar from Victorian designs. Inside, more than a quarter-million visitors each year study an incredible array of orchids, cacti, and tropical species in three crowded wings. Sadly, the abundant foliage permits no room for wheelchairs. Admirers periodically lobby the city for expansion, but the park's neighbors, fearing more traffic, object. ♦ Daily. 1400 E Galer St (off 14th Ave E). 684.4743

Monument to William H. Seward The weathered bronze statue is a likeness of the former US Secretary of State and real-estate tycoon who bought Alaska from the Russians in 1867 for two cents an acre. New York artist Richard Brooks created this piece for the 1909 Alaska-Yukon-Pacific Expo. ♦ In front of the Conservatory

Seattle Asian Art Museum This beloved building (the **Old Seattle Art Museum**) was given new life when it reopened in summer 1994 as a showcase for the **Seattle Art Museum**'s extensive assembly of Asian art, which ranks in the top 10 collections outside of Asia; its Japanese collection is one of the top five in the US. The works here reflect a span of many ages and cultures in India, China, Japan, Korea, and Southeast Asia. The museum is also an education venue for scholarly exchange about Asian art and culture.

Designed by **Carl Gould,** the building is an Art Deco gem. It was completed in 1933 and was a gift to the city from Dr. Richard Fuller, philanthropist and president of the Seattle Fine Arts Society, and his mother, Mrs. Eugene Fuller. At the time of its construction the museum was a fresh Protomodern design—with rounded corners, curved walls, and a foyer flowing gracefully toward side galleries and stairways. Admission; children under 12 free; discount for seniors and students. ♦ Tu-Su. 1400 E Prospect St (at 14th Ave E). 625.8901

Volunteer Park Water Tower

M. BLUM

Black Sun One of the park's focal points is this massive black granite sculpture—nine feet in diameter—created in 1968 by artist Isamu Noguchi (who also did *Landscape of Time,* a collection of carved granite boulders at Second Avenue and Marion Street). Area residents call it either "The Doughnut" or "The Black Hole." Not to discourage anyone, but if you choose to frame a photograph of the **Space Needle** through the hole in the middle, you won't be the first to do so. ♦ Across from the Seattle Asian Art Museum

30 **The Parker House** A vast Colonial Revival mansion was built in 1909 for George H. Parker, the West Coast fiscal agent for the United Wireless Company. Parker's $150,000 home, supported by Corinthian columns, boasted five covered porches, 12 bedrooms and 16 other rooms, seven fireplaces, five bathrooms, hardwood floors, muraled walls, and an adjoining coach house. Parker, however, was not to enjoy his mansion for long. In 1910 he was convicted of stock and mail fraud and given a two-year sentence at the federal prison on McNeil Island in south Puget Sound. It's a private residence. ♦ 1409 E Prospect St (at 14th Ave E)

31 **Roberta's Bed & Breakfast** $ This B&B (pictured above) offers five rooms with private baths and queen-size beds. The breakfast is a full, family-style vegetarian affair. There are lots of books for the borrowing, and *The New York Times* is available every day. Ask for the mountain view room. It's a one-block walk from here to **Volunteer Park.** No off-street parking is available. ♦ 1147 16th Ave E (between E Prospect St and E Highland Dr). 329.3326

32 **Capitol Hill Addition** Many of the comparatively modest residences found just east of **Volunteer Park** were part of the **Capitol Hill Addition,** a residential development begun around 1905. Spearheading that project was James A. Moore, the real-estate promoter who later built the **Moore Theater** downtown and created the University Heights district. Moore already had an interest in this neighborhood; in 1901 he'd acquired a good portion of it.

Moore's wife, Eugenia, named the development after an exclusive section of Denver, her hometown.

Before opening the area to occupants, Moore spent $150,000 on improvements (cement sidewalks, paved streets, sewers, and water) "a previously unheard-of procedure," wrote the *Seattle Times.* The subdivision attracted the construction of many Colonial Revival homes—a style now commonly referred to as the Classic Box—along a nearby streetcar line. The houses here still display with intricate details, such as squared-off corner bay windows, leaded glass, and Moorish keyhole windows. It's worth walking these thoroughfares to observe Moore's early legacy. One of the finer examples of the Classic Box can be found at 747 16th Avenue East and is identified by its shallow ground-floor bays. ♦ Bounded by E Galer and E Mercer Sts, and 15th and 23rd Aves E

33 **Isaac Stevens School** Early school district architect **James Stephen,** whose institutional artistry is also on display at **Summit Grade School** on First Hill, and **Latona Elementary** and **Interlake School** in Wallingford, designed this huge wooden Colonial Revival edifice in 1906. ♦ 1242 18th Ave E (between E Highland Dr and E Galer St). 281.6760

34 **Holy Names Academy** Beaux Arts styling receives grand exposition in this domed Catholic girls' school, designed by **C. Alfred Breitung,** who also created the tiny **Triangle Hotel Building** in Pioneer Square and Wallingford's **Home of the Good Shepherd.** ♦ 728 21st Ave E (between E Roy and E Aloha Sts). 323.4272

35 **St. Joseph's Catholic Church** Pay close attention to the tall, tapering belfry of this stripped-down Gothic house of worship, for it's there that you can find some relationship between this 1932 building and still-more-impressive structure also designed by architect **Joseph Wilson:** downtown's **Seattle Tower.** The facing of the church was apparently intended to be something grander than cast concrete, but the Depression forced **Wilson** to simplify his dreams. Don't miss the stained-glass window on the entrance face. ♦ 732 18th Ave E (between E Roy and E Aloha Sts). 324.2522

36 **Salisbury House** $ A Victorian charmer owned and operated by sisters Mary and Catheryn Wiese, this bed-and-breakfast can accommodate eight guests in four rooms, with queen-size beds and private baths. Family-style vegetarian breakfasts are served here, the library is comfy and well stocked, and **Volunteer Park** is two short blocks away. Off-street parking is not available. ♦ 750 16th Ave E (at E Aloha St). 328.8682

Restaurants/Clubs: Red   **Hotels:** Blue
Shops/ 🌲 Outdoors: Green   **Sights/Culture:** Black

37 Millionaires' Row This tree-lined cluster of Xanadus extends south from **Volunteer Park** along 14th Avenue East to East Roy Street. Seattle's most prominent families once found status and security here, as this mini-neighborhood was protected from mere mortals by a private gate. The gate is now gone, but the district retains much of its earlier elegance. As in other affluent Seattle neighborhoods, however, many of the mansions have been converted from single-family residences to apartments. ♦ 14th Ave E (between E Prospect and E Roy Sts)

Along Millionaires' Row:

Thomas Bordeaux House The builder of this house was a Canadian who arrived here in 1852 and later ascended to the presidency of the Mason County Logging Company and the Mumby Lumber and Shingle Company. Thomas Bordeaux was also a director of the First National Bank of Seattle. His home, complete with a decorated tower, was built in 1903. Designed by Seattle architect **W.D. Kimball,** it reflects the half-timber style then in vogue. ♦ 806 14th Ave E (between E Valley and E Aloha Sts)

Shafer Mansion $$$ When he died in 1951, at the age of 79, the *Seattle Times* wrote that Julius Shafer's career was "a typical success story of a poor immigrant boy." Born in Austria, he came to the US at age 12 and arrived in Seattle six years later, in 1890. He and his brother Issle had worked in Kansas and Texas, saved $700, and used that to start a secondhand clothing store in Seattle. The business prospered and, at the turn of the century, the Shafer brothers made a fortune outfitting men bound for the Alaskan goldfields. In 1921 he retired from the rag trade to pursue real-estate interests, and two years later, he and his brother built the **Shafer Building,** a 10-story office tower that still stands at Sixth Avenue and Pine Street downtown. Shafer later headed the Hebrew Immigrant Aid Society and assisted European refugees in resettling in this country.

As a reflection of his success, in 1914 he constructed this spacious and landscaped English manor overlooking Elliott Bay. Now a bed-and-breakfast, the mansion has 13 guest rooms, 10 with private baths. There's also a carriage house and a bridal suite. Current owner Erv Olssen has opened the mansion to a wedding and reception business, but that shouldn't detract from a pleasant stay here. After a buffet breakfast in the dining room, repair to the formal library or take a one-block stroll to **Volunteer Park.** Off-street parking is available. ♦ 907 14th Ave E (at E Aloha St). 322.4654

Cobb House Built in 1910, this house—"a fusion of the spirit of the German Black Forest and the English Arts & Crafts movement," as

A Guide to Architecture in Washington State so eloquently puts it—was designed by the prestigious early-20th-century firm of **Charles Bebb** and **Leonard L. Mendel.** It has lovely lead-glass windows and a sizeable second-floor balcony secluded by a parapet. The first owner was C.H. Cobb, a native of Maine, who moved west to California in 1876, then headed north to Seattle, where by the 1890s he had incorporated four logging and timber companies and the Marysville and Arlington Railroad Company. ♦ 1409 E Aloha St (off 14th Ave E)

38 Landes House $ This turn-of-the-century establishment—two adjacent houses connected by a garden courtyard—features a nice garden, a hot tub, off-street parking, and nine guest rooms (some with decks, some with private baths) and a two-bedroom apartment that can be rented by the week. Fresh-baked goodies are served as part of the expanded continental breakfast. And resident owners Tom Hanes and Dick Hurlocker are excellent and informative hosts. ♦ 712 11th Ave E (between E Roy and E Aloha Sts). 329.8781

39 Anhalt Apartments Dating to the late 1920s, these units are fine representations of the stylish but practical sort of brick apartment houses designed and constructed by developer/builder **Fred Anhalt.** Some apartments here have nine rooms, two baths, and a fireplace. To ensure soundproofing, **Anhalt** used double floors and double interior walls. The lovely landscaped courtyard and picturesque round-stair tower (an interesting and space-saving alternative to stairways) are Anhalt trademarks. ♦ 1005 E Roy St (at 10th Ave E)

40 Harvard-Belmont Historic District Many of Seattle's top industrialists, financiers, and business leaders, including **Great Northern Railroad** heir Sam Hill, lived in this venerable Capitol Hill enclave. Horace C. Henry, another railroader, who'd moved to Seattle in 1890 from his native Vermont to build the original belt line around Lake Washington for the **Northern Pacific Railroad,** also lived here.

Most of the mansions in the district were built between 1905 and 1910, with the predominant architectural styles being Tudor, Colonial, and Georgian Revival. In the 1920s a second wave of building brought a number of elegant brick apartment complexes to the area, many of them designed by **Fred Anhalt.** Unlike most of the city's old neighborhoods—which have largely succumbed to modern development—this area has remained a gracious retreat of tree-lined streets, professionally tended gardens, and majestic residential and institutional buildings. It is on the National Register of Historic Places. ♦ Bounded by E Highland Dr and E Roy St, and Broadway E and Belmont Ave E

40 Cornish College of the Arts This "quietly elegant building of Mediterranean persuasion," as it is described in *A Guide to Architecture in Washington State,* was designed in 1921 by the Seattle architectural firm of **Albertson, Wilson & Richardson.** Nellie Cornish, the piano-playing daughter of a Tennessee sheep farmer who moved to Seattle in 1900, founded the school without any initial support from the city. But with programs in art, music, theater, and dance, the institute has since played an important part in Seattle's cultural life. Renowned choreographer Martha Graham and painter Mark Tobey were members of the faculty. Nellie Cornish lived in an apartment on the top floor of this terra-cotta–ornamented edifice. ◆ 710 E Roy St (between Broadway E and Harvard Ave E). 323.1400

40 Rainier Chapter House of the DAR City architect **Daniel R. Huntington** designed the chapter house of the Daughters of the American Revolution in 1924 as a replica of George Washington's Mount Vernon estate. The building is rented out for parties, chamber-music concerts, and the like, and it is a favorite for wedding receptions. ◆ 800 E Roy St (between Broadway E and Harvard Ave E). 323.0600

40 The Bacchus Restaurant ★★$ The atmosphere here may remind you of an old wine cellar, although the walls are muraled over with an Alexander Pushkin folktale, painted by Russian artist Vladimir Pavlovich Shkurkin. (They're left here from an earlier restaurant.) The *paidakia* (lamb chops broiled with lemon, olive oil, and garlic) is a fine treat, as is the panfried baby squid appetizer (lots of onions and chopped almonds for crunch and color), and the *kefthethes* (meatballs served on pita and sprinkled with feta cheese). The Greek burger, buttermilk pancakes, and similarly shameful bows to American tastes could all be done without, but those are minor annoyances. Service is efficient, if somewhat overly familiar, and it's surprisingly quiet. ◆ Greek ◆ Daily lunch and dinner. 806 E Roy St (between Broadway E and Harvard Ave E). 325.2888

40 Loveless Building Designed in an English cottage vein by architect **Arthur B. Loveless,** this graceful block of first-floor shops and second-floor apartments arranged around a concealed courtyard was built in 1931. In his book Seattle Past to Present, Roger Sale refers to the "enchanting Loveless Block, stores and apartments of an elegance that Arthur Loveless alone among traditional Seattle architects seemed to have." Loveless was a master of well-sited period revival designs. His houses are dotted over Capitol Hill, and in 1930, he remodeled the Colman Building on First Avenue in an Art Deco style. ◆ 711 Broadway E (between E Roy and E Prospect Sts)

41 Harvard Exit Seattle's first luxury art theater makes its home in a building that once held a ladies' club. From the crowded entryway, pass through what once must have been an elegant drawing room or living room but is now a very comfortable, old-fashioned space to meet your moviegoing partners. Checkers are available for extended waits. The theater schedules some of the better flicks passing through town, and entries in the annual Seattle International Film Festival often play here. ◆ Box office opens one hour before show time. 807 E Roy St (at Harvard Ave E). 323.8986

41 Deluxe 1 Bar and Grill Amidst the Broadway area's fervid grab for glitz and its increasing dependence on patrons from beyond Capitol Hill, this spot has managed somehow to retain its down-home feeling—there are no bow ties behind the bar, no leather-skirted waitresses, no Art Deco menus. Warm a stool or pull up a chair and order a bacon, onion, and avocado burger that's guaranteed to put permanent frown lines in your doctor's forehead. Or try the pesto potato skins with a frosty pint of microbrewed beer. In summer a retractable wall out front allows for a maximum of people watching with a maximum of comfort. ◆ Daily until 2AM. 625 Broadway E (at E Roy St). 324.9697

41 Dancer's Series: Steps Look down as you're strolling either side of busy Broadway between East Pine and East Roy Streets. Periodically, you will spot arrangements of bronze footprints, accompanied by dance instructions, by Seattle artist Jack Mackie. Mackie, with assistance from artist Charles Greening, created these eight street-level artworks to be used, not just observed. He even mixed a few steps of his own creation (the Busstop, for instance, and the Obeebo) with the classic rumba, waltz, and tango. Mackie gave special treatment to the heels, imbedding parking tokens in those footprints outside a parking lot, and offering a simplified view of the skyline in a set near a bus stop. ◆ Broadway E (between E Pine and E Roy Sts)

41 Cafe Cielo ★★$$ Owner Larry Robinson brought in chef Andy Burgess to prepare a menu rich with tapas (try the roasted garlic with feta cheese and pita bread), pizzas, and toothsome boneless and herby chicken breast served over polenta. The interior is cozy, with subdued lighting and an expansive view of boisterous Broadway. ◆ Mediterranean ◆ M-F lunch and dinner; Sa-Su brunch and dinner. Reservations recommended. 611 Broadway (between E Mercer and E Roy Sts). 324.9084

42 Byzantion ★$ You'll find Greek food (and lots of it) at this place that's renowned for the quality of its *spanakopita* (spinach pie) and lamb dishes. Try the feta-cheese omelette at breakfast. ◆ Greek ◆ Daily breakfast, lunch, and dinner. 601 Broadway E (at E Mercer St). 325.7580

43 Siam on Broadway ★$ Regulars don't even consider sticking around here to eat—there's generally a 10- to 20-minute wait for a table. Instead, they call ahead, then fly by to pick up steaming orders of garlicky orange beef, *pad thai* noodles, or panfried butterfish. Be forewarned: the spice heat ratings of the dishes should be taken seriously. ♦ Thai/Takeout ♦ M-F lunch and dinner; Sa-Su dinner. 616 Broadway E (between E Roy and E Mercer Sts). 324.0892

43 Orpheum With compact discs galore, from heavy metal rock to old jazz, this store may be noisy, but it's ideal for browsing after a movie at the **Harvard Exit** or on a lazy weekend afternoon. ♦ Daily until midnight. 618 Broadway E (between E Roy and E Mercer Sts). 322.6370

44 Capons ★$ Chicken and more chicken—whole, half, and in sandwiches and soups—is what's on the menu here. The fowl is juicy and fresh, sometimes fresher than the steamed vegetables available on the side. Service is cafeteria-style, and the atmosphere pleasant and casual. ♦ Chicken/Takeout ♦ Daily lunch and dinner. 605 15th Ave E (at E Mercer St). 323.4026. Also at: Wallingford Center, 1815 N 45th St (at Wallingford Ave N). 547.3949

45 Matzoh Momma ★$ Seattle has nothing approaching the Jewish kosher delis of Detroit or New York City, but this place may be the next best thing. Food is "kosher style," rather than authentic kosher. But some of it is delicious. Try the chicken soup with matzoh balls or the Reuben sandwich. Every few months, the popular **Mazeltones** klezmer band will drop in to entertain at dinnertime. ♦ Jewish deli ♦ Daily breakfast, lunch, and dinner. 509 15th Ave E (between E Mercer and E Republican Sts). 324.6262

46 Olympia Pizza and Spaghetti House III ★$ Comfy booths, room for small parties, and killer pizza—what else do you need? ♦ Pizza/Takeout ♦ Daily. 516 15th Ave E (between E Mercer and E Republican Sts). 329.4500

46 City Peoples' Mercantile This small store somehow includes something for everyone. There's a well-stocked hardware department for the neighborhood wall-bangers, along with housewares, art supplies, and a trendy selection of clothing. The espresso cart out front provides nourishment and newspapers. Four women began this emporium in the 1970s and have since expanded their operations to include **City Peoples' Garden Store,** an upscale shop for gardeners (2939 E Madison Ave, between Martin Luther King Jr. Way and Lake Washington Blvd E, 324.0737) ♦ Daily. 500 15th Ave E (at E Republican St). 324.9510. Also at: 3517 Fremont Ave N (between N 35th and N 36th Sts). 632.1200

47 Jalisco ★$ A small, family-run Mexican operation, this restaurant is patronized almost exclusively by Hill residents. The standard dishes—especially enchiladas and burritos—are well done, and servers will help you design a combination plate. Or you could just order the delicious quesadillas. There are great margaritas and a wide selection of Mexican beers, but entertainment is limited mostly to the clientele, who seem anxious to practice their dubious Spanish on the patient and extraordinarily efficient staff. ♦ Mexican ♦ M-Sa lunch and dinner. 1467 E Republican St (between 14th and 15th Aves E). 325.9005. Also at: 122 First Ave N (at Denny Way). 283.4242; 12336 31st Ave NE (between Lake City Way NE and NE 123rd St). 364.3978; 115 Park La (at Lake Washington Blvd). 822.3355

48 Horizon Books An old house has been converted to a used-book cavern, where intrepid literati wander labyrinthine passageways in search of affordable reading. Your best bet is to ask for directions upon entering the maze. The science-fiction section is out of this world. ♦ Daily; M-F until 10PM. 425 15th Ave E (between E Harrison and E Republican Sts). 329.3586

49 Cafe Dilettante ★$ A chocoholic's fantasy, this place carries some of the most tempting truffles, butter crèmes, and dragées (nuts or dried fruits dredged through high-quality dipping chocolates) you will ever try to resist. There's a small menu offering such things as Romanian borscht and sandwiches. (Note that they also operate an imperfect-chocolates outlet store at 2300 E Cherry Street, at 23rd Ave E, 328.1955). ♦ Cafe ♦ M-Th, Su until midnight; F-Sa until 1AM. 416 Broadway E (between E Republican and E Harrison Sts). 329.6463

49 Bailey/Coy Books Covering a lot of area in a fairly confined space means that this bookstore, for all its efforts, must be very selective. Look for current best-sellers, a wide selection of gay and lesbian studies, lots of magazines, and respectable depth in the gardening and fiction categories. ♦ Daily until 10PM; F-Sa until 11PM. 414 Broadway E (between E Republican and E Harrison Sts). 323.8842

50 Broadway Market The market first came to life in 1928. The 32 stalls and shops with their fine prepared foods, fresh produce, and gift items served as the community center for Capitol Hill area residents for almost 50 years. In 1987, with a sense of history in mind, a **Fred Meyer** store was gutted and revamped into a new market housing a delightful florist, cafes, movie theaters, and a variety of shops. Musicians often entertain in the main gallery. There's a parking garage on East Harrison Street. ◆ Daily. 401 Broadway E (at E Harrison St). 322.1610

Within Broadway Market:

B&O Espresso ★$ Located right in the middle of the arcade, this is home to the hippest crowd and some of the best desserts and espresso in Seattle. ◆ Coffeehouse ◆ Daily; F-Sa until 10:30PM. First floor. 328.3290. Also at: 204 Belmont Ave E (at E Olive St). 322.5028

Bulldog News This little sibling of the expansive University District store of the same name carries a diverting array of magazine titles, from *Working Woman* to *Cigar Aficionado.* ◆ Daily until 11PM. First floor. 322.6397. Also at: 4208 University Way NE (between NE 42nd and NE 43rd Sts). 632.6397

Gravity Bar ★$ The setting is right out of *Star Wars,* futuristic and chromey with high-tech lighting. As with its larger branch in downtown, it's heavily into healthy juices and brown rice, and, of course, espresso. The staff is trendy, but then, so's the clientele. But you can do lots of sidewalk watching from the tall windows. ◆ Vegetarian ◆ Daily lunch and dinner. First floor. 325.7186. Also at: 113 Virginia St (between First and Second Aves). 448.8826

Rasa Malaysia ★$ Another in a popular chain of take-out or eat-in spots, this restaurant specializes in noodles, usually sautéed with fresh veggies; peanut or another mildly spicy sauce; and a variety of fish, shrimp, or meat dishes. ◆ Malaysian/Takeout ◆ Daily lunch and dinner. First floor. 328.8882. Also at: 7208 E Green Lake Dr N (at NE 72nd St). 523.8888; Pike Place Market (Sanitary Market Bldg). 624.8388

Sergio's ★$ An extremely unprepossessing place (it actually takes some work to find it off an obscure hallway), this eatery nonetheless serves pleasing burritos and tacos. The decor is modern mall, so order to go. ◆ Mexican/Takeout ◆ Daily lunch and dinner. First floor. 328.6055

Ticket/Ticket This counter operation offers day-of-the-show, half-price tickets (there's a service charge for each ticket, however) to music, theater, and dance performances. ◆ Daily. Cash only. Second floor. 324.2744

Urban Outfitters Totally hip apparel and housewares for the modern urban dweller are for sale here. ◆ Second floor. 322.1800.

Hamburger Mary's ★$ A gift from Portland, Oregon, and San Francisco, the kitchen cooks up hamburgers in all their thick and oozing glory. But don't ignore the omelettes (choose from a bewildering assortment of ingredients), which provide genuine comfort on inclement Northwest mornings. ◆ American ◆ Daily breakfast, lunch, and dinner until midnight; F-Sa until 2AM. Second floor. 325.6565

51 The Oven ★$ This is the fast-food affiliate of Belltown's **Mediterranean Kitchen.** In large part, the menu here is the same (yes, the renowned Farmer's Dish is available), but there are also gyro sandwiches and beef or chicken *shawarma* (marinated and broiled on a vertical rotisserie) plates. ◆ Middle Eastern/Takeout ◆ Daily lunch and dinner. 213 Broadway E (between E Thomas and E John Sts). 328.2951

51 Macheesmo Mouse ★$ Is there really such a thing as healthy fast food? Here you'll find south-of-the-border fare that's unfried, low fat, and low cholesterol. Tacos, enchiladas, and other entrées come with black beans, brown rice . . . and a calorie count. Burritos are best. ◆ Mexican/Takeout ◆ Daily lunch and dinner. 211 Broadway E (between E Thomas and E John Sts). 325.0072.

52 TestaRossa ★★$ Thick and flavorful Chicago-style pies are turned out by this second-floor pizza joint. The garlic, spinach, and mushroom pie is everyone's favorite. ◆ Pizza ◆ Daily. 210 Broadway E (between E Thomas and E John Sts). 328.0878

52 Steve's Broadway News Steve Dunnington, formerly a mustachioed fixture at **Read All About It** in **Pike Place Market,** has brought his love of magazines and other periodicals to hyperkinetic Broadway. The usual mix is available here, as well as some oddball foreign papers. A connoisseur of tabloid journalism, Dunnington keeps the scandal sheets prominently displayed ("Devil Escapes From Alaskan Oil Well!"), for laughs. ◆ Daily; F-Sa until midnight. 204 Broadway E (between E Thomas and E John Sts). 324.7323

52 Espresso Roma ★$ Here is a perfect spot to sip and read all those papers you bought next door at **Steve's.** Small and quiet, this is one coffeehouse where nobody's going to disturb you. Lots of students and artists come out here. ◆ Coffeehouse ◆ Daily. 202 Broadway E (at E John St). 324.1866. Also at: 4201 University Way NE (at NE 42nd St). 632.6001

Restaurants/Clubs: Red	**Hotels:** Blue
Shops/ 🌳 Outdoors: Green	**Sights/Culture:** Black

53 D'Afric ★★$ It's easy to miss this charming, little family-owned Ethiopian restaurant located behind a nondescript shopping arcade. But inside, food is served in the traditional manner on flavorful *injera,* the spongy flat bread that doubles as a plate and fork in Ethiopia. Of the appetizers, the pureed yellow split peas are among the tastiest. Meat dishes are generally spicy, with favorites including *yebeg wot* (beef and vegetables in a rich sauce) and *yesiga tibs* (beef mixed with green chili peppers). *Shifinfin* comes highly recommended by the hostess and is described by the menu in purple tones, but is in truth a less-than-satisfying, if well-spiced, mound of *injera.* Service is friendly, efficient, and helpful. If you've never had East African cuisine, order the combination plate, which includes three main dishes and three side dishes of your choice. ◆ Ethiopian ◆ Daily lunch and dinner. 112 Broadway E (between E John St and E Denny Way). 328.5117

54 Hill House $ Owners Ken Hayes and Eric Lagasca have lovingly restored a 1903 Victorian home. The five guest rooms (three with private baths) are individually decorated, and all have queen-size beds and down comforters. The location is excellent—close to Broadway and on bus routes to both downtown and the **University of Washington.** Breakfast is an expanded continental on weekdays, family-style on weekends. This is a nonsmoking place. ◆ 1113 E John St (between 11th and 12th Aves E). 720.7161

55 Prince of Wales $ Try to secure the attic suite here, with its westward deck view of the city, Puget Sound, and the Olympic Mountains. There are four rooms, two with private baths. Owners Naomi Reed and Burt Brun serve a full breakfast and will accept older, well-mannered children. The bus stops across the street, and it's only a one-mile walk to downtown's **Washington State Convention Center.** ◆ 133 13th Ave E (at E John St). 325.9692

56 Group Health Cooperative of Puget Sound In their efforts to find affordable medical care, farmers, union members, secretaries, and a handful of professional people defied the medical establishment of the 1940s to establish this cooperative in 1947. Today **GHC** is the nation's largest consumer-governed health-care organization, serving nearly a half-million residents of Washington and Idaho, and a model for accessible, cost-effective, quality health care. This central facility is Seattle's largest hospital and the neighborhood's major employment center, spawning an attendant flock of shops and restaurants on 15th Avenue East. Park in the underground garage. ◆ 200 15th Ave E (at E John St). 326.3000

57 Kidd Valley ★$ Unlike some other chain burger joints, this one succeeds at being both fun for children and culinarily satisfying for their accompanying adults. Hamburgers here are flavorful fistfuls of juicy meat and bun, best accompanied by the thick and not-too-greasy fries. The milk shakes are some of the best in town (order the chocolate or the root beer). Lines are common at the counter. ◆ American/Takeout ◆ Daily breakfast, lunch, and dinner. 135 15th Ave E (between E John St and E Denny Way). 328.8133. Also at: 4910 Green Lake Way N (between N 49th St and Stone Way N) 547.0121; 14303 Aurora Ave N (near N 145th St). 364.8493; 531 Queen Anne Ave N (at W Mercer St). 284.0184

58 The Corner House $ Of special note in this bed-and-breakfast (illustrated above) are the beds themselves, guaranteed to rival or surpass your own in comfort. There are only two rooms (each with a private bath), but the atmosphere is warm and inviting. Owners Julianne Nason and Oliver H. Osborn serve a continental breakfast and offer off-street parking. ◆ 102 18th Ave E (at E Denny Way). 328.2865

In 1907 moralist William Hickman Moore was elected mayor of Seattle and began a campaign to eliminate saloons and other vices from the city's borders. But Moore was out of office and his reform efforts were out of favor by 1910, when city councilman Hiram C. Gill was elected mayor. Gill favored a wide-open town. In fact, *McClure's* magazine reported that 30 to 40 gambling places opened under Gill's administration. Seattle's police chief himself was taking kickbacks from prostitution—$10 per person per month.

"The days here are full of mist from Puget Sound and of depression. I find it hard to keep cheerful."

   E.B. White, during his stay in Seattle, 1922-23

The Gaslight Inn

59 The Gaslight Inn $ This is a good bed-and-breakfast (illustrated above) choice if you want easy access to downtown: the *No. 10* bus stops right out front and goes all the way to the Waterfront. Antique Mission-style furniture graces the dining room, parlor, living room, and library. During the summer, guests can enjoy the heated pool surrounded with beautiful plantings and container gardens. Five of the nine rooms have private baths. One guest room has a city-view deck, and another has a fireplace. A continental breakfast is served. ♦ 1727 15th Ave (between E Howell and E Olive Sts). 325.3654

60 The Globe Cafe & Bakery ★$ Soy-milk *lattes* might seem too healthy for some, but the vegan tilt here is balanced by a relaxed atmosphere and outrageously good gingerbread. Toys are on hand for the young-uns. ♦ Coffeehouse ♦ Daily until 10PM. 1531 14th Ave E (at E Pine St) 324.8815

61 REI Founded in 1938, Recreational Equipment Inc. has become a Seattle institution, as well as the nation's largest consumer cooperative, with more than one million active members worldwide. The main headquarters have moved south to suburban Kent and REI has grown to a nationwide chain of 30 stores, but this hallowed temple remains the heart and soul of the operation, at least for outdoorsy Seattle natives. Everything you'll need for your next expedition to the Himalayas or just a jog around the block is here: gear and clothing for backpacking, climbing, water sports, cycling, and skiing. There's even an adventure-travel arm to the business now, and the mail-order catalog goes all over the world. ♦ Daily; W-F until 9PM. 1525 11th Ave E (between E Pine and E Pike Sts). 323.8333

62 Comet Tavern This pub is rather down-at-the-heels, and quite proud of it. The clientele is a Whitmanesque sampler of politicians, aspiring artists, writers, and escapees from nearby **Seattle University.** There's lots of graffiti but zero video games; it's just an honest drinking joint. ♦ Daily until 2AM. 922 E Pike St (at 10th Ave E). 323.9853

63 Egyptian Theater One of the city's classiest moviehouses is within an old Masonic temple that also serves as headquarters for the Seattle International Film Festival, held each May. Inside is **Cafe Cairo,** an espresso bar operated by Craig Donarum, who gave this city its first espresso cart. ♦ Box office opens one hour before show time. 805 E Pine St (between Harvard Ave E and Broadway). 323.4978

64 Neighbours By day, it's a mediocre restaurant, but at night it's a happening disco catering mostly to a gay crowd. Very-late-night patrons may be treated to a galley of over-fried foods just to keep up their strength to find their way around this truly cavernous space. ♦ Cover. M-Th, Su until 2AM; F-Sa until 4AM. 1509 Broadway (between E Pine and E Pike Sts). 324.5358

"Like any nouveau riche, Seattle is harder to love in her new finery than she was in her salad days. I grumble at her new greed, snarl at her misplaced snobbishness and then break down and admit: I love her still."

Eric Scigliano, *Seattle Weekly* columnist

First Hill

65 Stimson-Green Mansion As Seattle began to establish itself in the mid-19th century, the city's captains of industry all competed furiously to build grander mansions than those of their rivals. The first such examples graced First Hill, just east of downtown. It became Seattle's earliest status neighborhood, but the reign was brief, lasting only a generation or two before developments more remote from the city were settled. This baronial house (illustrated above) is a fine reminder of those times.

Built between 1899 and 1901 from designs by architects **Kirtland K. Cutter** and **Karl Malmgren** (whose efforts were heavily influenced by the European Arts and Crafts movement), the house was occupied from its completion until 1914 by the family of Ballard mill owner Charles D. Stimson. From then until 1975, it was the property of the Joshua Green family (Green was a prominent early Seattle banker). Today the mansion is a full-service catering facility. Tours for groups of 12 or more may be scheduled by appointment. ♦ Business office M-F. 1204 Minor Ave (at Seneca St). 624.0474

66 Summit Grade School/The Northwest School One of the finest among architect **James Stephen**'s many Seattle schools, this 1905 wood structure is a catalog of brick-and-stucco facing, stepped parapets, and decorative ironwork, with an octagonal bell tower. The local school district closed this building in 1965, but more than a decade later it was bought and rehabilitated by operators of **The Northwest School,** a private institution for grades 6 through 12. ♦ 1415 Summit Ave (between E Pike and E Union Sts). 682.7309

67 Cafe Sabika ★★$$ This bistro certainly deserves its rep for homey friendliness (it's not uncommon to hear the chef singing) and classic, elegant meals. Chef/owner John Rios's background in the food preparations of Provence has added an interesting dimension to all the dishes—from pork burritos to duck linguine to tender beef Wellington. ♦ International ♦ Tu-Sa dinner. 315 E Pine St (between Melrose and Bellevue Aves E). 622.3272

68 Re-bar Probably the best danceteria in Seattle, this club certainly boasts the liveliest disc jockeys (don't miss Queen Lucky if she's in town). The crowd is mixed straight and gay, but mostly gay on the signature **Queer Disco Nights.** You'll hear lots of Diana Ross and industrial dance—it all depends on the DJ. Live bands are scheduled irregularly. ♦ Cover. Daily until 2AM. 1114 E Howell St (off Boren Ave). 233.9873

69 Reiner's ★★★$$$ Chef/owner Reiner Greubel produces some fine fare in this small but elegant restaurant. Choice picks are the tender veal and fish dishes. He also serves the finest tortellini pesto-cream soup you've ever sunk a spoon into. The service is somewhat slow but very courteous. ♦ French ♦ Tu-F lunch and dinner; Sa dinner. Reservations recommended. 1106 Eighth Ave (between Spring and Seneca Sts). 624.2222

70 Sorrento Hotel $$ Built in 1908, this Mediterranean-style hotel boasted the city's first rooftop restaurant. (The architect was **Harlan Thomas**.) Restored to its original elegance, it's small by comparison with today's hotels, and guests sometimes complain that the dark-wood appointments look gloomy; it does, however, have an unusual intimacy. Some of the 76 guest rooms are small (a few have only narrow slices of view), but they're always comfortably appointed. Try to reserve a room with a view west over Puget Sound. The lobby's **Fireside Lounge** has an appealing clublike atmosphere, and complimentary limousine service is available within the downtown area. ♦ 900 Madison St (at Terry Ave). 622.6400; fax 625.1059

Within the Sorrento Hotel:

The Hunt Club ★★★$$$$ The executive chef here, Christine Keff, is an alumnus of Seattle's **McCormick & Schmick's** restaurant and former apprentice to the legendary chef Seppi Renggli of the Four Seasons in New York. Her menu combines Northwestern ingredients with Pacific Rim accents. At lunchtime try Keff's Seattle club sandwich: grilled king salmon and Dungeness crab cake on toasted sourdough, dressed with lemongrass mayonnaise, and served with paper-thin onion rings. For dinner, the classic braised osso buco, accompanied by a delectable saffron risotto, is a typical winner. The setting is elegant and intimate. ♦ Northwestern ♦ Daily breakfast, lunch, and dinner. Reservations recommended. 622.6400

Evergreen Point Floating Bridge is 1.4 miles long—the longest floating bridge in the world.

71 St. James Cathedral Imagine what this astonishing Neo-Baroque church, with its twin 175-foot-tall towers, would look like with a copper dome above its entrance. That was its appearance from December 1907 until January 1916, when the canopy (and a lighted cross on top of that) collapsed beneath the weight of 30,000 pounds of snow. "A roar like the boom of a heavy gun brought priest and layman to the cathedral," wrote the *Seattle Post-Intelligencer.* "They saw a huge jagged hole where the massive dome had soared and poured great clouds of mortar dust and flying snow." Months later, the church was reopened with a flat roof that lessened the building's visual impact (it was designed by **Heins & LaFarge** and **John Graham Sr.**) but actually improved interior acoustics. ♦ Ninth Ave and Marion St. 622.3559

71 Trinity Parish Episcopal Church This handsome, rough-cut stone landmark near the **Harborview Medical Center** and overlooking Pioneer Square is in the style of English-country parish churches. **John Graham Sr.** did the original design in 1891, then restored the building and gave it a new rectory after a terrible fire in 1901. ♦ 609 Eighth Ave (at James St). 624.5337

72 Temple de Hirsch Sinai Built in 1960 as a stylized mountain with exquisite stained glass, this Jewish sanctuary hardly seems like the work of the same man—**B. Marcus Priteca**—who many years earlier designed the downtown's **Coliseum** and **Paramount** theaters. But it is. ♦ E Pike St and 16th Ave. 323.8486

Central District and Madrona

73 Mount Zion Baptist Church This over-a-century-old church is a prominent feature of the Central District community. It seats a thousand people, and is packed to the rafters every Sunday. The church's 100-member gospel choir has become nationally famous through several acclaimed gospel recordings. The more than 2,000 members include several of the city's major politicians, and its pastor—the Reverend Samuel McKinney—is an assertive voice for African-Americans in Seattle. ♦ 1634 19th Ave (at Madison St). 322.6500

74 Madison Street Seattle's only waterfront-to-waterfront thoroughfare, this street stretches from Elliott Bay through the Central District to Lake Washington. Look at it as a core sample of local history and economics, taking in affluent neighborhoods, poverty-stricken pockets, new condominiums (especially in the area known as Madison Valley, from 23rd Avenue East to the lake), and old, single-family residences. ♦ Elliott Bay to Lake Washington

75 All the Best This upscale pet-supply store is typical of the stores now opening along a once slumlike stretch in the Madison Valley area which has undergone extraordinary gentrification in recent years. The pet foods sold here pack natural ingredients. Indulgent pet owners will appreciate the diversity of near toys and books in stock here, too. ♦ Daily. 2713 E Madison St (at Martin Luther King Jr. Way). 329.8565

76 Rover's ★★★★$$$$ Chef Thierry Rautureau's small, semiformal, and exquisitely intimate establishment in its frame-house setting is a French restaurant pa excellence. Perhaps it's because he gives familiar Northwestern fare a French accent, rather than simply producing Gallic classics.

Rautureau specializes in generous servings of seafood, including Columbia River sturgeon and halibut, the latter served with an embarrassment-of-riches lobster sauce. Ellensburg lamb, rabbit, and game entrées also make appearances on the menu. The chef's talents may be sampled best by ordering the five-course prix-fixe dinner, which can also be ordered with vegetarian components. Wines from the Northwest and France complement the meal. There are only about a dozen tables, plus a courtyard for warm weather dining. ♦ Northwestern/French ♦ Tu-Sa dinner. Reservations recommended. 2808 E Madison St (between 28th and 29th Aves E). 325.7442

77 Denny-Blaine Park Here is a tranquil little public beach (aka "Liberal Ladies' Beach") frequented mostly by lesbians. There's no bathhouse and no lifeguard on duty. ♦ Lake Washington Blvd (at 40th Ave E)

78 Madrona Park Bathing Beach Change in the bathhouse and then hit the beach. The water is pristine here (thanks to a major civic cleanup of Lake Washington back in the 1960s), but it's painfully cold, even in summer. For a less Arctic experience, take a seat in one of the usually unoccupied lifegua perches and watch the joggers, dog-walkers and picnickers do their thing. In clear weathe there is no better place from which to view 14,410-foot Mount Rainier, which (although 50 miles away) dominates the southern horizon. Clear skies also reveal other snowy peaks in the Cascade mountain range to the east, and the sharp-eyed may spy 10,778-fo Mount Baker north of the lake. It would be easy to forget that you're in a city, were it no for the jagged profile of Bellevue across the lake. ♦ Lake Washington Blvd (at E Marion S

79 Hi-Spot Cafe ★$ Owners Amanda Wood and Michael Kingsley revitalized this old-time coffeehouse in a Madrona home where the meal of choice is breakfast (hearty omelettes and terrific cinnamon rolls). Lunch, however, brings sumptuous burgers, terrific BLTs, and good vegetarian soups. Dinner is not yet offered, but plans were in the works at press time. ♦ American ♦ M-F breakfast and lunch; Sa-Su breakfast. 1410 34th Ave (at E Union St). 325.7905

80 Sam's Super Burgers ★$ This is a required stop on the hamburger lover's tour of Greater Seattle. The sandwiches are big, with lots of meat. The hot-links burgers purveyed by this unpretentious joint are also good. ♦ Soul food ♦ M-Sa lunch and dinner. 2600 E Union St (at 26th Ave). 329.4870

81 Catfish Corner ★★$ Talk about ultra-specialization: this eatery does have other things on the menu, but why stray when the breaded catfish is so superb? The potato salad is a bit mustardy, but still excellent. ♦ Soul food ♦ Daily lunch and dinner. 2726 E Cherry St (at Martin Luther King Jr. Way). 323.4330

82 Ezell's Fried Chicken ★★$ This is the take-out place that talk-show hostess Oprah Winfrey used to call to have the out-of-this-world fried chicken shipped to her overnight. Oprah's changed her diet these days, but thankfully this place hasn't. ♦ Fried Chicken/ Takeout ♦ Daily lunch and dinner. 501 23rd Ave (at Jefferson St). 324.4141

83 R&L Home of Good Barbeque ★★$ A Central District culinary landmark since Robert and Louise Collins opened the pit in 1952, this place serves excellent alder-smoked pork ribs, hot links, and baked beans. ♦ Barbecue ♦ Tu-Sa lunch and dinner. 1816 E Yesler Way (between 18th and 19th Aves) 322.0271

84 Frye Art Museum Dominated by the 19th-century European salon paintings of patrons Charles and Emma Frye, this small museum also includes Wyeth works and some by non-native Alaskan artists. The International Style building was designed in 1952 by **Paul Thiry** and is similar to his **Museum of History and Industry** in Montlake. ♦ Free. Daily. 704 Terry Ave (at Cherry St.) 622.9250

85 New Hong Kong Seafood Restaurant and B.B.Q. ★★$ Southeast Asians (mainly Vietnamese, but Cambodians, Laotians, and Thais as well) have recently made their mark in Seattle, just as the Chinese and Japanese did a century ago. The result is a new version of the International District, centered around the intersection of South Jackson Street and 12th Avenue South. You need only glance at the native-language storefront signs to know that these places draw their customers from the Asian community. This restaurant has a 200-item menu featuring Chinese, Vietnamese, and Thai dishes; word is that it serves some of the best wonton soup in town. ♦ Southeast Asian ♦ Daily lunch and dinner. 212 12th Ave S (between S Jackson St and Boren Ave). 324.4091

86 Tabernacle Missionary Baptist Church Certainly one of the most exuberant African-American churches in Seattle, the congregation here is inspired by Reverend Robert Manaway. The choir is loaded with energy and with talent. ♦ 2801 S Jackson St (at 28th Ave S). 329.9794

Leschi to Seward Park

87 Leschi Park The name comes from an 1850s Nisqually tribal leader who liked to camp here and who was accused by Territorial Governor Isaac Stevens of leading attacks against Seattle's pioneers in the Battle of Seattle; it was a bloody uprising and resulted in death on both sides. Chief Leschi, the focus of so much hatred, was tried for the deaths of two federal peacekeeping volunteers, and then shamefully hanged despite evidence of his innocence.

At the turn of the century a trolley carried Seattleites here to an amusement park and opera house, both long gone; and a cross-lake ferry docked here before the Interstate-90 floating bridge was opened in 1940. The Olmsted-designed park across the street from the marina is styled as a classic English garden and includes an ancient stone bridge (over which the trolley once rumbled). Until the 1970s the neighborhood was decidedly blue-collar and bohemian, and ascended to its present affluent status only in the last two decades—as indicated by the modern architecture of its homes and condos. Joggers and cyclists travel frequently over the 10 tree-lined and lightly trafficked miles between this greenbelt and **Seward Park** to the south. ♦ Lakeside Ave S and Leschi Pl

88 Leschi Lakecafe ★★$$ A busy bar (with 18 beers on tap) and a kitchen that does its best work with fresh- and saltwater fish, particularly salmon, are the main attractions. Diners may select a Dungeness crab right out of the fish tank. In warm weather the outdoor tables are packed with the tanned and single. Fish-and-chips from the cafe's adjacent **Koby's** take-out counter are delicious (some critics contend that they're even better than the greasefests dished up by **Spuds'**), but they're also overpriced. ♦ Seafood ♦ Daily lunch and dinner. 102 Lakeside Ave S (near E Alder St). 328.2233

89 Daniel's Broiler ★★$$$$ As the name
suggests, the emphasis is on flame-broiled
meat and seafood. Chef Russell Lowell
actually ventures out into the forests with bow
and arrow for duck, pheasant, and venison,
his personal specialties. If you prefer seafood,
try the swordfish. The restaurant offers a
terrific perspective of Mount Rainier and Lake
Washington to the east. There's a second,
more chichi venue in Bellevue. ♦ American
♦ Daily dinner. 200 Lake Washington Blvd (at
the Leschi Marina) 329.4191. Also at: Seafirst
Bldg (10500 NE Eighth Ave, at 105th Ave NE),
Bellevue. 462.4662

90 Remo Borracchini's A lot of Seattleites
wouldn't go anywhere other than this
landmark Italian bakery to get cakes for
special occasions. The confections are
outrageous: the chocolate Bavarian cream
should really be listed as a controlled
substance. The bakery also makes pasta and
breads, and sells Italian canned goods and
wines. And, while not officially a restaurant, it
has a few tables for snackers and serves
sandwiches, a rich lasagna, pizza, and baked
items. ♦ Daily from 6AM. 2307 Rainier Ave S
(between S Walker and S College Sts).
325.1550

91 Mutual Fish Company Here's the best
seafood store south of **Pike Place Market.**
Owned and operated by the Yoshimura family
since about the beginning of time, they'll pack
purchases for the trip home. ♦ M-Sa. 2335
Rainier Ave S (at S College St). 322.4368

92 Evans House This is the compelling work
of **Ellsworth Storey,** a Chicago native who
arrived in Seattle in 1903 and set about
building houses in the developing
neighborhoods along the west bank of Lake
Washington, especially Madrona and
Mount Baker. Apparently not interested in a
large-scale practice, **Storey** stuck with
residential design, an eminent example of
which is this wood home. Note the strong
diagonal emphasis. ♦ 2306 34th Ave S
(at Lonwood Dr S)

Restaurants/Clubs: Red   Hotels: Blue
Shops/ 🍸 Outdoors: Green   Sights/Culture: Black

Fowl Play

Northwesterners seem generally fascinated by the
peregrinations of birds, and Seattle residents are no
different. On almost any weekend you'll see clutches
of watchers bouncing high-tech binoculars on their
chests or toting cameras mounted with lenses big
enough to subdue a charging elk. Bird watching is
best here in winter, when migrating species make the
long flap down from the north in pursuit of warmer
climes. But early and late summer aren't without their
viewing opportunities.

The local Audubon Society recommends that bird
watchers scope out **Lincoln Park** in **West Seattle,**
Magnolia's **Discovery Park** (where more than 150
bird species have been sighted, including red-tailed
hawks, goldfinches, and ospreys), the **University of**
Washington campus, and the **Washington Park**
Arboretum (a stopping point—by last count—for
some 200 species). Endangered peregrine falcons
have been spotted in north **Ballard,** and another
threatened species—purple martins—have been
known to nest downtown, amazingly enough on the
skybridge of **The Bon Marché** department store.
Green Lake, in summer one of the best locations to
espy the "red-breasted Coppertone slatherer" and the
"oggle-eyed people peeper," is most attractive for
birders in the winter. Mergansers, mallards, and
other ducks swoop down from November through
January to grab bread crumbs, as do the visiting
Canadian geese on their migration southward. Bald
eagles are also known to perch in trees above **Green**
Lake, but they actually nest in **Discovery Park** and
Seward Park on the west bank of **Lake Washington.**

As is common with other port cities, sea gulls are
ubiquitous in Seattle. Their screeches are as
memorable as the blast of a ferry horn, and their
flight patterns as familiar as the march of rain clouds

If you have time for a day trip, about an hour's drive
to the south, amidst the docklands near Tacoma's
Lincoln Avenue bridge, is the **Gog-le-hi-te Wetland,**
an artificial estuary inhabited by more than a hundred
varieties of birds.

93 Stan Sayres Memorial Park On the first
weekend in August this park becomes—in
more ways than one—"The Pits" staging
area for the annual Seafair hydroplane
extravaganza. The race course is a long
oval just off the park, with straightaways
paralleling the shoreline. The usually quiet
park becomes a circus of noise, warm beer,
exposed flesh, and confusion, with attendees
angling for close-up looks at the monster
boats and their frenzied crews. For years,
young Seattleites anxiously awaited this
weekend, packing the shoreline and engaging
in a variety of creative behaviors, but that
tradition seems to be on the wane as Seafair
swings more toward the family values crowd
Race-day attendance is noticeably slimmer,
down from the half-million reported in the
1970s and 1980s. But neighbors still
complain about the traffic and the ear-splitting

roar produced by the **Blue Angels** aerial-acrobatics team, which rattles pets, windows, and nerves for miles around.
♦ Lake Washington Blvd S and 42nd Ave S

94 Seward Park According to the Olmsteds' comprehensive plan, this was intended to be a "wild" park, contrasting with more manicured garden spots like **Volunteer Park.** The peninsula's 277 acres of mainly Douglas fir trees are true old-growth forest; a 2.5-mile paved roadway circles the park's outer shoreline, offering strollers, joggers, in-line skaters, and cyclists a quiet respite. Somehow, the park never seems crowded.

A variety of pathways—some marked, some obscure—lace the woodlands, and a public fishing pier and swimming beach provide recreation on the northern end. Boaters will find a public ramp and city docks a short distance north. In addition to picnic tables, barbecue pits, and a small amphitheater atop the hill, there is a state trout hatchery out at the end of the point and Japanese gardens, which, while quite pleasant, are obviously outclassed by those at the **Washington Park Arboretum.**

A grouping of three traditional Japanese stone lanterns and an inscribed granite boulder stand sentinel at the park's entrance. These were placed here during the 1976 US bicentennial to commemorate the gift of one thousand cherry trees given by the citizens of Japan to the American people. Though shaped from Washington State granite, the lanterns were carved in Japan; the granite boulder carries an inscribed duplication of calligraphy painted by Takeo Miki, then prime minister of Japan. Translated, it reads "Congratulations on the bicentennial of the United States of America's independence."

Visitors may wish to avoid the parking lot along the southern shoreline, where local youths hang out and crank their cars' stereo equipment into the upper decibel ranges.
♦ S Juneau St and Lake Washington Blvd S

95 Kubota Gardens A Japanese immigrant to Seattle started this 20-acre garden in 1929 in the midst of a swamp which he transformed into a delight to the eye (not to mention the flora-loving nose). A creek trickles through the lush greenery, feeding five ponds. Among the many rare plants are tanysho pines and weeping blue atlas cedars. ♦ Renton and 55th Aves S. 725.4400

96 El Palacio ★★$ Any restaurant that has *menudo* on its menu is at least trying to serve authentic Mexican cuisine. The kitchen here prepares delicious *menudo* sausage, which in the old country is thought to be a hangover cure and is best left undiscussed as far as its preparation goes. Seafood dishes are also exquisite: try the shrimp, either *camarones gigantes* or the *camarones al mojo de ajo* (prawns with garlic and butter sauce). The

tortillas are homemade, of course. ♦ Mexican ♦ Daily lunch and dinner. 5212 Rainier Ave S (between S Alaska and S Graham Sts). 725.9139

97 Pho Hòa ★★$ The menu gets no more expansive than *pho*, a Vietnamese soup, but that's actually quite enough. The broth has a wide variety of spices and textures; diners select additional ingredients from a long list of meats and veggies. The growing clientele is no longer restricted to Vietnamese-Americans, but you may still overhear old-timers replaying the fall of Saigon.
♦ Vietnamese ♦ Daily breakfast, lunch, and dinner. 4406 Rainier Ave S (between S Genesee and S Alaska Sts). 723.1508

98 Museum of Flight Biplanes, military jets, early mail planes, and a giant B-47 dangle from the ceiling of this museum's glass-and-steel **Great Gallery.** Children especially love to wander among these relics; they can study a reproduction of Boeing's first seaplane and a real DC-13, or trace the history of flying in the adjacent **Red Barn,** which was the Boeing Company's original 1910 airplane factory.

Although the museum is often called "Boeing's Museum of Flight," it is, in fact, an independent operation adjacent to the **Boeing Development Center.** A gift shop is fully stocked with models, books, and leather bomber jackets.
♦ Admission; discounts for senior citizens and children. Daily; Th until 9PM.
9404 E Marginal Way S (at Boeing Field)

Bests

Bill Nye
Host/Writer, *Bill Nye—The Science Guy Show*

Red Door Ale House—The Halibut Chowder Soup is just too good.

The **Uptown Espresso**—Coffee, day-in, day-out. The best.

Ferry Boats—at the dock at **Pier 54.** The view is magnificent—actually, it's better than that.

Shirley Collins
President, Sur La Table

Fran's Chocolates on East Madison Street—chocolates (handmade) and candy bars that are divine, especially the gold bar.

DeLaurenti's Specialty Foods on First Avenue in **Pike Place Market**—an enormous selection of fine food products from Italy.

Pike Place Market from May to December—the heart and soul of Seattle.

Just how many hills are there in Seattle? Twelve: Capitol, First, Magnolia, Queen Anne, Beacon, West Seattle, Denny, Renton, Sunset, Crown, Yesler, and Phinney Ridge. Yesler was formerly called "Profanity Hill" due to the curses of citizens struggling up it.

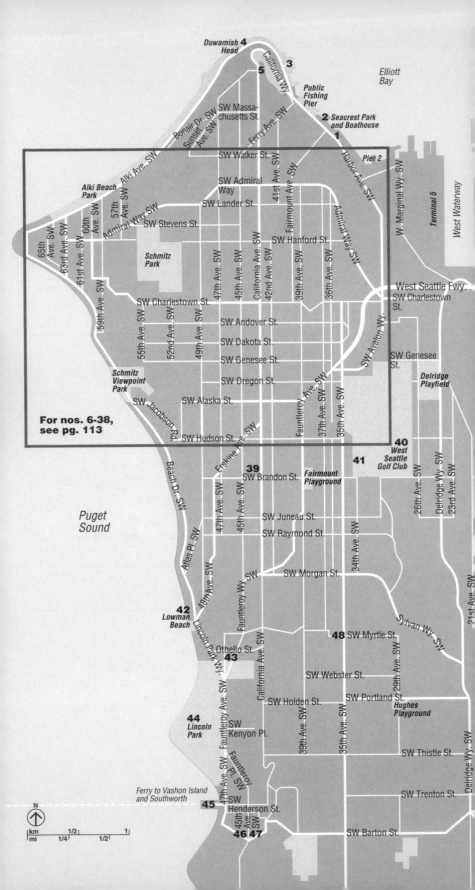

West Seattle

On balmy summer afternoons, **Alki Beach** in West Seattle is a polychromatic amalgam of people and vehicles and noise, noise, noise. Sunbathers stroll along the sand, boom boxes blare, and skaters, cyclists, runners, strollers, and families with tethered German shepherds jockey for position along the bike path. On the inland side of **Alki Avenue Southwest**, a variety of restaurants provide everything from elegant dinners to fast food. It's not exactly LA's Venice Beach, but then again it's not stereotypical Seattle either.

Today's scene is in marked contrast to that of November 1851, when a schooner dropped Arthur Denny's small cadre of pioneers at this very same spot. The settlers built their first cabins in the primitive Alki wilds and established relationships with the native Duwamish tribespeople before moving on to seek shelter on **Elliott Bay.**

Located southwest of downtown, across the **Duwamish River,** West Seattle is primarily a collection of residential areas distinguished by their views of downtown, **Harbor Island,** the **Cascade** and **Olympic Mountains,** and three **Puget Sound** islands: **Vashon, Blake,** and **Bainbridge.** Downtown West Seattle, as it is occasionally, if facetiously, called, is centered on the confluence of **California Avenue Southwest** and **Southwest Alaska Street,** and is best known simply as "The Junction." This central shopping area has had its ups and downs over the years; a number of businesses have made fleeting appearances, while others have stood almost unchanged for more than half a century. Although the growing number of high-rise condominiums on Alki Avenue Southwest attracts young urbanites, property values in many parts of West Seattle remain affordable, and the area retains some of its historic working-class spirit. But Alki Beach—which many residents claim is the only *real* beach in Seattle—is the area's principal attraction, boasting a wide expanse of sand, a long cycling/jogging/in-line skating lane, a boat launch, and grassy areas dotted with picnic tables.

1 Salty's on Alki ★$$ Owner Gerald Kingen claims no other place in the city commands as good a view as his upscale restaurant. That's debatable, but you do get a fine perspective on the downtown skyline and the ferries cruising across Puget Sound; it's especially beautiful at night. The food is a little pricier here than at most West Seattle restaurants, but it's served with more flair. Alder-smoked salmon stuffed with Dungeness crab, and clams steamed with vegetables and white wine are two favorites. Noise, however, can be a problem. ♦ Seafood ♦ M-Sa lunch and dinner; Su brunch and dinner. Reservations recommended. 1936 Harbor Ave SW (on Elliott Bay). 937.1600.

2 Seacrest Park and Boathouse This clean park has watercraft for hire, a simple coffee shop, and a fishing pier. You can rent fiberglass 13-foot-long double-hull fishing boats with six-horsepower motors for $11 an hour. A variety of other craft—including sea kayaks—are also available. Even if you never get so much as a bite on your line, views from out on the water are spectacular. ♦ W-Su 4:30AM-8PM July-Oct; 5:30AM-5PM Nov-June. 1660 Harbor Ave SW (on Elliott Bay). 932.1050

3 Don Armeni Park Boat Ramp A popular place for boaters to enter Puget Sound, this ramp was named after a deputy sheriff, active in fishing derbies, who was shot and killed in the line of duty in 1954. ♦ Harbor Ave SW (near California Way)

4 Duwamish Head Thanks to its views of Elliott Bay and downtown, this headland has long been a popular spot. In the late 19th and early 20th centuries the broad shoulders of beach were frequented by summer revelers and campers. In 1901 a former Klondike gold miner built the **Coney Island Baths,** which offered "a good bath and swim and use of fresh running water." Six years later, it became the site of the largest and showiest amusement park ever built in Seattle: **Luna Park.**

As with many other amusement parks of the early 20th century, this one sat on the water—actually and symbolically on the very edge of things. Created by Charles I.D. Looff, a German who had installed the first carousel at Coney Island, New York City, in 1876, **Luna Park** stretched over more than 10 acres, an imposing admixture of Atlantic City kitsch, Spanish Mission, and carnival gothic.

This fantasyland wanted to be all things to all people, and that's what finally got it in trouble. For along with the arcades and thrill rides, it also boasted "the longest bar on the bay," an easy target for reform-minded West Siders shocked by tales of drunkenness. The final straw came when Looff was implicated in a scandal involving the construction of a 500-room brothel on Seattle's Beacon Hill; when the park opened for the summer of 1913, Looff was gone. It didn't have a ninth season, although the natatorium (with its huge billboard exhorting, "Let's Swim!") remained in business until an arsonist set fire to the one-story frame building in 1931. All that's here now is a popular beach and some apartment buildings. ♦ Alki and Harbor Aves SW

5 Hamilton Viewpoint Generations of West Seattle teenagers have come to this lookout to, uh, "watch the submarine races." They couldn't help noticing also that it offers one of the most outstanding views of downtown Seattle across Elliott Bay. It's also a stop on **Gray Line**'s Grand City Tour (call 624.5213 for more information). Two coin-operated telescopes are available for a closer look. ♦ California Ave SW and SW Donald St

6 Cherry Blossom Teriyaki $ Seafood and, naturally, teriyaki dishes are the specialties of this small restaurant across the street from the beach. ♦ Japanese ♦ Daily lunch and dinner. 2620 Alki Ave SW (at 55th Ave SW). 933.0848

7 Alki Beach Park For many years this was the spot where teenagers showed off their cars and themselves. In the 1980s laws were passed that prohibited both cruising and amplified sound on the beach, thus cutting down considerably on the summer noise and traffic that had plagued local residents, but hardly decreasing the park's popularity. Today, the park is a two-and-a-half mile stretch with a sandy strip that's the closest thing Seattle can claim to a southern California beach. Volleyball courts on the sand are usually filled with players and lined with spectators when the sun shows its face. A bike path is active with skaters and runners. Picnic tables and shelters are available, and this is one of the few city parks that allows beach fires, although only in designated concrete rings. There are no lifeguards on duty, so swim at your own risk. ♦ Alki Ave SW (between Alki Point Light Station and Duwamish Head)

8 Alki Playground Facilities at this small playground about a block from the beach include a softball field, a soccer field, children's play equipment, and two lighted tennis courts. ♦ 58th Ave SW and SW Stevens St

9 Alki Community Center Local families come here to roller-skate on Friday nights, to shoot pool, or for basketball and volleyball games in the gym. ♦ Daily. 5817 SW Stevens St (at 58th Ave SW). 684.7430

10 Spud Fish and Chips $ Two English guys, Jack and Frank Alger, opened a summer fish-and-chips stand here in 1935. Fish-and-chips were then 10¢ per order, to go. Today, under the same ownership, the eatery is open year-round and seats as many as 82 people inside. The menu includes prawns, oysters, clams, and scallops, as well as chocolate chip cookies and milk shakes. ♦ Seafood/Takeout ♦ Daily lunch and dinner. 2666 Alki Ave SW (at 59th Ave SW). 938.0606. Also at: 6860 E Green Lake Way N (at Second Ave NE). 524.0565

11 Alki Bathhouse Art Studio The old bathhouse on Alki Beach is now open to all local artists as a free studio (available on a first-come basis). It's staffed by volunteers and administered by the **Alki Community Center.** ♦ M, W 10AM-3PM. Alki and 60th Aves SW. 684.7430

12 Alki Bakery & Cafe ★$ A local fave for weekend breakfasts (omelettes, fresh-baked bread, and cinnamon rolls), this long, narrow cafe also serves lunch and dinner. (Try the linguine primavera or the filling cheese tortellini with chicken and rosemary.) In 1996 cafe owner Kevin Piper (who also owns the **Point Grill**, see page 113) moved the bakery counter across the street and opened **Alki Bakery** (935.1352) in a former drugstore space. This is where they bake all the bread and pastries served in the cafe. You can pick up baked goods and espresso drinks to go. ♦ Continental ♦ Daily breakfast, lunch, and dinner. 2726 Alki Ave SW (at 61st Ave SW). 935.0616

13 Statue of Liberty The Boy Scouts of America dedicated this three-foot-high replica of New York City's harbor heroine to the City of Seattle in 1952. ♦ 61st and Alki Aves SW

Restaurants/Clubs: Red   Hotels: Blue
Shops/ ♣ Outdoors: Green   Sights/Culture: Black

Seattle's first public ordinance—passed in 1869—was a law against drunkenness.

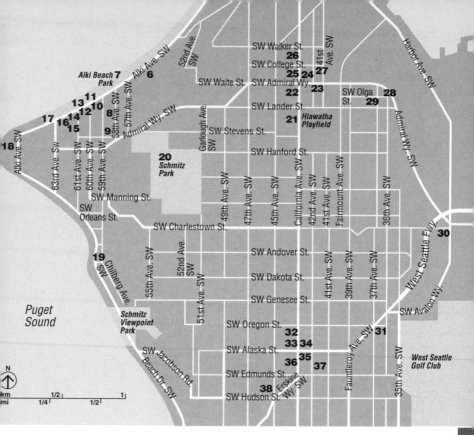

14 Pegasus Pizza & Pasta

★$ The pizza here has become legendary. One of the best varieties is Tom's Special, with mushrooms, green peppers, onions, olives, feta and mozzarella cheeses, spinach, pepperoni, fresh garlic, diced tomatoes, and sunflower seeds. The Greek pizza (with feta and mozzarella cheeses, spinach, onions, and ground beef), the feta bread, and the ravioli are also worth a taste. Expect a line on weekends. ◆ Italian ◆ Daily lunch and dinner. 2758 Alki Ave SW (between 61st and 62nd Aves SW). 932.4849

14 Point Grill

★$$ "Smoke 'em if you got 'em" is the culinary motto here. The kitchen smokes its own salmon, then serves it atop a fine Caesar salad. Ribs and chicken are also smoked, then barbecued. Also on the menu: pot roast and turkey dinners. ◆ Barbecue ◆ Daily lunch and dinner. 2770 Alki Ave SW (at 62nd Ave SW). 933.0118

15 Alki Homestead

$$ Originally a log cabin and a roadhouse for people who made the long journey by automobile from Seattle, this restaurant features a romantic ambience with lace curtains and light flickering from the cranberry glass lamps on the tables. The food is straight out of the 1940s—the specialty is panfried chicken with mashed potatoes, gravy, and green beans (which appear to be of the canned variety). The menu also includes steak, prime rib, and seafood. Cocktails are served in a spacious glassed-in porch. ◆ American ◆ W-Su dinner. 2717 61st Ave SW (near Alki Ave SW). 935.5678

16 Sunfish Seafood

$ You can get regular fish-and-chips here, or for a little more (and the difference is worth paying), halibut-and-chips. The influence of the Greek brothers who own this place shows up in such menu offerings as halibut shish kebab and calamari. Indoor and outdoor seating are both available. ◆ Seafood/Takeout ◆ Daily lunch and dinner. 2800 Alki Ave SW (at 62nd Ave SW). 938.4112

17 Monument to the Birthplace of Seattle

A concrete pylon marks the spot where Arthur Denny's pioneering party landed in 1851. Presented to the city in 1905 by Denny's daughter, Lenora, the column was originally installed beside the old **Stockade Hotel,** just across the street. It was moved to the beachside in 1926 when a piece of Massachusetts's famed Plymouth Rock was embedded in the pylon's base and a plaque was added to commemorate the occasion. The hotel, by the way, folded in 1936; apartments now occupy its former site. ◆ 63rd and Alki Aves SW

About 3,000 to 5,000 homeless people are out on Seattle's streets every day.

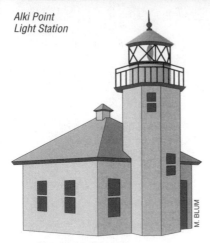

*Alki Point
Light Station*

M. BLUM

18 Alki Point Light Station Alki Point marks the southern entrance to Seattle's harbor, Elliott Bay. It's been the site of a warning beacon for ships since the mid-1870s, when Hans Martin Hanson, who bought the land from pioneer Doc Maynard, began lighting lanterns on the point every night. In the 1880s the US Lighthouse Service erected a lens-lantern on a scaffold. The present 37-foot-high octagonal tower (pictured above) was completed in 1913. Its light was converted to electricity five years later, and in 1984 its operation became fully automatic. Today, the lighthouse stands surrounded by apartments and condominiums. The station is maintained by the US Coast Guard. ♦ Tours Sa-Su, holidays; W noon-4PM. 3201 Alki Ave SW (on Elliott Bay). 217.6123.

19 Weather Watch Park Once a dock site for Puget Sound's ferry service from Seattle, this teeny lookout, on a small knoll between the apartments and cottages lining Beach Drive, was designed by local artist Lezlie Jane in 1991 and built with the help of many local residents. The centerpiece is an interpretive column—it's got a sundial, information on cloud formation and weather prediction, historical photographs, and it is topped off with a sculpture of ducks in flight. With its brick patio and benches, this makes a lovely spot to watch the weather over Puget Sound and the Olympic Mountains. ♦ Beach Dr SW and SW Carroll St

19 Dulce's ★$ This little cafe offers a great view through **Weather Watch Park,** as well as soup, salads, sandwiches, and delicious desserts and baked goods. ♦ Cafe ♦ Tu-F breakfast, lunch, and dinner; Sa-Su brunch and dinner. 4101 Beach Dr SW (at SW Carroll St). 933.8400

20 Schmitz Park Donated to the city by wealthy West Siders Ferdinand and Emma Schmitz in 1908 on the condition that the land be forever maintained as closely as possible to its natural state, this park is now home to one of the last stands of old-growth forest—some of the trees are more than 800 years old—within the city limits. It is also a 50-acre nature preserve where narrow trails through the thick woods can be hard to follow. There are no picnic areas or playgrounds. ♦ SW Stevens St and Admiral Way SW

21 Parkside News Cafe $ Espresso, salads, and sandwiches are the specialties at this friendly place. Try the excellent hazelnut torte, the tiramisù, and the carrot cake. In keeping with the shop's name, a wide variety of magazines and newspapers are for sale. ♦ Cafe ♦ Daily breakfast, lunch, and dinner. 2735 California Ave SW (at SW Lander St). 932.2279

22 Alki Bicycle Company This store has been outfitting local cyclists—and renting bicycles to visitors—for years. (Its name reflects the shop's original location on Alki Beach.) Besides peddling bikes and all manner of accessories, it also provides repair services, sells used bikes on consignment, and offers classes in road safety. The Alki Bicycle Club operates out of this shop, with free Wednesday night rides and guided tours available to groups of five or more. ♦ Daily. 2611 California Ave SW (between SW Admiral Way and SW Lander St). 938.3322

23 Starbucks ★$ No Seattle neighborhood seems complete anymore without its own branch of this coffee chain, selling pastries, espresso drinks, coffee by the pound, and all the equipment you need to brew your own beans at home. ♦ Coffeehouse ♦ Daily. 4101 SW Admiral Way (at 41st Ave SW). 937.5010

24 Rock City Sports Bar & Grill With something for almost everyone, this sports bar features live Top-40 dance music on weekends, a big-screen TV, pool tables (tournaments on Tuesdays), dart boards (Wednesday tourneys), and karaoke singing on Thursday and Sunday nights. ♦ Cover varies. Daily until 2AM. 2306 California Ave SW (between SW Admiral Way and SW College St). 933.9500

24 Peace Cafe ★$$ According to co-owner (with Bashar Al-Nakhala) Madeleine Khass, this establishment got its name because "It's about time for peace in this world." Falafel and *shawarma* (rotisserie-roasted meat) sandwiches, as well as more typical American dishes, are offered. Be sure to save room for an espresso and one of the savory cakes, pies, tortes, biscotti, and brownies that come from Capitol Hill's **B&O Espresso.** ♦ Middle Eastern ♦ Daily breakfast, lunch, and dinner. 2352 California Ave SW (between SW Admiral Way and SW College St). 935.1540

Painting the Town

Historical murals have become increasingly familiar sights in West Seattle. Located primarily in the **Junction** area, these paintings reflect a variety of artistic styles, ranging from a stylized folk-art look to trompe l'oeils, but most are lifelike images of West Seattle in the late 1800s and early 1900s.

After admiring murals in southwestern Washington and in Chemainus, British Columbia, where more than 25 murals serve as that town's primary tourist draw, area resident Earl Cruzen decided that his neighborhood should adopt the popular public-art theme. Most of the 11 murals painted in West Seattle have been funded by local donations, city matching funds, and contributions from building owners. Brochures are available from the West Seattle Chamber of Commerce (4151 California Ave SW, near SW Genesee St, 932.5685). Here's a brief guide to the works of art:

The Junction depicts the intersection during the 1920s, when the old streetcar lines converged here. The work of Eric Grohe, this trompe l'oeil looks so realistic that local wits have suggested the city hang a traffic light in front of the painted streetcar tracks. You'll find it framed by a mock concrete arch on the south wall of the **Junction Feed & Seed Store** (4747 California Ave SW, near SW Genesee St).

Part of the west side of **Morton's Drugs** (4707 California Ave SW, at SW Alaska St) is covered with a montage that includes images of onetime local attraction **Luna Park,** the old **West Seattle Cable Railway,** and turn-of-the-century ferries. Artist William Garnett of Portland, Oregon, completed the mural in 1989 and dubbed it *West Seattle Ferries.*

A deep-blue nighttime scene of a horse-drawn wagon dashing away from the 1913 Junction Fire Station brightens the south side of the **Don Swanson Insurance Building** (4711 44th Ave SW, near SW Alaska St), across from where that fire station once stood. Seattleite Don Barrie painted the mural, titled *Midnight Call,* in 1990.

The First Duwamish Bridge, a panorama of the old swing bridge that crosses the **Duwamish River,** is the work of Louisiana artists Robert and Douglas Dafford. Located on the north wall of the **Jacobson Building** (44th Ave SW and SW Edmunds St), it shows a trolley crossing the river, with the Cascade Mountains in a background of dreamy sunset shades.

A colorful 1937 view of the old *Morgan Street Market* was painted in 1990 by Nova Scotian artist Bruce Rickett on the west wall of **Olsen's Drugs** (6501 California Ave SW, at SW Fauntleroy Way). The original market stood across the street.

Another artist from Nova Scotia, Susan Tooke Crichton, depicted a 1910 landing by the old steamships that hauled freight and passengers between **Puget Sound**'s ports. *Mosquito Boat Landing* can be seen on the east wall of the **Campbell Building** (California Ave SW and SW Alaska St).

● **Huling's Chevrolet** dealership (4755 Fauntleroy Way SW at SW Alaska St) is the site of another Bruce Rickett mural, this one entitled *Alki in the Twenties,* a portrait of a 1919 Chevrolet and a woman painting. In the background is an Alki community with residences, a streetcar line, and ferry dock.

● *Tuesday's Bank Day* is the subject of the mural on the north side of the **Washington Mutual Bank** building (California Ave SW and SW Oregon St). It commemorates a project begun in 1923 to teach school children about saving money; at the time, this was the only bank that was willing to take the pennies, nickels, and quarters that kids wanted to deposit, and they even offered interest on accounts exceeding a few dollars. British Columbian Alan Wylie was the artist.

● Lany Little of Gresham, Oregon, depicted the *Wizard of Oz* float from a 1973 parade in a mural on the wall of the **West Seattle Post Office** (4412 California Ave SW, between SW Oregon and SW Genesee Sts).

● *The Old Mud Hole* by Mike Svob of Coquitlam, British Columbia, shows the old swimming area that Laurence Colman created in what is now Lincoln Park, complete with Puget Sound saltwater. In 1940, the Colman family donated funds for a modern pool at the same site. The mural is on the side of an apartment building (44th St SW, between Alaska and Oregon Sts).

● The days of hot metal type are revived in *Press Day,* a mural illustrating putting the *West Seattle Herald* to bed. Painted by Alan Wylie of Fort Langley, British Columbia, the mural is on the **Seawest Building** (44th St, between SW Alaska and SW Edmunds Sts).

24 Admiral Benbow Inn $ This replica of an old English inn was modeled after the fictional hostelry where pirates planned their voyage in Robert Louis Stevenson's *Treasure Island.* The **Chart Room Lounge,** a replica of the fictional ship *Hispaniola,* is a good place to stop in for a cocktail. In the dining room, fare ranges from seafood to prime rib, but the place isn't as interesting as Stevenson's story promises. ◆ American ◆ M-Sa lunch and dinner. 4212 SW Admiral Way (between California and 42nd Aves SW). 937.8348

The Unidentified Flying Objects (UFOs) Reporting and Information Service estimates that Seattleites report 20 to 100 UFO-type incidents per year.

25 Angelina's Trattoria $ Here is yet another in Dany Mitchell's stable of Seattle trattorias. Like the others (including **Stella's** in the University District and Pioneer Square's **Trattoria Mitchelli**), this restaurant provides Italian fare at reasonable prices. Entrées range from simple pastas of the day with marinara sauce to the more elaborate *fettuccine con pollo e nocciole* (pasta in a velouté sauce with roasted hazelnuts and chicken). ♦ Italian ♦ Daily breakfast, lunch, and dinner. 2311 California Ave SW (between SW Admiral Way and SW College St). 932.7311

25 Ristorante di Ragazzi ★$ In a comfortable setting replete with murals, faux marble walls and and deep-green wicker furniture, "The Boys' Restaurant"(as its name translates) serves great salads, innovative pastas and good pizzas (try the pie with pesto and artichoke hearts). It's also a good stop for an after-movie cappuccino or glass of wine. ♦ Italian ♦ M-F lunch and dinner; Sa-Su dinner. 2329 California Ave SW (between SW Admiral Way and SW College St) 935.1969

25 Admiral Theater Originally built as the **Portola Theater** in 1919, this playhouse has had a colorful history. In the 1920s the theater—along with the nearby **Olympus** and **Apollo** theaters—screened feature films, newsreels, and comedy shorts, all for a mere 20¢ per customer. An $18,000 pipe organ was added in 1924, talkies followed in 1929, and, in response to the realities of the Depression, in 1933 admission was dropped to 15¢.

In 1942 the moviehouse was expanded amid great fanfare. John Danz, the owner, held a contest for West Seattle residents to name the picture palace. The architect was **B. Marcus Priteca,** famed designer for Alexander Pantages's nationwide theater chain, whose local work may be remembered best in the **Coliseum** and **Paramount** theaters in downtown Seattle. **Priteca** used the winning moniker as a theme, adding nautical allusions to the facade (note the portholes, anchors, and a giant mast with crow's nest on the "upper deck," as well as the seahorses riding exit signs). Usherettes sported naval uniforms. A gala opening in 1942 drew 3,000 people to a showing of *Weekend in Havana,* starring Alice Faye, Carmen Miranda, and John Payne. In 1953 the theater put in "the first panoramic wide screen installed in a suburban theater."

Twenty years later it was converted to a "twin" with two 430-seat viewing rooms. But the theater closed in 1989, after several years of false hopes that its Canadian owners would restore its original majesty. A campaign by the Southwest Seattle Historical Society finally led locals to purchase the theater in 1991 and open it as a second-run movie palace. There are now five to six shows per week at about $ a seat, a bargain price these days. ♦ 2343 California Ave SW (between SW Admiral Way and SW College St). 938.3456

26 Pailin Thai Cuisine ★★$ A relative newcomer, this comfortable restaurant has become a neighborhood favorite. The food—especially the *pad thai* noodles—is good and the prices can't be beat. ♦ Thai ♦ M-F lunch and dinner; Sa-Su dinner. 2223 California Ave SW (between SW Walker and SW College Sts). 937.8807

27 West Seattle Library This attractive 1910 brick building was created by **W. Marbury Somervell** and **Joseph C. Cote,** who in the same year also designed two other Carnegie libraries: the **University Branch Library** on Roosevelt Way North and the **Green Lake Public Library.** In addition to the usual services, free special programs are offered for children and adults. ♦ M-W, F-Su. 2306 42nd Ave SW (between SW College St and SW Admiral Way). 684.7444

28 Belvedere Viewpoint The totem pole here, carved by Boeing engineers Michael Morgan and Robert Fleishman and dedicated in 1966, is modeled after one that had been presented to the city in 1939 by J.E. "Daddy" Standley, owner of downtown's **Ye Olde Curiosity Shop.** (Standley's original, crafted by the Bella Bella tribe of British Columbia's Queen Charlotte Islands, had decayed beyond repair.) There's an excellent view over Harbor Island to downtown. Be forewarned: There are only a few parking spaces. ♦ SW Admiral Way and SW Olga St

29 Hainsworth House $ An 18-room 1906 Tudor mansion offers excellent views of downtown Seattle, lovely landscaped grounds, and two guest rooms with private baths. The larger room, decorated in French country style, has an antique Austrian king-size bed, a private deck, a fireplace, and a full view of the city. The second has a partial view, a deck, and an antique oak bedroom set. Guests are treated to coffee half an hour before a full champagne (or sparkling cider) breakfast served by owners Carl and Charlotte Muia. No smoking is allowed, and visitors with animal allergies beware: there are two resident dogs. ♦ 2657 37th Ave SW (at Olga St). 938.1020

Restaurants/Clubs: Red	Hotels: Blue
Shops/ 🌳 Outdoors: Green	**Sights/Culture:** Black

30 Luna Park Cafe $ Eat 1950s-style food beneath a black-velvet Elvis painting. A neon-lit Seeburg jukebox (the remote selectors at each table actually work) spins 200 eclectic selections from Elvis to Frank Sinatra, Bob Marley, and Annette Funicello, and costs an amazing dime per play. A 1946 Wurlitzer 1015 Bubbler is a display jukebox only. Other kitschy decor includes an impressive collection of children's lunch boxes along with old business signs.

The food here is basic but good. (Try the meat loaf on whole wheat or the Cobb salad—turkey, bacon, blue cheese, egg, Swiss cheese, tomato, and olives.) The milk shakes (root beer, coffee, fresh fruit, and more) are much in demand on steamy days. The name is taken from the amusement park that once graced Duwamish Head (see page 111). ◆ American ◆ Daily breakfast, lunch, and dinner. 2918 SW Avalon Way (near SW Spokane St). 935.7250

31 YMCA The main branch of the West Seattle Y is also the most deluxe. There's a swimming pool, a weight room with free weights and exercise machines, basketball and volleyball courts, a running track, two racquetball courts, and a spa. All facilities, except regularly scheduled classes, are available on a drop-in basis: $7.50 per day for adults, $3 for children 18 and younger, and $5 for senior citizens. ◆ Daily. 4515 36th Ave SW (at SW Oregon St). 935.6000

32 Foreign Accents For aromatherapy and all kinds of soaps, lotions, potions, and gifts in more than 85 fragrances, this is the place. ◆ Daily. 4511 California Ave SW (between SW Oregon and SW Alaska Sts). 932.3747

32 Capers ★$ The kitchen here whips up terrific scones, muffins, and cobblers, as well as an estimable seafood salad and a daily quiche. It's a popular lunch spot for local office workers. A variety of Martha Stewart-ish decorator items for the kitchen and dining room, as well as Dilettante chocolates and coffee by the pound, are also sold. ◆ Cafe ◆ Daily breakfast and lunch. 4521 California Ave SW (between SW Oregon and SW Alaska Sts). 932.0371

33 Reflections West Seattle's metaphysical shop carries tarot cards, relaxation audiotapes, art objects crafted by Native Americans, incense, and more. Interested people gather here on Wednesday and Thursday evenings for Lakota singing and drumming. ◆ M-Sa. 4537 California Ave SW (between SW Oregon and SW Alaska Sts). 937.6032

33 West Seattle Speedway and Hobby Behind the stacks of plastic and intricate wooden model kits, this shop boasts a 135-foot, Euro hill-climb slot-car track, one of only a few left in the city. The sport owes its historical debt to auto racers of the 1920s, who, before the advent of dragsters and mud racers, gunned Duesenbergs and Millers around 24 steeply banked board tracks (none of which survived the Depression years). In addition to renting the slot cars and track time, the shop also sells the cars, parts and accessories, and baseball cards. ◆ Daily. 4539 California Ave SW (between SW Alaska and SW Oregon Sts). 932.9620

33 Pegasus Book Exchange This bookshop buys, sells, and trades used books. Its principal stock is in paperback fiction, but the owner also has an interest in metaphysics and will help you find anything in that category that isn't already available here. ◆ Daily. 4553 California Ave SW (between SW Alaska and SW Oregon Sts). 937.5410

34 Bonvechio's Book & Bean Here is the ultimate Seattle combo—books, coffee, and *The New York Times*. An in-store espresso cart makes this bookstore a favorite. In addition to a good general selection of titles, there's a large children's department, a well-stocked gardening section, *and* several tables, chairs, and benches for browsing. Call for information on special programs, such as theatrical readings. ◆ Daily. 4554 California Ave SW (between SW Oregon and SW Alaska Sts). 935.1003

The term "flying saucer" was first used after Civil Air Pilot Kenneth Arnold, who was searching on 24 June 1947 for a military plane that had gone down near Mount Rainier, spotted instead a formation of nine brilliant, boomerang-shaped objects flying from Rainier toward Mount Adams. Asked to describe his odd encounter, Arnold compared the flight of his bogeys to an undulating kite tail or a "saucer skipping across the water." Thus was born one of the most popular unsolved mysteries of the 20th century.

35 California and Alaska Street Brewery
Brewmaster Charles McElevy of this tiny brewpub trained in Germany and was formerly with the Rainier Brewing Company and Fremont's Red Hook Brewery. The beer names reflect local geography: Junction Ale, Alki Ale, Fauntleroy Stout. Alki Ale is red, with medium body. Hi-Yu Brown Ale (which means "Big Time" in Chinook jargon and also applies to an annual festival held in West Seattle since 1934) is rich and malty. Pub grub is limited, covering the short span betwixt chili and sandwiches. For entertainment, there are dart boards and board games. ♦ Tu-Th until 11PM; F-Sa until midnight; Su until 9PM. No smoking permitted. 4720 California Ave SW (at SW Alaska St). 938.2476

36 Husky Delicatessen A local institution since 1933, this family-owned establishment grew from an ice-cream parlor specializing in large chocolate-covered cones to a full-fledged deli. It attracts customers from all over Seattle with its homemade ice cream; also available are cold cuts, salads, beers and wines, and truffles. ♦ Daily; Tu-Su until 10PM. 4721 California Ave SW (at SW Alaska St). 937.2810

36 Northwest Art & Frame One-stop shopping for graphics needs: calligraphy pens and paper, rubber stamps, fabric painting supplies, watercolors, oils, enamels, children's art supplies, stationery, gifts, and cards. Picture framing is also available—do-it-yourself or pay more and have it done professionally. ♦ Daily. 4733 California Ave SW (between SW Alaska and SW Edmunds St). 937.5507

37 ArtsWest This nonprofit organization (formerly the West Seattle Cultural Society) has established a cultural center within **Jefferson Square,** a retail/residential complex named for the brick elementary school that stood at this site from 1912 to 1985. The center offers educational theater, music, dance, and other arts programs. There's also an art gallery that displays local talent. ♦ Tu-Sa. 4734 42nd Ave SW (between SW Alaska and SW Edmunds Sts). 938.0963

38 Villa Heidelberg $ A converted 1909 house (constructed and named by a German immigrant), this bed-and-breakfast inn has lead-glass windows, beamed ceilings, a finely landscaped yard (from which the owners pick their decorative flowers), and a covered porch. Four guest rooms share two baths. One of the rooms offers an Olympic-view sundeck; another has a fireplace. Popovers are a treat at breakfast. ♦ 4845 45th Ave SW (at Erskine Way SW). 938.3658

39 West Seattle Nursery This is a wonderful place to find answers to your gardening dilemmas. The nursery carries a full line of seeds, bulbs, bedding plants, perennials, vines, shrubs, trees, landscaping paraphernalia, gardening videos, plus horticultural books for gardeners of all ages and stages, charming gifts, and botanical items. The staff is friendly and knowledgeable. ♦ Daily. 5275 California Ave SW (at SW Brandon St). 935.9276

40 West Seattle Golf Club Set on relatively hilly terrain, this public 18-hole course features tree-lined fairways and great views of the city skyline. ♦ Greens fees. Daily. Reservations required. 4470 35th Ave SW (between SW Genesee and SW Brandon Sts). 935.5187

41 Camp Long One of the city's few parks to offer overnight facilities, this 68-acre patch is open to organized groups for camping and wilderness-skills programs. There are cabins for rent ($15 per night), picnic shelters, and a rustic lodge which is a popular spot for weddings. There's a rock wall for climbing practice and instruction ($15 for a one-and-a-half-hour session, with a minimum class size of 15). Free nature walks are scheduled on Saturdays, and there are educational programs for youngsters; call ahead for a rundown. ♦ Park ranger station Tu-Sa. 5200 35th Ave SW (at SW Dawson St). 684.7434

42 Lowman Beach Named for a former Seattle parks commissioner, this tiny park offers not only access to the sand but a swing set and one tennis court. In December locals gather here to watch Seattle's ceremonial Christmas ships make their loop through Puget Sound. Walkers can take pleasant strolls down an access road into the lower portion of adjacent **Lincoln Park.** ♦ 48th Ave SW and Beach Dr SW

43 Cat's Eye Cafe $ Most of the sandwiches served at this deli feature cute feline names: the Kit Cat (sliced chicken, avocado, tomato, and sprouts), the Cat on a Hot Tin Roof (a classic Reuben), and the Cat in Heat (tuna melt with tomato). Other menu items include pesto lasagna, quiche, chili, and salads. The deli does brisk business in espresso, although the richness falls far short of **Starbucks.** On sunny days sit outside at one of the picnic tables on the grass. ♦ Deli ♦ Daily breakfast, lunch, and dinner. Fauntleroy Way SW and SW Othello St. 935.2229

44 Lincoln Park Designed by Frederick Law Olmsted Jr. and John Charles Olmsted, who developed Seattle's 1903 comprehensive greenery plan, this park comprises 130 acres of wooded and waterfront trails, with picnic areas, tennis courts, softball fields, horseshoe pits, and children's playground equipment. Access is limited to foot traffic; park roads are open only to park vehicles or for emergencies. As with most beach parks on Puget Sound, no lifeguards are on duty even during summer months. A bit of historical trivia: the park was named at the request of the local Young Men's Republican Club, which promised to erect a statue of Honest Abe at the park entrance. The promise was never kept. ♦ Fauntleroy Ave SW and SW Kenyon Pl

Within Lincoln Park:

Colman Pool This heated, outdoor, Olympic-size pool is filled with both chlorinated fresh-water and saltwater. One negative: It's open only during summer vacation for the Seattle School District. ♦ Admission; discount for senior citizens, disabled persons, and children 18 and younger. Daily noon-7PM late June-Aug. 684.7494

45 Fauntleroy Ferry Dock Washington State Ferries leave this dock to take passengers to Vashon Island, a 28-minute ride that's packed with commuters on weekday mornings and late afternoons. Vashon is a charming rural area; many residents work in town, but others have found work on the island itself in industries such as ski manufacturing (K2 Corporation), orchid growing, or food processing. ♦ 47th Ave SW and SW Henderson St. 464.6400, 800/542.0810

46 Bakery The Original A working bakery, specializing in gooey cinnamon rolls, birthday cakes, and bread, this place also has a small seating area and serves espresso. ♦ Bakery Tu-Su. 9253 45th Ave SW (at SW Wildwood Pl). 938.5088

47 Georgie Cafe $$ This eatery offers hummus, gyros, and a variety of other Greek and Middle Eastern specialties. Sit in the outdoor dining area above the restaurant on sunny days. ♦ Greek/Middle Eastern ♦ Daily breakfast, lunch, and dinner. 9214 45th Ave SW (at SW Wildwood Pl). 933.8413

48 High Point The highest point in Seattle, this intersection tops off at 518 feet above sea level, higher even than lofty Queen Anne Hill. The views, from Puget Sound to the Olympic Mountains, are expansive. ♦ 35th Ave SW and SW Myrtle St

---

Seattle's location in the Pacific Northwest puts it closer to the Orient than any other port in the Continental United States. It's nearly 300 nautical miles closer to Japan than San Francisco, and 600 miles closer than Los Angeles.

Bests

Greg Kucera
Owner, Greg Kucera Gallery

Spend an intimate, quiet evening dining at **Chez Shea** overlooking **Pike Place Market** and Elliott Bay. It's a small, elegant restaurant with a seasonal prix-fixe menu featuring the kind of dishes one can never talk one's mate into fixing—better to go out and have a romantic candlelit supper.

Other favorite bites to eat include fried calamari at **Adriatica,** overlooking Lake Union; grilled sweet-breads in mustard sauce at **Maximilien-in-the-Market** and pork gypsy at **Labuznik,** both in the **Pike Place Market** area.

My favorite bit of architecture is the old **Federal Court House** at Fifth Avenue and Madison Street. It's a wonderful lesson in rhythm, repetition, and above all else, restraint. A few of the newer buildings could take a lesson.

The best views of the **Space Needle** are experienced while heading south on the Aurora Bridge or east on Olympic Boulevard near **Kinnear Park.** In either instance the top section of the **Space Needle** appears for only a few seconds and, at first glance, looks like an alien spacecraft hovering above the trees; it's a shocking illusion that is scary only the first time and is amusing thereafter. . . depending on the state of your inquiring mind.

Don't miss **Second Avenue,** which has become a "public-art street." Beginning with a view of Jonathan Borofsky's *Hammering Man* at the **Seattle Art Museum** and continuing south on Second Avenue toward **Pioneer Square,** one can see large-scale public sculpture by such notables as Manuel Neri, Isamu Noguchi, Beverly Pepper, and Anne and Patrick Poirier. Other major works by Robert Irwin and Henry Moore are nearby on Third and Fourth Avenues, respectively.

Additional concentrations of public art can be seen in **Seattle Center,** the **Downtown Bus Tunnel** (especially in the **Westlake Station** downtown), the **Washington State Convention and Trade Center,** and **Sea-Tac Airport.** The airport includes large works by luminaries Louise Nevelson, Robert Rauschenberg, Frank Stella, Ross Palmer Beecher, Francis Celentano, Robert Make, and Alden Mason; looking at all the art is a great way to kill time while waiting for a delayed flight.

On the first Thursday of each month, the **Pioneer Square** and downtown galleries open their exhibitions in unison between 6PM and 8PM. While the **First Thursday** gallery walk no longer holds the same thrill for me (I've hosted more than a hundred of them in the past decade), it's a great crowd-pleaser for art collectors and art enthusiasts.

Bushell's Auctions has public auctions every Tuesday of consigned material, mostly furniture and collectibles. The occasional find proves that one person's junk is another's treasure.

Queen Anne/ Magnolia

In 1853 Seattle pioneer Thomas Mercer staked a claim to 320 heavily forested acres on what is now **Queen Anne Hill.** Looking out at **Puget Sound** and the **Olympic Mountains,** you will no doubt understand why Mercer called his new home "Eden." At a dizzying crest elevation of 457 feet above sea level, this is the second-highest point in the city (surpassed only by the intersection of 35th Avenue Southwest and Southwest Myrtle Street in West Seattle, which tops out at 518 feet).

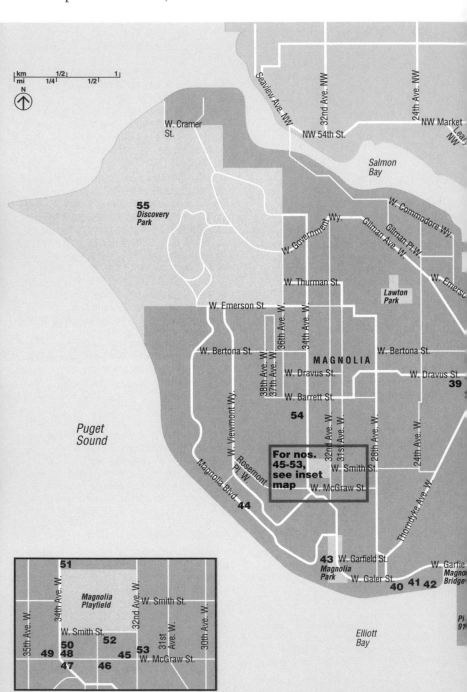

To much of Seattle's old guard, Queen Anne and adjacent Magnolia *did* represent idyllic escapes from the burgeoning city. After First Hill and Capitol Hill were developed, it was to this area that the wealthy retreated, erecting their capitalist castles as the 20th century made its debut. "The Hill," as residents called it, looked down its nose—both literally and figuratively—at the city's center. The exclusive area adopted an air of elegance; so many of the homes on its south flank were designed in an Americanized spin on classic Queen Anne architectural style that by the 1880s the district had been dubbed **Queen Anne Town.** Unfortunately, most of the towered villas that

For nos. 6-34, see pg. 124

inspired this name a century ago are now gone. Many of the other older dwellings have been carved into duplexes and triplexes to make room for the neighborhood's growing population (upwards of 30,000).

Bordered by water on three sides (**Elliott Bay** to the south and west, **Lake Union** to the east, and the **Lake Washington Ship Canal** connecting them), for years Queen Anne managed to maintain the atmosphere of a place set apart. In time it was conquered by cable-car lines and then annexed to the city of Seattle in 1891. Today hideous 500-foot-tall television towers—which, ironically, disturb TV and radio reception in the immediate neighborhood—have been thrust up against the sky here. But still, Queen Anne strives to rise above it all.

Magnolia is even more luxuriously isolated. Connected to Queen Anne and the rest of the city by only three streets and a bridge, this hamlet—named in 1865 after a United States Coast Survey misidentified a stand of madrona trees as magnolias—used to be dominated by single-family houses. Along with the properties bordering **Magnolia Bluff** and the waterfront homes hugging **Perkins Lane**, the area now has many apartment and condo complexes. A clear indication of Magnolia's shifting profile is the main shopping district along **West McGraw Street** between **32nd** and **35th Avenues.** More than half the businesses in "The Village," as Magnolians call the area, have opened since the mid-1980s. Successful thirtysomething couples are moving in, drawn to Magnolia's manageable size (only about 16,000 residents so far), natural beauty, and relative calm.

Queen Anne

1 Kinnear Park This 14-acre park of majestic trees, sloping lawns, and mountain and Puget Sound views was donated to the city by Midwesterner George Kinnear, who visited Seattle in 1874 and invested his money in local real estate. Unfortunately, in addition to natural views, the park also looks down on the Port of Seattle grain terminal, which is second only to the **Kingdome** among Seattle's few real eyesores. ♦ Bounded by W Olympic Pl and W Mercer St, and Eighth and Sixth Aves W

2 Queen Anne Counterbalance The name for the steep ascent on Queen Anne Avenue north of Roy Street dates back to the late 1800s and early streetcar technology. While other Seattle cable-car lines employed conventional underground mechanical power until 1940, the car that ran through these parts was converted in 1900 to draw electricity from overhead wires. But to scale the 20-percent incline of Queen Anne Hill the streetcar needed assistance from a pair of special counterweight arrangements. Here's how it worked: one streetcar could go up the hill and one could go down, each linked via cable to a 16-ton "truck," which ran on tracks through a tunnel beneath the street. As the truck went downhill, it helped pull the heavier streetcar uphill. Going the other direction, the ascending truck restrained the descending streetcar. At eight miles per hour, it was slow going.

In a race up the **Counterbalance** on 5 March 1937, a more modern trackless trolley loaded with 92 passengers "embarrassed the Queen Anne streetcar, making the 2,150-foot hill in less than half the time required by the street car," reported the *Seattle Times* the next morning. The **Counterbalance**'s last two cable cars were retired in 1943, but the pair of tunnels remain in place under Queen Anne Avenue. ♦ Queen Anne Ave N (between N Roy and N Galer Sts)

3 Adriatica Cucina Mediterranea ★★★★$$$ From this immensely popular restaurant's hillside location—you have to climb a couple of flights just to reach the front door—diners can look out over the south end of Lake Union and its twinkling lights after dark. An upstairs bar offers a second level of gorgeous views, and a more casual atmosphere than in the dining room.

The kitchen is the province of talented Nanci Flume, a graduate of **Seattle Central Community College**'s acclaimed culinary-arts program, who plans the menu with the collaboration of co-owner Connie Malevitsis. No one in Seattle makes better fried calamari, and, t entrées, the prawns served on a bed of angel hair pasta with cilantro and roasted-red-pepper cream are wonderful, as are the lamb loin chops. Co-owner Jim Malevitsis, an engaging and gregarious host, is always happy to recommend a wine from his carefully chosen list of fine European and California labels. ◆ Mediterranean ◆ Daily dinner. Reservations recommended. 1107 Dexter Ave N (between N Prospect St and N Highland Dr). 285.5000

4 Latitude 47 The dance floor of this club is small, mirrored, and circled by TV sets playing rock videos. A stop here is often the opening act for an evening's cruise of wilder joints around Belltown or Pioneer Square. Latin salsa cuts in on the Top-40 repertoire on Wednesday and Sunday nights. Like some other Seattle area clubs, this place operates as a restaurant during the earlier hours, serving your basic American food for lunch and dinner daily. ◆ Cover. M-Sa until 1:30AM; Su until 11PM. 1232 Westlake Ave N (between N Mercer and N Garfield Sts). 284.1047

5 Arrowhead Cafe ★$ This triangular cafe blends Southwestern specialties (don't miss the spicy all-beef chili) with classics that have been adapted to the Northwest setting. Anybody for an oyster club sandwich? Accompaniments are sometimes the biggest surprise; a toss of red onions and fruit, for example. ◆ Southwestern ◆ M-F lunch and dinner; Sa-Su breakfast, lunch, and dinner. 1515 Westlake Ave N (at N Garfield St). 283.8768

6 The Williams House $ Doug and Sue Williams are the owners of this charming bed-and-breakfast located in a quiet residential neighborhood on the east side of the hill. It has five spacious guest rooms with private baths; most offer commanding views east and west. A winning sun porch on the first floor faces south. ◆ 1505 Fourth Ave N (at N Galer St). 285.0810

7 Bhy Kracke Park Werner "Bhy" Kracke donated 1.5 acres of his property to the city, along with $20,000 to develop the land as a park, but his casket was closed before the deal was made. In 1970 the city bought the property from Kracke's heirs and named the park in his memory. Visit here for the views, sweeping from Lake Union and the Cascade Mountains to the **Space Needle.** The park is constructed on several levels; follow the winding paved path. You'll feel you've discovered a little gem that most locals don't know exists—and you'll be right. For parking, look for the street sign signaling Comstock Place and Bigelow Avenue North, ignore the Dead End sign, and head east to the three-car parking area just ahead. ◆ Bigelow Ave N and Comstock Pl

8 Queen Anne High School Apartments A successful conversion from institutional to residential, this school closed its doors in 1981 and now has 139 apartments on five floors. Many of the units have expansive views; from a top-floor apartment, for instance, you can see all the way to Canada.

The school was designed in 1909 by **James Stephen,** the accomplished son of a Scottish cabinetmaker, who received his architectural training through a Chicago correspondence course and served as the Seattle School District's resident architect from 1899 to 1908. (He also created **Summit Grade School** on First Hill, **Latona Elementary** and **Interlake School**—now **Wallingford Center**—in Wallingford, and many other educational facilities needed to service the city's growing population during its early boom years.) The building was converted by **Bumgardner Architects,** in 1988 and is still the most visible landmark on the hill, especially when it's lit up at Christmastime. ◆ 201 N Galer St (between Second and Third Aves. N). 285.8800

9 Riddle House Proving the diversity of architectural vision along Highland Drive is this 1893 Queen Anne–Shingle style residence (pictured above), with its colonial allusions and great rounded bows of windows. The designer was **E.W. Houghton,** who 15 years later would put his finishing touches on the ambitious **Moore Theater** downtown. ◆ 153 Highland Dr (at Warren Ave N)

10 Gable House This house of 14 gables was completed in 1905 by Harry Whitney Treat, an investment banker who came to Seattle in 1904. His first act—a confirmation of his wealth and stature—was to commission the firm of **Charles Bebb** and **Leonard L. Mendel** (responsible for downtown's **Hoge Building** and the vast **University Heights Elementary School**) to design a Queen Anne residence that would accommodate his family of four, plus a domestic staff of 14, and would cost exactly $101,000.

Treat kept coaches and horses and a tallyho pulled by blooded steeds purchased from the New York Vanderbilts. Not content with his existing fortune, he bought hundreds of acres just north of Ballard, creating Loyal Heights (named after one of his two daughters) and

Restaurants/Clubs: Red
Shops/ 🌳 Outdoors: Green
Hotels: Blue
Sights/Culture: Black

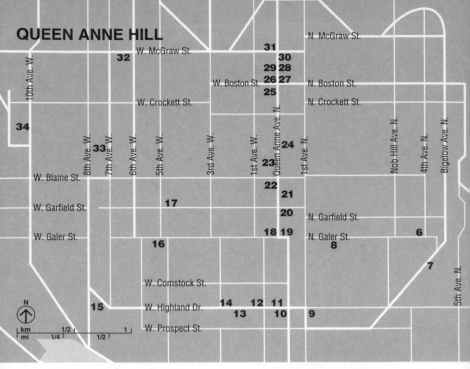

establishing **Golden Gardens Park.** An acquaintance of Colonel William F. "Buffalo Bill" Cody, Treat had Cody's entire Wild West troupe come to Queen Anne Hill to entertain his daughter on her ninth birthday. It was also in this house that Treat and Cody planned the acclaimed Whitney Gallery of Western Art in Cody, Wyoming. Originally, 61 rooms occupied the 18,000 square feet of living space; it now has 15 private residential suites. ◆ 1 W Highland Dr (at Queen Anne Ave N)

11 Highland Drive Heading west from Queen Anne Avenue and about halfway up the hill, this elegant residential street reflects a variety of architectural styles in its mix of mansions and lovely brick apartment houses. For many years, beginning at the turn of the century, Highland Drive was *the* finest address in Seattle. One of the most prominent residents there was Alden J. Blethen, a bombastic former lawyer from Maine who'd entered journalism in the Midwest and lost a fortune there before moving to Seattle in 1896 to found the *Seattle Times.* So proud was Blethen of his pillared manse and the neighborhood in which it sat that for years he paid out of his own pocket to have Highland Drive gaslit every night.

Leisurely strolls are highly recommended along this route; at the end of Highland Drive notice the brick-in-concrete retaining walls at Seventh and Eighth Avenues, designed by W.R.B. Wilcox in 1913. The steps, railings, and lights are all part of the design. ◆ Between Queen Anne Ave N and Seventh Ave W

11 Ballard-Howe Mansion This stately white house, built in 1906, was designed in the Colonial Revival style by **August Heide,** whose larger-scale work can be seen in the **Lowman Building** at Pioneer Place. It now contains apartments. ◆ 22 W Highland Dr (between Queen Anne Ave N and First Ave W)

12 Victoria Apartments Built in 1921, this large, Tudor-style brick apartment building, enclosing a lovely, expansive courtyard, was designed by prolific architect **John Graham Sr.** It was later refurbished as Seattle's first condominium complex. ◆ 100 W Highland Dr (at First Ave W)

13 Kerry Park From this small, rectangular park, views of the **Space Needle,** downtown office spires, and Elliott Bay are stunning, day or night; the sight of Mount Rainier will take your breath away. Also worth appreciating: *Volumetric Space Frame,* a steel sculpture of giant framed holes created by local artist Doris Chase in 1969, and a seemingly out-of-place totem pole across from Kerry Park at 222 West Highland Drive. ◆ 211 W Highland Dr (between Second and Third Aves W)

In 1850 a ship sailing north from San Francisco, the *G.W. Kendall,* entered Puget Sound in the misguided belief that icebergs floated there. The plan was to break down the bergs and use the ice to keep drinks cool in saloons along the Barbary Coast. Instead, the *Kendall* returned home with a load of wood piling.

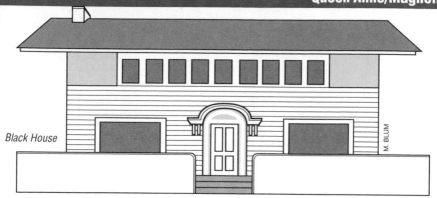

Black House

M. BLUM

14 Black House Architect **Andrew Willatsen,** who worked in **Frank Lloyd Wright**'s Chicago office, designed this precisely lined residence (illustrated above), built in 1912. According to Sally B. Woodbridge and Roger Montgomery in *A Guide to Architecture in Washington State,* the home's "strong Prairie School character is revealed by the low-pitched, broadly overhanging gable roof, the band of second-story windows tied to a belt course, and the large, boldly framed ground-floor windows." ♦ 220 W Highland Dr (at Third Ave W)

15 Betty Bowen Viewpoint Tony Bennett would be the ideal musical accompaniment on a visit to this romantic spot at the end of Highland Drive. From here the views of Puget Sound, the Olympic Mountains, and the dying blaze of sunsets are unrivaled. The overlook was designed in 1977 by **Victor Steinbrueck,** the architect and preservationist who brought the **Space Needle** to concrete reality and fought successfully to save **Pike Place Market.** ♦ Seventh Ave W and W Highland Dr

16 West Queen Anne Elementary School This historic brick structure, with its whimsical medieval hints, was created in 1896 by the Seattle architectural firm of **Skillings and Corner** (responsible also for the **Old Main Building** at Bellingham's **Western Washington University**). It was used as a school until the 1980s, when it was converted into condominiums by local architect **Val Thomas** (who reserved the former gymnasium for himself). The building rests on lovely landscaped grounds in a neighborhood of residential grandeur. ♦ 515 W Galer St (at Fifth Ave W)

17 Queen Anne Branch Library On New Year's Day 1914, this library was opened in a festive celebration attended by more than a thousand people. *Seattle Times* owner Alden J. Blethen had contributed $500 to help buy the land, and the city kicked in the remaining $6,500. Pennsylvania steel-and-iron magnate Andrew Carnegie had donated the money for the building: $32,667. And a couple of heavy

architectural hitters had been brought out to develop the handsome library in a style that might best be labeled English Scholastic Gothic: **W. Marbury Somervell,** who, along with partner **Joseph C. Cote,** already had the **Providence Hospital** in the Central District and the **West Seattle Public Library** on his curriculum vitae; and **Harlan Thomas,** best remembered for downtown's 1924 **Chamber of Commerce** building on Columbia Street.

During the library's first year, it circulated 71,623 books and became an active community center. Interior highlights include small-pane, leaded-glass windows, oak-panel doors with bronze mortise handles and locks, and stained-glass entry windows. In 1978 a vividly colored art-glass mural, created by Seattle artist Richard Spaulding, was hung on the north wall. ♦ M-Th; Sa. 400 W Garfield St (at Fourth Ave W). 386.4227

18 La Tazza di Caffe ★$ Coffee imported from Italy and unusually well-brewed *lattes* pack the patrons in at this handsome coffee bar, which also serves four kinds of *panini* (sandwiches), including the tasty *Fresca:* fresh mozzarella, tomatoes, and fresh basil on focaccia. ♦ Coffeehouse ♦ Daily. 1503 Queen Anne Ave N (at W Galer St). 284.8984

19 Olympia Pizza & Spaghetti House ★$$ There are several branches of this pizzeria around town now, but this one, perched at the top of the **Counterbalance,** was the very first. Choose from 30 pizzas, including the three house specialties: the Spiro (pepperoni, Canadian bacon, shrimp, mushrooms, olives, green peppers, cheese, and tomato sauce), the Olympia (sausage, Canadian bacon, fresh garlic, mushrooms, olives, onions, and fresh or cooked tomatoes), and the House Special (salami, pepperoni, sausage, Canadian bacon, green peppers, olives, cheese, mushrooms, and tomato sauce). Delivery is available, of course. ♦ Pizza/Takeout ♦ Daily. 1500 Queen Anne Ave N (at W Galer St). 285.5550. Also at: 516 15th Ave E (at E Mercer St). 329.4500; 4501 Interlake Ave N (at N 45th St). 633.3655

19 The 5-Spot ★★$ Peter Levy, the high-energy cofounder (with Jeremy Hardy) of Wallingford's attitude-intensive **Beeliner Diner,** has stretched himself here to develop a menu strong on regional American cooking. Some representative dishes: salmon linguine from the Northwest; shrimp enchiladas *con queso* (with cheese) from the Southwest; steaming bowls of smoked chicken and corn chowder à la New England; and, from the heart of Dixie, Hoppin' John (seasoned black-eyed–pea pancakes topped with sour cream and salsa). There's also a dynamite red-flannel hash served for breakfast and a different dinner special every day, dished up from 5PM "till it's gone." Portions are plentiful and the **Counterbalance Room** bar, set off near the kitchen, is a surprisingly peaceful place, rarely crowded. Weekend mornings, there's a line out the door for the dining room. ♦ American ♦ Daily breakfast, lunch, and dinner. 1502 Queen Anne Ave N (between W Galer and W Garfield Sts). 285.7768

20 Pasta Bella ★$$ Owner David Rasti has created a cozy decor in this restaurant, where deep, rich green predominates. A very pleasant deck enhances warm-weather meals (try to ignore the monstrous TV tower next door). *Linguini amatriciana* (fresh tomatoes, pancetta, chili, garlic, and wine), *linguini con vongole* (clams, garlic, wine, butter, and cheese), and *pollo piccata* (breast of chicken with capers, garlic, butter, and wine in a lemon-cream sauce) are highly recommended. The selective wine list is 80 percent Italian. ♦ Italian ♦ Daily lunch and dinner. Reservations recommended. 1530 Queen Anne Ave N (at W Garfield St). 284.9827. Also at: 5909 15th St NW. 789.4933

21 Nelly Stallion For wonderful unconstructed casual garments or designer suits and dresses, visit this specialty womenswear shop. ♦ Daily. 1622 Queen Anne Ave N (between W Blaine and W Garfield Sts). 285.2150

22 Queen Anne Avenue Books Alice Osborne and Randy Brownlee are the founders and owners of this fine small bookstore. It's a general interest store, especially strong on fiction, with a good selection of travel books, magazines, and children's literature as well. ♦ Daily. 1629 Queen Anne Ave N (between W Blaine and W Garfield Sts), Suite 101. 283.5624

22 Herbfarm This is the city outlet for the legendary **Herbfarm's** (see "Eastside Wine Country" section in the "Day Trips" chapter) rural bounty. In addition to culinary herbs and sauces, there are supplies for organic gardening, as well as terrific body oils, lotions and soaps. Information about **Herbfarm** classes and workshops on everything from crafts to herbal medicine is also available here. ♦ Daily. 1629 Queen Anne Ave N (between W Blaine and W Garfield Sts), Suite 102. 284.5667

23 Standard Bakery For a real treat, bite into one of the biggest apple fritters on the planet. This bakery also makes and sells breads, scones, muffins, and made-to-order cakes—all well above standard. ♦ Daily. 1835 Queen Anne Ave N (at W Howe St). 283.6359

24 Queen Anne Thriftway Seattle's first—and many would say its best—upscale supermarket has an espresso counter and flower stand out front, and a car-wash service in the parking lot. Inside, there's everything from an exceptionally good wine department, with depth in European, California, and Northwest labels, to an organic gourmet salad bar. The bakery section features French breads, croissants, and other fresh comestibles from the justly celebrated **Boulangerie** on North 45th Street. The seafood department is likewise estimable, and the staff is helpful and friendly, even at 3AM. ♦ Daily 24 hours. 1908 Queen Anne Ave N (between W Howe and W Crockett Sts). 284.2530

25 Queen Anne Cafe $ Breakfast all day, 11 kinds of burgers, French dip and hot turkey sandwiches, onion rings, and shakes are featured at this hilltop institution. ♦ American ♦ Daily breakfast and lunch. 2121 Queen Anne Ave N (between W Boston and W Crockett Sts). 285.2060

26 Starbucks ★$ Here's yet another outpost of this granddaddy of the coffee revolution in the Northwest. Limited, uncomfortable seating discourages lingering so order your *caffè latte*—make it a *grande*—to go. ♦ Coffeehouse ♦ Daily. 2201 Queen Anne Ave N (at W Boston St). 285.3711

When they were built by the Port of Seattle in 1915, Piers 90 and 91 below Magnolia were the longest earth-filled piers in the world.

Restaurants/Clubs: Red	**Hotels:** Blue
Shops/ ♥ Outdoors: Green	**Sights/Culture:** Bla

26 Teacup Order a cup of tea from the counter at Mary Noe's charming shop, then place your bulk-tea order from a list of more than a hundred selections. She sells fine English marmalades and other imported goodies, too. ♦ Daily. 2207 Queen Anne Ave N (between W Boston and W McGraw Sts). 283.5931

26 McCarthy & Schiering Wine Merchants This is the second location for the friendly and knowledgeable team (the original shop is in Ravenna) who are as attentive to your request for a $10 Chardonnay as they are to someone else's interest in a case of Batard-Montrachet. The owners have built a state-of-the-art wine-cooling room, so you can order a case of Taittinger Blanc de blancs in the morning and pick it up chilled for the evening's dinner party. ♦ Tu-Sa. 2209 Queen Anne Ave N (between W Boston and W McGraw Sts). 282.8500. Also at: 6500 Ravenna Ave NE (at NE 65th St). 524.0999

27 Maybe Monday Caffe ★$ The engaging Emmon Pitaksakpong owns this cheerful place, named after her response to the repeated query: "When are you going to open?" She specializes in good sandwiches and delicious soups. ♦ Deli ♦ Daily breakfast, lunch, and dinner. 10 Boston St (at Queen Anne Ave N). 283.7118

27 Westside Stories This charming small bookstore sells new, used, and rare books in all subjects. While there are good selections in art, history, travel, and biography, the fiction selection is especially good. ♦ Daily. 12 Boston St (between Queen Anne and First Aves N). 285.2665

28 The Broadway Clock Shop Certified master clockmaker Brian Varner moved his business from Capitol Hill some years ago but kept the original store's name. Browsing among the antique wall clocks and wonderful grandfather timepieces is like stepping back in, well, time. ♦ Tu-F noon-6PM; Sa 10AM-3PM; or by appointment. 2214 Queen Anne Ave N (between W Boston and W McGraw Sts). 285.3130

28 Pirosmani ★★$$$; A cozy restaurant in a converted house, the kitchen dishes up Mediterranean-influenced cuisine ranging from the south of France to Tunisia. Food from the Republic of Georgia, a former state of the USSR, is also featured. Located on the Black Sea, Georgia is a southern clime, which is reflected in its cooking—recipes emphasize fresh herbs, as well as plentiful fruits and vegetables. One good example is the *badrijani* appetizer (slivered eggplant wrapped around a puree of walnuts, coriander, and garlic). Combination Georgian/Mediterranean plates are also served. ♦ Georgian/Mediterranean ♦ Tu-Sa dinner. 2220 Queen Anne Ave N (between W Boston and W McGraw Sts). 285.3360

29 Nancy's Sewing Basket Amateur and professional tailors alike will enjoy all the exotic silks, imported cottons, and designer fabrics for sale. There's even a separate **Ribbon Room,** with a sumptuous selection of brocade, embroidered, silk, cotton, and rayon ribbons from whisper-thin to six inches wide. ♦ Daily. 2221 Queen Anne Ave N (between W Boston and W McGraw Sts). 282.9112

30 Ristorante Buongusto ★★$$ Hailing from Naples, the Varchetta brothers, Salvio and Roberto, and Anna, Salvio's wife, operate one of Seattle's favorite Italian restaurants. The space, a former house, is warm and inviting. Dinner highlights include the superb *gamberoni alla brace* (grilled jumbo prawns with garlic, olive oil, parsley, and red pepper), *agnello alla griglia* (grilled lamb chops), and *linguine alla pescatora* (with shellfish and calamari in a fresh tomato sauce). Eggplant parmigiana and panfried calamari lead the list of appetizers. Choose from a strong selection of fine Italian wines. ♦ Italian ♦ Daily lunch and dinner. Reservations recommended. 2232 Queen Anne Ave N (at W McGraw St). 284.9040

31 A&J Meats In addition to the usual meat market offerings, this shop purveys convenient prepared specialties: Bavarian Rouladen (rolled beefsteak stuffed with bacon, Italian salami, mushrooms, and Parmesan cheese), chicken Cordon Bleu, meatballs, chicken puff pastries, and more. There's a variety of fine sausages, too. ♦ Tu-Sa. 2401 Queen Anne Ave (at W McGraw St). 284.3885

In a backlash against the Seattle hype of the 1980s, Emmett Watson, the *Seattle Times*'s longtime columnist and curmudgeon, resorted to half-truths and a few pointed prevarications regarding Seattle's resolute smugness, its notorious rainfall, and its general backwardness. "Plainly," Watson stated, "only a fool would want to live in Seattle, fools like me. . . ."

32 McGraw Street Bakery Jessica Reisman has gone from baking a few batches of her patented mazurka cookies in her apartment to turning out more than 3,500 of them weekly from the brick oven in this storefront. Adapted from a Polish recipe (mazurka is the name of a Polish folk dance), the cookies—crumbly, fruit-filled squares similar to a Linzer torte—are made from all natural ingredients.

Reisman's regular clients include **Nordstrom** espresso carts, some of the city's better supermarkets, and the Eastside's natural-food stores. The bakery also makes cinnamon rolls, blueberry, bran, and apple-cardamom muffins, cookies and brownies, and an outstanding apple-walnut coffee cake. It's a popular neighborhood hangout where regulars linger over a pastry, a cup of good coffee, and the house copy of *The New York Times*. ♦ Daily. 615 W McGraw St (between Sixth and Seventh Aves W). 284.6327

33 Queen Anne Hill Bed & Breakfast $ Mary and Chuck McGrew own this charming B&B situated at the top west side of Queen Anne Hill. There are three guest rooms upstairs, including one with a private deck which affords glorious views of the Olympic Mountains and the sunsets, and another that boasts the place's sole private bath. (The shared bath, however, is big and airy, and has a claw-foot tub.) There are two more bright and cheerful bedrooms downstairs. Common areas include a deck facing west, a cozy living room, and a small sun porch. The lovely English garden is a good place to relax. The full breakfast often includes croissants and quiche. The house is decorated with attractive artwork—from original works to posters. ♦ 1835 Seventh Ave W (at W Howe St). 284.9779

34 Cadiz Espresso ★$ The wall hangings and other art decorating the walls of this intimate coffeehouse are the legacy of owner Jean Villagas's extensive world travels. She believes in expressive art and real espresso; no coffee milk shakes here. The delectable pastries are baked in the neighboring whole-sale bakery, **Sweet Success**. ♦ Coffeehouse ♦ M-F until 1PM, Sa until 3PM. 1905½ 10th Ave W (between W Howe and W Crockett Sts). 282.0779

35 Canlis ★★★$$$$ For almost 50 years Peter Canlis's restaurant—now in the capable hands of his son, Chris—has occupied a commanding position high above Lake Union at the south end of the George Washington (better known as the Aurora) Bridge. And the service is impeccable—from the moment you walk in, you'll be pampered by the kimono-clad waitresses (a **Canlis** tradition).

For an appetizer, try the Dungeness crab legs with mustard sauce and the lobster bisque. The mahimahi broiled over Kiawe wood and the butterfly prawns with pork are highly recommended main courses. The place made its rep as a steak house, and many people think the cuts of beef here are the very best in town. And the ever-popular **Canlis** salad ("with no apologies to Caesar," as the menu says) is prepared at your table; pick up the recipe at the reception desk on your way out. ♦ Steak house ♦ M-Sa dinner. 2576 Aurora Ave N (at the south end of George Washington Memorial Bridge). 283.3313

36 Turret House This arresting residence is a multigabled, cedar-shake structure, complete with solarium, turret, and a widow's walk. In the 1970s this was the home of the commune of the controversial Love Israel Family. It's since been carved up into apartments. ♦ W Halladay St and Sixth Ave W

37 Seventh Church of Christ-Scientist Built in 1926, this impressive, if somewhat squat looking, red tile–roofed structure anchors the northwest corner of Eighth Avenue West and Halladay Street. It was designed in Neo-Byzantine/Early Christian Revival church style by the firm of **Thomas, Grainger & Thomas**, which a few years later created **Harborview Hospital** on First Hill. ♦ 2555 Eighth Ave W (at W Halladay St)

Hoping to shed the raw wooliness of its frontier roots, in 1903 Seattle hired the Olmsted Brothers landscaping firm of Massachusetts to develop a comprehensive city plan. Like their firm's founder, the renowned Frederick Law Olmsted (who designed Boston's park systems and New York's Central Park), Frederick Law Olmsted Jr. and his cousin, John Charles Olmsted, believed that the most beautiful cities integrated natural areas with commercial and residential ones. After surveying Seattle, John explained that one of his principal ideas for the town was to provide a park or playground within a mile of every home. Unfortunately, much of the best land here had already been scooped up by business and industry, and the city had to exercise its broad powers to acquire barely developed or undeveloped land wherever possible.

Magnolia

38 Panda's ★★$ Like its much-praised older sibling in Wedgewood, this restaurant is known for relatively inexpensive, high-quality food, and fast, friendly service. Soup noodles, dumplings, buns, and sauces are made fresh daily. The Orange Beef (tender beef slices with an orange sauce) and Happy Family (stir-fried scallops, shrimp, and breast of chicken) specials are outstanding. Sit at the counter and observe firsthand the kitchen staff's skill. ♦ Chinese/Takeout ♦ Daily lunch and dinner. 1625 W Dravus St (between 15th and 16th Aves W). 283.9030. Also at: 7347 35th St NE (between NE 73rd and NE 74th Sts). 526.5115

39 Romio's Pizza ★$$ One of this chain's five Seattle locations, this joint is just west of **Burlington Northern**'s main railroad yard. It's a popular, busy stop, with a constant stream of deliveries going out the door. While all the pizzas are good, the Zorba (onions, tomatoes, Greek feta cheese, olives, and gyro meat with a housemade yogurt-cucumber sauce), and the GASP (an acronym for garlic, artichoke hearts, sun-dried tomatoes, and pesto) are the most memorable. ♦ Pizza/Takeout ♦ Daily until 11PM. 2001 W Dravus St (between 20th and 21st Aves W). 284.5420. Also at: 8523 Greenwood Ave N (between N 85th and N 86th Sts). 782.9005; 3242 Eastlake Ave E (at Fuhrman Ave E). 322.4453; 917 Howell St (at Ninth Ave). 622.6878; 616 First Ave (between James and Cherry Sts). 621.8500

40 Runions House Built in 1972 on a triangular site, this striking home was designed by Seattle architect **Ralph Anderson.** With its expanse of glass, wide eaves, decks, and fine integration with the natural environment, it represents a late flourishing of what's come to be known as Northwest Style architecture—a regional, mostly residential style that took root in the 1930s. Northwest Style was organic in nature and functional in form, drawing from modernism, common barn design, the early 20th-century Western Stick Style (itself a derivative of florid Victorian architecture), and even Japanese design. **Anderson,** along with Seattleite **Paul Thiry** and Oregon architects **Pietro Belluschi** and **Van Evra Bailey,** helped create the look. ♦ 2587 W Galer St (near 26th Ave W)

41 Elliott Bay Marina This privately owned state-of-the-art marina, located at the base of Magnolia Bluff, can accommodate 1,200 boats. An interesting mix of graceful old boats and sleek new yachts are moored here, some of them one hundred feet long. This is a select sight-seeing spot for all recreational sailors. ♦ 2601 W Marina Pl (at Elliott Bay). 285.4817

At the Elliott Bay Marina:

Palisade ★★$$$ Rich Komen, the man behind Restaurants Unlimited (**Triples, Palomino, Cutters Bayhouse**) never does anything without a splash. And this high-concept, $4-million Polynesian restaurant is no exception. With 13,000 square feet, it seats 300 patrons inside, another 30 out on the deck. The main dining room, designed by interiors architect **Gary Dethlefs,** is a soaring space, complete with an elevated piano trellis and player piano.

To get to the dining room, you cross a 60-foot-long bridge over a 1,000-square-foot pool of seawater filled with Pacific Northwest finfish and shellfish. The 180-degree view spans the Port of Seattle grain terminal, past downtown, across Elliott Bay to West Seattle and Alki Point, and out to Puget Sound and the Olympic Mountains.

Fish, poultry, and meat dishes are prepared here in a variety of ways: from the wood-fired oven, searing grill, wood-fired rotisserie, or apple-wood broiler. Menu highlights include a shellfish chowder, Dungeness crab cakes (listed on the lunch menu only, but ask for them at dinner), wood-oven roasted black tiger prawns, and applewood-grilled salmon (king or silver). ♦ Northwestern ♦ Daily lunch and dinner. Reservations recommended. 285.1000

Maggie Bluffs $ This cafeteria-style restaurant below **Palisade** specializes in pizza, burgers, and breakfasts. Unfortunately, it is almost impossible to escape the TV, but those who want to catch the latest sports scores with their burgers will do well here. ♦ American ♦ M-F lunch and dinner; Sa-Su breakfast, lunch, and dinner. 283.8322

Elliott Bay Yachting Center If you've always wanted to lease a yacht—sail or power, 27 feet to 50 feet—you've come to the right place. Various options are available, starting at $145 a month. Expert instruction is provided when you sign up. ♦ Daily. 285.9499, 800/422.2019 in Washington and Oregon

42 Smith Cove Park On the Elliott Bay waterfront between Pier 91 and the **Elliott Bay Marina,** this small spot of greenery is a fine place to catch sea-level views of the harbor and watch the car-carrying ships docked at Pier 91.

Two men played key roles in establishing this place. The first and more powerful was James J. Hill, of the **Great Northern Railroad.** After Hill muscled his tracks to Seattle in 1893, he constructed giant double docks at Smith Cove to service the steamers *Minnesota* and *Dakota,* which carried silk from the Orient to be loaded onto trains in Seattle and shipped to East Coast markets. It was a lucrative trade until about 1940, when nylon replaced the demand for silk.

Smith Cove was taken over for a time by the US Navy, but the Port of Seattle bought it back in the 1970s and created this park, named for Dr. Henry A. Smith, who arrived from Ohio and built a log cabin here in 1853. A well-liked gentleman farmer, poet, and surgeon, known for anesthetizing patients through hypnotism and promoting the therapeutic use of dream analysis, Smith was King County's first school superintendent and a territorial legislator. He also supposedly translated Duwamish Indian Chief Sealth's famous 1854 caution to invading white men that their day of decline would come as surely as had the Native Americans'—a speech that became controversial in the early 1990s when questions were raised about its authenticity. ♦ 23rd Ave W and W Marina Pl

43 Magnolia Park Take a break, enjoy the breeze and the quiet, and gaze up at the trees or out to the water. This spot is excellent for picnics. Look for a small parking area on the boulevard's west side. ♦ W Garfield St and Magnolia Blvd W

44 Magnolia Boulevard This scenic route west of the Magnolia Bridge (it's called West Galer Street until **Magnolia Park**) is noteworthy for its distinctive madrona trees and views of Puget Sound and the Olympic Mountains. Heading west on the boulevard leads to Seattle's largest park, **Discovery Park.** ♦ Between 32nd Ave W and W Emerson St

45 Magnolia's Bookstore Thanks to owner Molly Cook, this neighborhood has a bookstore to call its own. There's a good selection of general fiction and mysteries, along with travel, self-help, cooking, reference, and other categories. A surprising variety of alternative magazines greets you up front, and more conventional magazines are found in the back of the store. ♦ Daily. 3206 W McGraw St (between 32nd and 33rd Aves W). 283.1062

46 Caffè Appassionato ★$ At this unusually handsome coffeehouse, the beans are roasted on site, so the coffee could hardly be fresher. The eponymously named beans are featured in many Seattle restaurants. *Caffè latti* are consistently tasty, and the pastries, made off premises by a "cottage-industry" baker, are also delicious.

Lightly grilled *panini* (sandwiches)—including a variety with prosciutto, provolone, tomato, and fresh basil served on *schiaciatta* (Tuscany's version of focaccia)—make a satisfying lunch. A second, slightly larger store operates in Bellevue. ♦ Coffeehouse ♦ Daily; F-Sa until 11PM. 3217 W McGraw St (between 32nd and 33rd Aves W). 281.8040. Also at: Bellevue Square (NE Eighth St, between 100th Ave NE and Bellevue Way NE) Bellevue. 450.0886

47 Szmania's ★★★$$$ Thanks to owners Ludger and Julie Szmania, Magnolia finally has a restaurant of the first order. Chef Ludger uses regional ingredients but reveals his German roots in the signature sauerkraut "à la Szmania," with smoked pork loin and homemade sausages. The imaginative dinner menu includes dishes like cinnamon-roasted chicken breast in white Zinfandel sauce and superb grilled prawns with asparagus, olive oil, and basil on linguine. Some regulars opt to sit at the bar with a glass of wine and appetizers (try the blackened scallops and the risotto with mushrooms and asiago cheese). An outside deck, unusual in these wet parts, has been rebuilt and expanded. ♦ German/Northwestern ♦ Tu-F lunch and dinner; Sa-Su dinner. Reservations recommended. 3321 W McGraw St (at 34th Ave W). 284.7305

48 Starbucks ★$ The tentacles of this company reach into every neighborhood. But the *lattes* are dependable. ♦ Coffeehouse ♦ Daily. 3320 W McGraw St (at 34th Ave W). 298.3390

49 Loco Cafe ★$ As the name suggests, there's a friendly, playful attitude about this spot, owned and operated by the youthful team of Brigid McVeigh and Linda Hegg. The customer mix reflects the changing neighborhood, with younger, freer spirits alongside Magnolia's old guard. You can order meat loaf here—*good* meat loaf, too—as well as prime rib, grilled or poached king salmon (with papaya salsa), and a pesto pasta. The tasty omelettes and the three-egg scramblers are served all day. ♦ American ♦ M, Sa-Su breakfast and lunch; Tu-F breakfast, lunch, and dinner. 3416 W McGraw St (between 34th and 35th Aves W). 281.9233

50 Hot Cha Cha Interactive art reaches a boisterous high in this kinetic sculpture, created in 1987 by artist Kenny Schneider and located beside Fire Station No. 41. Seventy-seven identical stainless-steel firefighters, arranged in 11 rows, dance at a speed determined by turning a wheel on the sculpture's side, a peculiar ode to hand-cranked motion pictures of the early 20th century. The piece's name is a humorous allusion both to the movement of the figures and to the working environment of firefighters everywhere. ♦ 34th Ave W and W McGraw St

51 Catherine Blaine Elementary School Built in 1952, this school was designed by Seattle architects **J. Lister Holmes and Associates,** with **Robert Dietz** and **Charles MacDonald.** "An outstanding example of the large public school in the full-fledged post-war Modern idiom," enthuses *A Guide to Architecture in Washington State,* "with natural lighting through sawtooth skylights, antiglare ceiling baffles, window walls, and modular construction." ♦ 2550 34th Ave W (between W Smith and Raye Sts)

52 Eleganza Ltd. Despite its obscure location on an alleylike street, this nationally known porcelain gallery and importer of fine statuary is worth a visit. ♦ Daily; irregular hours on Saturday, call ahead. 3217 W Smith St (between 32nd and 33rd Aves W). 283.0609

53 Village Pub ★$ Popular for lunch, this friendly public house draws all segments of the Magnolia community: long- and short-termers, old and young, well-to-do and just barely squeaking by. Though known for its juicy hamburgers and "snowshoe fries" (huge, wide, and flat), the kitchen also turns out good fish-and-chips. ♦ American ♦ M-Sa lunch and dinner; bar until midnight. 2410 32nd Ave W (at W McGraw St). 285.9756

54 Magnolia Library Designed by Seattle architect **Paul Kirk,** this handsome modern institution occupies three lots acquired from the Catholic Diocese. **Kirk** used weathered cedar shingles and large plate-glass windows to "bring the beauty of the outside inside." Clerestory windows face north to admit the best light for reading. Even the furniture is noteworthy: hand-crafted solid walnut chairs and tables made by Pennsylvania artist George Nakashima. Outside, a bronze sculpture by Glen Alps graces the courtyard wall; inside, you'll find a fused-glass screen by Steven Fuller, and two ceramic sculptures by Ebba Rapp McLauchlan.

The building was dedicated in 1964, and two years later won awards from the American Institute of Architecture, the National Book Committee, and the American Library Association. Despite those laurels, the library has not won unanimous neighborhood approval; occasional complaints about the "raw shingles" and "big, bare windows" can still be heard. ♦ M-Th; Sa. 2801 34th Ave W (near W Barrett St). 386.4225

55 Discovery Park When Captain George Vancouver was exploring Puget Sound in 1792, he reportedly anchored nearby; the park is named after his ship, the *Discovery*. This is the largest park in Seattle, comprising 527 acres of richly varied terrain—woods, bluffs, beach, meadows, and trails. The farthest link in the 20-mile string of Frederick L. Olmsted's planned parklands was built north and west from **Seward Park** on Lake Washington during the early 20th century; it is a haven for Seattleites desperate to escape urban forests of concrete and steel.

Walking or jogging along the 2.5-mile loop trail will take you through a quiet forest, across colorful meadows, and up to windy bluffs with panoramic views west to the sound and mountains. Follow signs for trails to the beach. Bald eagles are a common sight here (you'll know where they are by the crowds of people milling about with their faces craned to the sky). In 1982 a cougar also turned up in the park; mercifully, restraint and sensitivity prevailed, and the creature was captured without harm. Picnic possibilities are endless and playing fields abound. ♦ Bounded by W Cramer and W Emerson Sts, and 36th Ave W and Puget Sound). 386.4236

Within Discovery Park:

Daybreak Star Indian Cultural Center Built in 1977 on a piece of parkland leased for 99 years to the United Indians of All Tribes Foundation, this dramatic timbered building was designed by **Arai Jackson** in collaboration with **Lawney Reyes.** The place is filled with interesting works of art by Native American artists including: John J. Hoover's carved polychromed cedar panel, *Ancestor Spirit Boards; Buffalo Hunt,* a ceramic-tile mural by Glenn LaFontaine; and Marvin Oliver's painted and carved fir tree, *Raven/Eagle and Bear.* There's also a small gallery of rotating Native American art, and the center sponsors a variety of Native American activities. Energetic children will delight in the well-equipped playground, and everyone will enjoy relaxing at the picnic tables and savoring the spectacular view. ♦ W-Su. 285.4425

A C-700 seaplane carried the first international airmail from Vancouver, British Columbia, to Seattle's Lake Union on 3 March 1919. Eddie Hubbard was the pilot. His only passenger was aircraft company founder William E. Boeing, Sr.

Restaurants/Clubs: Red		**Hotels:** Blue
Shops/ 🌳 **Outdoors:** Green		**Sights/Culture:** Black

Ballard

Located north of the **Lake Washington Ship Canal** and extending west to **Puget Sound**, Ballard was once home to a settlement of Shilshole Indians. (*Shilshole*, meaning "tuck away a bit" in the Salish dialect, aptly describes old Ballard's protected position on **Salmon Bay**.) Concealed from raiding parties, the village's location served the natives well, and their population grew to about 1,000. But Ballard was eventually discovered and repeatedly attacked by northern tribes. By the beginning of the 19th century, the population of the village had dwindled to a mere dozen families. Enter Ira Wilcox Utter, who in 1852 filed a claim to become the first white settler at Salmon Bay, then an area of pristine beauty, with a virgin forest of giant thousand-year-old cedars. By 1870, 50 to 100 white settlers had staked claims in the area; before the decade was over, the logging of the bay's shore—which was to change this place forever—had begun.

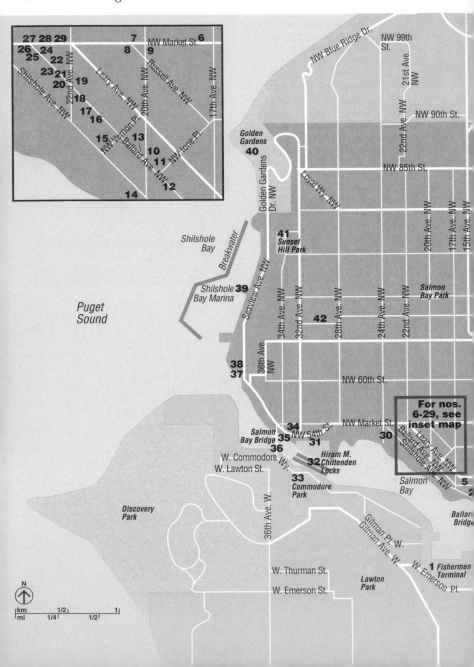

n 1890, with a population of 1,636, Ballard was the first community to ncorporate as a city after Washington became the 42nd state. It started out s an industrial city with a predominantly Scandinavian population, boasting ive shingle mills, three sawmills, a sash-and-door factory, a steel- and iron-vorks, a boiler works, three shipyards, a blacksmith shop, and a booming aloon district to service all of the workers. The sawmills provided much of he wood used to rebuild Seattle after the devastating fire of 1889. The mills louded the skies with a blizzard of what was termed "Ballard snow"—air)ollution dense enough to produce a "vast wall of smoke which makes an mpenetrable barrier between the city and Salmon Bay," in the words of one rustrated photographer.

'he waterfront was equally bustling: Salmon Bay had become a harbor for log hipping, the commercial fishing fleet brought in tons of halibut, salmon, ind cod, and oceangoing ships docked at nearby shipyards for hull repairs.

(Today it's still home to one of the largest fishing fleets in the world.)

By 1906 Ballard had more than 10,000 residents and was the seventh-largest town in the state. Such rapid growth brought inevitable problems, none more urgent than finding an adequate water supply. Annexation to the city of Seattle, which was eager to expand northward, became a hot topic. After a bitter, divisive battle, the citizens of Ballard narrowly approved the merger.

Separated geographically from the main body of Seattle, Ballard continues to exist very much as a small town within larger metropolitan boundaries. The community has managed to maintain its historic character while gentrifying its older sections. Young professionals are moving in, attracted to the abbreviated skyline, classic main street, unpretentious style, and reasonably priced housing. They describe their neighbors in the most generous of terms. "A typical native Ballardite," says one, "is a down-to-earth sort of person, careful with money but generous with friendship."

1 **Fishermen's Terminal** Owned and operated by the Port of Seattle since 1913, this terminal, located at the south end of the Ballard Bridge on Salmon Bay, is home base to more than 700 commercial fishing vessels, ranging in length from 30 to 300 feet. Here are the trollers, gillnetters, seiners, longliners, crabbers, and trawlers that make up the North Pacific fleet, one of the largest commercial fishing fleets in the world. Every year, Washington fishers harvest 2.3 billion

pounds of fish and other seafood, more than half the total edible catch in the United States. The huge factory trawlers that moor at the terminal—some as long as a football field—catch 85 percent of the bottom fish taken in US waters. The moorage provides not only a good location for sightseers and photographers but opportunities to buy whole fish right off the boat. Take a peek at the bulletin board inside, advertising everything from Puget Sound seine permits to all manner of ships for sale, for a glimpse into the world of commercial fishing. ♦ 3919 18th Ave W (off W Emerson Pl). 728.3395

At Fishermen's Terminal:

Chinook's ★★$$ As you might expect, fresh Northwest seafood is featured—as is a wall-to-wall view of the fishing boats—at this popular addition to the **Anthony's Homeport** restaurant fleet (see page 139). The grilled Copper River salmon (seasonal) is superb, and the mussels are fresh and flavorful. ♦ Seafood ♦ M-F lunch and dinner; Sa-Su breakfast, lunch, and dinner. Reservations recommended. 283.4665

Bay Cafe $ Specialties of the house include a three-egg omelette of havarti cheese, bacon, fresh mushrooms, onion, and green pepper; and the grilled Alaskan halibut. If you're seated at a window booth, you'll be close enough to the fishing boats to read their registration numbers. ♦ American ♦ Daily breakfast and lunch. 282.3435

Wild Salmon From Alaskan king salmon to Dungeness crab, the catch is always the freshest at David Leong's superb seafood market. One of the best in Seattle, this place will also ship anywhere in the US. The canned tuna here will make you forget all about the stuff you buy in the super-market. ♦ Daily. 283.3366

E.F. Kirsten Tobacconist Get a world-renowned Kirsten pipe and choose from a broad selection of pipe tobaccos, including the unusual Mariner's Mixture and Dutch

Harbor Blend. The cigar humidor is as big as a walk-in closet. You'll also find a serious selection of knives, card decks, and flasks. ♦ M-Sa. 286.0851

Seattle Ship Clothing The heavy-duty outdoor gear sold here is designed for professional fishers. The Stormy Seas Clothing line was developed by commercial fisherman Michael Jackson after he had been swept overboard in Alaska's Bering Sea. ♦ M-Sa. 283.0830

Seattle Fishermen's Memorial The gathering point for the ceremonial blessing of the fleet, held annually in May, this memorial (pictured at left) was created by Seattle sculptor Ron Petty in honor of the 400 Seattle fishers lost at sea during this century; their names are inscribed on a plaque at the base. Dedicated 8 October 1988, the memorial is a bronze-and-concrete sculpture, with a variety of North Pacific marine life sculpted at the base and a lone bronze fisherman perched at the top.

2 **Mike's Chili Parlor** ★$ This little, red-brick place looks like a diner you'd see somewhere along Route 66. Mike Semandaris started out here in 1933 with a sidewalk stand and the popular tavern is still owned by the Semandaris family. The chili—beans on the side for nonpurists—is still good. The eatery was a featured location in filmmaker Bud Yorkin's 1985 movie *Twice in a Lifetime*. ♦ American ♦ M-Sa lunch and dinner. 1447 NW Ballard Way (at 15th Ave NW). 782.2808

3 **Bardahl Manufacturing Corp.** Manufacturers of the best-selling motor-oil additive Bardahl, this company was founded in 1939 by Ole Bardahl, a native of Norway. By 1952 the company was an industry leader in automotive and industrial additives. Today, it produces more than 100 oil and fuel additives, which are sold in 80 countries. The company's hydroplane, *Miss Bardahl,* has won five gold cups and six national championships, and has set numerous world records. The gigantic sign—"ADD BARDAHL OIL"—clearly visible from the Ballard Bridge, announces the company's location (and stature). ♦ 1400 NW 52nd St (at 14th Ave NW). 783.4851

4 **Le Gourmand** ★★★$$$ One of the city's finest French restaurants, this intimate dining spot is located in a nondescript building at the eastern edge of Ballard. Ingredients are fresh and the menu is limited so owner/chef Bruce Naftaly's kitchen can concentrate on—and unfailingly deliver—excellence. Roast duckling with black currant sauce and sautéed rabbit with chanterelles are a pair of aces in a deck of kings. The wine list is as selective as the menu items—and just as good. ♦ French ♦ W-Sa dinner. Reservations recommended. 425 NW Market St (at Sixth Ave NW). 784.3463.

Seattle Fishermen's Memorial

M. BLUM

5 St. Charles Hotel When it was built in 1902, this place, with its projecting bays and 100 feet of building frontage, was an imposing presence in early Ballard. Now painted an appalling lavender, the building is home to Ballard Mini Storage. ♦ 4714 Ballard Ave NW (near NW 48th St)

6 The Old Pequliar Ale House The only thing peculiar about this place is the spelling of its moniker. Before it went *veddy veddy* British, it was known as the **Valhalla Tavern**—a tad more in keeping with Ballard's Scandinavian heritage. There is a good selection of Northwest brews on tap. ♦ Daily. 1722 NW Market St (between 17th and 20th Aves NW). 782.8886

7 Carnegie Library Raised in 1904 with a $15,000 grant from the Andrew Carnegie Foundation, this was the first Carnegie library built in King County. (A total of 10 were eventually erected in the Seattle area.) The structure was designed by local architect **Henderson Ryan,** and it served bookish Ballardites for nearly 60 years, until it was replaced by a new and much less interesting facility in 1963. Today, it hosts a nondescript mall filled with antiques vendors and a law firm. ♦ 2026 NW Market St (near 20th Ave NW)

8 Old Ballard Firehouse Built in 1908, **Firehouse No. 18** was designed by the successful Seattle partnership of **Charles Bebb** and **Leonard L. Mendel.** It served Ballard for 62 years before being replaced in the early 1970s by a new station just a few blocks away. Now a hot spot on the Ballard nightclub scene, this is a big space, with lots of room for dancing to the blues, country, reggae, and rock bands that play here nightly. You can also grab lunch or dinner; the kitchen features Italian fare. ♦ Cover. Daily until midnight. 5429 Russell Ave NW (at NW Market St). 784.3516

9 Andre's Pizza ★★$$ The eponymous Andre is Andre Goldberg, a professional baker trained in his native France, who's been turning out superb pizza for years in an unassuming brick building just big enough for himself, his equipment, and a countertop; the food is takeout only. The pizza dough could very well be the best in town, and the toppings—you name the combos—include pesto, sun-dried tomatoes, and sausage made on the premises. ♦ Pizza/Takeout ♦ Tu-Sa. 5402 20th Ave NW (at Russell Ave NW). 783.0479

10 Cors and Wegener Building Once the grandest edifice in town, it had an elegant wine room on the ground floor in the 1890s and early 1900s, and the *Ballard News* occupied the second floor for years. One of the first of the city's old buildings to be renovated, it now has apartments on the top floor and offices along the street level. ♦ 5000-5004 20th Ave NW (at Ballard Ave NW)

11 Conor Byrne's Soccer Stadium This traditional Irish pub features the requisite dark-wood bar, stained-glass lamps, and brick walls. There's live contemporary music Friday and Saturday nights at 9PM and traditional Irish music on Sunday afternoons. ♦ Cover. Daily until 2AM. 5140 Ballard Ave NW (off 20th Ave NW). 784.3640

12 Ballard Avenue Named a Historic Landmark District in 1976, this seven-block stretch—slanting southeast off Market Street toward Salmon Bay—represents the heart, if not also the soul, of Ballard. It contains many of the community's oldest buildings (and newest businesses). The majority went up between 1890 and 1930: brick, stone, and stucco constructions of no more than two or three stories in height. Thanks to a shift of commercial development north to Market Street in the 1930s, these buildings were still sitting here, just waiting to be revitalized, in the 1970s. Pick up a Historic Ballard Avenue Walking Tour brochure, available from most avenue merchants. The **Ballard Historical Society** (784.3086) also conducts guided excursions, sometimes with docents in 1890s attire; call for schedules and reservations; donation requested. ♦ Between 17th and 24th Aves NW

13 The Junction Block Built in the late 1890s, this was once a three-story structure (now it's two), complete with elaborate turret, and one of the largest brick buildings on Ballard Avenue. It was a gathering place for locals, who held meetings and dances here. Today, the edifice is home to a community arts center which offers classes in printmaking, painting, and watercolor. ♦ 5202-5210 Ballard Ave NW (at 20th Ave NW)

14 Salmon Bay Cafe ★$ Hearty breakfasts draw a devoted clientele every morning and a lined-up-out-the-door crowd on weekends. Among the many egg dishes, the Ballard omelette—bacon, cream cheese, green onion, tomato—and the crab, shrimp, and green onion omelette topped with hollandaise stand out. You can also get eggs with Polish or Italian sausage or steak. A side order of the huge french fries is a satisfying meal in itself. ♦ American ♦ Daily breakfast and lunch. 5109 Shilshole Ave NW (at 20th Ave NW). 782.5539

Sam Spade may be San Francisco's most famous fictional private eye, but he got his start elsewhere. In Dashiell Hammett's renowned novel *The Maltese Falcon,* Spade explains that in 1927 "I was with one of the big detective agencies in Seattle."

Restaurants/Clubs: Red   **Hotels:** Blue
Shops/ 🌳 **Outdoors:** Green   **Sights/Culture:** Black

15 C.D. Stimson Company Charles D. Stimson, the one-armed scion of a wealthy Michigan lumber family, arrived in Seattle just in time to help fight the Great Fire of 1889. When the nascent milling industry moved from what's now Pioneer Square north to Lake Union and Ballard, Stimson went with it and founded the huge Stimson Mill Company. This surprisingly modest single-story dark brick building was designed in 1913 in a modern English style by noted Spokane architect **Kirtland K. Cutter** (who also created the **Rainier Club** in downtown). It still houses the Stimson offices, although that company is no longer in the lumber business. The combination of declining markets and escalating tariffs sent Ballard's shinglemaking industry into a tailspin in the early 20th century and eventually forced the mill to close. The Stimson operation now leases commercial real estate in the Seattle metropolitan area and operates a pleasure-boat marina on Salmon Bay. ♦ 2116 NW Vernon Pl (at Shilshole Ave NW)

16 Cafe Illiterati ★$ Bobby Beeman's refreshingly idiosyncratic restaurant serves such specialties as hearty beef, chicken, and veggie dinner pies; baked tomatoes stuffed with ricotta and spinach; grilled pork sandwiches with provolone cheese, red onions, and roasted peppers; bread pudding French toast; and cappuccino eggs—three eggs steamed using the steam wand on an espresso machine, with fresh herbs and cheese. The deck out back, cats and all, is a most salutary place for weekend brunch. ♦ American ♦ Daily breakfast and lunch. 5327 Ballard Ave NW (between NW Vernon Pl and 22nd Ave NW). 782.0191

17 Jay White Law Offices This wood-frame structure is a combination of two pre-1890 houses, looking much like those that lined Ballard Avenue around 1900. In 1976 the Historic Seattle Society rescued the buildings from development in the International District and moved them to their present location. A bordello reportedly occupied the houses in their first lives. ♦ 5341 Ballard Ave NW (near 22nd Ave NW)

18 Guitar Emporium Owner Robb Eagle's merchandise ranges from fine inexpensive imported instruments to handmade acoustic masterpieces. He'll also recommend instructors—and offer encouragement—to would-be Segovias. ♦ Tu-Sa. 5349 Ballard Ave NW (at 22nd Ave NW). 783.7607

19 Sunset Building This three-story brick-veneer construction, with arched windows and decorative cornice work, was built in 1901. In the 1940s a local public market occupied the street level. The residential **Sunset Hotel** still takes up the upper floors. ♦ 5400-5404 22nd Ave NW (at Ballard Ave NW)

Within the Sunset Building:

Jones Brothers Meats Carnivores can buy everything from a 35-pound "pork package" (pork chops, ham, bacon, sausage, spareribs) to a side of beef—anywhere from 250 to 400 pounds—at this butcher shop. ♦ M-F. 5404 22nd Ave NW (at Ballard Ave NW). 783.1258

20 Portland Building Erected in 1901, this two-story brick pile was home to various well-established businesses—**Cascade Drug** and **J.C. Penney** among them—before Ballard's commercial district moved to Market Street. Taverns anchored the corner storefront for 40 years until its renovation in 1985. Now, a seafood trading company, picture frame shop and hair salon occupy the ground floor; there are studio apartments upstairs. ♦ 5403 Ballard Ave NW (at 22nd Ave NW)

21 Ballard Centennial Bell Tower Ballard **City Hall** (pictured above), built in 1899, stood proudly on this corner for more than 60 years. The three-story structure, one of the first on Ballard Avenue, included the usual administrative warrens and a jail, community meeting rooms and, on the top floor, a dance hall. There was also a bell tower, whose occupant—a 1,000-pound brass noisemaker—was saved when the building was torn down in 1965 after extensive earthquake damage. Thanks to efforts by former state senator Ted Peterson, who grew up hearing the bell, it has been returned to its original site and is now housed in a copper-capped cylindrical obelisk designed by architect **Thom Graham**. ♦ 22nd and Ballard Aves NW

22 Julia's Park Place ★★$$ Julia Miller, a social worker turned restaurateur, and her boatbuilder husband, David, own this handsome, spacious eatery that turns out well-prepared natural foods. Salads are very good, especially the signature "Julia's Caesar," and the nutburgers (made of ground nuts) are surprisingly tasty. Penn Cove mussels and pasta, seafood marinara, and peppercorn steak top the dinner selections.

Dishes can be overpriced, but it is still one of Seattle's most popular breakfast stops, especially on weekends, when you may have to cool your heels in line for some time. If and when you finally get in, try the whole-wheat pancakes with blueberries and pure maple syrup. Pick up a peanut-butter-and-mocha cookie at the espresso counter to go with your requisite *caffè latte*. ◆ Natural ◆ M breakfast and lunch; Tu-Su breakfast, lunch, and dinner. 5410 Ballard Ave NW (near 22nd Ave NW). 783.2033. Also at: 4401 Wallingford Ave N (at N 44th St) 633.1175.

23 Burk's Cafe ★$$ The joys of gumbo and crayfish (in season) await at Terry Burkhardt's lively cafe. Spicy sausages, catfish, and exceptional pecan pie are likewise memorable draws. Try the mild pickled okra—there's a jar of it on every table. The building, erected in 1891 to house a tavern, was remodeled in 1968 to revive its wooden-frame origins. A serene fenced courtyard buffers the dining room from the sidewalk. ◆ Creole/Cajun ◆ Tu-Sa lunch and dinner. 5411 Ballard Ave NW (near 22nd Ave NW). 782.0091

24 Ballard Computer One of the largest computer retailers on the West Coast, this store sells laptops, PCs, notebooks, printers, software, books, cables and switch boxes, memory boards, templates, dust covers, and...well, you get the idea—the price list is 36 pages long. Salespeople are knowledge-able and welcome questions, even over the phone. The service department is in a separate building. ◆ Daily. 5424 Ballard Ave NW (between 22nd Ave NW and NW Market St). 781.7000

25 Ballard Smoke Shop $ It's not a smoke shop at all (although it is smoky inside) but a simple, old-fashioned restaurant (with a separate entrance to the bar), where you can still get an eight-ounce New York steak for $10. Built in 1903, this is one of the last frame structures left from Ballard's early days. Remodeled in the 1920s, it is now Spanish-style white stucco with a red-tile roof. ◆ American ◆ Daily breakfast, lunch, and dinner. 5443 Ballard Ave NW (between 22nd Ave NW and NW Market St). 784.6611

26 Scandie's at Ballard $$ This may be the only restaurant left in Ballard that specializes in Scandinavian cuisine. Look for such delicacies as *kokt torsk* (poached cod) and *friskadeller* (Swedish meatballs). ◆ Scandinavian ◆ M-W lunch; Th-Su lunch and dinner; Sa-Su breakfast, lunch, and dinner. 2301 NW Market St (at Ballard Ave NW). 783.5080

27 Olsen's Scandinavian Foods Everything from *rullepøise* (lamb sandwich meat) to *kransekake* (marzipan cake) can be found here. Erik Olsen took over from his parents Reidar and Ebba, who ran the shop for more than 20 years, and continues a line of homemade specialties, including outstanding lamb sausage, fish cakes, fish loaf, and smoked salmon. There are also imported foods, such as dry soups from Norway, Swedish peas, and cloudberries. ◆ Daily. 2248 NW Market St (between 22nd and 24th Aves NW). 783.8288

28 American Eagles Inc. A paradise for serious hobbyists, this store packs in precisely detailed train sets and models of virtually every airplane that's ever caught an updraft. ◆ M-Sa. 2220 NW Market St (between 22nd and 24th Aves NW). 782.8448

29 Ballard Building This four-story Second Renaissance Revival edifice—representing the only large-scale use of terra-cotta in Ballard—was erected in the early 1920s by the Fraternal Order of Eagles. Ballard's community hospital occupied the second floor from 1928 to 1954, with doctors' offices on the third floor. The second level now contains offices of the *Ballard News-Tribune*. ◆ 2208 NW Market St (at 22nd Ave NW)

Within the Ballard Building:

The Backstage A showcase venue for national acts, this basement club features live blues, rock, jazz, and folk. Get here early for a good seat. ◆ Cover. Th-Sa (call ahead for other nights); box office: M-F. 781.2805, box office 789.1184

Lombardi's Cucina ★$$ The former home of **Lafferty's Drugstore and Soda Fountain** (which moved—sans soda fountain, alas—to 5312 17th Avenue NW), this place serves such honest Italian cuisine as *gamberoni di scampi* (shrimp sautéed with garlic, capers, red pepper, white wine, and lemon juice). There's a select list of good Italian wines, moderately priced, and pleasant outdoor seating in warm weather. ◆ Italian ◆ M-F lunch and dinner; Sa-Su breakfast, lunch, and dinner. 783.0055

30 Yankee Diner ★$$ This location on the Salmon Bay waterfront is the third Seattle venue for the chain. Emphasizing home-style cooking, the dinner menu features meat loaf, breaded veal cutlets, chicken-fried steak, Yankee pot roast, and roast turkey. Fresh seafood and daily breakfast specials are available, too. ◆ American ◆ M-Sa breakfast, lunch, and dinner; Su breakfast and dinner. 5300 24th Ave NW (off NW Market St). 783.1964. Also at: 1645 140th Ave NE (at Bel-Red Rd), Bellevue. 643.1558; 4010 196th Ave SW (at 40th Ave W), Lynnwood. 775.5485

31 LockSpot Cafe & Tavern You can't miss this place, sitting at the eastern edge of the Chittenden Locks, with its sign boasting the "World's Best Fish and Chips." The claim is open to

debate, but the restaurant does have a long history here; it opened in the early 1930s to take advantage of traffic at the locks and along Seaview Avenue. There's a convenient take-out window. ◆ Seafood/Takeout ◆ Daily breakfast, lunch, and dinner. 3005 NW 54th St (off NW Market St and 32nd Ave NW). 789.4865

32 Hiram M. Chittenden Locks Completed in 1917, after decades of indecisiveness, legal delays, and government red tape, the eight-mile-long Lake Washington Ship Canal—winding through the Ballard, Fremont, Wallingford, University, and Montlake districts—is a protected route connecting the saltwater of Puget Sound and Shilshole Bay with the higher-elevation freshwater of Salmon Bay, Lake Union, and Lake Washington. Attended by much fanfare, the locks were officially opened two months after completion of the canal, on 4 July, when the *Roosevelt*, flagship of Admiral Robert Edwin Peary's North Pole expedition, led a procession of ships through the canal. In 1956 the locks were named for Major Hiram M. Chittenden, who, as Seattle's district engineer of the Army Corps of Engineers from 1906 to 1908, had chosen and designed the site for this project. (Lock buildings, however, were created by renowned Seattle architect **Carl Gould**.)

In an average year, 100,000 commercial and pleasure craft, and two million tons of cargo and logs pass through the locks. People line up on weekend afternoons to watch the regatta rise and fall. The shorter of the two locks—150 feet long and 28 feet wide, with a wall 42 feet high—is used for small pleasure boats; larger vessels are "locked" through the bigger portal: 825 feet by 80 feet, with a 55-foot-high wall. Depending on tides and lake levels, the lift varies from 6 feet to 26 feet. ◆ Visitors' Center: daily 10AM-7PM; guided tours: daily 1PM and 3:30PM. 3015 NW 54th St (off NW Market St and 32nd Ave NW). 783.7059

At the Hiram M. Chittenden Locks:

Fish Ladder In 1976 this $2.3-million, 21-level fish ladder—connected by walkways to the locks—was opened on the south shore of the canal adjacent to **Commodore Park.** More than a half-million salmon, steelhead, and trout scale the ladder annually, bound for spawning areas in the Cascade range. You can watch (and even cheer on) their progress from an interior viewing port. In the mid-1980s sea lions, recognizing a feast when they smelled one, caused quite a stir with their extended stay near the fish ladder. Officials were determined to send them packing, and locals were equally determined that the creatures—known collectively as Herschel—not be harmed. After defeating a number of human (and humane) efforts to discourage them, Herschel was sent to California; undaunted, some of the sea lions turned right around and swam back home to Seattle. ◆ South shore

Carl S. English Jr. Ornamental Gardens These lovely seven acres of lawn, trees, shrubs, and flowers—a thousand plant species in all, including palm trees—were developed from a handful of plantings in 1916. A fine spot for picnicking, the gardens are named for the man who, as head of the Corps of Engineers' gardening staff, spent 34 years cultivating them. ◆ South shore

33 Commodore Park Across the locks in the Magnolia neighborhood, this aptly named park is a secluded spot for picnicking underneath the trees while watching boats cruise by. ◆ W Commodore Way and 33rd Ave W (nearGilman Ave W)

34 Totem House $ Originally opened in 1937 as an Indian artifact shop, the building that houses this restaurant is a replica of an Indian *haiat* house (resting place). It became a fish-and-chips place during World War II, and that dish is still a specialty here, as is the homemade clam chowder. ◆ Seafood ◆ Daily lunch and dinner. 3058 NW 54th St (at 32nd Ave NW). 784.2300

35 Hiram's At The Locks ★★$$ This restaurant overlooking the ship canal gives you a front-row seat for the passing boat parade. The kitchen uses grain-fed Midwestern beef for its top sirloin and filet mignon steaks. Seafood specialties include mesquite-grilled king salmon, Dungeness crab-shrimp-scallop cakes with a delicious roasted-red-pepper sauce, and a zesty pesto salmon sandwich. A lavish Sunday brunch, popular with locals, includes many kinds of fresh fruit, grilled or chilled salmon, made-to-order pasta dishes and omelettes, and a weight-watcher's nightmare—a dessert buffet. In warm weather the patio is a favorite spot for after-work drinks. The corrugated metal building was designed in 1977 by **Barnett Schorr & Co.,** which also refurbished the **Legislative Building** in Olympia. ◆ American ◆ M-Sa lunch and dinner; Su brunch and dinner. Reservations recommended. 5300 34th Ave NW (near 32nd Ave NW). 784.1733

36 Salmon Bay Bridge Built in 1914 by the **Great Northern Railroad** (now **Burlington Northern**) to limit congestion along the Ballard waterfront and to handle the boat traffic from the locks, this imposing bascule bridge can be raised quickly to allow passage for big ships (and high-masted sailboats). Normally suspended, the bridge is lowered only for approaching trains. ♦ Just west of Hiram M. Chittenden Locks and Commodore Park

37 Ray's Boathouse ★★★$$ Begun in 1946 as a coffee shop at a charter-fishing boat dock, this place has passed through several incarnations on its way to becoming one of Seattle's best—some say *the* best—seafood restaurants. The kitchen makes good use of fresh regional ingredients and, thanks to executive chef Wayne Ludvigsen, both the steamed clams and the pasta with smoked salmon have won raves from food critics. So popular is the main-floor restaurant that you may want to head upstairs to the less-pricey, blond-wood-and-glass cafe level with a similar, but smaller, menu. Both floors have views of the water, the Olympic Mountains, and tremendous sunsets. ♦ Seafood ♦ Daily lunch and dinner. Reservations recommended. 6049 Seaview Ave NW (on Shilshole Bay). 789.3770

38 Anthony's Homeport ★★$$; With its waterfront location and plentiful outdoor seating, this restaurant is a great place for views of Puget Sound and the Olympic Mountains, especially radiant at sunset. Fresh seafood is the order of the day, with cioppino a particular palate-pleaser. ♦ Seafood ♦ M-Sa lunch and dinner; Su brunch and dinner. Reservations recommended. 6135 Seaview Ave NW (on Shilshole Bay). 783.0780. Also at: Des Moines Marina, Des Moines. 824.1947; Edmonds Marina, Edmonds. 771.4400; Homeport Marina, Kirkland. 822.0225

39 Shilshole Bay Marina In 1950 the waterfront at Shilshole was not a pretty sight, what with its derelict ferry dock, scattered boathouses, vacant, untended land, a shipyard in decline, and what one writer derisively described as an "expanse of beach with a perimeter road that kept slipping off into the water." Today, after a 30-year effort to build a breakwater (completed in the early 1980s), the marina is the preferred moorage of Seattle's sailboat fleet; the waiting list to win berth space there is a mile long. The boat ramp is a terrific place to waste an afternoon watching boat owners curse their craft onto or off of trailers. ♦ 7001 Seaview Ave NW (on Shilshole Bay). 728.3385

Within the Shilshole Bay Marina:

Charlie's Bar & Grill $ Come early for a quiet waterfront breakfast, or enjoy a late afternoon drink while gazing at the sailboats and the sunset. ♦ American ♦ M-F lunch and dinner; Sa-Su dinner. 783.8338

Sharky's Beach Bar Dancing is the main attraction here, with traditional rock 'n' roll bands mounting the stage five nights a week. ♦ Cover. Tu-Sa 3PM-2AM; live music starts at 9:30PM. 784.5850

Wind Works Take a basic sailing course or (if you've passed the official qualifying course) rent a sailboat from this enterprise, one of Seattle's leading big-boat sailing schools. The instructors, friendly and helpful, all US Coast Guard–licensed captains, teach on 28-foot to 54-foot crafts. ♦ Daily; but call ahead. 784.9386

40 Golden Gardens Harry Whitney Treat, a New York investments mogul and real-estate mover, established this park soon after he moved to Seattle in 1904. Treat even built a special trolley line (the fare: 3¢) from downtown Ballard, which was later incorporated into the Seattle transit system. Much of this 95-acre reserve is covered in woods and scratched with trails, but it is always the expanse of beach north of the marina—where Ballard families used to camp for weeks at a time during the summer—that receives the most attention. It's perfect for beachcombing, walking, or just looking out to Puget Sound and breathing in what is arguably this city's freshest air. Windsurfers test their mettle nearby, in part because the sound is warmer than Lake Washington during the wintertime. Be warned, however, that hardly anyone else would call this water warm; it's only for the hardy.

Lawrence Beck's enamel and welded-steel sculpture, *Atala Kivlicktwok Okitun Dukik (The Golden Money Moon),* is at the park's south end. ♦ North of Seaview Ave NW at NW 80th St, to NW 95th St

41 Sunset Hill Park From here, high above Golden Gardens, the unobstructed view is, in a word, spectacular. ♦ NW 75th St and 34th Ave NW

42 Nordic Heritage Museum Founded in 1979, this is the only museum in the United States that covers all five Scandinavian countries: Denmark, Finland, Iceland, Norway, and Sweden. Its emphasis is on the Nordic people who settled in the Pacific Northwest. Permanent exhibits include *Promise of the Northwest,* which describes life in early Washington, and *Ballard Story,* a richly detailed history of the community. The museum also offers Scandinavian language classes, lectures, and films, and sponsors ethnic festivals. ♦ Admission; discount for children. Tu-Su. 3014 NW 67th St (between 28th and 32nd Aves NW). 789.5707

Restaurants/Clubs: Red	**Hotels:** Blue
Shops/ 🌳 Outdoors: Green	**Sights/Culture:** Black

Selling Seafood by the Seashore

When it comes to supplying savory salmon and other seafood delectables, Seattle is not only Washington's largest seaport, but Alaska's as well. The salmon, halibut, and sablefish caught in Alaskan waters generally pass through this city to be processed or shipped to international markets. Seattle also has easy access to seafood from all around Washington state: mussels from **Penn Cove** on **Whidbey Island,** pink swimming scallops from the **San Juan Islands,** octopus from **Puget Sound,** Pacific oysters from the Hood Canal and Willapa Bay, Olympia and Kumamoto oysters from southern Puget Sound, and Dungeness crab from offshore waters. Oysters and salmon are the big favorites here, and there are so many species of each of these available—all with different flavors and textures—that it can easily boggle the mind of the average landlubber. Here's a reference guide to the local catch.

 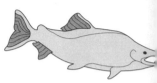

Oysters

Four varieties of oysters are commonly found in Seattle-area restaurants and seafood markets, from the native Olympia to the often pricey European Flat. In general, these oysters are in season from late October through May or June—as long as the Puget Sound waters remain cold. Oysters prepare to spawn and turn milky and soft during warm weather, which is why they are usually not at their best during the summer months (but that's all right, since summertime is when salmon is most abundant in local waters). They're all best served raw on the half-shell.

European Flat Oyster Often erroneously called "belon," after the most famous French beds of this delectable mollusk, they have a delicate yet satisfying flavor. Primarily raised in the pristine waters off San Juan Island (especially in Westcott Bay), supplies are limited and often more expensive than the other varieties raised hereabouts, so feast on them whenever they are available. (Some Seattle restaurants serve a related oyster, the Chiloë, in midsummer when local oysters are out of season.)

Kumamoto Oyster Deeply cupped, thus better preserving their tasty juices, the Kumamotos have a complex and subtle flavor. At their best they surpass the renowned Olympia oyster.

Olympia Oyster The tiny Olympia oysters' superb taste—one reason for their scarcity—more than compensates for their drab exterior. This is the Northwest's only native oyster; all other species were first raised from spawn shipped in from Asia or Europe.

Pacific Oyster Seattle's primary commercial variety is a plump, lusciously flavored bivalve, originally imported from Japan but now ubiquitous in Washington's inland waters. Fatter than other shellfish, they have a rich, satisfying flavor that's excellent raw or cooked. Pacific oysters are often named after the areas they're grown in, such as Samish Bay, Hood Canal, Shoalwater Bay, and Skookum Inlet.

Salmon

There are five species of salmon caught in Seattle's local waters. The earliest to migrate are the spring salmon, which are also the last to spawn. Sockeyes run in August, silver salmon in August and September, pinks in summer, and chums in fall. These dates are important to know, because most local salmon are caught just before they enter the rivers to spawn. Since it's often difficult to tell salmon apart in the markets, a few identification tips may prove helpful:

Chum Salmon They're similar in shape to silver salmon but have a more deeply forked tail with a rounded slender base. Sometimes sold as "silverbrite," chum is low in oil and should be grilled or smoked. Don't miss the superb chum salmon caviar served at **Ray's Boathouse** (6049 Seaview Ave NW, on Shilshole Bay, 789.3770).

Pink Salmon Large oval spots on the tail and back and small scales are the predominant features of these fish. Pink salmon get their name from the color of their flesh, which is low in oil (they're delicious when smoked).

Silver Salmon Also known as "coho," they have dark spots on the back and upper tail, and are smaller and more slender than spring salmon. Silvers are commonly featured on local menus, since they are farmed in Washington and caught in the wild. Farmed silver salmon are smaller than others but are still very flavorful, and they're especially good served with sauces made from fresh, tart berries.

Spring Salmon These fish, also called "chinook" or "king," have gray or brown spots on the upper body, tailfin, and head (other salmon don't have spotted heads). The flesh is rich in oil and often deep red in color, but it may be white or even streaked with white, red, and pink (particularly in the rainbow king variety). Whatever the color, spring salmon make for great eating.

Sockeye Salmon The bodies are slender, with a few tiny specks on the back but none of the spots found on other salmon. These are the oiliest and most richly flavored of salmon. Their flesh is deep red.

onsider yourself lucky if you find Fraser River
ockeyes in a Seattle seafood market; they're
rought in from British Columbia.

Vhen buying salmon look for fish with red gills, a
omplete coat of scales, and bright, unclouded eyes.
o avoid buying fish that has turned sour, smell the
tomach cavity. The flesh should be firm, glossy,
rightly colored, and resilient to the touch (meaning
our finger shouldn't leave an impression when you
oke it). Atlantic and silver salmon can be farmed,
ut try to buy wild fish whenever possible for their
uperior texture and flavor. **University Seafood &
oultry** (1317 NE 47th St, 632.3900) and **Mutual
ish Company** (2335 Rainier Ave S, 322.4368)
ell the best seafood in town.

If you prefer to have your oysters shucked by a
professional or want to have the catch of the day
cleaned and cooked for you, Seattle offers a wide
assortment of first-rate seafood restaurants. For
example, **Elliott's Oyster House & Seafood
Restaurant** (Pier 56, off Alaskan Way, 623.4340)
on the Waterfront is renowned for its oysters on
the half-shell. **Ray's Boathouse** on Shilshole Bay
specializes in salmon dishes, while its neighbor,
Anthony's Homeport (6135 Seaview Ave NW, on
Shilshole Bay, 783.0780), features a superbly rich
Yukon River king salmon in the spring. And for
salmon and pasta entrées, don't miss **Saleh al Lago**
(6804 E Green Lake Way N, between First and
Second Aves NE, 522.7943) at Green Lake.

Bests

awrence Kreisman
uthor, *Art Deco Seattle*

ly favorite places are the outstanding pre-1930
uildings in Seattle's downtown and some of its
arks and boulevards, proposed by the Olmsted
rothers in the first decade of the century:

orthern Life Tower (now called the **Seattle Tower**)
a wonderful 1928 Art Deco skyscraper by
lbertson, Richardson, and Wilson. It's a mountain
f multicolored brick over a steel frame, with terra-
otta trim recalling the snowcapped peaks of Mount
ainier. Three stylized evergreen trees crown the
ower. Be sure to see the extraordinary lobby. The
rnamentation was inspired by Northwest Coast
dian art and by the Chinese, Japanese, Hawaiian,
nd Maya cultures, which were associated with trade
utes along the Pacific Rim.

he **Artic Club Dome Room** in the **Arctic Building**
as built in 1916 for a private club and is now owned
nd used by the City of Seattle. The club's former
ning room is a great opalescent glass-domed space
ch with Renaissance plasterwork that represents
uits and vegetables. Note the great terra-cotta
alrus heads on the exterior of the building.

ioneer Building in **Pioneer Square.** Many are
miliar with the exterior of this brick and stone
omanesque building, but few venture past the
ntrance and up to the first floor. Here, this 1890
kyscraper" opens up into two light-filled
ourtyards that rise six floors to a skylit roof.

he **Stimson-Green Mansion** is not open to the
eneral public but is accessible by appointment
uring business hours. This home is a beautifully
eserved 1901 English-style manor house
esigned by **Kirtland Cutter.**

or students of the American Arts and Crafts
ovement, a visit to the **Sorrento Hotel** lobby will
ward you with a fine Rookwood tile fireplace. Or
op by the **John Leary House** (now the Episcopal
ocese headquarters) on 10th Avenue East just
rth of **St. Mark's Cathedral.** The Rookwood tile
eplaces and bathroom wall tiles here are
onderful, as is the Renaissance great hall. The
ffany glass windows that originally hung in this

hall are now on display in the **Burke Museum** on
the **University of Washington** campus.

The Suzzallo Library at the center of the **University
of Washington**'s **North and South Quadrangles** was
modeled after King's College Chapel at Cambridge,
England, and a peek into the main reading room on
the second floor is a must. The **North Quadrangle**
becomes a sea of cherry blossoms during late
February or early March.

One of my favorite drives is through the **Washington
Park Arboretum** south of the **University of
Washington** and along **Lake Washington Boulevard,**
which borders **Lake Washington,** all the way south
to **Seward Park.** En route, stop a while for a walk
through the **Japanese Tea Garden** or **Azalea Way**
in the arboretum. Drive into the residential
neighborhood of **Washington Park** to experience
the cathedral-like canopy of American elm trees
along 36th Avenue. This street and the chestnut-lined
boulevard of 17th Avenue Northeast just north of the
university campus, known as **Greek Row,** are two of
Seattle's loveliest tree-lined streets.

Another outstanding city drive is the **Kerry
Viewpoint** on West Highland Drive, with **Mount
Rainier** as its backdrop. It is worth walking farther
west past the early Seattle mansions. Then, around
Seventh Avenue West the road turns north. Newly
repaired balusters and reconstructed lighting
fixtures frame views of **Puget Sound** and the **Olympic
Mountains.** The stairways and concrete retaining
walls that comprise this portion of the boulevard
are themselves works of art.

"Seattle is an old gold-mining stopover peopled
by too many boring Canadians to have any real
style. . . . The personality is that of a Boeing
engineer—a guy who still wears wide-wale
corduroy pants and a pullover sweater. . . .
I suppose I might be missing the charm of the
area, whatever it is. I say this because Seattle
dwellers always talk about going back as if the
burg were some sort of Mecca. The stay-put
locals seem content enough in their pretty little
environment. There must be drugs in the water."

San Francisco Examiner

Fremont/Wallingford

The two neighborhoods to the north and west of **Lake Union** were once suburban, but today Fremont and Wallingford are about as citified as they can get without actually having high-rises in their midst. In fact, Fremont is home to one of the city's most popular public works of art, *Waiting for the Interurban,* a sculpture reflecting that ultimate urban experience—public transportation. Both areas are filled with funky shops, friendly taverns, and inexpensive restaurants, and teem with traffic. (In a tizzy over parking congestion caused by Wallingford's popularity, residents have won restrictions that make it near impossible to park within a quarter-mile of a given destination on a Friday or Saturday night.)

Fremont was originally a mill town, plotted first as the **Denny-Hoyt Addition** in 1888, where sawmills operated until 1932. Wallingford was stitched together from the rural communities of **Latona** and **Edgewater**—an area that once supported dairies, a furrier, and a candy store that made Easter eggs to order. In 1907 the Seattle Gas Company plant opened on Lake Union and transformed Wallingford into a working-class district showered with sparks and soot from the burning of coal. The gasworks shut down in 1956, and 25 years later were transformed in the high-tech **Gas Works Park**.

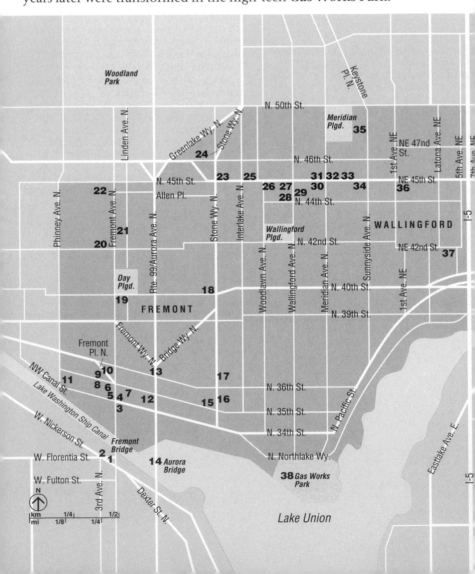

oday both neighborhoods come across as confident and cool, almost folksy, ut they have a history of protest and civic activism, as well: Fremont eclared itself one of the city's earliest Nuclear-Free Zones—no nuclear waste r power plants here, and Wallingforders have rallied variously against the attle of streetcars along **North 45th Street**, seaplane noise from the nearby ake, and garbage dumping; they've even succeeded in prohibiting IcDonald's from raising a set of golden arches at its local franchise. During ne 1960s and early 1970s, as the whole city went through some trying conomic times, these districts became somewhat shabby. But as the Seattle eal estate market began to boom in the 1980s, there was renewed interest in he ungentrified character found in this part of town. Many of the original omes built here were vacation cottages of the gable-and-shingle design so opular at the turn of the century; bungalows are still this neighborhood's uintessential digs, but those that once cost $1,000 are now considered a argain at $150,000 or more. And while there are still many older single- imily homes, many have been made over into apartments and duplexes for owntown commuters who can reach their offices in 20 minutes or less.

Fremont

1 318 Tavern $ You may find yourself seduced by the barbecued beef sandwich or beef stew, but your heart will long be faithful to the big, sloppy cheeseburgers and long, slender fries served here. Burgers made this place what it is—a narrow, dark, often crowded joint where patrons are known to insult duded-up business folks; the hired help can be surly too. ♦ American ♦ M-Sa lunch and dinner. 318 W Nickerson St (at the Fremont Bridge). 285.9763

2 Ponti Seafood Grill ★★$$$ The location—right on the south lip of the Lake Washington Ship Canal, with a direct watch on the tiny blue-and-orange Fremont Bridge—cries out for a restaurant with big windows. And that's exactly what owners Jim and Connie Malevitsis (also of **Adriatica**) and Richard and Sharon Malia (ex-**Malia's Northwest**) created in this upscale establishment. Chef Alvin Binuya offers wonderfully fresh seafood salads, and the dishes are often influenced by Mediterranean or Asian cooking styles. One gripe is the stingy portion sizes of the appetizers; a serving of peppered tuna, for instance, could hardly satisfy a squirrel, much less a hungry human. The wine list is on the expensive side, and service can be slow when the house is packed. In summer ask for seating on the porch, where the views compensate for the restaurant's few

deficiencies. ♦ Northwestern/Seafood ♦ M-Sa lunch and dinner; Su brunch and dinner. Reservations recommended. 3014 Third Ave N (at W Nickerson St). 284.3000

3 Waiting for the Interurban Created by Richard Beyer, this sculpture portrays a motley clutch of people anticipating the approach of a bus or train or some other public transportation. Installed in 1978, *Interurban* has become the most popular work of art in Seattle, a cast-aluminum tableau decorated appreciatively through the seasons by "Fremonsters" who enjoy its gentle reflection of everyday life. Beyer, who has lived in Seattle since 1957, is also responsible for a number of other art pieces around town, including the wooden *Sasquatch* at **Pike Place Market** and *The Itinerant*, which portrays a newspaper-draped man sleeping on a bench in Capitol Hill's Broadway district. ♦ Fremont Ave N and N 34th St

4 Frank and Dunya Here's the place to shop for outrageous and colorful home furnishings and accessories. Canines are popular motifs in the statuary, jewelry, and hangings, but so are other members of the wild kingdom—a two-legged drinking cup painted like a cow, or a huge green frog perfect for mounting on your dining room wall. ♦ Daily. 3418 Fremont Ave N (between N 34th and N 35th Sts). 547.6760

The Puget Sound Council of Governments predicts that between 1988 and the year 2000 about $500-million worth of gasoline will be wasted by vehicles waiting on crowded roadways in the central Puget Sound region.

Restaurants/Clubs: Red   **Hotels:** Blue
Shops/ 🌳 Outdoors: Green   **Sights/Culture:** Black

4 The Daily Planet Fremont has a rep as the North End's vintage and retro capital, thanks to places such as this one, dense with old lamps, fans, hats, clocks, mirrors, globes, and even a motorbike or two. ◆ Daily. 3416 Fremont Ave N (between N 34th and N 35th Sts). 633.0895

5 Red Door Ale House One of several upscale groggeries in Fremont, this is the neighborhood's best-known and most crowded after-work hangout. (Don't even *try* to get in on a Friday night.) The least claustrophobic seating can be found on a small back deck. Inside, try for a bar seat—no easy task. Twenty-two beers are on tap, and there's a small menu which is strongest on steamed mussels, burgers, and french fries. ◆ Daily until 2AM. 3401 Fremont Ave N (at N 34th St). 547.7521

5 Fremont Sunday Market On Sundays a parking lot behind the **Red Door Ale House** fills up with vendors of jewelry, pottery, produce, and hot dogs. In classically lowbrow Fremont fashion, there are also people here selling recycled castoffs—old radios and books, used videotapes, clothes, shoes, and lamps. Musicians provide entertainment, as do the shoppers themselves, a cross section of hippie holdouts and slumming stockbrokers. ◆ Su May-Dec. 670 N 34th St (at Fremont Ave N)

6 Fremont Antiques Mall The entrance is at street level, but the goods—collectible toys and appliances, along with some larger antique furniture—are in the basement of this mall, built in 1901. Take a nostalgic browse. ◆ Daily. 3419 Fremont Pl N (between N 34th and N 35th Sts). 548.9140

6 Fritzi Ritz A Marlene Dietrich fantasy of a vintage store where you'll find feathered boas and sequined dresses on display. Well-preserved wing-tip shoes and fedoras wait for Fred Astaire to waltz through the door. ◆ Daily. 3425 Fremont Pl N (at N 35th St). 633.0929

6 Simply Desserts Some of the baked delights you've enjoyed at several of the more upscale movie theaters around town can now be savored with a cup of espresso from this dinky outlet store. The white-chocolate strawberry cake is outstanding. ◆ Daily; F-Sa until 11:30PM. 3421 Fremont Ave N (at N 35th St). 633.2671

6 Fremont Place Book Company For a small shop, this general bookstore carries a lot of feminist and ecological titles, as well as a good selection of regional literature. ◆ Daily. 621 N 35th St (at Fremont Pl N). 547.5970

7 Still Life in Fremont ★$ This unpretentious coffeehouse once epitomized the hippie attitude of Fremont. But hey, the 1960s are over and the place is rapidly earning anachronism status. It continues to serve some of the better cafe grub in town: pasta specials are usually terrific, soups are chunky and sandwiches are thick and savory. The sidewalk seating is pleasant—much better than enduring the interior stagnation in summer. And it's a quiet spot for coffee drinking. There is jazz or folk music some Thursday nights from 8PM to 10PM. ◆ Vegetarian ◆ Daily breakfast, lunch, and dinner. 709 N 35th St (between Fremont and Aurora Aves N). 547.9850

8 Guess Where There's something classy about this retro resource—from the winged cherubs that decorate the front windows to the statuary that looks as if it's waiting to decorate some dear departed's grave. Take a look at the wide array of vintage men's shoes and suits, now back in style. ◆ Daily. 615 N 35th St (between Fremont and Evanston Ave N). 547.3793

8 Yoohoo $ Tables are covered in comic-book collages, the lights appear to be crafted from bulbs and old pizza trays, drinks are squeezed from fresh fruit, and calzones or waffles prove satisfying and filling. Wear a black outfit and cat's-eye sunglasses to dine here. ◆ Vegetarian ◆ Daily breakfast and lunch. 607 N 35th St (between Fremont and Evanston Aves N). 633.3760

9 Triangle Tavern ★★$ Some of the ancient pensioners who knew this place as the **Classic** (and still weave in here on occasion) may have trouble getting used to its new look. Odd-shaped tiles crawl up the support pillars; old phones dangle from the walls; the dining room ceiling has an earthquake-distressed look. It's a hip spin on the traditional tavern—"Cheers" by way of MTV. Lots of finger foods are featured on the typo-pocked menu, leaping from mediocre burgers to delightful two-person pizzas with soft crusts and a spinach lasagna layered with roasted-red-pepper pasta. There's a cold Oriental noodle pork plate and a vegetarian Middle Eastern plate. *Bruschettas du jour* (spicy Italian bread baked with different toppings) should be ordered straightaway, as they're invariably satisfying. Salads, including the Caesar, make a lesser showing. The broad pick of beers specializes in West Coast craft varieties. ◆ American ◆ Daily lunch and dinner; bar until 2AM. 3507 Fremont Pl (at N 35th St). 632.0880

10 Deluxe Junk A stock of mid-20th century clothing (which rotates seasonally), furniture, housewares, and stacks of kitschy doodads are all on display in a onetime funeral parlor. ♦ Daily. 3518 Fremont Pl N (between Fremont and Evanston Aves N). 634.2733

11 The Redhook Ale Brewery Seattle's first microbrewery has an unusual setting: Fremont's 1905 Seattle Electric Company streetcar barn. Trolleys used to roll out of this building on their various routes, but when the city converted to trackless trolleys in 1940, the barn went first to the US Army for use as a wartime warehouse and later to a garbage company. Redhook owners Paul Shipman and Gordon Bowker ultimately bought the barn and commissioned architect **Skip Satterwhite** to turn it into their new brewery, and the beer started rolling in 1988. ♦ Free. Daily one-hour tours; call for times. 3400 Phinney Ave N (at N 34th St). 548.8000

Within the Redhook Ale Brewery:

Trolleyman Pub As expected, all Redhook brews are on tap at this tavern, from the ESB (extra special bitter) to the Blackhook porter and the seasonal Winterhook Christmas Ale. It's a bit harshly decorated for a pub—all white walls and neatly arranged tables—but it has cozy elements too, like a good-sized fireplace and a piano. The snack menu is small, highlighted by black-bean burritos served with two cheeses, sour cream, and salsa. ♦ M-Sa until midnight; Su until 7PM. 548.8000

12 Fremont Public Library This was the last of 10 Carnegie-financed libraries raised in the Seattle area during the early 20th century. Money for construction—$35,000—had been promised from the Carnegie Corporation in 1917, but work didn't get underway until after World War I, and the library didn't open until 1921. **Daniel R. Huntington,** for many years Seattle's city architect, designed this excellent neighborhood library in an echo of California Mission style. ♦ M-Sa. 731 N 35th St (between Fremont and Aurora Aves N). 684.4084

13 Fremont Troll Come face to face with a Brothers Grimm nightmare: the crook-nosed, long-haired, malevolent looking troll that hides beneath the north end of the Aurora Bridge. Constructed in 1990 of ferroconcrete, with a real Volkswagen Bug squeezed in its left hand, the 18-foot-high sculpture was a whimsical community project from the Fremont Arts Council, built with money from the Seattle Neighborhood Matching Funds Program. Adults and children seem equally ready to climb all over it. ♦ Heading east on N 34th St, turn left up the hill under the Aurora Bridge

14 Aurora Bridge Nobody uses its proper name—George Washington Memorial Bridge—and most don't even know it. (The bridge's 1932 dedication to the first US President can only be found on a plaque at its south end, not on regular city maps.) And sometimes this span is referred to as Suicide Bridge because of the number of people (an average of three per year) who leap from its 135-foot height into Lake Union below. The sidewalk across is narrow; walk at your own risk and never on rainy days, when taking a bath in your clothes would leave you less soaked than the speeding traffic does. ♦ Aurora Ave N (over Lake Union)

15 Pacific Inn Although this pub is pocket-sized, it has disproportionately large windows and assertively spiced fish-and-chips. There are 10 microbrews on tap, and espresso drinks are also served. ♦ Daily until 2AM. 3501 Stone Way N (at N 35th St). 547.2967

16 Archie McPhee's This is *the* place to shop for Halloween creepy crawlies or wacko party favors—there are hundreds of spiders, fish, rubber slugs, and similar creatures here. The owner, Mark Pahlow, is a natural-history buff and a stickler for anatomical correctness in his plastic wildlife. Apparently he's had some trouble convincing manufacturers to produce cockroaches that look exactly like they do in real life! An adjacent espresso stop, the **Tacky Tiki Hut,** provides refreshments. ♦ Daily. 3510 Stone Way N (between N 35th and N 36th Sts). 547.2467

17 Stone Way Cafe ★$ Don't expect any "heart smart" entrées at this restaurant. Do anticipate outstanding plates of biscuits and gravy or corned-beef hash, not to mention weighty, onion-slathered hamburgers and omelettes stuffed shamelessly with meats and cheeses. Owner Charlene Iverson usually has a few healthful soups cooking (don't miss the vegetable or navy-bean varieties), and there are always muffins on hand. Expect to wait in line on weekends. ♦ American ♦ Daily breakfast and lunch. 3620 Stone Way N (just north of N 36th St). 547.9958

"They're backpacky, but nice."

The New Yorker, in a cartoon about residents of Seattle

18 Pizzeria Pagliacci ★$ There are four sit-down restaurants of this name scattered across Seattle, but this branch is takeout or delivery only. Pizza Centioli features an extra-thin crust coated with olive oil, fresh garlic, peppers, and mozzarella and fontina cheeses. The South Philly is topped with Italian sausage, mushrooms, and onions. And if somebody asks you whether you'd like to buy the Brooklyn Bridge (pepperoni, Italian sausage, mushrooms, black olives, and green peppers), by all means say yes. Calzones and pasta are also on the menu. ♦ Pizza/Takeout ♦ Daily. 4003 Stone Way N (at N 40th St). 632.1058. Also at: 4529 University Way NE (between NE 45th and NE 46th Sts. 632.0421; 426 Broadway Ave E (at E Republican St). 324.0730; 550 Queen Anne Ave N (at W Mercer St). 285.1232

19 B.F. Day Elementary School While other classic Seattle schools have been torn down or closed, this brick structure was restored to return to the grandeur it enjoyed at its 1892 dedication. Originally designed by **John B. Parkinson**, this is the city's oldest school in continuous operation. Its history predates the building: Classes were held in private homes for some years before this edifice was built. ♦ 3921 Linden Ave N (at N 40th St)

20 Buckaroo Tavern Most of the motorcycles have disappeared from out front, and there are more young white-collar businesspeople in the crowd, but the "Fabulous Buckaroo" has hardly lapsed into respectability. Billiard balls still crack against one another, voices rise in cursing contraltos, and nimbuses of cigarette and cigar smoke loom over the knife-scarred booths in the back. It is still possible to disappear here, to sink your elbows into the bar and drink beer for hours without anyone disturbing you.

Founded in 1938, the establishment has so far warded off the forces of civil gentrification that prey so merrily on Fremont. The food—burgers, thick potato wedges, steaming bowls of chili mountained with cheddar and onions—hasn't yet become "cuisine." Distinctly nongourmet hot dogs go for 25¢ apiece on Monday nights from 6PM until they run out. Twenty tap beers, many of them microbrews, can be had, too. ♦ Daily until 2AM. 4201 Fremont Ave N (at N 42nd St). 634.3161

21 Swingside Cafe ★$ This small, divided, and low-ceilinged dining room, fielded with baseball paraphernalia, is best enjoyed with one close friend (who isn't averse to repeatir sentences several times to be heard above the din). Come in the morning, when you can linger over delicious *huevos rancheros* o buckwheat pancakes, generous helpings of toast, and black coffee that hasn't been adulterated by Seattle's espresso militancy. Omelettes are whipped together in several worthy variations, but the best usually appea on the specials board; try the spicy Cajun wit sausage, chicken, and prawns. Lunch turns t barbecued chicken and sandwiches, and dinners built around pastas. Expect a line at the door but the wait is worthwhile. ♦ Mediterranean ♦ Daily breakfast, lunch, an dinner. 4262 Fremont Ave N (between N 42n and N 43rd Sts). 633.4057

22 City Cafe $ Situated in a corner of a mode apartment building, this cafe is a handsome and convivial spot. Expect generously sized coffee drinks, muffins, and sandwiches or soup at lunch. Dawdling is encouraged, and there are copies of *Vanity Fair* and the local dailies conveniently strewn around. ♦ Coffeehouse ♦ M-Sa. 4459 Fremont Ave N (between N 44th and N 45th Sts). 633.2139

Wallingford

23 Blue Star Cafe & Pub ★★$ The interior of this tavern/restaurant, with its rich wood booths and a handsome mirrored bar, is quite tasteful, and the cuisine matches the decor. Chef Greg Tushar's combination soups are usually delicious, even if they sound egregiously chichi (yam, pear, and cinnamon, for example). The roasted lamb and garlic sandwich, skillet-fried chicken with mashed potatoes, and Caesar salad are all excellent choices; burgers, however, are merely passable. Save room for the peanut butter ice-cream pie drizzled with chocolate sauce and nuts—merely sniffing it increases your belt size. For smaller appetites, there a half-orders of fettuccine Alfredo or the fine black-bean chili, both with salad. Eighteen beers, mostly microbrews, are on tap, but the alehouse atmosphere is disrupted by a blanket no-smoking policy, even at the bar. ♦ American/Continental ♦ Daily dinner; bar until 2AM. 4512 Stone Way N (between N 45th and N 46th Sts). 548.0345

24 Sorel's ★$ This place is one of the neighborhood's friendliest coffee stops. Espresso drinks are rich and poured large, perhaps to match the size of the danishes a scrumptious apple fritters sold here. Severa types of sandwiches can be ordered at lunc but try the thick chili and the soups instead. warm weather take your coffee and the pape to the outside deck. Service is excellent. ♦ Coffeehouse ♦ Daily. 4613 Stone Way N (between N 46th and N 47th Sts). 547.7835

Restaurants/Clubs: Red   **Hotels:** Blue
Shops/ ♀ Outdoors: Green   **Sights/Culture:** Black

Grave Matters

Like any town worth its salt—not to mention its weight in garlic cloves and silver bullets—Seattle boasts a host of ghost stories. Here are some of the more popular tales of ghoulish gallivantings:

Pike Place Market—normally as crowded and cheery as can be—seems to have more than its share of active ectoplasm. One legend involves the ghost of a 300-pound woman who, apparently during the market's more rickety days, fell through a ceiling there and landed on a table. Another is told about the spirit of an elderly Native American woman. Those who have seen her say she's stocky, beatific, and wrinkled. She wears a quilted shawl and her hair hangs in two long braids; she carries a couple of baskets and appears only in the evening, when the market is closing. By the way, it's believed that anyone who spots this Indian matron will die an unusual death, so watch out.

The nearby **Butterworth Building,** halfway between Virginia and Stewart Streets on First Avenue, was constructed in 1903. The builder was one of Seattle's best-known morticians, Edgar Ray Butterworth, which may help explain the structure's reported apparitional population.

The **Butterworth**'s bottom floor, now home to **Kell's Restaurant & Pub** on Post Alley, once held stables, a hearse garage, cremation oven, and vault for ashes of the dearly departed. The chapel, sitting parlor, visitation rooms, and choir loft were on the first floor, where **Cafe Sophie** does business today. Customers rode a hydraulic elevator—the first in Seattle—to the third story, where they could shop for caskets and where embalming and cosmetic work were practiced. (The mortuary moved from this building in 1923, relocating to Capitol Hill.)

Mysterious mumbling has been heard in the bathrooms at **Kell's Restaurant & Pub,** long after it has closed for an evening. But the best story comes from **Cafe Sophie,** where an electrician, working past midnight to rewire one of the restaurant's chandeliers, once encountered two shadowy gents sitting at a table, talking. He tried his best to ignore the reveling revenants, until they came over to help him steady a ladder. Then suddenly, a woman dressed in "an unearthly white linen dress" ventured into the dining room, provoking the other two ghosts to shout insults in her direction, until the terrified electrician rushed from the premises.

The venerable **Arctic Building,** on Third Avenue in downtown, is supposedly inhabited by the specter of someone who leapt from one of its windows during the stock-market collapse of 1929.

The building that once housed the **Burnley School of Professional Art** on **Capitol Hill** (now the south annex of **Seattle Central Community College**) has seen thousands of students in its day, and many of them swear they've encountered the school's poltergeist—an elderly man who walks the corridors with a heavy gait and sometimes unlocks doors or turns on coffee machines. Speculation has it that he's the ghost of a student from long-gone **Broadway High** (the original institution on the college site) who got into a fight during a basketball game in the school's third-floor gym, fell down a flight of stairs, and died.

The **United Methodist Church** on Capitol Hill, built at the turn of the century, has a couple of resident spirits: a woman in a flowing gown and a gaunt, white-bearded gentleman. Both have been seen by a variety of folks over the years. Some theorize that they are the Reverend Daniel Bagley, Seattle's first Methodist minister, and his wife.

Whatever the reason, Seattle's ghosts especially seem to like movie houses and theaters. The **University of Washington**'s **Showboat Theater,** which has floated in **Portage Bay** since the 1930s, has been home to such diverse actors as Lillian Gish and Kyle MacLachlan. According to students and teachers, however, it's also the residence of a mysterious presence who performs harmless tricks like supplying cue lines and playing the onstage piano. Some say it's the ghost of Glenn Hughes, the father of **UW**'s **School of Drama.**

Belltown's **Moore Theater** was built in 1907 as Seattle's first vaudeville house. (It's now used mainly for rock shows.) One night during its tenure as a movie palace in the 1970s, the theater's owner-operators swore they encountered . . . well, something that sighed, smelled bad, and gave them a cold, tingling sensation. When they reluctantly reported it to their employees, the reaction was, "Oh, so you've seen it, too?"

The **Neptune Theater,** a venerable repertory film house in the **University District,** is (according to persistent stories told by workers there) also the haunt of things not quite human. One is a lady with long dark hair, swathed in white and surrounded by light, who likes to hang around in the organ loft. Another leaves behind the odor of fresh tobacco, and still another—the only one of the three who appears somewhat malevolent—loiters menacingly near the upstairs men's room.

25 Musashi's ★$ This place has lots of fans, and they may all be trying to get one of the few tables on the night you visit. (Thankfully, takeout is available.) A wide variety of excellent sushi is offered, and there are a few other choices—try the teriyaki chicken. *Bento* box meals, including rice, a crab cake, sashimi, and a teriyaki chicken skewer, are available at lunchtime. Cooks tend to throw extra items in for the restaurant's regulars. ♦ Japanese/Takeout ♦ Tu-F lunch and dinner; Sa dinner. 1400 N 45th St (at Interlake Ave N). 633.0212

26 Firehouse No. 11 Erected in 1913, this building is surprisingly unimposing, even given its tower (where they dry out the hoses), which was long ago blocked on the skyline behind taller structures. Architect **Daniel R. Huntington** covered the building with cedar shakes, shutters, and trellises surrounding the accordion-style doors through which horse-drawn fire wagons once charged. The design was meant to blend in with Wallingford's growing predominance of bungalow homes. At one time both police and firefighters occupied this building, but since 1984 it has been home to a community health clinic. The Wallingford-Wilmot branch of the **Seattle Public Library** shares part of the ground floor, as well. ♦ N 45th St and Densmore Ave N

27 Guadalajara ★$ This unassuming Mexican outpost can be easily (and unjustly) overlooked amid the proliferation of chic restaurants. Although service can be curt, the kitchen turns out fine and filling burritos and enchiladas. The tacos are so-so, but the Guadalajara nachos (chicken or beef), topped with guacamole and sour cream, are excellent. A chunky salsa of veggies marinated in pepper juice is some of the hottest around. And the bartenders usually have a heavy hand on the tequila bottle when mixing margaritas. ♦ Mexican ♦ M-Sa lunch and dinner; Su dinner. 1715 N 45th St (between Wallingford and Woodlawn Aves N). 632.7858

Who invented the Happy Face, that lemon-yellow symbol of goodwill that was ubiquitous during the Vietnam War years and continues to make passersby smile . . . or cringe, depending on their kitsch threshold? A San Francisco button-store owner once tried to take the credit. Other wags say the noseless, browless, guileless character with the vapid grin has no single parent but rather a variety of folk sources. Seattle advertising exec David Stern contends, however, that he was actually responsible for making the Happy Face the world's third-most-recognizable symbol (the red octagonal traffic STOP sign is the most recognizable, while the circle with a bar through it that silently screams "don't, don't, don't" takes second place).

27 Alfi News Domestic and international newspapers, and a wide array of magazines—particularly bounteous in nature, sports, and home or craft publications—are available here. Clerks sometimes are slow to get new issues racked and allow back issues of some magazines to hang around long after their usefulness has expired. ♦ Daily; F-Sa until 11PM. 1717 N 45th St (at Wallingford Ave N). 632.9390.

28 Julia's in Wallingford ★★$$ The health-conscious menu here includes build-your-own omelettes (20 possible ingredients), pancakes, and *huevos rancheros* at breakfast; nutburgers and other sandwiches and soups for lunch; and Greek salads and pasta at dinnertime. A popular upscale place (with another location in Ballard), this restaurant may be becoming a victim of its own success. Regulars complain about crowds or the rising cost of meals; there also has been grumbling about the sometimes superior attitude of the servers. Expect to wait for a table on weekends; wise folk bring along a book or newspaper to occupy the time. ♦ Natural ♦ Daily breakfast, lunch, and dinner. 4401 Wallingford Ave N (at N 44th St). 633.1175. Also at: 5410 Ballard Ave NW (at 22nd Ave NW). 783.2033

28 The Store Next Door This annex of **Julia's** (literally located right next door to the restaurant) serves the fresh baked goods—breads, cinnamon rolls, and other pastries—from the restaurant, only without the wait. It's a great early morning coffee stop but has only three tables for lingerers. ♦ Daily Su until noon. 4405 Wallingford Ave N (at N 44th St). 547.3203

29 Wallingford Center There were plans in the 1950s to condemn or relocate this three-story, Neo-Classical wooden behemoth that was then the **Interlake Public School.** The neighborhood's population of children was in decline, and business leaders argued that soon there would simply not be enough of them left to justify continued operation. The school had originally been the community's pride and joy, one of Wallingford's first public buildings, created by the prolific architect **James Stephen,** who also designed **West Queen Anne Elementary** and **Latona Elementary School.** It was finally closed in 1981, but before commercial interests could even aim a wrecking ball at the building, preservationists joined forces with community officials to gentrify the structure. The edifice became a warren of stores selling jewelry, clothing, and books. Outside, on the corner of North 45th Street and Wallingford Avenue North, look for *Wallingford Animal Storm,* a 1984 bronze and aluminum totem created by neighborhood resident Ronald W. Petty.

A tribute to local wildlife, the installation features raccoons, Canadian geese, cats, pigeons, and even slugs. ◆ 4400 Wallingford Ave N (between N 44th and 45th Sts). 632.2781

Within the Wallingford Center:

Capons Rotisseria ★$ You'd better like chicken, because that's about all there is—whole marinated rotisserie chickens, half chickens, chicken sandwiches, chicken potpie, and chicken soup. The fowl is fresh and juicy. Some feathers have been ruffled by scant servings, but for the most part, both the vegetables and the salads are satisfying if only second-fiddle accompaniments to the birds. Service is cafeteria style, with an atmosphere that's pleasant and casual. ◆ Chicken/Takeout ◆ Daily lunch and dinner. Main level. 547.3949. Also at: 605 15th Ave E (at Mercer St E). 323.4026

Garden Spot Plentiful supplies of potted flowers and hanging plants, as well as a wide range of pots, can be found here. In summer the outside courtyard is an excellent place to browse and sniff, but even the interior space seems warm and earthy. The staff is knowledgeable and helpful. ◆ Daily; M-F until 8PM. Main level. 547.5137

Simpatico ★$ There's a secluded, brick-walled wine bar in the back and lots of white-draped tables out front where flavorful pasta dishes are served. But when the weather allows, head for the expansive sunken patio. Order a pizza (versions with chicken and pesto top the list) and a cold microbrew, then sit in the shade provided by umbrellas, listen to the burbling fountain, and chill out in the peaceful setting. ◆ Italian ◆ Daily dinner. Main level. 632.1000

Spot Bagel Bakery Grand, doughy, and kosher bagels are available in garlic, pumpernickel, pesto, jalapeño, and other flavors. Try any of them spread with herb cream cheese or layered with lox. Because it's so popular, service can be slow. If you grow impatient, you can buy the same bagels across North 45th Street at **Food Giant** or at this bagel bakery's second location—downtown in the **Newmark Building**. ◆ Daily; M-F from 6:30AM. Main level. 633.7768. Also at: 1401 Second Ave (at Pike St). 625.1990

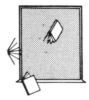

Second Story Bookstore Along with broad offerings in new general fiction and children's lit, this bookstore provides a rental service that makes it possible to read the latest best-sellers or listen to recent books on tape. Armchairs in the back provide the proper setting for thinking over any purchases. ◆ Daily; M-F until 8PM. Second level. 547.4605

Zanadia Among the many nicely designed accessories for the kitchen and home are a wide array of glassware and some intriguing candlesticks, perfect for gift giving. ◆ Daily; M-F until 8PM. Second level. 547.0884

30 Teahouse Kuan Yin ★$ Running distinctly against the grain in this coffee-lover's town is this quiet teahouse owned by Frank Miller and Miranda Pirzada. Miller, a former travel agent with a special interest in Asia, tasted teas all over Hong Kong before selecting the black, green, herbal, and oolongs that grace the menu. Quiche, focaccia, and other light edibles provide nice supplements to a cup of tea. In a brilliant synergistic move, the teahouse has a door-way connecting it to neighboring **Wide World Books.** Readers can dive right into their newly purchased pages while sipping an aromatic brew. Staffers are always willing to educate customers about the characteristics of the different teas. ◆ Teahouse ◆ Daily; F-Sa until midnight. 1911 N 45th St (between Burke and Meridian Aves N). 632.2055

30 Wide World Books Here are shelf upon shelf of guidebooks and travel literature, plus staffers who've probably already been where you want to go and can help you make the most of your visit. The shop also features maps, some luggage, and a passport-photo service. ◆ Daily. 1911 N 45th St (between Burke and Meridian Aves N). 634.3453

31 Ace Hardware Very organized, very well stocked, and very old-fashioned, this is the sort of small store your parents knew as kids. Tradition dies hard here: you can still make your check payable to the business's sweetly enduring former moniker, **Tweedy & Popp.** ◆ Daily. 1916 N 45th St (between Burke and Meridian Aves N). 632.2290

In 1992 a dozen Seattle-based bands got together to record "Hey Joe," the first song ever released that was all about coffee.

---

estaurants/Clubs: Red   **Hotels:** Blue

hops/ ☂ Outdoors: Green   **Sights/Culture:** Black

31 Murphy's Pub This relocated Irish pub (shown above) has a facade displaying Old World charm, and dark furnishings that give the interior the almost reverential atmosphere familiar to so many historied taverns. Fifteen tap beers (primarily substantive microbrews and imports) and a trio of alcoholic ciders are on hand, accompanied by a limited menu that makes its biggest splashes with the enormous nacho platter and the cider stew. There are the requisite dart boards to one side of the bar. Wednesday is open-mike entertainment night, with live Irish music played (usually too loudly) on Friday and Saturday. ◆ Cover. Daily until 2AM. 1928 N 45th St (at Meridian Ave N). 634.2110

32 Starbucks ★$ Local resentment ran high when this ubitiquous chain took over the old premises of **Murphy's Pub.** People worried about the coffeehouse's close commercial proximity to the much-loved **Boulangerie** bakery. But so far, this venue—large, compared with some of its brethren around town—has had no negative effects on the neighborhood. In fact, it's a pleasant hangout before and after films at the **Guild 45th Movie Theater** across the street. ◆ Coffeehouse ◆ Daily; F-Sa until 11PM. 2110 N 45th St (between Bagley and Meridian Aves N). 548.9507

32 Beeliner Diner ★★$ This narrow, attitude-heavy dispensary of rapid service (based on the old "Eat It and Beat It" policy) is brought to you by Peter Levy and Jeremy Hardy, the same pair who later created Queen Anne's **5-Spot Cafe.** Servers joke with diners, chiding them lightly for not cleaning their plates or for sitting around talking while a line forms outside. The valiant few who sit at the counter rather than in one of the vinyl booths have the dubious pleasure of being harassed by the cooks, too. Orders yelled into the tiny kitchen are masterpieces of short-order–speak: "Bossy in a bowl!" (beef stew); and "Adam and Eve on a raft—and wreck 'em"

(scrambled eggs on toast). The wine list lampoons trendy tastes and prominently offers "cheap white wine."

The regular menu sounds pedestrian, but the chicken-fried steak is spicier and made from better cuts of beef than you'll find at a roadhouse, and the hot turkey sandwich consists of really huge slabs of white meat atop homemade bread and doused with a buttery gravy. There are blue-plate specials daily, the best of which is Wednesday night's meat loaf. Try the hot cabbage salad marinated in vinegar and sprinkled with blue cheese. Top it all off with a slice of hot apple pie à la mode. Almost anything here is worth lying about in your diet diary. ◆ American/Takeout ◆ Daily breakfast, lunch, and dinner. 2114 N 45th St (between Bagley and Meridian Aves N). 547.6313

33 Boulangerie Repeatedly chosen by Seattleites as their favorite bakery, this place specializes in crusty baguettes and other French loaves, as well as such memorable sweets as the Tarte Normande, made of Granny Smith apple slices arranged within a nutty pastry. It's also a very popular take-out coffee and pastry stop. Try the *pain au chocolate* (croissant filled with chocolate) ◆ Daily. 2200 N 45th St (at Bagley Ave N). 634.2211

Café VIZCAYA

33 Café Vizcaya ★★$$ While some diners find the laissez-faire demeanor of servers here off-putting, others say that it lends further authenticity to this dimly lit Spanish restaurant. It's best to just forget about the time and order several different small plates of tapas to share, and toast the experience with sherry. In Spain, diners make whole dinners of these often heavily spiced finger foods; Seattleites tend to use the tasty morsels as appetizers. Favorites include the *gambas brava al ajillo* (prawns sautéed in a marinade of onion, garlic, paprika, cayenne, and olive oil); the more basic *crostini* (round of toasted bread with a variety of toppings) are accompanied by a cilantro pesto.

The entrées are a balance of Spanish and citrus-accented Cuban dishes (the owner, Barbara Soltero, is a native Cuban who moved to Vizcaya, Spain). One specialty is a marinated fillet of red snapper baked on a bed of potato slices and served with a white sauce with peppers, capers, olives, and plenty of onions. The *pollo asado* is a half-chicken marinated in lime juice, garlic, and pepper, then roasted and garnished with a delightful papaya-tomatillo salsa. Or try the roasted pork smothered in onions. Unfortunately, salads here are less inventive, and the bread served before your meal is cold and tends to be dry. But don't let such things dissuade you from what can be a thoroughly novel and romantic experience. ♦ Spanish/Cuban ♦ Daily dinner. Reservations recommended. 2202 N 45th St (between Bagley and Corliss Aves N). 547.7772

33 Twice Sold Tales Spun off a popular used-books outlet on Capitol Hill, this shop is most densely packed with general fiction, science fiction, and mystery novels. Former best-sellers crowd an extra-cheapo cart on the sidewalk outside. The owners' political leanings are reflected in newspaper clippings hanging on the front windows and walls. Money, not credit, is given in exchange for books sold. ♦ Daily; F-Sa until 10PM. 2210 N 45th St (between Bagley and Corliss Aves N). 545.4226. Also at: 905 E John St (at Broadway Ave E). 324.2421

34 Kabul ★★$$ Chef Sultan Mahmoud Malikyar has introduced the rich pleasures of Afghan cuisine into Wallingford's culinary melting pot. Kebabs are a good introduction, especially the tender fillets of chicken marinated in turmeric, garlic, and cayenne. A hands-down favorite is the *qorma-i tarkari* (fresh vegetables and lamb tossed with dill, saffron, turmeric, and cumin). The *ashak* (flat dumplings stuffed with scallions, leeks, and cilantro and covered in a sauce of yogurt, garlic, and ground beef) is also popular. For an appetizer, try the *burta* (crushed eggplant blended with yogurt, sour cream, garlic, cilantro, and mint) served with a somewhat dry but satisfying pita bread. The room is filled with small tables and pleasant sconce lighting. Service is friendly and efficient. ♦ Afghan ♦ M-Sa dinner. 2301 N 45th St (at Corliss Ave N). 545.9000

34 Erotic Bakery As you might expect, this bakery specializes in creating party cakes designed to look like male or female sex organs. It's all done in good humor and not really as ribald as it sounds. ♦ Daily. 2323 N 45th St (at Sunnyside Ave N). 545.6969

35 Good Shepherd Center Built in 1906 from a plan by architect **C. Alfred Breitung** (who designed other Seattle edifices such as the **Triangle Hotel Building** in the International District), this was originally a Catholic convent and residence, the **Home of the Good Shepherd.** In more recent years it has become something of a political football, fought over by historic restoration forces and Wallingforders, who can't agree on its appropriate use. Presently, Greenpeace, private art and elementary schools, and the Seattle Tilth Association all occupy some portion of the building and grounds. The grounds and the Tilth gardens are a good place for a stroll. ♦ 4649 Sunnyside Ave N (off N 50th St). 547.8127

36 Dick's Drive-In $ The long, pencil-thin fries here are best consumed from the grease-spotted bag in great gangly handfuls. Complete your feast with a thick chocolate milk shake. You might be able to find better fast food in this town, but there are few more interesting human-study environments than this drive-in's parking lot. The scene is especially entertaining just before closing time on Friday and Saturday nights. ♦ Fast food ♦ Daily lunch and dinner until 2AM. 111 NE 45th St (at First Ave NE). 632.5125. Also at: 115 Broadway E (between E Denny Way and E John St). 323.1300; 9208 Holman Rd NW (at 12th Ave NW). 783.5233

37 Latona Elementary School You may see this great wooden building from Interstate 5, just north of the North 45th Street overpass. If you have a chance, get closer for a better view. Dating back to 1906, this is the only one of architect **James Stephen**'s many Seattle schools to feature Queen Anne–style towers. ♦ NE 42nd St and Fifth Ave NE

38 Gas Works Park Twenty-five years after the Seattle Gas Company plant belched its last coal dust in 1956, the gasworks at the north end of Lake Union reopened as a park for picnickers and kite fliers, its industrial towers retained as totems of the industrial age. It's like that scene from *Planet of the Apes* where Charlton Heston rides his horse past the submerged Statue of Liberty and realizes just how much the world has changed.

Children now scamper over ground that was once so polluted it demanded intensive purifying before it was safe to walk upon. Landscape architect Richard Haag (who had earlier remodeled the Century 21 fairgrounds into **Seattle Center**) was responsible for seeing aesthetic value in this industrial wasteland and saving the plant as a bizarre relic. His modifications were relatively minor—bright primary colors in some covered areas, a huge symbolic sundial (created by artist Charles Greening in 1979) that's mounted atop a knoll to the west, and outdoor dining tables on the beautified grounds. Visitors have an unobstructed view of boats chopping over the lake. The park marks the beginning of the 12.5- mile **Burke-Gilman Trail** (see the "University District" chapter on page 168.) ♦ Lake Union (off N Northlake Way)

"A rust-brown smudge ballooned over Seattle, end to end, a thousand feet thick. Mac knew the locals were telling themselves that if they were getting headaches and their eyes were bloodshot and their noses ran, it must be something else. Seattleites had a stunning town, but it grew dirtier by the minute. It was only Northwest vanity that kept people calling it fog."

Earl Emerson, *Black Hearts and Slow Dancing*

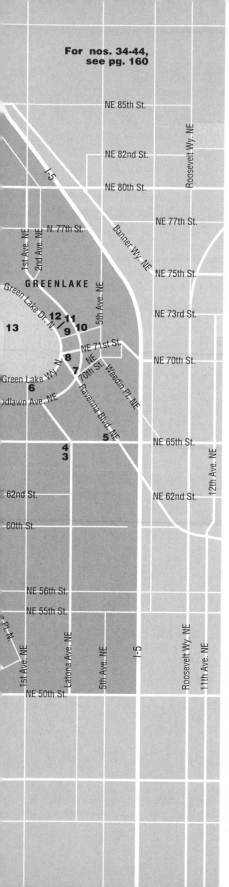

For nos. 34-44, see pg. 160

NE 85th St.

NE 82nd St.

NE 80th St.

NE 77th St.

Roosevelt Wy. NE

I-5

N. 77th St.

1st Ave. NE

2nd Ave. NE

Banner Wy. NE

NE 75th St.

GREENLAKE

Green Lake Dr. N.

5th Ave. NE

NE 73rd St.

12 11

13   9 10

8   NE 71st St.

NE

7   70th St.

Green Lake Wy. NE   Weedin Pl. NE

6   Ravenna Blvd. NE

Odlawn Ave. NE

5   NE 65th St.

4

3

62nd St.   NE 62nd St.

12th Ave. NE

60th St.

NE 56th St.

NE 55th St.

Roosevelt Wy. NE

11th Ave. NE

PL. N.

1st Ave. NE

Latona Ave. NE

5th Ave. NE

I-5

NE 50th St.

NE 70th St.

Green Lake/ Greenwood/ North Seattle

A quiet residential district, the Green Lake/Greenwood area is bordered by **Ballard** to the west, **Wallingford** and **Fremont** to the south, and the **University District** on the east. Its houses range from modest bungalows to some of the most desirable homes in Seattle—the large turn-of-the-century residences and modern dream houses atop **Phinney Ridge**, for instance, command views of both the **Olympic** and the **Cascade Mountains.**

The centerpiece of the area is **Woodland Park,** located at the south end of Phinney Ridge, where the **Woodland Park Zoo,** playgrounds, tennis courts, a rose garden, and acres of wooded trails and picnic areas can be found. Bisecting the park is **Aurora Avenue** (Highway 99), which in the early 1930s—following bitter public debate—was extended north from downtown Seattle. The benefits of this bit of progress are dubious: The highway created what Washington writer Ivan Doig called "a concrete gorge" in the park—the western half contains the zoo, while most of the rest of its attractions, including Green Lake, are in the eastern half.

Green Lake, with two paths circling it, is "Jogging Central" and *the* center of summertime fun in Seattle. Aside from running, there's plenty of kayaking, bicycling, in-line skating, windsurfing, pram-pushing, golfing, baseball playing, fishing, or just plain people watching here. A couple of small commercial areas on the east and north sides of the lake service the area year-round, and seasonal businesses (such as Rollerblade and Windsurfer rentals) pop up in the summer. And, of course, this is Seattle, so you won't need to travel far before encountering an espresso stand.

Parallel to Aurora Avenue on the park's western edge—along the spine of Phinney Ridge—runs **Phinney Avenue**, which becomes **Greenwood Avenue** farther north. With its secondhand stores spanning the gamut from junky to sublime, the avenue is ripe territory for antiques lovers. The Greenwood district, centered at the intersection of **North 85th Street** and **Greenwood Avenue North,** retains a funky charm that has endured nobly against encroaching gentrification.

A little farther afield is North Seattle. The city limits used to end at North 85th Street, but as Seattle has grown (the line now stands at **North 145th Street**), the various smaller communities embraced by the North Seattle rubric—**Lake Forest Park, Northgate, Broadview, Maple Leaf,** and **Wedgewood** among them—have developed. North Seattle is primarily home to auto dealerships, budget motels, strip malls, modest housing, and the world's first shopping mall, **Northgate Shopping Center.**

Green Lake

1 Green Lake Small Craft Center
Located at the lake's southwest corner, this concession offers year-round canoe and kayak instruction, as well as hosting special sailing events. It's also home to the Seattle Sailing Association, which rents its small boats for an annual fee. The lake is active on weekday mornings when rowers embark on their journeys. ♦ M-F 3PM-6PM; Sa 9AM-2PM. 5900 W Green Lake Way N (off Stone Way N). 684.4074

2 Honey Bear Bakery ★$ Dropping by this place for a cup of joe and a sourdough cinnamon roll is a morning ritual for many folks. Crowded and convivial, this nonsmoking bakery has become a neighborhood institution where you can linger over conversation or grab a quick bite. The breads are locally famous, and the enormous chocolate-chip cookies or the white-chocolate brownies are excellent. Dinner is a dicier matter, although the black-bean chili is a safe bet. ♦ Bakery ♦ Daily breakfast, lunch, and dinner. 2106 N 55th St (at Meridian Ave N). 545.7296

3 Cafe Los Gatos ★★$ The subtle flavors of Central and South America, redolent with such herbs as cilantro and cardamom, are featured at this tiny restaurant. Fish, meat, chicken, and vegetarian specials are available nightly. Or try the pork stew, a rich sargasso of fruit and nuts with pork. Be sure to leave room for one of the nut tarts for dessert.

Friendly service makes up for the dimly lit decor. ♦ Central/South American ♦ Tu-Su dinner. Reservations recommended. 6411 Latona Ave NE (between NE 64th and NE 65th Sts). 527.9765

4 Latona Pub This funky, friendly neighborhood tavern offers a good selection of wines and a frequently changing assortment of microbrews, including products from the Rogue Brewery in Ashland Oregon, and the Maritime Pacific Brewing Company in Seattle. Bartenders are happy to give recommendations. The pub grub menu is limited, but salads are a good choice. There's also something called the Haystack—chips and bean dip smothered in cheese.

Sit at the bar; avoid the balcony overlooking the main floor, where the service is glacially slow and you'll feel cut off from the action. A variety of local musicians, usually of the folk or jazz persuasion, play Thursday through Sunday evenings. A small cover is sometimes charged, but if you're inside when the music starts, you can usually slide. A mailing list will keep you apprised of new brews. ♦ M-Sa until 12:30AM; Su until midnight. 6423 Latona Ave NE (at NE 65th St). 525.2238

5 Boehm's on Ravenna It's somewhat off the beaten path, but this shop is worth a visit. Old man Boehm, a Swiss immigrant, was a master candy maker and a legendary mountain climber and skier; for years his original shop in the town of Issaquah has been a regular stop for travelers headed east across Snoqualmie Pass. This small retail outlet caters mostly to fans of its splendid handmade chocolates, oversize muffins, buttercream-filled chocolates, and espresso drinks. ♦ Daily. 559 Ravenna Blvd NE (at NE 65th St). 523.9380

Restaurants/Clubs: Red	**Hotels:** Blue
Shops/ ♣ Outdoors: Green	**Sights/Culture:** Bla

Saleh al Lago

6 Saleh al Lago ★★★$$$ You wouldn't think this sleek restaurant with its modern and minimal pastel decor, set in an ordinary block of shops, would be one of Seattle's top Italian *ristoranti*. And the owner/chef, Saleh Joudeh, is not even Italian (he's Syrian). Joudeh studied cooking (and medicine) in Italy; his imaginative blendings of various Mediterranean influences can make even plain fare remarkable. Fresh pasta and veal dishes are consistently delicious. Special praise goes to the garlicky calamari antipasto and the chef's *ravioli al mondo mio* (sauces and fillings change daily). Seafood dishes are prepared simply and excellently.
♦ Italian/Mediterranean ♦ M-F lunch and dinner; Sa dinner. Reservations recommended. 6804 E Green Lake Way N (between First and Second Aves NE). 522.7943

6 Spud Fish and Chips $ The ambience is a big zero, but this is a choice spot on sunny days when all you want is to grab a quick lunch and burn off a few skin cells beside the lake. The fish is remarkably flaky and the fries are filling and salty, but everything's a bit on the greasy side. ♦ Seafood/Takeout ♦ Daily lunch and dinner. 6860 E Green Lake Way N (at Second Ave NE). 524.0565. Also at: 2666 Alki Ave SW (at 59th St SW). 938.0606

Gregg's Greenlake Cycle

7 Gregg's Greenlake Cycle This is the biggest and busiest of several shops around Green Lake that rent bicycles, Rollerblades, and skateboards for a nominal fee. All these types of wheels are also for sale here, and there's a helpful service department for when things go bewilderingly wrong. ♦ Daily; M-F until 9PM. 7007 Woodlawn Ave NE (at Ravenna Blvd NE and NE 70th St). 523.1822

8 Kyllo's Lakeside Deli ★$ A bustling cafe with good sandwiches and home-baked items provides a nice break before, during, or after a rousing walk around the lake. ♦ Deli ♦ M-F breakfast and lunch until 4:30PM. 315 NE 71st St (between Woodlawn Ave NE and E Green Lake Way N). 522.9088

9 My Friends Cafe ★$ Fresh fruit and other healthy ingredients whipped up into good breakfasts and tasty sandwiches are the offerings here. ♦ American ♦ Daily breakfast and lunch until 4:30PM. 310 NE 72nd St (between Woodland Ave NE and E Green Lake Dr N). 523.8929

10 Rosita's ★$ Just a couple blocks off the lake, this place is commonly crowded and uncommonly efficient. Try any of the combination plates or the *chiles rellenos*. The super nachos platter is a winning appetizer. A plus for parents: The place is extremely kid-friendly. ♦ Mexican ♦ Daily lunch and dinner. 7210 Woodlawn Ave NE (between NE 72nd St and NE Maple Leaf Pl). 523.3031

11 Rasa Malaysia ★★$ The emphasis at this popular dining spot is on noodles, usually served sautéed with very fresh vegetables and a variety of fish, shrimp, or meat, and such mildly spicy sauces as a peanut topping. Fruit smoothies and not-too-sweet lemonade are the drinks of choice. ♦ Malaysian ♦ Daily dinner. 7208 E Green Lake Dr N (at NE 72nd St). 523.8888. Also at: Broadway Market (401 Broadway), 328.8882; Pike Place Market, 624.8388

12 Green Lake Public Library Perched on a grassy knoll, this well-maintained building shows Mediterranean and Chicago School influences. Opened in 1910, it is one of eight libraries still standing in the Seattle area (two were lost to wrecking balls) that were built thanks to the largess of iron-and-steel-magnate Andrew Carnegie. Designers were **W. Marbury Somervell** and **Joseph C. Cote**, who in the year of its opening would also see two of their other library projects inaugurated: the **University Branch Library** on Roosevelt Way North and the **West Seattle Public Library** on 42nd Avenue SW. Not surprisingly, these three structures bear some resemblance to one another. ♦ M-W; F-Sa. 7364 E Green Lake Dr N (at Fourth Ave NE). 684.7547

13 Green Lake Boat Rentals Rent a canoe, small boat, or paddle-wheel craft at this Parks Department concession. Windsurfing equipment and lessons are also available. ♦ Daily May-Sept. 7351 E Green Lake Dr N (near NE 73rd St). 527.0171

14 The Urban Bakery ★$ Early morning and late-night hours make this a convenient spot for runners and walkers to pick up an espresso or iced *latte*. Hearty sandwiches, soups, fresh pastries, and a full line of juices are also on hand. ♦ Coffeehouse/Bakery ♦ Daily. 7850 E Green Lake Dr N (at Wallingford Ave N). 524.7951

15 Ed's Juice and Java ★$ Tiny but convivial, this joint features just what the name advertises. A variety of unusual concoctions are available in the juice department, such as carrot and wheatgrass; the coffee-based drinks are more conventional. ◆ Coffeehouse ◆ Daily. 7907 Wallingford Ave N (at E Green Lake Dr N). 524.7570

15 Secret Garden Bookshop The oldest and best bookstore in the Seattle area exclusively for children carries hundreds of titles, many at bargain prices. There's a table of toys, an inviting reading area, a loose-brick floor that makes great crunching noises, and a helpful staff. The store sponsors weekly story times and regular author signings. ◆ Daily; Th until 8PM. 7900 E Green Lake Dr N (at Wallingford Ave N). 524.4556

15 Guido's Pizzeria ★$ Buy it by the slice or by the pie, thin crust or thick, with the usual toppings or more uncommon choices like fresh basil and sun-dried tomatoes at this minuscule and crowded place (most of the business here is takeout). Calzones, salads, a variety of juices and mineral waters, and—as you might expect—espressos and *lattes* are also available. Several picnic tables beckon from just across the street in **Green Lake Park**. The cheerfully brash New York–style attitude of the employees is free. ◆ Pizza ◆ Daily. 7902 E Green Lake Dr N (between Densmore and Wallingford Aves N). 522.5553.

16 Greenlake Jake's ★$ Good burgers and breakfasts can be ordered here to take to the lake or enjoy on site. The mushroom burgers, biscuits with gravy, and blueberry muffins are all especially recommended. Portions are traditionally copious. An outdoor eating area beats the sterile interior. ◆ American ◆ Daily breakfast, lunch, and dinner. 7918 E Green Lake Dr N (at Densmore Ave N). 523.4747

17 Bathhouse Theatre Under the auspices of its irrepressible artistic director, Arne Zaslove, this theater mounts six productions annually on a year-round schedule, specializing in innovative updates of classics. In addition, it produces numerous free public shows in Seattle parks throughout the summer. The building was originally erected in 1927 as—you guessed it—a brick bathhouse; it becam a theater in 1970. ◆ Box office: Tu-Su noon-7PM. 7312 W Green Lake Dr N (between N 76th St and Aurora Ave N). 524.9108

18 Beth's Cafe $ This greasiest of spoons, located between **Twin Teepees** restaurant an **Butch's Gun Shop,** attracts plenty of college students who finish up their all-nighters with a stop here to wolf down inexpensive 12-egg omelettes (be prepared to share!), layered over a two-inch bed of hash browns, toast or the side. Half orders can be had by the less gluttonous. Breakfast is served all day. Burgers and enormous french fries carry on the stomach-busting tradition. It's a real scene. ◆ American ◆ Daily 24 hours. 7311 Aurora Ave N (at Winona Ave N). 782.5588

19 Twin Teepees Restaurant ★$ A classic of roadside kitsch on the west side of Green Lake, this place is a mishmash of Native American design motifs. The structure was apparently prefabricated in California and then trucked up Highway 99 to this site. Inside, you'll find substantial breakfasts and other forms of good, solid American food. ◆ American ◆ Daily breakfast, lunch, and dinner. 7201 Aurora Ave N (at N 72nd St). 783.9740

20 Woodland Park Zoo Origins of this zoo a the surrounding park go back to Guy Phinne a flamboyant Englishman who made his fortune in Canadian real estate before moving to Seattle at the end of the 19th century. Phinney built a private park on his estate, at the southern end of the ridge that bears his name. He included—among other amenities—a trolley line, flower garden, conservatory, picnic grounds, a zoo, bathing beach, and music pavilion. The city bought the park from him in 1900 for the then-extravagant sum of $100,000.

Today, Seattle's zoo is one of the nation's best. In 1992 a $9-million tropical rain-fores exhibit opened, complete with artificial vegetation (created by a technique pioneere in Hollywood) and digitally recorded sounds from a real rain forest piped in over hidden speakers. In 1994 a rejuvenated version of t popular family farm petting zoo was unveile and, at press time, an Alaskan exhibit with bears, owls, otters, and mountain goats, an a tropical Asian exhibit were scheduled to open.

In many of the exhibits animals are free to wander in near-natural settings: There's an African savanna (where you can peer from afar at giraffes and gazelles); an Asian elephant forest, including a replica of a Thai logging camp; and a lush, lowland gorilla enclosure, the largest of its kind in the world, in which you can get up close and personal (behind glass) with these fascinating creatures.

The zoo offers lectures, summer musical performances, and educational series for youngsters. Older children will love the periodic exhibits of raptors in flight.
♦ Admission; children under 2 free; discount for senior citizens, disabled persons, and children ages 3 to 5. Daily. 5500 Phinney Ave N (at N 55th St). 684.4800

21 The Santa Fe Cafe ★★★$$ Sparse but elegant decor combines with consistently high-quality, innovative cuisine to create Phinney Ridge's classiest restaurant. A couple of the appetizers alone—an order of garlic custard, say, and a luscious artichoke ramekin—could make a meal. And the green-chili stew, enchiladas, and green-chili burritos made with blue-corn tortillas are all delicious entrées.

The owners, both from Albuquerque, New Mexico, import tons of red and green chilies from their home state. If your server warns you that something like the red-chili burrito may be too hot for most palates, take his or her word for it. There's another branch in Ravenna. ♦ Southwestern ♦ M-F lunch and dinner; Sa-Su lunch. Reservations recommended. 5901 Phinney Ave N (between N 59th and N 60th Sts). 783.9755. Also at: 2255 NE 65th St (between 22nd and Ravenna Aves NE). 524.7736

22 The 12-Step Bookstore and Gift Shop For books on a multiplicity of dysfunctions, lists of various meetings, gifts for fellow 12-steppers, bumper stickers for those who want to be less than anonymous, and notices of upcoming workshops and speakers, check out this store. ♦ Daily; M-F until 8PM. 6300 Phinney Ave N (at NE 63rd St). 789.6300

23 Mae's Phinney Ridge Cafe ★★$ Mae is the shared *nom de cuisine* of three women owners who have created this congenial nook for breakfast and lunch. The sandwiches, burgers, and cinnamon rolls are all wonderful. Omelettes are the top pick at breakfast, but for the truly famished, a cheese-covered mountain of hash browns is served as a main course. The **Moo Room** (formerly a bar) features a soda fountain, great milk shakes, a jukebox, and more cow-related art than you can shake a hoof at. Service can be slow, and the lines form quickly on weekends, but the wait isn't usually too long. ♦ American ♦ Daily breakfast and lunch. 6412 Phinney Ave N (between NE 64th and NE 65th Sts). 782.1222

24 Terra Mar This shop features an eclectic assortment of handmade items—including masks, clothes, and artwork—by a wide variety of local and international artists. The emphasis is on unusual folk art and primitive designs. ♦ Daily. 7200 Greenwood Ave N (at N 72nd St). 784.5350. Also at: 7904 E Green Lake Way N (at Wallingford Ave N). 526.5869

25 2nd Hand Hube Furniture and kitschy stuff from the 1930s to the 1950s, some of it high-quality collectibles and some of it near junk, is featured in this browser's delight of a shop. ♦ Daily noon-5:30PM. 7217 Greenwood Ave N (between N 72nd and N 73rd Sts). 782.1335

25 The Couth Buzzard This dusty bookstore with the peculiar moniker contains a treasure trove of unlikely and sometimes unheard-of finds in used hardcovers and paperbacks. Mainstream fiction is the strongest section here. Look for sidewalk sales. ♦ Tu-Su. 7221 Greenwood Ave N (between N 72nd and N 73rd Sts). 789.8965

25 Greenwood Bakery The excellent pastries, breads, cookies, and other delectables made here are complemented by the good espresso drinks. ♦ Tu-Su. 7227 Greenwood Ave N (between N 72nd and N 73rd Sts). 783.7181

25 Ken's Market This better-than-average grocery store caters to an upscale crowd with its wealth of coffee beans, delicious deli sandwiches (try the meat loaf), and fresh pasta. The espresso drinks served here are just as good as those sold next door at **Greenwood Bakery,** and the service is faster. ♦ Daily 6AM-11PM. 7231 Greenwood Ave N (between N 72nd and N 73rd Sts). 784.3470

26 George's Corner A charmingly eccentric shop full of goofy collectibles showcases an impressive selection of cowboy paraphernalia. Indulge your inner John Wayne. ♦ M, Th-Su. 7400 Greenwood Ave N (at N 74th St). 781.0973

27 74th Street Ale House ★★$ This former hard-drinker's dive has been reincarnated as an airy neighborhood tavern serving an excellent array of Northwest microbrews and standard-issue beer (16 taps in all), along with wine. The brains behind this operation are Jeff Eagan, formerly of **Roanoke Park Place Tavern** on Capitol Hill and the **Mark Tobey** restaurant in downtown, and Jeff Reich, who runs the kitchen. The menu is brief but thoughtful. Try the big burgers (decked with grilled onions and peppers), the sausage sandwich, or the Reuben. The vegetarian sandwich, a neat orchestration of Montrachet and cream cheese, sun-dried tomatoes, artichoke hearts, and heaps of roasted garlic on country bread, is another fine choice. Some fans claim this alehouse serves Seattle's best chicken sandwich, but critics have found it to be rather dry and unexciting compared with other offerings here. Try the white clam chowder served on Fridays. ♦ American ♦ Daily lunch and dinner. 7401 Greenwood Ave N (at N 74th St). 784.2955

27 Yanni's Lakeside Cafe ★★$ Huge portions of good Greek cooking are offered at this congenial neighborhood hangout. Try the gyro platter for lunch and any of the lamb dishes or moussaka for dinner. The appetizer plate of calamari can make a whole meal. Desserts are less interesting. There's a simple, no-nonsense wine list. ♦ Greek ♦ M-Sa dinner. 7419 Greenwood Ave N (between N 74th and N 75th Sts). 783.6945

28 Pelayo's Antiques This large, well-stocked store is at the upper end of the price continuum. Specialties are pine furniture, toys (such as elegant hobbyhorses), and crockery. ♦ Daily. 7601 Greenwood Ave N (at N 76th St). 789.1999. Also at: 8421 Greenwood Ave N (at N 85th St). 789.1333

29 Patty's Eggnest ★$ It's all about comfort foods like Denver omelettes, blueberry pancakes, liver and onions, and gyro sandwiches. Decor is nothing to write home about: checkered tablecloths and walls covered with black-and-white photos of local TV personalities. But proprietor Patty Papadopoulos (she's the one with the long black hair, slinging plates and instructing her staff to keep pouring the coffee) remembers regulars and always greets them on their visits. The breakfast menu is served all day. ♦ American ♦ Tu-Su breakfast and lunch. 7717 Greenwood Ave N (between N 77th and N 78th Sts). 784.5348

30 Bizango Within these flamingo pink walls are all manner of gift items—jewelry, posters, flying angels, candles, clocks, you name it—all hand-crafted, and all with a touch of silliness about them. ♦ M-Sa. 759 N 80th St (at Linden Ave N). 784.7455

31 Arita Japanese Restaurant ★★$ This very pleasant family-run restaurant serves Japanese dishes, slightly altered for the American palate. The atmosphere is calm and cool, with gentle music in the background and simple furnishings. There's no sushi bar, but the sashimi and sushi dinners are fresh and reasonably priced. ♦ Japanese ♦ M-F lunch and dinner; Sa-Su dinner. 8202 Greenwood Ave N (at N 82nd St). 784.2625

32 Phad Thai ★$ There's been an explosion of Thai restaurants in Seattle over the past several years. This eatery is informal in decor and cheerful in service; employees have been known to take fussy children in hand for a kitchen tour, giving grateful parents a chance to eat. The food is fresh, well-presented, and cooked without MSG. Try the vegetable curry or the chicken in peanut sauce. ♦ Thai ♦ Daily dinner; M-Tu, Th-F lunch. 8530 Greenwood Ave N (between N 85th and N 86th Sts). 784.1830

33 El Tapatio ★$ A venerable Greenwood institution, this Mexican restaurant offers few culinary surprises, but it's cheerful, inexpensive, and informal. The standards are all available—taco combination plates, burritos, enchiladas—with heaping sides of rice and beans. Kids are welcome, too; they receive helium balloons and lots of attention. ♦ Mexican ♦ Daily lunch and dinner. 8564 Greenwood Ave N (between N 85th and N 86th St). 782.7545

North Seattle

34 Carkeek Park This 198-acre greensward bordering Puget Sound has been left mostly to wilderness, though there are a number of forest trails and picnic areas for nature lovers. Crews of Camp Fire Girls conduct weeklong summer camps out here, and folks run their dogs or enjoy lunch by the water. ♦ NW Carkeek Park Rd and Ninth Ave NW

35 Bella Luna ★$ The northernmost in Dany Mitchell's local Italian chain (which includes **Trattoria Mitchelli** in Pioneer Square, **Trattoria Angelina** in West Seattle, and **Stella's Trattoria** in the University District) is housed in a former pizza parlor. It serves hearty, consistently good fare—pasta specials change daily and there's decent pizza, too— plus some more unusual dishes like the garlicky spinach linguine with walnuts and red peppers. The wine list is simple but effective. The decor is spacious, featuring a fireplace for chilly days and a plant-bedecked atrium for sunny ones. ♦ Italian ♦ M-F lunch and dinner; Sa-Su breakfast, lunch, and dinner. 14053 Greenwood Ave N (at N 143rd St). 367.5862

36 Tan Duc ★$ This quiet restaurant specializes in Chinese and Vietnamese food. Especially recommended are the Vietnamese box dinners—huge platters of barbecued shrimp, bean sprouts, cooked meats, vegetables, and other savories. Wrap them all up in a delicate rice-flour pancake, dip it in the sweet sauce, and enjoy! Friendly advice from the staff is available for novices. ♦ Chinese/Vietnamese ♦ Daily lunch and dinner. 10009 Aurora Ave N (at N 100th St). 525.0511

Mail carriers don't hesitate to identify Seattle's most exclusive neighborhood: The Highlands. The houses in this area west of Aurora Avenue on the bluff above the Shilshole Marina don't even have addresses. Letters and packages to residents are simply addressed, "The Highlands, Seattle, Washington 98177."

Seattle, more than most cities, is wary of outsiders."

New York Times Magazine

Restaurants/Clubs: Red Hotels: Blue
Shops/ ♦ Outdoors: Green Sights/Culture: Black

37 Doong Kong Lau ★★$ Hot and spicy Hakka regional cuisine is served in this usually busy Chinese restaurant. The hot pots—the name is quite literal—are prepared in an assortment of styles (vegetarian, seafood, pork, etc.), and the garlic eggplant should not be missed. ♦ Chinese ♦ Daily lunch and dinner. 9710 Aurora Ave N (between N 97th and N 98th Sts). 526.8828

Aurora—Another Roadside Distraction

Aurora Avenue North, also known as **Highway 99,** used to be the main north-south highway running through Seattle. Today, it's a comparatively minor thoroughfare. At the city's heart, Aurora is an elevated highway running along the Waterfront; south of downtown, it's known as **Pacific Highway South.** But north of Seattle, rolling out into the suburban hinterlands of Lynnwood, now, that's a different kettle of kitsch. There, this road becomes the car culture equivalent of a Marrakech bazaar, bordered by blinding neon, strip malls and strip joints, questionable motels, taverns, used-car lots, and assorted other businesses—alternately cheerful and new or grim and shopworn, but always unique. Aurora Avenue's style evokes three essential aspects of American life: fast cars, quick bucks, and a high tolerance for personal weirdness.

"Aurora is the homely and affordable face of American capitalism. . . . " writes Jonathan Raban, a British author expatriated to Seattle. "Driving Aurora is like riffling at speed through the text of an eccentric illustrated encyclopedia. The entries rush past too rapidly to follow, and they couple promiscuously with each other: Something about pest control gets tangled up with something about foam rubber and chiropractors and The Love Pantry."

For example, the **Twin Teepees Restaurant** (7201 Aurora Ave N, at N 72nd Ave, 783.9740) is a loony tribute to Native American culture. Built in 1937, it cheerfully mixes Northwest Coast and Plains Indian clichés with no particular regard for accuracy; case in point are the paintings that flank the entrance to the "teepees"—they look like bears, or maybe whales.

Another classic is an extremely ratty looking life-size elephant that advertises the **Aurora Flower Shop** (8808 Aurora Ave N, between N 88th and N 89th Sts, 522.5336). It was also built during the Depression, as were so many of these highway come-ons. Legend has it that a florist who once owned this shop kept the paunchy proboscidean in his backyard for years before hoisting it onto a pole above busy Highway 99. **Seal's Motel** (12035 Aurora Ave N, between N 120th and N 122nd Sts, 363.9009) displays a seal balancing a ball on its nose.

And, all along the way the signs reel by, each more outlandish than the last until you reach some true showstoppers such as "Do bugs, not drugs," which promotes an exterminator.

38 Larry's Market Welcome to Grocery Land USA, a pop-culture spin on the classic American supermarket. Larry McKinney was a grocer's son who inherited his first store in the 1960s and has since expanded the family business into a chain of fine food emporiums in the suburbs. The stores have a faux-industrial appearance—exposed ventilation pipes and rafters and metal racks supporting boxes of unpacked supplies. But interior design is theater, so enjoy the show. The sheer quantity and quality—of everything from fresh flowers to fresh sushi—is mind boggling. ♦ Daily 24 hours. 10008 Aurora Ave N (at N 100th St). 527.5333

39 Northgate Shopping Center Holding the dubious distinction of being the world's first shopping mall, this structure was designed in the 1950s by architect **John Graham Sr.**, who also invented the revolving restaurant and

helped develop the **Space Needle** for the 1962 World's Fair. Oddly enough, considering Seattle's prevailing weather, it was originally uncovered; only later was a roof added. All the usual suspects can be found here: **Nordstrom, The Bon, B. Dalton Bookseller, Lamonts,** and **The Tux Shop.** ♦ Daily; M-Sa until 9:30PM. NE Northgate Way (off I-5). 362.4777

40 Maple Leaf Sports Grill ★★$ Don't let the name fool you; the fresh flowers on the tables are a tip-off that this is not a typical sports bar. It's a true neighborhood hangout, serving an excellent assortment of beers and wines. The decor has lots of old wood and open space. Lunch and dinner choices include one of the most succulent burgers in town and a changing array of imaginative specials featuring fish, chicken, and pasta. ♦ American ♦ M-F lunch and dinner; Sa dinner. 8909 Roosevelt Way NE (at NE 89th St). 523.8449

41 Cooper's Northwest Alehouse It's technically not a brewpub (no beers are prepared on the premises), but this crowded and cheery tavern is a mecca for Northwest microbrews: 21 of its 22 tap brews are West Coast specialties. The staff is knowledgeable about the subtle distinctions of each type, and sipping samples of new brews are accompanied by enthusiastic debate over their relative merits and flaws. Wine and some bar food (like fish-and-chips) is served, but beer is the draw. Darts tournaments are held on a regular basis. ♦ M-Sa until 2AM; Su until midnight. 8065 Lake City Way NE (near 15th Ave NE). 522.2923

42 Panda's ★$ Known for inexpensive high-quality food and fast, friendly service, the kitchen staff here makes its soup noodles, dumplings, buns, and sauces fresh daily. The orange beef, Happy Family (stir-fried scallops, shrimp, and breast of chicken), and *moo shu* pork (stir-fried vegetables and pork wrapped in crepes) are all outstanding. Delivery is free within the North End. ♦ Chinese/Takeout ♦ M-Sa lunch and dinner; Su dinner. 7347 35th Ave NE (between NE 73rd and NE 74th Sts). 526.5115. Also at: 1625 W Dravus St (between 15th and 16th Aves W). 283.9030

43 Wurdemann Mansion Situated in **Lake Forest Park,** this two-story Georgian manse was built in 1914 for eye surgeon Harry Wurdemann. The mansion stood on five acres of land at the entrance to the park, just off Victory Way (later rechristened Bothell Way). The grounds were planted with rose bushes, apple trees, and a cherry orchard that had given the estate its name, Cherry Acres.

Ten years later local banker (and later, embezzler) Adolph Linden bought the house and sank as much as $100,000 into improvements: a wading pool in the side yard; a fence encircling the property, made partly of white-wood latticework, partly of brick and iron; a gate from Victory Way onto a driveway that curved up to the white, pillared mansion, then swept around to a porte cochere at the rear. (This grand entrance eventually had to be locked because travelers continually mistook the mansion for a roadhouse and would come at all hours in search of lodging). The mansion fell into disuse but, after decades of decrepitude, it has been restored as the centerpiece of a small, upscale housing community, and is now privately owned. ♦ Bothell Way NE and NE Ballinger Way

44 Charlie Mac's Sports Club This sports bar replaced **Parker's,** a legendary North Seattle teen hangout of the 1950s and 1960s, and later a more sophisticated music venue. There's still dancing Wednesday through Saturday nights, but the dance floor can be converted to a basketball or volleyball court at will. There are dart boards, pool and Foosball tables, and 30—that's right 30—color monitors and three giant screens for watching televised sports. ♦ Daily until 2AM. 17001 Aurora Ave N (at N 173rd St). 542.9491

Green Lake, which has an average depth of only 15 feet, is what's left of a huge Ice Age lake that once stretched between the present cities of Everett and Olympia. Haller and Bitter Lakes, in the northern part of Seattle, are also remnants of that ancient body of water.

43

km 1/2 1
mi 1/4 1/2

N

Lake
Washington

35th Ave. NE
39th Ave. NE
Riviera Pl. NE
Hwy. 513/Sand Point Wy. NE
20th St.
40th Ave. NE
15th
NE 110th St.
owbrook
eld NE 105th St.
40th Ave. NE
45th Ave. NE
Lake Shore Blvd. NE
00th St.
Matthews
Beach
Park
35th Ave. NE
NE 85th St.
Sand Point Wy. NE
NE 80th St.
NE 75th St.
2

| Restaurants/Clubs: Red | Hotels: Blue |
| Shops/ 🌳 Outdoors: Green | Sights/Culture: Black |

Froula
Playground

NE 70th St.

I-5

NE 68th St.

NE 65th St.

30

NE 63rd St.

NE 62nd St.

29

NE 60th St.

20th Ave. NE

23rd Ave. NE

32
33

12th Ave. NE

31
Cowen
Park

Cowen Pl. NE

34
Ravenna
Park

NE 58th St. **35**

NE 60th St.

Ravenna Blvd. NE **36**

RAVENNA

27th Ave. NE

37

Latona Ave. NE

NE 55th St.

24

NE 52nd St.

15th Ave. NE

17th Ave. NE

Ravenna Ave.

Burke-Gilman Trail

NE Blakeley St.

25
26
University
Playfield

23

22
21

NE 50th St.

19

Latona Ave. NE

Roosevelt Wy. NE

12th Ave. NE

Brooklyn Ave. NE

University Wy. NE

NE 47th St.

20th Ave. NE

25th Ave. NE

18

17
16

28

27

11th Ave.

15

13 **14**

NE 45th St.

Burke Memorial Museum

20

Hwy. 513

Clark

12 **11**

Stevens Wy.

8th Ave. NE

9th Ave. NE

NE 43rd St.

10
9

Pend Oreille Rd.

Montlake Blvd. NE

Walla Walla Rd.

NE 42nd St.

5

NE 41st St.

8 **7**
6

2
University of
Washington

Edmundson
Pavilion

NE Campus Pkwy.

1
3

Husky
Stadium

NE 42nd St.

4
NE Northlake
Wy.

Burke-Gilman Trail

NE 40th St.

NE Pacific St.

NE Boat St.

Stevens Wy.

Lake Washington
Ship Canal Bridge

University
Bridge

Pacific Pl. NE

Columbia Rd.

University of
Washington
Medical Center

Eastlake Ave. E.

Fuhrman Ave. E.

San Juan Rd.

Walla Walla Rd.

Montlake
Bridge

Waterfront
Activities
Center

N

Portage
Bay

km
mi

1/4   1/2   1/2   1

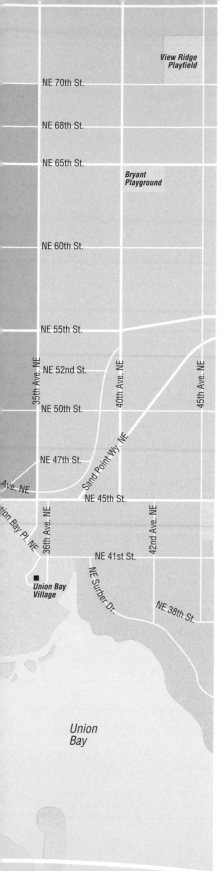

University District/ Ravenna

Centered around the **University of Washington (UW)**, the University District has grown with the institution, which opened its doors downtown in 1861, then relocated to this area just north of **Lake Union** in 1895. Around the beginning of the 20th century the "U District," as it's called, was sparsely populated, without paved streets, sewers, lights, or sidewalks. It could take half a day just to journey downtown by streetcar. Residents called it "Brooklyn" back then, trusting that this neighborhood, like New York City's Brooklyn, would thrive because it was adjacent to a big city.

In 1909 their faith was rewarded when Seattle located the Alaska-Yukon-Pacific Exposition (AYP) at the **UW** campus. This, the city's first World's Fair, was heavily promoted by business burghers who wished to attract East Coast attention and stimulate regional growth. University officials eagerly volunteered their land for the fair's site, hoping to reap a legacy of buildings and development for what was then a backwoods campus.

The AYP was a stunning success. It took two years to build, cost $10 million, drew 3.7 million visitors, turned a small profit ($62,676) despite the fact that liquor was banned in the district at the time, and stamped Seattle as a young city on the move. Exhibits showcased 26 countries and featured dozens of Classical-style buildings set amid stately grounds laid out by the Olmsted Brothers of Massachusetts, the nation's foremost landscape architecture firm and principal players in Seattle's early planning. The AYP opened when President William Howard Taft pressed a golden telegraph key in Washington, DC, and switched on the fair's opening lights. (That same key would be used by President John F. Kennedy 53 years later to kick off the 1962 Century 21 Exposition.) It lasted more than four months, drawing visitors to hundreds of industrial, educational, and carnival exhibits. When the exposition was over, the neighborhood was left with sewers, water mains, and other modern amenities, and the university ha been given a parklike campus and about 20 buildings. With the Olmsteds' help, the fairgrounds were adapted to university use.

Over the years the school and its neighborhood have often been the center of controversy. In 1948 a state-appointed commission scrutinized the campus fo "un-American activities." In the dark days that followed, the Board of Regent: dismissed three faculty members, and put three others on probation for their Communist Party associations. Later the tumultuous 1960s brought long hai rock music, marijuana, and the counterculture. Tensions ran high and in 196 the Black Student Union took over part of the **Administration Building.** The next year, antiwar demonstrators bombed university structures. In 1970 som 10,000 people marched from the campus down Interstate 5 to downtown in protest over the deaths of four students at Kent State University in Ohio.

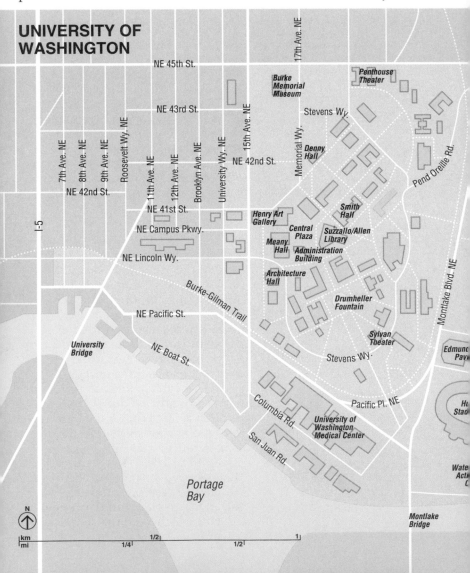

UNIVERSITY OF
WASHINGTON

Today the **University of Washington** is one of the largest single-campus universities on the West Coast. Its 694-acre tract, hosting nearly 34,000 students in 16 schools and colleges, occupies nearly half the neighborhood. A number of its component schools—including health sciences, engineering, and computer science—are counted among the nation's top 10. The neighborhood mirrors the school's diversity and energy. Streets are filled with bookstores, clothing shops, coffeehouses, and informal, inexpensive cafes. This area is a big reason why Seattle consistently ranks so high in per-capita movie attendance, book purchases, and espresso consumption. The district's spine, as well as its heart, is represented by **University Way** (better known as "The Ave"). During the noon hour each day, more than a thousand pedestrians move through this lengthy corridor. The Ave also hosts the annual University Street Fair, a popular arts and crafts fest held in May, which brings long-haired vendors selling necklaces, street musicians, and the scent of patchouli oil back to these streets.

Colorful as it is, the U District isn't as interesting as it could be. Outside of the campus, it's dominated by dull, modern apartment buildings. It's loaded with bargain-filled restaurants, but few are among the city's finest. And there is a dearth of places that have good music or dancing. More seriously, the Ave is frequently besieged by panhandlers and drug dealers. Generally, however, this and other streets are safe to stroll after dark, which is a relief, because the district's flat topography invites walking.

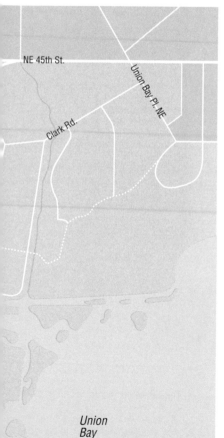

NE 45th St.

Union Bay Pl. NE

Clark Rd.

Union Bay

Named for the large, lovely park that graces its center, Ravenna lies just north of the University District. It is a safe, well-tended, middle-class enclave where many **UW** professors and other staff members reside in 1920s and 1930s "bungaloids"—remodeled two-bedroom houses that have retained the neighborhood's original character. A decade or two ago mainly middle-aged and older people dwelt here, but many families with young children have moved in and the playgrounds are full again. Nightlife in this neighborhood is practically nonexistent, but several good restaurants have popped up.

Seattle boasts more than 300 parks and playgrounds, for a combined 5,000 acres of parkland.

"It's cute. Why are they tearing it down?"

Fran Leibowitz, humorist, commenting on Seattle and the signs of its obsessive growth.

University District

1 Visitors' Information Center An ideal starting point for a tour of the neighborhood, the center offers campus maps, restaurant, lodging and bus info, and local events' schedules. ◆ M-F. 4014 University Way NE (at NE Campus Pkwy). 543.9198

2 University of Washington The upper campus is the classic evocation of academia: ivy-covered Gothic-style buildings grouped around formal, brick-paved quadrangles; majestic sycamores, maples, and oaks; and curved walkways leading through nicely landscaped grounds. There's no denying that this is a beautiful place to stroll (see the map of **UW** on page 164), whether you're dazzled by the architecture, the cherry trees in bloom, or the million-dollar views of Lake Washington and the Cascade peaks from the student dorms. The lower campus, marked by newer, 1950s concrete edifices, merits little attention by comparison. Today, the university has an enrollment of about 34,000; its most popular graduate schools are arts and sciences, engineering, medicine, law, and dentistry.

The main entrance is at the intersection of 17th Avenue NE and NE 45th Street, from which you travel along Memorial Way beneath a dramatic archway of sycamores to arrive on campus. At NE 41st Street, a pedestrian overpass crosses 15th Avenue NE to reach the university via Central Plaza. The entrance to a large parking garage (located below the plaza) is here, too. A third point of entry is on the eastern backside of campus, at 25th Street NE, about one-eighth of a mile north of **Husky Stadium.** ◆ 17th Ave NE and NE 45th St

On the University of Washington campus:

Central Plaza Commonly referred to as "Red Square" (attributable to its expanse of red bricks, not to any Bolshevik incidents), this campus crossroads was designed in 1972. The vast, almost treeless plaza is surrounded by stark, hard-surfaced buildings constructed in a mishmash arrangement of architectural styles. It's overpowering and strikes many people as depressing and inhuman, but on sunny days this spot functions as an Italian piazza, alive with students strumming guitars, throwing Frisbees, and enjoying brown-bag lunches. ◆ 15th Ave NE and NE 41st St

Suzzallo/Allen Library Certainly the most impressive building on campus, this ornate Tudor Gothic library was designed by **Carl Gould** and dates from about 1926. Founder of the university's architecture department, **Gould** laid out plans for 18 campus buildings (as well as **Volunteer Park**'s old **Seattle Art Museum** and, with partner **Charles Bebb,** the **Times Square Building** downtown).

This library was the crowning achievement—and also the downfall—of Henry Suzzallo, former university president (1915-1926), who is often recalled as **UW**'s "modern father." Suzzallo wanted an ambitious, cathedral-like building, believing that "the library is the sou of the university." Washington Governor Roland Hartley didn't agree: He looked at the $900,000 invoice, dubbed it "Suzzallo's extravagance," and fired the respected educator, who went on to head the philanthropic Carnegie Foundation.

Outside, observe three sculptures perched over the entrance: *Thought, Inspiration,* and *Mastery,* created by Tacoma artist Allan Clark (see **Art Around the Plaza** below). Inside, follow the curved staircase from the building entrance to the mezzanine-level **Graduate Reading Room,** where vaulting and 36-foot-high stained-glass windows tower above. ◆ Daily; M-Th, Su until midnight (hours are more restricted during school breaks). Central Plaza

Smith Hall Twenty-eight gargoyles decorate the exterior of this 1940 building, which houses the history and geography departments. Designed by faculty member **Dudley Pratt,** each gargoyle symbolizes something different. Six figures at the east entrance signify humankind's primitive need while those on the southeast corner depict concepts of weather. Those on the northeast corner stand for the power and war of Europ the magic of Africa, and the knowledge of th Orient. A book-laden egghead in the groupin stands for the intelligent democracy of America. Groups on the north side depict Seattle's history. ◆ Adjacent to the Suzzallo/Allen Library

Meany Hall Named in honor of a popular and longtime history professor, Edmond S. Meany, this performing arts center contains a 1,200-seat theater, a 200-seat studio, and dance facilities. Excellent acoustics and intimate seating make it one of the city's premier venues for chamber music series, dance recitals, and concerts. ◆ Central Plaz 543.4880

Art around the Plaza The west facade of the **Suzzallo/Allen Library** hosts 18 terra-cotta figures of famous people, including Shakespeare, Beethoven, and Plato. The original design for Darwin featured a small ape thumbing its nose at the humans below but the university president vetoed that concept. (Look closely at Darwin, and you'll see a hole at the bottom of the figure where the ape should be.) Hidden behind oak trees the Gothic-style **Administration Building** o the south side of the plaza is ringed by 24 gargoyles and other figures, each one representing an academic discipline. The square contains *Broken Obelisk,* a two-ton, 26-foot steel work that resembles an upside down pencil and is a rare sculpture by Barnett Newman, a New York painter known mostly for abstract color fields. The three campaniles that soar into the sky are visually striking but have a more quotidian purpose as well: they are vents to disperse car exhaust fumes from the underground garage. A bronze statue of *George Washington* on the square's west side was sculpted in 1909 by Lorado Taft and unveiled for the AYP Expo.

Henry Art Gallery This **Carl Gould**–designed museum boasts classical lines: Tudor Gothic architecture, striking decorative brickwork, and handsome skylit exhibition galleries. Opened in 1927, its construction was funded by Horace C. Henry, a local real estate and railroad magnate, who also donated an art collection worth more than $400,000 to it. The gallery blends past and present, so you might stumble upon a video exhibition just as easily as you would a display of historical Western landscapes or modern Chinese painting. The permanent collection contains the 19th- and early 20th-century American and European paintings from Henry's original contribution. ◆ Donation requested. Tu-Su; Th until 9PM. Central Plaza. 543.2280

Denny Hall Built circa 1895, this turreted French Renaissance structure was the first—and for some time the only—building on campus. Given the hall's original importance, its very ordinary location (with no expansive view over Lake Union) seems curious. But campus legend has it that officials argued for so long over the building's proper site that one exasperated regent finally stuck his umbrella into a fallen fir tree and said, "You fellows can put the building where you want it; I'm going to put it here." And there it's been ever since. ◆ Off Memorial Way

Thomas Burke Memorial Washington State Museum Exhibits in natural history, anthropology, and geology from Pacific Rim cultures span many epochs in this museum. High on the list of must-sees is the collection of Northwest Coast Indian artifacts. An

Alaskan Arctic collection of basketry, ivory, beadwork, and masks (like the three pictured below left) wins accolades. Children will enjoy the dinosaur skeletons, fossils, and totem poles. Take a look at the stained-glass window portraying a peacock in the **Burke Room**: It's by master Louis Comfort Tiffany himself. The museum was designed in 1962 by **James J. Chiarelli** in honor of Judge Thomas Burke, an attorney who negotiated early Seattle land acquisitions for **Great Northern Railroad** builder James J. Hill. ◆ Donation requested. Daily; Th until 10PM. NE 45th St (between 15th Ave NE and Memorial Way). 543.5590

Within the Thomas Burke Memorial Washington State Museum:

The Boiserie ★★$ The museum's basement contains the toniest and one of the most pleasant coffeehouses in Seattle. The high-ceilinged room features 18th-century French pine panels and artwork, antique wooden tables, classical music, and very tasty pastries. It's a favorite spot for students between classes, and a rest stop for campus cops. Desserts are plentiful and delicious; the carrot cake comes from the Broadway Baking Company. The tree-shaded patio is ideal for lounging on warm days. ◆ Coffeehouse ◆ Daily; M-F until 8PM. 543.9854

Penthouse Theater Built in about 1940 as the nation's first theater-in-the-round (the frescoes and seats have been restored to their original state), this is the stage for the **School of Drama**'s productions. Tickets are available here at the box office or at the **UW Ticket Office** (4001 University Way NE, at NE Campus Pkwy, 543.4880), which is open Monday through Friday from 10:30AM to 6PM. ◆ Box office opens one hour before show time. Near NE 45th St and 17th Ave NE. 543.4880

Architecture Hall This is the only major structure built for the Alaska-Yukon-Pacific Expo that is left standing. San Francisco's **John Galen Howard**, who in 1909 was campus architect for the University of California, Berkeley, created the eclectic classical style design. Today, the building houses the **Department of Urban Planning.** ◆ NE Lincoln Way

Frosh Pond, Rainier Vista During the AYP Exposition this body of water was a geyser basin. Afterward it became a spot where first-year students received honorary dunkings from sophomores. And today it's a decorative pool with a fountain—officially the *Drumheller Fountain*—that's especially appealing when surrounding roses are in bloom. Proud moms and dads snap Polaroids of students here. The walkway down to the Montlake Bridge was designed by the Olmsted Brothers in 1909 as a culminating viewpoint from which fairgoers could eyeball Mount Rainier. ◆ Between Stevens Way and Pend Oreille Rd

Sylvan Theater The grassy glade, site of an annual summer Shakespeare series, is easily missed. Tucked away within a grove of trees, it contains a cool, shady amphitheater and four white columns standing by themselves with nothing to support. These columns, shaped of cedar poles, were transported—at the insistence of Professor Edmond Meany—from their positions at the entrance to the original downtown **Territorial University** building, when that old edifice was finally being torn down in 1908. Each of the four columns has a name—Loyalty, Industry, Faith, and Efficiency—the first letters of each spelling LIFE. ♦ Stevens Way

Husky Stadium Football-crazed fans watch the **Huskies** (often called "The Dawgs" but never "Dogs") here in the Northwest's largest stadium, which seats 72,500 people. It's said that the Wave was invented here in 1981 by the marching band director and cheerleader, Robb Weller. The south section of the cantilevered steel balcony and roof was finally erected in 1987, after a calamitous construction accident in which steel support beams weakened and the entire section crumbled into a massive pile of twisted metal. No one was hurt, but the scene was immortalized when a photographer, John Stamets, riding by on his bicycle, snapped a frame-by-frame account of the collapse and published it in a local newspaper. ♦ Montlake Blvd NE. 543.2200

Waterfront Activities Center Rent canoes or rowboats to cross Union Bay and then wander through the soft, lily-padded backwaters near the **Washington Park Arboretum** (see the "Capitol Hill" chapter on page 93) for a Monet-like experience. Bird-watchers might want to go north from the center, creeping along the shore to see blue herons, eagles, and other wild creatures in a protected reserve. ♦ M-F Feb-Oct. Walla Walla Rd (on Union Bay). 543.9433

3 College Inn Guest House $ Popular with visiting professors and other university types on a budget, this renovated 25-room bed-and-breakfast was built as a hotel for the 1909 AYP, and is on the National Register of Historic Places. Rooms are very plain, spare (no TV, no telephones) but clean and generally pleasant. Bathrooms are shared. ♦ 4000 University Way NE (at NE 40th St). 633.4441

4 Burke-Gilman Trail This beloved, 12.5-mile recreational route runs along an abandoned **Burlington Northern** railbed. More than a million people bike, jog, or walk here each year. The scenic trail hugs Lake Union and then crawls east and north, virtually through the backyards of lakefront homes, until it reaches Kenmore's **Logboom Park** at the northern tip of Lake Washington. One caveat: 70 percent of trail users are bicyclists, so walkers should take extra care. ♦ From Gas Works Park, Fremont, to Logboom Park, Kenmore

4 Northlake Tavern & Pizza House ★★$ The principal wall decorations here are cartoons from the *Seattle Post-Intelligencer*'s David Horsey, but there's nothing comic about the pizza here. Crusts (including a respectable whole-wheat variety) are chewy without threatening to yank out your wisdom teeth, and the cooks have nothing against piling on the toppings. Build your own pie from a 14-ingredient list, or just order the Italian Special (salami, Italian beef sausage, mushrooms, onions, and tomatoes). You can even buy an uncooked pizza to pop in the oven later on. ♦ Pizza/Takeout ♦ Daily lunch and dinner. 660 NE Northlake Way (at I-5). 633.5317

5 University Inn $ A $2.5-million addition added a sleek touch to this small, friendly, modern hotel (pictured above). There are 102 comfortable rooms—none with a view worth mentioning, however—a small heated outdoor pool, a coffee shop, and complimentary continental breakfast. ♦ 4140 Roosevelt Way NE (between NE 41st and NE 42nd Sts). 632.5055; fax 547.4937

6 European Restaurant & Pastry Shop ★ German-style food (Hungarian goulash, stuffed cabbage rolls, sausage sandwiches) is served in an Old World atmosphere. Most people, though, come here for the pastries, especially the Black Forest cake. ♦ German ♦ M-Sa breakfast, lunch, dinner; Su lunch. 4108 University Way NE (between NE 41st and NE 42nd Sts). 632.7893

7 Folk Art Gallery-La Tienda Begun in the early 1960s by an anthropology aficionado who brought back a carload of trinkets from Tijuana, this small shop has flowered into a folk art treasure trove. Gift-hunters can choose items from 80 countries: Chilean rain sticks, Guatemalan ceremonial *huipils* (woven ponchos), Balinese masks, and Indonesian shadow puppets. ♦ M-Sa; Th until 9PM. 413

University Way NE (between NE 41st and NE 42nd Sts). 632.1796

7 Shultzy's Sausage $ The homemade sausages served at this hole-in-the-wall are ground and stuffed with Uncle Norm's recipe. Lines form out the door for the spicy-hot Ragin' Cajun and milder andouille choices. ◆ Deli ◆ Daily lunch and dinner. 4142 University Way NE (between NE 41st and NE 42nd Sts). 548.9461

8 Big Time Brewery and Alehouse This tavern-turned-brewpub offers four kinds of beer made on the premises, all flavorful, unpasteurized, and heavier than your standard-issue Bud. An 80-year-old back bar, hardwood floors, vintage signs, and a jukebox create a traditional American alehouse atmosphere. Large front windows allow for a maximum of people watching. A small kitchen produces hefty sandwiches and very acceptable nachos. ◆ M-Th, Su until 12:30AM; F-Sa until 1AM. 4133 University Way NE (between NE 41st and NE 42nd Sts). 545.4509

9 Magus Bookstore Unswept floors, books stacked precariously high, a guy who has a PhD and speaks 11 languages working behind the counter—this is your quintessential college used-book seller. Don't expect to find Judith Krantz among the piles of literature, philosophy, history, and art books. ◆ Daily; F-Sa until 10PM. 1408 NE 42nd St (at University Way NE) 633.1800

9 Cafe Allegro ★$ Reputed to have introduced Seattle to espresso during the 1960s and still a funkier, more traditional coffeehouse than most in the city, this small, smoky, brick-lined cafe enjoys a remarkably loyal clientele. There's great coffee, ordinary pastries, and a staff that will let you curl up in a corner to read *War and Peace* in its entirety. The political graffiti in the bathrooms is not to be missed. ◆ Coffeehouse ◆ Daily until 11PM. 4214 University Way NE (in the alley around the corner from Magus Bookstore). 633.3030

10 Bulldog News The largest, most eclectic newsstand in the Northwest carries everything from the *New Yorker* and *National Review* to *Spin, Story*, British *Esquire, The Hockey News*, and *British Columbia Report*. Hundreds of alternative weeklies, out-of-town papers, and foreign periodicals are also on hand. Service can sometimes be indifferent to your requests. An espresso counter dispenses drinks to sidewalk patrons; watch out, the lines here can get long. ◆ Daily 8AM-9PM. 4208 University Way NE (between NE 42nd and NE 43rd Sts). 632.6397. Also at: Broadway Market (401 Broadway E). 328.2881

11 University Book Store Banished from campus in 1925 when its location was deemed a fire hazard, the business landed here, the former site of a pool hall that was closed by state authorities to protect students from "distractions." The present store, now the largest bookstore in Seattle and one of the largest college bookstores in the nation, offers an extensive selection of general fiction, mysteries, science fiction, and travel books. The children's department is estimable, and textbooks and academic press offerings can be found in almost overwhelming proportions. There's free gift wrapping on the second floor and frequent sale prices on general-interest books. ◆ Daily; Th until 9PM. 4326 University Way NE (between NE 43rd and NE 44th Sts). 634.3400. Also at: 990 102nd Ave NE (at NE 10th St), Bellevue. 632.9500

12 Toscana ★★$$ Sit down to a candlelit dinner with white tablecloths and imagine yourself in an intimate, no-name *ristorante* off the Via Veneto. The homemade pastas are light and zesty, the stuffed chicken and sautéed squid are expertly prepared, and the desserts are wonderful. ◆ Italian ◆ M, W-Su dinner. 1312½ NE 43rd St (between University Way NE and Brooklyn Ave NE). 547.7679

13 Safeco Building At 23 stories in height, the tallest—and some would say the ugliest—in the district is corporate headquarters for an insurance company. More interesting, the company has assembled a $1-million, 600-piece collection of modern Northwest art and makes some of it accessible to the public. Go into the lobby or up to the mezzanine to see rotating exhibitions of Pilchuck School glass and abstract paintings. The bronze fountain outside was created by famed local sculptor George Tsutakawa. **Naramore, Bain, Brady & Johanson** (precursors of today's **NBBJ Group**) designed the tower. ◆ M-F. 4333 Brooklyn Ave NE (at NE 45th St). 545.5000

14 Neptune Theater One of Seattle's first-run movie houses, this elaborate palace was built in 1921 to showcase silent movies. It was renovated in 1993, when plastic "stained glass" was removed and the original plasterwork featuring renditions of Neptune's head was restored. Grillwork over the organ pipes features tridents and starfish. ◆ 303 NE 45th St (between Brooklyn Ave NE and University Way NE). 633.5545

estaurants/Clubs: Red   **Hotels:** Blue

ꞁops/ 🌳 **Outdoors:** Green   **Sights/Culture:** Black

15 Meany Tower Hotel $$ The district's first luxury hostelry, this 14-story building opened to great fanfare in 1931. The architect was **Robert C. Reamer**, who also designed those oversize mountain cabins known as the Old Faithful Inn and the Canyon Hotel in Yellowstone National Park (a far cry from the Art Deco column here). Today, it's one of the neighborhood's nicer hotels—not as luxurious as some of the downtown spots, but much more economical. **Reamer** (whose other credits include the **Skinner Building** and the **1411 Fourth Avenue Building** downtown) shaped the hotel so that each of the 155 guest rooms provides a broad corner view. (Ask for a room facing either south to the city or east across Lake Washington.) On the first floor, the **Meany Grill** serves prime rib, steaks, and seafood in an undistinguished setting. The lounge has a big-screen TV and an oyster bar. ♦ 4507 Brooklyn Ave NE (at NE 45th St). 634.2000, 800/648.6440

16 Danken's Gourmet Ice Cream This rich, creamy ice cream is for serious junkies and gets lots of publicity for owner Dan Samson. The Chocolate Decadence Bar—reputed to be a whopping 22-percent fat—and the coffee ice cream are tops. ♦ Tu-Th noon-11PM; F-Sa noon-midnight; Su noon-10PM. 4507 University Way NE (at NE 45th St). 545.8596

17 New Seattle Massage A longtime district fave for relaxing, hands-on treatments, this salon offers a variety of techniques including Swedish, Shiatsu, and Sports styles by 35 licensed massage therapists. ♦ Daily until 9PM. Call for an appointment. 4519½ University Way NE (between NE 45th and NE 47th Sts). 632.5074

18 The Continental Restaurant ★$ Old-timers play backgammon, the postgrad crowd sips retsina in an unhurried atmosphere, and parents of young children return time and again because owner Demetre Lagos works magic with unruly tots. The souvlakia sandwiches, Greek fries, and feta cheese omelettes are all good. ♦ Greek ♦ Daily breakfast, lunch, and dinner. 4549 University Way NE (between NE 45th and NE 47th Sts). 632.4700

18 University Bar & Grill ★$ This was once a hip place to hang out, but now it's a quiet location for drinking and conversation. The menu's strength is in its fettuccine dishes, but the restaurant's real raison d'être is its full bar, surprisingly a rarity in this neighborhood. Grab a front table for people watching along the Ave or slip into the back room for privacy. ♦ Italian ♦ Daily lunch and dinner. 4553 University Way NE (between NE 45th and NE 47th Sts). 632.3275

18 University Seafood & Poultry Very fresh high-quality gifts from the sea—Dungeness crabs, local oysters, salmon, halibut, caviar—are sold at this third-generation, family-owned business. The shop will pack and ship your fish by overnight courier or put it in an airline-approved, odorless, leakproof carton good for 48 hours. ♦ M-Sa. 1317 NE 47th St (at University Way NE). 632.3900

19 Greek Row Six blocks of stately, traditional, brick-faced fraternity and sorority houses set amid a long archway of tall trees will make you want to get out your college letter sweater and yell, "Sis boom bah!" Of the 31 frat houses and 18 sororities, the most interesting include the **Sigma Nu House** (built in 1926 and designed by architect **Ellsworth Storey**), showing Wrightian overtones (1616 NE 47th St); the **Alpha Tau Omega House** (completed in 1929 and designed by **Lionel Pries**), the work of a onetime teacher at **UW's Department of Architecture** (1800 NE 47th St); and the **Phi Gamma Delta House** (built in 1927 and designed by **Mellor, Meigs & Howe** with **J. Lister Holmes**), a Tudor Revival edifice (5404 17th Ave NE).

Sadly, this Ivy League atmosphere was also the setting for the 1975 disappearance of Georgann Hawkins, an 18-year-old coed living at a nearby sorority house. She was among the victims of serial killer Ted Bundy, a good-looking, smooth-talking former **UW** psychology student who terrorized Seattle during the 1970s before he was caught and finally executed in Florida in 1989. Bundy confessed to more than a dozen murders in Washington, Oregon, and Utah, but detectives suspect he actually committed somewhere between three dozen and one hundred. ♦ Between NE 45th and 50th Sts, and 17th and 22nd Aves NE

20 University Village Several large stores anchor this shopping center, and more than 60 independent shops sell clothes, gift items, and home furnishings. Brick walkways, a fountain, and a casual pace suited to browsing help cut back on shopper's frenzy. **Caldwell** (522.7531) carries ethnic and decorative home accessories such as New England crafts, Mexican folk art, African pots, as well as wicker tables, chairs, baskets, and boxes. **VIVA** (525.8482) and **Marlee** (522.6526) are popular for their exclusive women's apparel. **Teri's Toybox** (526.7147) sells kids' playthings and games. **Pasta and Co.** (523.8594) offers tempting appetizers and salads; try the marinated chicken breasts, tortellini, or Chinese vermicelli. ♦ 25th Ave N and NE 45th St. 523.0622

Restaurants/Clubs: Red   **Hotels:** Blue
Shops/ 🌳 Outdoors: Green   **Sights/Culture:** Black

21 Grand Illusion This independently owned theater regularly books experimental or political films. The screen is small and the viewing room is claustrophobic, but a blue velvet couch in the back row gets a thumbs-up for romance. ♦ Box office opens a half-hour before show time. 1493 NE 50th St (at University Way NE). 523.3935

22 Sala Thai ★★$ Consistently good Thai soups, curries, and coriander chicken are served at this unassuming restaurant. ♦ Thai ♦ M-Sa lunch and dinner; Su dinner. 5004 University Way NE (at NE 50th St). 522.2297

23 University Heights Elementary School Established in 1902, the district's first primary school grew in the 1920s to become the largest in Seattle. Contending that major repairs were needed, the school district closed the school down several years ago, despite widespread community protest. The wooden-framed structure, designed by **Charles Bebb** and **Leonard L. Mendel** (who together would later create the **Old Ballard Firehouse**), is now used by nonprofit organizations and community groups. ♦ 5031 University Way NE (between NE 50th and NE 52nd Sts). 527.4278

24 Giggles Comedy Nite Club Stand-up comics with national reputations (including Jerry Seinfeld, Ellen DeGeneres, and Pat Paulsen) have appeared here. ♦ Cover. Shows Th 8:30 PM; F-Sa 8PM and 10PM. Reservations recommended. 5220 Roosevelt Way NE (at NE 53rd St). 526.5653

25 University Branch Library Architects **W. Marbury Somervell** and **Joseph C. Cote** were busy in the year 1910. Not only were they putting the final touches on this building but also on two other Seattle libraries that opened that same year: the **Green Lake Public Library** and the **West Seattle Public Library.** All three structures look eerily similar, all showing Mediterranean touches, as perhaps was their intention. In any case, this building, like its brethren, is a handsome legacy of an ambitious project. It is one of eight libraries still standing in the Seattle area that were built thanks to the largess of iron-and-steel-magnate Andrew Carnegie. ♦ M-Sa. 5009 Roosevelt Way NE (at NE 50th St). 684.4063

26 Mamma Melina Ristorante ★★★$$ Excellent Neapolitan cuisine is served in an open, elegant room decorated with bright frescoes. The sounds of Puccini (sometimes too loud) flow through the air and Mamma herself may be in the kitchen. Reviewers rave over the lasagna, which is strewn with tiny meatballs, but you can't really go wrong with any of the dishes. The appetizers, the spinach cannelloni, and the veal dishes all deserve stars. ♦ Italian ♦ M-F lunch and dinner; Sa-Su dinner. 4759 Roosevelt Way NE (at NE 50th St). 632.2271

26 Cinema Books A major find for film buffs, this specialty shop sells movie picture books, celebrity bios, screenplays, guidebooks to shows, technical and analytical treatises, and some film memorabilia (posters, stills, a hundred different Marilyn Monroe postcards). ♦ M-Sa. 4753 Roosevelt Way NE (between NE 47th and NE 50th Sts). 547.7667

26 Seven Gables Theater Once upon a time there was a single theater in Seattle that showed high-quality films. Called **Seven Gables,** it grew into a chain and then sold out to a California operator. Now with nine theaters and 28 screens in town, it operates on the premise that people will support movies of literary and/or noncommercial styles. Often used as a test market for independent productions, Seattle has "saved" several small films (among them *The Black Stallion, The Stunt Man,* and *Never Cry Wolf*) that Hollywood had written off. This theater is the chain's flagship and shows fine foreign films. Its viewing room is small, but the antiques-decorated lobby is lovely. ♦ 911 NE 50th St (between Ninth Ave NE and Roosevelt Way NE). 632.8820

27 Metro Cinemas With 10 screens, Dolby sound, and a mix of good-quality, first-run commercial and independent films, this theater is a sanctuary on a rainy afternoon. There's even a soundproof room for infants. ♦ 4500 Ninth Ave NE (at NE 45th St). 633.0055

27 Stella's Trattoria ★$ This lively, bistrolike establishment is ideal for grabbing a quick bite before or after a movie at the adjacent **Metro Cinemas.** Nighthawks, rejoice: one of Seattle's rare all-night eating spots, this joint is still jumping at 3AM. Pastas, fish, and breakfast are served after 11PM when the full menu isn't available. This is one of a small chain of restaurants that also includes **Trattoria Mitchelli** in Pioneer Square and **Angelina's** in West Seattle. ♦ Italian ♦ Daily 24 hours. 4500 Ninth Ave NE (at NE 45th St). 633.1100

Seattle has more equity theaters than any US city except New York.

28 Blue Moon Tavern Poet Carolyn Kizer once described this tavern as "a grubby oasis just outside the university's one-mile-limit Sahara. Here, the jukebox roars, Audrey the waitress slaps down schooners of beer, and poets, pedants, painters, and other assorted wildlife make overtures to each other." She wrote that in 1956, but not much has changed. This fabled bar, supposedly frequented by Ginsberg, Kerouac, Roethke, and Tom Robbins, still attracts free spirits and loosely wrapped crazies. In 1990 it was scheduled to be razed, but an 11th-hour campaign to save the bar prevailed. Sunday night the tape deck plays only **Grateful Dead** music; Monday is Opera Night. ♦ Daily noon-2AM. 712 NE 45th St (near Seventh Ave NE). No phone

Ravenna

29 Salvatore Ristorante Italiano ★★★$$$ Specializing in Southern Italian cuisine, including veal so tender you could cut it with a plastic fork, this dining spot serves a varied selection of delicious pastas and features an extensive wine list with gentle prices to complement your meal. ♦ Italian ♦ M-Sa dinner. 6100 Roosevelt Way NE (at NE 61st St). 527.9301

30 Sunlight Cafe ★$ This vegetarian restaurant serves a full menu, including soyburgers, tofu scrambles, and various stir-fry concoctions. Whole-wheat waffles, blueberry pancakes, and nutritious muffins draw healthy crowds on weekends. ♦ Vegetarian ♦ M-F breakfast, lunch, and dinner; Sa-Su breakfast and dinner. 6403 Roosevelt Way NE (at NE 64th St). 522.9060

31 Cowen Park Donated in 1907 by Charles Cowen, an Englishman reared in South Africa, this area was undeveloped until the city filled and flattened it with dirt from freeway construction in 1961. The result is an eight-acre patch of picnic grounds with a playfield used for softball. The park is used heavily by the neighborhood despite periodic incursions by transients. ♦ University Way NE and NE Ravenna Blvd NE

The Big Snow of 1880 marked the worst winter this city ever experienced. Snow began to fall on 5 January and within a week was heaped in six-foot-high drifts. The *Seattle Post-Intelligencer* confessed that "we shall have to admit hereafter that snow does occasionally fall in this country. . . . The average citizen walks nowadays as though he were drunk." The 64-inch snow total from that week brought the city (including vital railroad lines) to a complete standstill.

32 Bagel Oasis ★★$ Some of the best bagels in town are available here: big, soft, chewy, and often sold hot right out of the oven. Nosh on any of these with cream-cheese spreads and Port Chatham lox, or order them as part of a sandwich. Also served are homemade soups, salads, and filling omelettes in the morning. ♦ Jewish deli ♦ Daily breakfast and lunch. 2112 NE 65th St (between 21st and 22nd Aves NE). 526.0525

33 The Santa Fe Cafe ★★★$ Enjoy New Mexican cooking at its best. Blue-corn tortillas are used in many of the zingy, flavorful dishes. One longtime favorite is the artichoke ramekin appetizer, baked with green chilies and kasseri cheese. The *chiles rellenos* tart is also outstanding. Try any of the dishes that come with the house green sauce. And the margaritas have won newspaper polls as the best in the city. ♦ Southwestern ♦ M-F lunch and dinner. 2255 NE 65th St (between 22nd Ave NE and Ravenna Ave). 524.7736. Also at: 5910 Phinney Ave N (between N 59th and N 60th Sts). 783.9755

34 Ravenna Park Clarence Bagley, a Seattle pioneer and local historian, complained in the early 20th century that this 52-acre park was "a dark, damp, dismal hole in the ground for which the city paid an outrageous price." Bagley must have been a sourpuss to cast such a poor light on this urban gem.

A creek bed once ran from Green Lake through this heavily wooded ravine and drained into Lake Washington. History buffs say the area was home to an invigorating mineral springs and a magnificent stand of trees—giant evergreens 30 to 60 feet in diameter. It so impressed a realtor named William W. Beck, who bought it as part of a 300-acre tract, that he named it after the parklike Italian town of Ravenna. Beck also named the largest trees after famous people—Teddy Roosevelt and Robert E. Lee among them—and charged visitors 25¢ a head to enter his sanctuary. The city coveted his land and eventually acquired it through condemnation in 1911. But it promptly destroyed much of the park's grandeur by lowering Green Lake and cutting off the creek, then constructing an underground drainage system and toppling the great trees Beck had so admired, to be sold as cordwood.

Today, the park is minus its virgin timber, but it still feels like a small piece of wilderness within city limits. It boasts two large playgrounds on either end (in **Lower Ravenna Park** and in **Cowen Park**), joined together by a natural ravine and small creek. Quiet and unsculpted, this ravine sometimes seems imbued with magic (one writer called it a hobbit's realm) as it follows Ravenna Creek through steeply sloped brush- and fern-covered forestland. A wide trail here provides a 20-minute walk for strollers and a shorter but still soothing escape for runners during the daytime. Come night, however, transients may use the park, so be cautious. ♦ Bounded by NE 62nd and NE 55th Sts, and 25th and 15th Aves NE

35 Lower Ravenna Park Walking east of the main park, the ravine empties into a broad field and baseball diamond. Above it, you'll come across a small playfield, playground, and tennis courts with full sun exposure. Keep walking up the hill and wind through a series of small, serene meadows where you can picnic at tables, read in solitude, or just listen to the many songbirds. Go farther, and you'll dead-end at a larger meadow that has a covered barbecue pit area. ♦ 20th Ave NE and NE 58th St

36 Ravenna Boulevard Designed by the Olmsted Brothers to be part of their chain of Seattle parks linked by boulevards, this once marked the Ravenna neighborhood's northern boundary. Now, the wide, grassy, tree-lined strip is a favorite for runners. ♦ Between 25th Ave NE and Green Lake

37 Killing Time It's a mystery bookstore, what else? They stock new hardcovers, paperbacks, books-on-tape, even mysteries for children. Staff members are happy to discuss and recommend authors, and there are frequent author readings and signings. ♦ Tu-Su. 2821 NE 55th St (between 28th and 29th Aves NE). 525.2266

37 Queen Mary ★★$$$ This could very well be the site of the Mad Hatter's Tea Party—from the shards of lovely crockery imbedded in the sidewalk outside to the flowered chintz curtains inside. Owner Mary Greengo has created a perfect spot for a leisurely afternoon tea of tomato-and-basil sandwiches and lemon curd tart. And, if you're late for a very important date, pick up a sweet morsel from the pastry case. ♦ American ♦ Daily breakfast, lunch, and tea; Th-Sa dinner. 2912 NE 55th St (between 29th and 30th Aves NE). 527.2770

Bests

om Douglas
wner/Chef, Dahlia Lounge

ood:

& L Home of Good Barbeque at 19th Avenue and esler Way where the people are as good as the ribs.

oast pork and dumplings with caraway gravy and auerkraut at **Labuznik** restaurant, First Avenue and irginia Street.

isotto at **Al Boccalino** with their great Italian ine list.

isotto at **Lampreia**, total simplicity, great flavor.

elato from **Procopio Gelateria** on the Pike Street illclimb. My favorites: green tea, cantaloupe, nger.

ne satay bar at **Wild Ginger** restaurant, open until 00 AM.

progressive stomp through the **Pike Place Market** r "apps" and cocktails starting with the **Pink Door** the deck, then **Campagne** in the bar, then **Shea's unge,** then **Place Pigalle,** and finally ending up at **Bistro** in the bar. Finish with a ride on Rachel, the g under the **Pike Place Market** clock!

ores:

utual Fish Co. on Rainier Avenue South. This place extraordinary!! The freshest fish in Seattle. ousemade traditional Japanese fish cakes, Kasu, aweed salads. Family run from the heart!!

llard Computer in beautiful downtown Ballard. er friendly.

e low stalls at the **Pike Place Market** where the mers display and sell their prize possessions.

Pike & Western Wine Shop in the **Pike Place Market.** The best selection of new and old Northwest wines.

Stroll through **Elliott Bay Books** and dream.

Peter Miller
Owner, Peter Miller Books

Pike Place Market is Seattle's soul. Get there early—the fruit and vegetable stands and the fish markets are all set up by 7:30 AM. In season, the raspberries come in early in the morning, as do the chanterelles and the salmon. The bakeries are open then, for croissants, crumpets, muffins—always with good coffee.

Everyone asks, "Where is the best seafood?"; then off they go to some chain restaurant. Instead, I recommend **Labuznik,** where Peter Cipra cooks every dinner. If the restaurant is full, I eat in the cafe. Try **Campagne.** Or just outside **Pike Place Market,** the **Queen City Grill.** All of these places know fish—what is in, what is out.

Have a beer or glass of wine at the **Virginia Inn,** still the best tavern in town.

Louis runs the finest Italian deli in the Northwest, **DeLaurenti's Specialty Foods.**

Seattle's *Virginia V,* built in 1922 as part of Puget Sound's Mosquito Fleet and still chartered for celebratory cruises, is the last inland-water, passenger-carrying steamer operating west of the Mississippi.

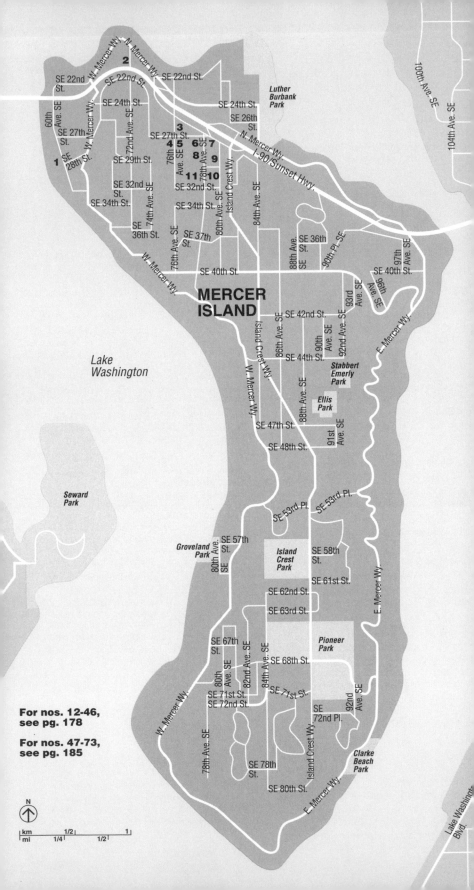

MERCER
ISLAND

Lake
Washington

Seward
Park

Luther
Burbank
Park

Stabbert
Emerly
Park

Ellis
Park

Island
Crest
Park

Groveland
Park

Pioneer
Park

Clarke
Beach
Park

Lake Washington Blvd.

60th Ave. SE
SE 22nd St.
SE 27th St.
SE 28th St.
W. Mercer Wy.
N. Mercer Wy.
W. Mercer Wy.
N. Mercer Wy.
SE 22nd St.
SE 22nd St.
SE 24th St.
SE 24th St.
SE 26th St.
72nd Ave. SE
SE 27th St.
SE 29th St.
76th Ave. SE
76th Ave. SE
78th Ave. SE
SE 32nd St.
SE 32nd St.
74th Ave. SE
SE 34th St.
SE 34th St.
SE 36th St.
SE 37th St.
80th Ave. SE
Island Crest Wy.
84th Ave. SE
SE 40th St.
86th Ave. SE
88th Ave. SE
SE 36th SE
SE 40th St.
90th Pl. SE
97th Ave. SE
96th Ave. SE
N. Mercer Wy.
I-90/Sunset Hwy.
100th Ave. SE
104th Ave. SE
SE 42nd St.
90th Ave. SE
93rd Ave. SE
92nd Ave. SE
E. Mercer Wy.
SE 44th St.
88th Ave. SE
SE 47th St.
91st Ave. SE
SE 48th St.
Island Crest Wy.
W. Mercer Wy.
SE 53rd Pl.
SE 53rd Pl.
SE 57th St.
80th Ave. SE
SE 58th St.
SE 61st St.
SE 62nd St.
SE 63rd St.
SE 67th St.
80th Ave. SE
82nd Ave. SE
84th Ave. SE
SE 68th St.
92nd Ave. SE
SE 71st St.
SE 71st St.
SE 72nd St.
SE 72nd Pl.
78th Ave. SE
SE 78th St.
Island Crest Wy.
E. Mercer Wy.
SE 80th St.
W. Mercer Wy.
E. Mercer Wy.

1
2
3
4 5   6   7
8   9
11 10

For nos. 12-46,
see pg. 178

For nos. 47-73,
see pg. 185

N

km
mi
1/2   1
1/4   1/2

Eastside

Places separated from others by water—Venice, Valhalla, the New World—have traditionally held certain allure. So it's not surprising that the suburban communities nestled on the near-east side of **Lake Washington**—principally **Mercer Island, Bellevue,** and **Kirkland**—always have been and probably always will be somebody's dreamland.

Pioneer Peter Kirk set out in the 1880s to build the "Pittsburgh of the West" on the forested slopes above **Moss Bay.** But this industrial capital of belching steel- and ironworks never materialized. And in 1928, before the first bridge was built across the lake, real estate baron James Ditty laid out a plan for an eastside utopia that included blimps traveling to and from downtown Seattle and huge observation towers in the midst of Mercer Island; this dream also was unrealized. An advertisement from the 1940s solicited interest from Seattleites with the slogan "15 Minutes to Your Home in the Country." It seems a cruel joke now, when even a fairly athletic slug might outpace the heavy rush-hour traffic across the lake.

But thousands of new residents continue to be drawn here by the quality of life (including the fairly safe schools) and by booming high-tech industries (computer giant Microsoft and cellular phone purveyor McCaw Communications among them). Neighborhood strip malls and well-groomed suburban lawns characterize the Eastside of today. It's the fourth-largest urban area in Washington state, and very much ruled by the automobile. Only a few enclaves, such as **Beaux Arts Village,** southwest of downtown Bellevue, have escaped the rule of the road. Founded in 1908 as a rustic artists' commune (and for a while it was a nudists' colony), this lovely residential hideaway is still woven with streets barely wide enough for two cars to pass.

The look and attitude of the Eastside varies greatly from one district to the next. Mercer Island is primarily residential, bisected at its north end by Interstate 90. It boasts only a small commercial zone and is a leisurely ride for bicyclists. Kirkland has several art galleries, antiques shops, and good restaurants. Bellevue, the most urban of the three areas, is characterized by businesses set back from the street in retail and office valleys in the legacy of one of the Eastside's most successful dreamers, Kemper Freeman Sr., who believed businesses that provided parking in front of their buildings would flourish. A rare Bellevue exception is **Main Street** in "Old Bellevue," an area just off the downtown core that resembles compact Kirkland.

Aside from some obvious sites in Kirkland, historic buildings are in short supply throughout the Eastside, partly because of the area's relatively recent settlement, and partly because the value of its first structures was not recognized in the furor of slapdash post–World War II development. Much of the architecture of the past 45 years has failed to consider the Eastside's potential; many of the structures raised were clearly second-class. But that's changing. Several award-winning multiuse projects, such as **Carillon Point** and **Bellevue Place,** have taken great steps in making huge complexes accessible to the public and compatible with the environment. As everywhere else, developers are, for better or worse, changing the face of the area in an effort to accommodate growth, while preservation-minded citizens strive to save what they can for future generations.

Mercer Island

1 Calkin's Landing Charles Cicero Calkins was a lawyer from Illinois who abandoned the bar to become an entrepreneur, real estate gambler, and Mercer Island's best-remembered dreamer. He arrived in Seattle in 1887 and soon determined that Lake Washington's only island should shed its pioneer image. He raised a three-story hotel just up the hill from the present-day landing, which must have been a magical sight—it was an architectural amalgam of an American railroad station and a Swiss chalet, with dormers, turrets, and chimneys punctuating its tile roof, and broad elegant porches skirting its lower levels. The grounds boasted mazes, promenades, a huge greenhouse with 635 varieties of roses, and 25 fountains, one with a 60-foot-wide bowl. A bathhouse held 100 boats and 28 dressing rooms, as well as a complete system of Turkish baths. The **Hotel Calkins** was designed to be the centerpiece of a new, nonindustrial community called **East Seattle**—Puget Sound's version of Newport, Rhode Island. Hoping to start a trend, the developer built a lavish home for himself on the north tip of what is now **Luther Burbank Park.**

But misfortune put an end to Calkins's schemes. Within the span of a few years, his daughter died, his wife divorced him, and the depression of 1893 ripped away his fortune. Calkins's mansion and later his hotel burned to their foundations. He set out in despair for southern California, where he again tried (and failed) to make his fortune in gold mining before he died in 1948 at the age of 98. It's sad that the only thing remaining of the elegance Calkins brought to Mercer Island is a mispunctuated sign on this tiny wedge of lawn and sand, where his hotel once had a dock. ◆ 60th Ave SE and SE 28th St

2 Roanoke Inn Bartenders here are generally versed in the colorful history of Mercer Island's longest-operating business. They'll explain how this place was a general store when it opened in 1916; how there was once a pinball machine here that would pay off in quarters; and how it used to be a popular drinking spot for city swells. Those were the good old days, back when a ferry still connected the north end of Mercer Island with Seattle, before I-90 took all the **Roanoke**'s drive-by business away and left it baby-sitting a dead-end route to a dark pier. Late owner Hal Reeck's stepfather was known to pack pistols into this place and fire them at inconvenient times, blowing holes in various walls and pieces of furniture.

Today most of the action takes place on the TV screen, but much of the tavern's classic atmosphere endures. A giant fireplace sits opposite the front door, gold trophies elbowing each other for room upon its mantel. Beer paraphernalia crowds the walls, and there's a dingy pool room in the back, although it's too cramped for anyone to properly wield a cue. During warm months the place to be is on the long front porch, swapping tall tales and watching Lake Washington capture moonbeams.

The bar stocks a minuscule selection of craft beers like Henry Weinhard and Rainier. Seltzers and wine coolers are available, too. Food selections run to burgers, oyster stew, and taco salads. Spaghetti dinners are served on Thursday nights. ◆ M-Sa until 2AM; Su until 10PM. 1825 72nd Ave SE (just north of I-90). 232.0800

3 Cafe Italia ★$$ This airy and cheerful trattoria offers few real surprises, but the food is fresh and pretty good. Try the Chianti chicken. ◆ Italian ◆ M lunch; Tu-F lunch and dinner; Sa-Su dinner. 2448 76th Ave SE (at SE 27th St). 232.9009

4 Oh Chocolate! Tempting confections (including more than a dozen varieties of truffles) are handmade on the premises. ◆ M-Sa. 2703 76th Ave SE (at SE 27th St). 232.4974

5 Finders A small store, chockablock with gift ideas: toys, handmade crafts, quilts, children's books, journals, stationery, and a wide selection of cards. ◆ M-Sa. 7607 SE 27th St (between 76th and 77th Aves SE). 236.1110

5 Nature's Pantry Based on the evidence here, Mercer Island has gone full circle—from a bucolic rural island to asphalted suburbia and now back to nature. Shoppers will find a good selection of organic produce, bulk foods, vitamins, cosmetics, and books. ◆ M-Sa. 7611 SE 27th St (between 76th and 77th Aves SE). 232-7900

6 Thai on Mercer ★★$$ Roast lamb and halibut with tamarind sauce are two of the favorites at this consistently excellent restaurant. Sit back and enjoy the restful, inviting ambience and the well-prepared, well-presented food. ◆ Thai ◆ M-F lunch and dinner; Sa-Su dinner. 7691 SE 27th St (at 77th Ave SE). 236.9990

7 Addison's For many years, this eclectic gift shop—first named **Crosby's**, then **Riley's**—was *the* place on the island to find that special something. It still is, but the name has changed—again. The emphasis is on such thoughtful items as elegant household goods, soaps, clothing, and greeting cards. ◆ M-Sa. 7811 SE 27th St (between 78th and 79th Aves SE). 232.0833

Restaurants/Clubs: Red   **Hotels:** Blue
Shops/ 🌳 Outdoors: Green   **Sights/Culture:** Bl

8 Alpenland Delicatessen ★$ First look for **Island Video,** then you can spot this tiny place next door. Behind a small storefront is a well-stocked deli offering sandwiches and other treats for eat-in or take-out lunches and picnics. ◆ Deli/Takeout ◆ Daily. 2707 78th Ave SE (between SE 27th and SE 28th Sts). 232.4780

9 Mercer Island Cyclery Those touring the island by bike can get competent repairs or buy cycling equipment here. ◆ Tu-Su. 2827 80th Ave SE (between SE 27th and SE 28th Sts). 232.3443

10 Island Books This excellent general bookstore has a large stock and a friendly staff made up of genuine readers. The spacious back room is devoted to kid's lit; there's also a huge playhouse and enough toys to keep any number of small-sized nonreaders occupied. As expected, an espresso bar—the ever-popular **Espresso Sam's**—is just inside the door. ◆ M-Sa; Th until 8PM. 3014 78th Ave SE (between SE 30th and SE 32nd Sts). 232.6920

10 Island Beads and More In the same shopping center as **Island Books,** this shop sells more beads than you'll ever be able to twirl around your neck, wrists, *and* ankles. Classes and restringing services are also available. ◆ 3024 78th Ave SE (between SE 30th and SE 32nd Sts). 232.8121

11 Pon Proem Restaurant ★$ Colorful, cool decor and well-prepared Thai food are the offerings here. Try the chicken with cashews or fresh ginger. ◆ Thai ◆ M-F lunch; daily dinner. 3039 78th Ave SE (between SE 29th and SE 30th Sts). 236.8424

Bellevue

12 Red Lion Hotel $$ Some say the addition of this mammoth first-class hotel to Bellevue's hospitality trade marked the city's coming of age as a business destination. Indeed, its 353 rooms and meeting space for 1,400 people are usually occupied. All rooms have balconies, and executive suites come with complimentary continental breakfast, hors d'oeuvres, and a newspaper delivered to your room. ◆ 300 112th Ave SE (between Main and SE Fourth Sts). 455.1300, 800/547.8010; fax 455.0466

Within the Red Lion Hotel:

Velato's ★$$ Color and spaciousness are the signatures here. One wall features a mural of a Venetian canal scene, while another—full of large windows—overlooks a garden, fountain and, in the distance, freeway traffic. The seafood pasta and the lasagna are both good choices. ◆ Italian ◆ M-Sa breakfast, lunch, and dinner; Su brunch. 455.1300

13 Bellevue Hilton $$ The 180 comfortable rooms here are all decorated in soft color tones, with cable TV and movies available. But it's the other amenities that win this place most of its plaudits. Hotel vans take guests around at no charge within a five-mile radius, which is ample reach for Bellevue's main attractions. Indoor activities include an indoor pool, sauna, and Jacuzzi. And security is great; upon request, solo guests are walked to their cars. ◆ 100 112th Ave NE (between Main and NE Second Sts). 455.3330; 800/235.4458; fax 451.2473

Within the Bellevue Hilton:

Sam's Bar and Grill $$ Northwestern and continental cuisine are served in a low-key stucco and tile-roofed setting just across the breezeway from the hotel's main entrance. The chicken Dijon sautéed with onions and shallots is a good choice, as are the clam and salmon chowders. ◆ Northwestern/Continental ◆ Daily breakfast, lunch, and dinner. 455.3330

14 Bellevue Botanical Gardens In 1947 Calhoun and Harriet Shorts bought a seven-acre cherry orchard on Wilburton Hill where they built a home and created a rhododendron glen. Today, that property is the center of a 36-acre public botanical garden. Some of the rhododendrons are 20 feet tall, and the garden contains a special collection of native and exotic trees, as well as rare shrubs and groundcovers. Near the entrance of the **Shorts Visitors' Center** (which includes a botanical library, gift shop and meeting rooms) a miniature waterfall cascades from a granite boulder through the courtyard; bricks appear to "float" in the small stream of water on its way to a small pond that contains water plants. Beyond the visitors' center are trails to the 17,000-square-foot botanical border on a hill high above downtown Bellevue. There's also a wheelchair-accessible garden loop trail about a half-mile long, as well as individual gardens devoted to groundcovers, dahlias, herbs, fuschias, the **Yao Garden** (a sister-cities project with Yao, Japan), and a rock garden. ◆ Daily. 12001 Main St (at 124th Ave NE). 462.2749.

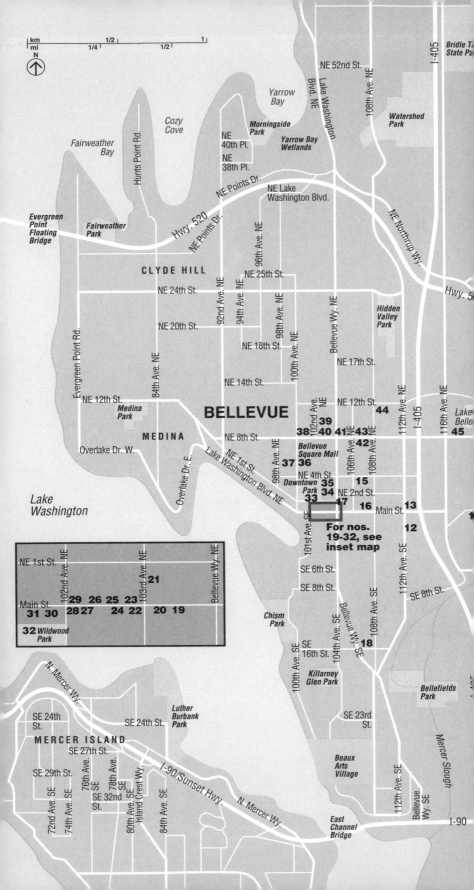

15 Spazzo ★★★$$ *Spazzo* is Italian slang for "a good time," and that's exactly what you'll have in this bright restaurant atop the Key Bank Building. Diners are surrounded by murals on one side and views of the skyline and Lake Washington on the other. The food is from the cuisines of Greece, Turkey, and North Africa: lamb with vegetables, olives, and artichokes over saffron couscous, for example. There's also a fun tapas bar, where the chefs whip up tasty appetizers; and a childrens' menu. ♦ Mediterranean ♦ Daily lunch and dinner. Reservations recommended for lunch. 10655 NE Fourth St (between 106th and 108th Aves NE). 454.8255

16 Pogacha ★★$ Named for the distinctive Yugoslavian bread crust that makes pizzas served here so unusual, this affordable restaurant is an Eastside favorite. The crunchy-yet-soft bread is made fresh daily and served in three sizes: dinner rolls, sandwich bread, and the hefty pizza disks. The best pizza is topped with goat cheese, sun-dried tomatoes, and spinach. Owner Helen Kranjcevich Brocard also serves chicken and lamb dishes, and has a wine list containing about 30 selections. ♦ Pizza ♦ M lunch; Tu-Sa lunch and dinner. 119 106th Ave NE (between NE Second and Main Sts). 455.5670

17 Rubato Records Bellevue's best-loved platter pawnshop carries 10,000 used compact discs, an extensive collection of old 45s, and thousands of vinyl albums. ♦ Daily; M-Sa until 9PM. 136 105th Ave NE (between NE Second and Main Sts). 455.9417

17 Giuseppe's ★$$ Like a rare plant that grows without sunlight, this Italian restaurant and lounge thrives despite its basement strip-mall location in the shadow of a colossal hardware store. Try the veal cognac. ♦ Italian ♦ M-Sa dinner; lounge M-Sa until 2AM. 144 105th Ave NE (between NE Second and Main Sts). 454.6868

18 Chace's Pancake Corral $ If you like a hearty stack o' cakes served with a smile at the crack of dawn, this friendly flapjack and coffee stop is for you. It's the only place of its kind left in Bellevue. Owner Bill Chace quit counting birthdays at age 82 and still takes time to sit down with the customers, whether he knows them or not. A favorite is banana pancakes with coconut syrup, but if you want to play the field, try the Joe Adams assortment: Joe was a customer who could never make up his mind whether to have buttermilk, buckwheat, potato, or strawberry pancakes, so Chace came up with this satisfying sampler. ♦ American ♦ Daily breakfast and lunch; Th dinner. 1606 Bellevue Way SE (between SE 16th St and 108th Ave SE). 454.8888

19 Stamp Gallery Proprietor John Kardos's philatelic shop specializes in European issues, but also has one of Seattle's largest collections of international stamps. ♦ Tu-Sa. 10335 Main St (between Bellevue Way NE and 103rd Ave NE). 455.3781

20 Toy's Cafe ★$ Good Chinese food at irresistible prices has made this a neighborhood institution for decades. It's not fancy, but the service is quick and courteous. Combos are the way to go; sample three or four foods for not much more than each would cost separately. ♦ Chinese/Takeout ♦ Tu-F lunch and dinner; Sa-Su dinner. 10311 Main St (between Bellevue Way NE and 103rd Ave NE). 454.8815

21 Azalea's Fountain Court ★★$$$$ Coming to this restaurant is like visiting your favorite auntie at her light-green farmhouse tucked away under the trees. Inside this somewhat preciously overdone space, you'll find a gracious staff and excellent chef preparing Northwestern cuisine with French overtones. Seafood is the specialty, especially the crab cakes, local mussels, and the baked salmon. The atmosphere is romantic and the service is good. ♦ Northwestern ♦ W-F lunch and dinner; M, Sa dinner. No smoking allowed. 22 103rd Ave NE (between Main and NE First Sts). 451.0426

22 Bellevue Barber Shop Nothing has changed since the days when your dad was a kid and your grandfather brought him into a place just like this to get his ears lowered. The Russel family has been giving no-frills haircuts here for almost 50 years. Their collection of Bellevue High School yearbooks, which you're welcome to peruse, predates the shop's 1926 building by two years. Opinions are plentiful and free, and haircuts are $10, which includes being finished up with a straight razor. ♦ Tu-Sa. 10251 Main St (at 103rd Ave NE). 455.0980

23 La Cocina del Puerco $ In this cafeteria-style restaurant you pay for food—handmade tortillas and generous helpings—not for the overhead of fancy furnishings. Decor is upscale functional, but there are enough piñatas, posters, and other paraphernalia on the walls and ceiling to make you feel you've gotten tangled up in a *Cinco de Mayo* parade. Try the *chiles rellenos*. ♦ Mexican ♦ Daily lunch and dinner. 10246 Main St (between 103rd and 102nd Aves NE). 455.1151

Sixty percent of the airline jets operating outside of the former Soviet Union were manufactured by Boeing. They transport 675 million passengers each year—that's 12 percent of the planet's population.

24 Cuttysark There's a blinding assortment of brass goods salvaged from old ships for the nautically inclined: coat hooks, portholes, soap dishes, lanterns, binnacles, telegraphs, telescopes, and more. There are also thousands of nonbrass items, including flags, books, paintings, charts, and ship models. ♦ M-Sa. 10235 Main St (between 103rd and 102nd Aves NE). 453.1265

25 Christmas House This year-round ornament and gift shop has expanded to include three buildings (two are in the back alley) carrying an ever-larger selection of knickknacks, bric-a-brac, baubles, bangles, and gewgaws to stuff every stocking. Don't miss the traditional linden-wood carvings from the German Erzgebirge and several sizes of the hand-painted Fontanini nativity figures. ♦ Daily Nov-Dec; Tu-Sa Jan-Oct. 10230 Main St (between 103rd and 102nd Aves NE). 455.4225

26 Ross and Co. Ross Bendixen has been bending metal in this neighborhood for more than 25 years, specializing in custom-designed iron-and-steel furniture. His dynamic wall sculptures have become a hallmark of Old Bellevue. ♦ M-Sa. 10220 Main St (between 103rd and 102nd Aves NE). 455.4111

27 Main Street Kids Book Company The very best thing you can do for your children is turn them loose in this marvelously stocked bookstore and let their curiosity go to work. And for adults, there are books on parenting in the back. ♦ M-Sa. 10217 Main St (between 103rd and 102nd Aves NE). 455.8814

According to the *Washington Almanac*, if Puget Sound's coastline could be stretched from end to end, it would reach from Seattle to Chicago, a distance of 2,031 miles.

27 Fortnum's European Cafe ★$ The name underscores the continental theme here. You will find the regular round of soups and sandwiches, a zucchini frittata, and a wonderful artichoke tart. Floral-print tablecloths add a touch of elegance. ♦ Continental ♦ Daily breakfast and lunch. 10213 Main St (between 103rd and 102nd Aves NE). 455.2033

28 Oriental Interiors This shop specializes in rosewood furniture from China, but the building in which it's housed is equally interesting. Ostentatiously named the **City of Paris,** it was Bellevue's first bank, but became a casualty of the Depression as soon as it opened. The structure once housed Bellevue's first library as well as the first offices of the *Bellevue American* newspaper, now the daily *Journal American.* ♦ Daily. 10203 Main St (between 103rd and 102nd Aves NE). 637.0860

29 Dilly Dally The wooden cow that hangs out on the sidewalk during business hours was ticketed for being an illegal sign, but owner Nadine Lukoff took her cow to court and won. Look closely; baskets, cards, boxes of cookies, and most of the items carried here can't be found anywhere else in the Northwest. ♦ M-Sa. 10202 Main St (between 103rd and 102nd Aves NE). 454.1518

30 The Collection This shop carries lines from about eight different contemporary women's sportswear collections. ♦ Daily. 10149 Main St (between 102nd and 101st Aves NE). 453.5791. Also at: Rainier Square. 622.4147; 2654 NE University Village Mall. 524.6954

31 Bloomingals "Sportswear for fun" is the slogan intended to draw women who shun trends and want distinctive designs from New York and San Francisco. ♦ Daily. 10133 Main St (between 102nd and 101st Aves NE). 451.2880

32 Wildwood Park This little lawn surrounded by trees is all that's left of a park that once reached west to what is now the **Meydenbauer Yacht Club.** In the first years of the 20th century Seattleites crossed Lake Washington on a ferry to picnic on the grass here, dance in a pavilion, and mess about in canoes. ♦ 260 101st Ave SE (just south of Main St)

Restaurants/Clubs: Red	Hotels: Blue
Shops/ 🌳 Outdoors: Green	Sights/Culture: Black

33 Bellevue Downtown Park At a total cost of $20 million, the City of Bellevue purchased nearly four blocks of prime downtown real estate and set it aside (ostensibly forever) as sacred, idle space, dedicated to daydreams and dawdling. From the park, a proper study can be made of downtown Bellevue's skyscraper growth during the late 20th century. The two blue ones most in evidence to the east, **Security Pacific Plaza** (10620 NE Eighth St) and **One Bellevue Center** (411 108th Ave NE), were built during the 1980s as bookends to anticipated heavy development along 108th Avenue NE (alas, the "books" never materialized). Depending on the sky, they can become beacons of fire or disappear altogether. The copper-toned **Koll Center** (500 108th Ave NE), at 27 stories Bellevue's tallest building, incorporates multiple angles and sides on a common center to suggest one building exploding out of another. All three reflective glass structures were designed by Seattle architect **Gerald Geron.**

The most active area is the west side of the park, where kids play on a colorful, turreted jungle gym and swings. Elsewhere, workers and shoppers can enjoy a low waterfall and a hypnotic canal crossed by charming little bridges. Perhaps the leveling of two of Bellevue's oldest grade schools for this park will prove forgivable (the foundation of one remains as a topographic attraction), as people take refuge not far from the madding crowd. A stone marker and four elms planted in 1926 in memory of three World War I soldiers were left undisturbed. ♦ 10201 NE Fourth St (at 100th Ave NE)

34 Games and Gizmos The back half of this store is dedicated to role-playing games of the Dungeons and Dragons sort, but up front you'll find all the old favorites—tiddledywinks, chess, Twister. There are some interesting cribbage and backgammon boards, and plenty of brainteasing puzzles for those who've mastered the Rubik's cube. The floor is checkered black and white, of course. ♦ Daily; M-F until 9PM. 211 Bellevue Way NE (between NE Second and NE Fourth Sts). 462.1569

PSYCHO 5

34 Psycho 5 Die-hard superheroes Thor and Spiderman rub elbows with Spawn, Ren and Stimpy, and such Japanese animated creations as Youngblood in this comics, video, and card shop. The owner knows his stuff and relates to kids on their own level, enthusing about soon-to-be-released issues or a rare Steve Largent football card. ♦ Daily. 221 Bellevue Way NE (between NE Second and NE Fourth Sts). 462.2869

35 DeLaurenti's Specialty Foods A familiar name from **Pike Place Market,** this international food market (emphasis on the Italian) is also one of the relative oldies in downtown Bellevue. There's a sandwich and espresso bar, so you can try the pâtés, salads, cheeses, meats, and fresh breads on the spot. Walk it off among the shelves of imported olives, olive oils, pastas, beans, ground semolina, basmati rice, teas, jams, and cookies. ♦ M-Sa. 317 Bellevue Way NE (between NE Second and NE Fourth Sts). 454.7155. Also at: Economy Market, Pike Place Market. 622.0141

36 Bellevue Square Mall About one-third of Bellevue's retail business is conducted under this roof, which has skylights along its entire length to lend the mall below an ambience that architects **Cober-Slater** hoped would suggest a narrow European street. Real ficus trees planted here support this effect, as do the indoor clock tower (with a late 19th-century bell and movement salvaged from Mississippi's Winona County Courthouse) and the bow window storefronts and blade signs protruding into the mall. The usual heavyweights can be found here: **Nordstrom, J.C. Penney,** and **The Bon Marché.** ♦ NE Eighth St (between 100th Ave NE and Bellevue Way NE). 454.8096

Within Bellevue Square Mall:

The Nature Company It's like stepping into an expensive rain forest, with its very green gallery of pricey gadgets, learning devices, and offbeat entertainments. There are globe puzzles, fish ties and bird shirts, telescopes, polished geodes, birdhouses, posters, children's science kits, CDs of ocean sounds, tea, Saturn holographs, and life-size inflatable Emperor penguins. In a bind for some quartz? This store stocks it in four colors. ♦ Daily; M-Sa until 9:30PM. First floor. 450.0448.

Kenneth Biehm Art Gallery Dalí and Matisse prints vie for wall space with limited editions by Michel Delacroix and Jiang. The leaning is toward big, busy, and bright, but the gallery has presented a collection of small monochrome sketches and engravings by Rembrandt, two of which are part of the inventory. ♦ Daily; M-Sa until 9:30PM. First floor. 454.0222

The Body Shop This international chain of soap and lotion shops is known for its politically active business policies. In the "Trade, Not Aid" program, founder Anita Roddick buys nature-friendly products from Third World countries. Items include paper from Nepal, acacia footsie rollers from southern India, and Brazil-nut oil from the Kayapo Indians of South America. High prices separate the dedicated from the curious. ♦ Daily; M-Sa until 9:30PM. First floor. 637.9535

Cellophane Square Anyone who knows the funky used records, tapes, and CDs store in Seattle's University District will be happy to know that this posh mall location hasn't altered its bottom line. The selection of new and used music is as good as ever. ◆ Daily; M-Sa until 9:30PM. First floor. 454.5059. Also at: 1315 NE 42nd St (between University Way NE and Brooklyn Ave NE). 634.2280

Northwest Discovery About 70 percent of the jewelry and decorations sold here are by Northwest artists, including vases by Bremerton glassblowers Scott and Linda Curry and wall designs by Seattle tilemaker Paul Lewing. ◆ Daily; M-Sa until 9:30PM. First floor. 454.1676

Lucca's Pasta Bar $ An anomaly among mall dining choices, this small cafe radiates cheerfulness. It's bright, clean, judiciously decorated with tinted photographs of Venice and Rome, and staffed by a youthful crew. Focaccia with a Caesar salad is a good quick lunch. Of course, they serve espresso. ◆ Italian ◆ M-Sa breakfast, lunch, and dinner; Su lunch and dinner. First floor. 451.2278

The Bombay Company

The Bombay Company The home of a retired English colonel could not be more stuffed with fox-hunt paintings, cricket tables, Italian leather decanters, and solid-brass lamps. Queen Anne and other reproductions are mostly of cherry or birch with mahogany finish, many adapted to the modern function of housing files, VCRs, or tapes. ◆ Daily; M-Sa until 9:30PM. Second floor. 455.8544

Pendleton In the 1800s the Bishop family of Pendleton, Oregon, began making wool blankets based on Native American designs. The wool is still cleaned, dyed, spun, and woven at Washougal on the Columbia River, and all garments are made in the US. The Chief Joseph blanket is the same pattern that has been made and sold since the 1920s.

◆ Daily; M-Sa until 9:30PM. Second floor. 453.9040. Also at: 1313 Fourth Ave (between University and Union Sts). 682.4430

Port Chatham Smoked Seafood A handwritten note from Julia Child on the wall calls the salmon here the best she's ever had. Whether cold-smoked or kippered, the Alaskan king salmon and other seafoods prepared in Ballard and sold in this shop can be packed to travel. There's also wild capers and caviar for sale. ◆ Daily; M-Sa until 9:30PM. Second floor. 453.2441

Excalibur The quantity of sharp edges alone makes this shop an intrigue: kitchen cutlery by such household names as Henckel, Mundial, and Forschner; reproduction Viking and Samurai swords by Marta of Spain; Buck and Victorinox pocket and hunting knives. There are even battle-axes, just in case you've been looking for one. ◆ Daily; M-Sa until 9:30PM. Second floor. 451.2514

Mrs. Field's Cookies Treat yourself after an afternoon's mall walking. Pick any semi-sweet chocolate variety. ◆ Daily; M-Sa until 9:30PM. Second floor. 454.1790

Bellevue Art Museum Not your typical mall resident, this small museum does not exhibit a permanent collection but offers rotating exhibits, primarily of Northwest crafts. Strengths are jewelry and all manner of wearable art. ◆ Admission; free Tuesday. Daily. Third floor. 454.3322

37 La Residence Suite Hotel $ This 24-unit inn caters to the corporate traveler, but is also a good choice for families on a budget: all apartments have fully equipped kitchens. Views, unfortunately, are mostly of a parking garage, but elegant rosewood and leather furnishings, a friendly and hard-working staff, and complimentary fax service make it an attractive choice right on the edge of the Bellevue business district. There is no restaurant. ◆ 475 100th Ave NE (between NE Fourth and NE Eighth Sts). 455.1475, 800/800.1993; fax 455.4692

38 Veneto's Grab a paper from the news-stand across the hall and indulge in a good espresso. ◆ Daily from 6:30AM. 10116 NE Eighth St (between 100th and 102nd Aves NE). 451.8323

38 Mr. "J" Kitchen Gourmet Everything you need to operate your professional-level kitchen is available here. Hanging baskets, skillets, and giant utensils form a junglelike upper canopy. Bins full of citrus peelers, honey dippers, butter spreaders, and poultry lifters are constantly restocked so that no peg or shelf space is empty. An electric pepper grinder with a light (for poorly lit romantic dinners?), a crumb box with a removable trivet, a tripod-mounted solid-brass cork extractor, and a marble rolling pin can be found near more familiar Waterford crystal and Henckel's cutlery. ◆ Daily. 10116 NE Eighth St (between 100th and 102nd Aves NE). 455.2270

39 University Book Store The University District original is so successful that branching out seemed inevitable, but the selection of specialty literature, such as mysteries or science fiction, pale against those found at the older main store. This outlet, however, contains two packed aisles of volumes about cooking, nutrition, and international cuisines. Browse to your heart's content. ◆ Daily; M-F until 9PM. 990 102nd Ave NE (at NE 10th St). 632.9500. Also at: 4326 University Way NE (between NE 43rd and NE 44th Sts). 634.3400

40 Starbucks ★$ Along with some of the best espresso made in the Seattle area, this coffee-teria sells everything for the home *latte* junkie. ◆ Coffeehouse ◆ Daily; M-F from 5:30AM. 10214 NE Eighth St (between 102nd Ave NE and Bellevue Way NE). 454.0191

40 Silberman/Brown Stationers Owner Sue Silberman sums up the selection of new and antique pens, inkwells, and letter openers with a smile and a quip: "There's nothing in here you *need*." But there may be many things you *want*—like a one-in-500 Lorenzo de' Medici sterling-silver fountain pen ($1,500)—making this a gift shop for the executive that has almost everything. ◆ M-Sa. 10220 NE Eighth St (between 102nd Ave NE and Bellevue Way NE). 455.3665

41 Bellevue Place This high-rise complex was the first multiuse project of such magnitude in the Northwest, but as architecture it is only mediocre. The complex includes the **Seafirst Building,** the **MGM Building,** and the glass-domed **Wintergarten,** linking the towers. ◆ 10500 NE Eighth St (at 105th Ave NE). 453.5634

Within Bellevue Place:

St. Michael's Alley Named after the famous London back street where the 17th-century intelligentsia and literati hung out, this espresso shop and bookseller, wedged into an awkward space on the first floor of the **Seafirst Building,** has captured the work force's coffee-break and last-minute-gift market. The two or three shelves of new and old books (perhaps 1,300 of them, total) are there mainly to whet the appetite; the owners are happy to order and gift wrap. ◆ M-Sa. Seafirst Bldg, First floor. 453.9456

Daniel's Broiler ★★$$$$ Simultaneously chic in appearance (dark woods, onyx table-tops) and simple in its meal preparations, this is an ideal spot for entertaining. Its 21st-floor setting in the **Seafirst Building** provides Bellevue's best dining views. A specialty is the veal Daniel's—tenderloin sautéed with wild mushrooms, olives, garlic, herbs, and stock. And in both the 1987 and 1990 Puget Sound Chowder Off competitions, this eatery has served up the prize-winning bowl.

There's live piano music Tuesday through Saturday nights, a jazz trio plays on Sunday, and a jazz guitarist riffs on the deck Monday nights. The **Oyster Bar Lounge** is frequented by designer-suited people. ◆ American ◆ M-F lunch and dinner; Sa-Su dinner. Seafirst Bldg, 21st floor. 462.4662. Also at: 200 Lake Washington Blvd (at Leschi Marina). 329.4191

You can identify a tourist in a snap by the way he or she pronounces the name of Seattle's least-understood, elephantine-appendaged shellfish: the geoduck. Repeat slowly: *goo*-ee-duck.

Cucina! Cucina! ★★$$ Bicycles hanging from the ceiling reflect the offbeat spirit of the after-work crowd that keeps this hot spot going. Try the focaccia as an appetizer. Dinner choices range from pizzas and pastas to seafood, soups, salads, and more. The veal scallopini sautéed with fresh sage, prosciutto, pine nuts, and garlic is a specialty. ◆ Italian ◆ Daily lunch and dinner; bar until 1AM. MGM Bldg, First floor. 637.1177. Also at: 901 Fairview Ave N (between Mercer St and Eastlake Ave). 447.2782

41 Hyatt Regency at Bellevue Place $$$
The 382 rooms here are the most centrally located in Bellevue. Appointments are classy, without being ostentatious, decorated in neutral and pastel hues with cherry trim. Best choices are those rooms located high up on the south side, which feature views of Mount Rainier and Lake Washington. The **Regency Club** on the 23rd and 24th floors is a luxury hotel within a hotel, offering complimentary concierge and executive business services. All the usual Hyatt amenities apply.
◆ 900 Bellevue Way NE (at NE Eighth St). 462.1234, 800/233.1234; fax 451.3017

Within the Hyatt Regency at Bellevue Place:

Eques ★★$$$ Northwestern cuisine—especially seafood—is served in an elegant venue among paintings and stone sculptures of horses. Natural-wood floors and private alcoves make this a great place to relax. One of the most popular entrées is the salmon fillet with roasted-red-pepper sauce, but the grilled ahi with pineapple cilantro relish is also a winner. ◆ Northwestern ◆ Daily breakfast, lunch, and dinner. 451.3012

42 Tower Books The fire marshal must make special dispensation for this book-jammed store that's an even better resource for bibliophiles than its other location in Belltown. Especially generous are the mystery and science fiction sections. ◆ Daily until midnight. 10635 NE Eighth St (between 106th and 108th Aves NE). 451.1110. Also at: 20 Mercer St (at First Ave N). 283.6333

42 Barnes & Noble Bookstore The green arches of a former bowling alley shoulder this chain's superstore. Largest departments are general fiction, business, and computer books. ◆ Daily until 11PM. 626 106th Ave NE (at NE Eighth St). 451.8463.

Thinker TOYS

43 Thinker Toys A large, imaginatively decorated shop full of toys, games, and puzzles designed to entertain and challenge. Besides the popular construction sets by Lego, Brio, Erector, and Playmobile, you'll find fingerprint kits, chemistry sets, and other intriguing toys from around the world. ◆ Daily; M-F until 9PM. 10680 NE Eighth St (at 108th Ave NE). 453.0051

44 Rosalie Whyel Museum of Doll Art
This Victorian-style museum was built slightly oversize to make visitors feel a little . . . well, doll-like. The exhibits showcase antiques and collectibles—not reproductions—from ivory Eskimo dolls to Barbie gift sets. ◆ Admission children 4 and under free. ◆ Daily; Th until 8PM. 1116 108th Ave NE (at NE 12th St). 455.1116

45 The Pumphouse ★$ In such a car-oriented place, "neighborhood joint" has more to do with camaraderie than location. Aggressively nonglitzy, this tavern is Bellevue's version of "Cheers." Burgers are large and juicy (order the bacon-and-cheese version), and potato skins are stuffed with green onions, melted cheese, and sour cream. ◆ American ◆ M-Sa lunch and dinner; bar until midnight. 11802 NE Eighth St (between 116th and 118th Aves NE). 455.4110

46 I Love Sushi ★★$ Chef Tadaski Sato creates delectable raw-fish delicacies at this very popular restaurant. Specialties include tuna sashimi in the shape of a rose, an excellent *futumaki* roll of pink fish cake and mushrooms, and even Dungeness crab sushi ◆ M-Sa lunch and dinner; Su dinner. 11818 NE Eighth St (at 118th Ave NE). 454.5706. Also at: 1001 Fairview Ave N (at Lake Union). 625.9604

Kirkland

47 Carillon Point The six bells or carillons in the center of this office and hotel complex were forged in France and chime every half hour, giving it the atmosphere of a small European plaza. The public dock, ample parking, and waterfront paths make the place accessible by boat, car, and foot, and the low-rise buildings don't jar against the wooded hillside to the east. This bulge in the shore-line started out as the **Lake Washington Shipyards** and later became the training grounds for the **Seattle Seahawks** football team for a time; the new buildings are the world headquarters of such firms as McCaw Cellular Communications and Univar, and the street level offers a healthy handful of retail shops and restaurants, including the inevitable **Starbucks**. Lots of parking is available, mostly underground. ◆ Off Lake Washington Blvd NE (at 102nd Ave NE). 822.1700

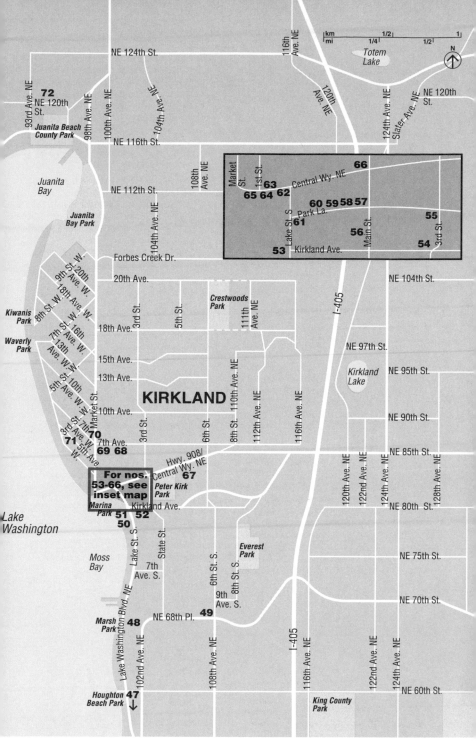

KIRKLAND

For nos. 53-66, see inset map

At Carillon Point:

Toppers This florist specializes in English floral design, using Northwest natives such as salal and huckleberry as a base and flowers from all over the world as accompaniments. The shop doubles as an art gallery, presenting glassworks ranging from a $12 vase to a $500

Dab Bergsma glass sculpture. ◆ M-Sa; irregularly extended summer hours. 1260 Carillon Pt. 889.9311

Hannigan/Adams Goldsmith Frank Hannigan is an avowed constructivist, but he will make whatever you can dream up. Partner Beth Adams's more organic, sculpted pieces complement Hannigan's Bauhaus designs, and if you like the classic Tiffany look, they can do that in their tiny workshop, too. The prices are realistic for hand-crafted gold jewelry. ◆ M-Sa. 1230 Carillon Pt. 889.9450

Yarrow Bay Grill and Beach Cafe ★$$$
One small staff and kitchen create sophisticated dishes for both the restaurant upstairs and the lower outdoor deck, where yups chill after work. There are at least three fresh seafood entrées daily and, if you're tired of fish, this is a good place to get your teeth into a 12-ounce New York steak topped with a green-peppercorn-and-brandy sauce. But that's not all; for a further change of pace, you can order venison or rack of lamb. Downstairs in the **Beach Cafe,** order a gin-and-tonic, one of the appetizer-size snacks (ravioli stuffed with three cheeses is a good choice, as is the zesty bowl of Cajun popcorn shrimp), and sit back comfortably on the deck to watch the sun set upon Seattle. ◆ Seafood/Italian ◆ M-F lunch and dinner; Sa-Su dinner. Reservations recommended for the Grill. 1270 Carillon Pt. 889.9052

Woodmark Hotel $$ A bright atrium flanked by a curved staircase and filled with piano music welcomes you to the only hotel on the shores of Lake Washington. All 100 rooms and suites have TVs and VCRs, and most boast balconies with views westward. For the insomniac with an appetite, a "Raid the Pantry" program offers complimentary late-night snacks. If you really live it up, stay in the **Woodmark Suite,** a 1,456-square-foot apartment with two balconies and a fireplace enjoyed by the likes of Paul McCartney, Arnold Palmer, and Harry Connick Jr. Expensive but satisfying meals are available at the **Carillon Room,** where the salmon fillet comes with some of the best crab cakes to be found in these parts. ◆ 1200 Carillon Pt. 822.3700, 800/822.3700

48 Marsh Estate In the exclusive residential park called **Marsh Commons** sits an elegant 1929 Tudor-style home (illustrated below) that is anything but common. It was erected by Louis Schuster Marsh, born in Wisconsin in 1892, who moved his family to the Seattle area in 1904. Marsh studied engineering at th **University of Washington;** in 1916 he went to work for William Boeing's airplane company, becoming that outfit's chief metallurgist.

Marsh was the engineer who invented all-metal fuselages, and Boeing stock made a small fortune for him. Just over 10 years after joining the company, Marsh commissioned the architectural firm of **Edwin J. Ivey,** to build a home reflecting his success. It's been said that much if not most of the design work was done by **Ivey**'s partner at the time, **Elizabeth Ayer,** the first woman graduate of **UW**'s architecture program and the first female architect licensed in Washington state. The finished estate included a series of waterfalls tremendous hand-carved beams in the living and dining rooms, a darkroom in the basement, a pistol range, and an extensive wine cellar. A weather vane on the rooftop features the likeness of Marsh, an avid golfer dressed in his sporting knickers. It remains a private residence. ◆ 6604 Lake Washington Blvd NE (across from Marsh Park)

49 Shamiana ★★★$$ The kitchen at this popular eatery (it's best to come on weeknights, when the crowds are smaller) prepares a westernized derivation of traditional Indian fare, mixing in Northwest ingredients and toning down spices somewhat for tender American palates; the results are pleasing and provide a slightly exotic gustatory experience. A lunchtime buffet offers the opportunity to sample many dishes, including cardamom-flavored lamb curry; meltingly tender butter chicken, cumin-scented, in a tomato and cream sauce potatoes studded with crushed peanuts; and

Marsh Esta

COURTESY OF THE KIRKLAND HERITAGE SOCIETY

a smooth *dal* of pureed lentils. At dinner, try the intensely flavored pork vindaloo, marinated in vinegar, ginger, and chili. The restaurant's moniker is taken from the name used for the colorful tents that hang bannerlike from the dining room ceiling. ◆ Indian ◆ M-F lunch; Sa-Su dinner. 10724 NE 68th Pl (at Sixth St S and 108th Ave NE). 827.4902

50 Anthony's Homeport ★★$$$ Some people come here for the sunset view over Lake Washington, but even if this first of many branches were located in an underground parking garage people would visit for the sautéed scallops, grilled salmon, and oysters. Try the pear crisp for dessert. For views, the next best **Anthony's** choice is on Shilshole Bay, in Ballard. ◆ Seafood ◆ M-Sa dinner; Su brunch and dinner. Reservations recommended. Moss Bay Marina, 135 Lake St S (at Second Ave S). 822.0225. Also at: 6135 Seaview Ave NW (on Shilshole Bay). 783.0780; Des Moines Marina, Des Moines. 824.1947; Edmonds Marina, Edmonds. 771.4400

50 Third Floor Fish Cafe ★★$$$ Just yards from the famous **Anthony's** is this classy upbeat upstart. The views are as good as any on Moss Bay, and such thoughtful entrées as grilled sea scallops with cider butter, apple-onion relish, and walnuts are complemented by some of the best appetizers and desserts around. Service here is consistently efficient. Kathy Casey, the wunderkind who made her reputation originally at **Fuller's** restaurant downtown, created this cafe's concept. ◆ Seafood ◆ M-F lunch and dinner; Sa-Su dinner. Reservations recommended. 205 Lake St S (at Second Ave S). 822.3553

51 Gunnar Nordstrom Gallery Contemporary original prints and paintings by international and local abstract expressionists are found at this gallery. Featured are Robert Motherwell's works, James Rizzi's 3-D paper constructions, and prints by Toko Shinoda, the grande dame of Japanese abstract expressionism. ◆ Tu-Su. 127 Lake St S (between Kirkland Ave and Second Ave S). 827.2822

52 Danish-Swedish Antiques The country furniture carried here is mostly unpainted, old country pine and turn-of-the-century antiques imported from Sweden and Denmark by Scandinavian owners Ib and Alaina Knoblauch. Here and there among the armoires are china cabinets, washstands with marble tops, porcelain accessories, and Mora clocks with hand-painted faces. The shop has expanded into the space once occupied by **Charing Cross** gift shop. ◆ Daily. 207 Kirkland Ave (between Third St and Lake St S). 822.7899

53 Davinci's Flying Pizza and Pasta ★$ By day the bar is a quiet sports pub and the restaurant's garage-door front is opened to create a relaxing sidewalk cafe. But at night, the dance floor becomes a quasar of Kirkland nightlife. Mannequin parts spin from the ceiling among neon planets. Inventive poultry and seafood pizzas are available in the bar, but if you're really hungry, try the restaurant where the pasta is a savory alternative. The Cajun chicken fettuccine or the seafood cannelloni are top draws. ◆ Daily lunch and dinner; bar until 2AM. 89 Kirkland Ave (at Lake St S). 889.9000

53 Kirkland Clock Captain John Anderson, who ran ferries and steamboats on Lake Washington for more than 40 years, gave this handsome pedestaled timepiece to the City of Kirkland in 1935. Lake St S and Kirkland Ave

54 Avoir Gallery One of Kirkland's first art galleries (and certainly its narrowest) is squeezed into a sliver of an old downtown building (shown above). Owner Scott Fitzgerald exhibits traditional, contemporary, and three-dimensional works by such established local artists as Take Hama and Marilyn Schultzky. There's also a museum-quality framing service offered. ◆ Tu-Su. 216 Kirkland Ave (between Main and Third Sts). 827.8349

55 Old Heritage Place Seventy-two dealers are represented under this one roof, each occupying a small space jammed with relics from yesteryear. The rub is that the dealers are not present, so there's no one to answer your questions about the old banjo or bookshelf or set of fine china that catches your eye. You're on your own—great if you know just what you're looking for and don't like sales pressure. ◆ Daily. 151 Third St (at Park La). 828.4993

"Seattle floats along on Mr. Toad's Wild Ride, stuck in the quicksand of consensus, unfocused, unclear about much except that it would be, well, nice to keep things the way they are."

Seattle Times

Restaurants/Clubs: Red   Hotels: Blue
Shops/ 🏕 Outdoors: Green   **Sights/Culture:** Black

56 Coyote Coffee Company Technically, this is a retail store, not a restaurant, but there are three tables inside. The shop sells Michaelo's coffee, a full-flavored espresso, as well as sandwiches, salads, and desserts. Try the *zufolo*—ambitiously seasoned Italian bread with provolone cheese, salami, tomato, green pepper, onion, and sweet basil—served, if you're lucky enough to come on the right day, with a delicious tabbouleh. Leave room for the hazelnut chocolate mousse. Pottery, masks, paintings, prints, and basketry by local artists are also for sale. ♦ M-Sa until 8PM. 111 Main St (between Kirkland Ave and Park La). 827.2507

57 The Norsemen This Scandinavian gift shop is loaded with such things as wooden plaques declaring "It's a Blessing To Be Finnish." What the store lacks in class is perhaps made up for in variety. Sweatshirts, books, crackers, shelves of dolls and Swedish crystal, and even open-faced sandwiches are all for sale. It's the ultimate in niche marketing. ♦ M-Sa. 140 Park La (at Main St). 822.8715

58 Parklane Gallery A cooperative effort, this gallery is owned and operated by the artists represented. Among the regular painting selections are Loreita Richards's depictions of Native Americans and some powerful Vietnam images by Norm Bergsma. ♦ Tu-Su; F-Sa until 8PM. 130 Park La (between Lake St S and Main St). 827.1462

59 Moss Bay Gallery Original Northwest paintings by a variety of artists are featured, including some by Alaskan artist Rie Muñoz. ♦ Daily. 128-A Park La (between Lake St S and Main St). 822.3630

60 Ristorante Paradiso ★★$$ Sardinian Fabrizio Loi's Mediterranean cafe has a terrifi location on Kirkland's most charming street, and in good weather several tables materializ on the sidewalk outside. Inside or out, the cioppino—mussels, scallops, shrimp, clams and the fish of the day served in a marinara sauce with homemade croutons—is a house specialty, as is the *vitello scampi* (veal pounded thin and wrapped around tender sage shrimp with butter, garlic, and a white-wine-and-lemon sauce). The wonderful, soft bread is made fresh at least twice daily. ♦ Mediterranean ♦ M-Sa lunch and dinner; Su dinner. 120 Park La (near Lake St S). 889.8601

61 Wood 'n' You This gallery carries originals and limited edition prints by national and loc artists. Ken Ledbetter's elegant hand-crafted picture frames of teak, koa, purple heart, and other exotic hardwoods are equally original. ♦ Daily; F until 9PM. 107 Park La (between Lake St S and Main St). 827.6835

62 The Corner Shop One of the best newstands on the Eastside, this shop still carries a wide variety of periodicals, from local to international in scope. ♦ Daily; M-Th until 9PM; F-Sa until 10PM; Su until 8PM. 11 Lake St S (at Central Way NE). 827.6486

62 Triple J Cafe $ You'll have trouble getting your mouth around one of the huge sandwiches at this tiny lunch joint owned by brothers Jim, Jeff, and Jason Harnasch. Spli the meat loaf, the veggie, or the turkey and cranberry with a friend. Or enjoy an espresso and homemade muffins while you ponder th local artists' paintings featured on the walls. ♦ American ♦ Daily lunch. 101 Central Way NE (at Lake St S). 822.7319

63 Ballard Furniture Twice as deep as it looks from the sidewalk, this successful Seattle furniture store is packed with reproductions and antique-looking originals. You'll see the distinctive hand-painted corne of the venerable Hitchcock line, as well as some of Lexington's hard-to-find solid cherr pieces. The earth-friendly accessories are by Robert Beauchamp, who uses only fallen tre for his ducks and other woodcrafts. Ask to s in the Amish rocker made of steamed hickor boughs. ♦ Daily; M-F until 8PM. 108 Central Way NE (between First St and Lake St S). 827.3331

64 Kirkland Roaster & Ale House ★$$ Thi dazzling place has lots of glass and brass an a nine-foot-high vertical spit. Roasted meats including lamb and ham, are the specialty, though they also serve a hearty bowl of clam chowder. And there are 19 draught beers on tap. It's generally crowded and noisy on Frid and Saturday nights. ♦ American ♦ Daily lunch and dinner. 111 Central Way NE (between First St and Lake St S). 827.4400

65 Hale's Ales Brewery In the past decade, the Northwest has seen the rise of a strong microbrewery craft, including this distinctive Eastside business. Hale's doesn't officially give tours, being a small operation in a tight space, but staffers have been known to let the odd passerby in for a closer look when time allows. If the brewery is hopping, go next door to the **Kirkland Roaster & Ale House** (see page 188), where six of their ales are on tap. ◆ 109 Central Way NE (between Lake St S and Market St). 827.4359

65 The Yuppie Pawn Shop This business is based on the concept that while young urban professionals may have it all, they may also be willing to hock it all (or at least some of it) for ready cash. The result is a store full of such high-end used goods as computers, keyboards, espresso machines, radar equipment, sailboards, and riding lawn mowers, as well as the usual watches and cameras. It doesn't buy weapons. ◆ M-Sa. 107 Central Way NE (between Lake St S and Market St). 827.9438

66 Cousins ★$ Plenty of natural light shows off the high ceilings and Art Deco interior of this family-run deli. The blintzes are great for breakfast, served in homemade crepes. For lunch, try their cheese-steak sandwich, roast beef simmered au jus, topped with onions, mushrooms, bell peppers, and melted Swiss, and served on a long French roll. The matzo ball soup also comes highly recommended. ◆ Deli ◆ M-F breakfast and lunch; Sa-Su breakfast. 140 Central Way NE (between First and Third Sts). 822.1076

67 Parkplace Unlike a typical mall, this blissfully uncovered shopping center seems more like a collection of creative and accessible shops. The complex also includes a five-story office tower with a clock on the top. Nestled among the 45 shops and restaurants are the **Parkplace Theater** (with six screens), a health club, and, needless to say, a **Starbucks**. ◆ 401 Park Pl (between Central Way NE and Kirkland Ave)

Within Parkplace:

The Wallflower This shop features an inventory rich in Victorian stock—antiques, cards, and even some apparel. It's a good place to find unusual gifts—laces and linens are the specialties. ◆ Daily; M-F until 8PM. 827.5337

staurants/Clubs: Red   Hotels: Blue
ops/ 🌳 Outdoors: Green   Sights/Culture: Black

Pinocchio's Toys Stuffed with puzzles, games, things that snap together, things that come apart, and things that just sit there waiting for parents to trip over them, this toy shop looks like a kid's dream closet. In the midst of all this are some noteworthy collectibles, including hand-painted Russian *matruschkas* (stacking dolls). The owners quit this business once but couldn't stay away for long. ◆ Daily; M-Th until 8PM; F until 9:30PM. 827.1100

City Thai ★$ Visit this small, quiet, and surprisingly elegant restaurant where owner Joe Suwanvichit takes much care with the presentation of food. For beginners, the *pad thai* noodles (with shrimp, egg, vegetables, and tofu in a peanut sauce) make a great introduction to an often daunting cuisine. Also tasty is the house special beef dish, cooked with carrots, potatoes, and roasted peanuts and served in a spicy curry with coconut milk. They'll be happy to turn down the temperature in any dish. ◆ Thai ◆ M-Sa lunch and dinner; Su dinner. 827.2875

COURTESY OF THE KIRKLAND HERITAGE SOCIETY

68 Dr. Trueblood/Creger Home In 1907 this slender wood-frame house (pictured above) was bought by Kirkland's first physician, Dr. Barclay Trueblood. The now-quiet street in front of the house was once the busiest avenue in town. It's a private residence. ◆ 127 Seventh Ave (near Market St)

Microsoft Corporation chairman Bill Gates, who lives on the east side of Lake Washington, may be one of the wealthiest people in America (with a net worth, based on his stock holdings, of at least $7 billion), but he's not the only one enriched by his Seattle-area company. According to one Wall Street research firm, some 2,200 Microsoft employees—almost one in five—are millionaires.

COURTESY OF THE KIRKLAND HERITAGE SOCIETY

69 Peter Kirk Building Kirk's urban dream began to materialize with the construction of this handsome 1891 brick edifice (illustrated above). Refurbished by the Creative Arts League, it now houses the **Kirkland Arts Center,** which holds classes and presents shows in all media. ◆ Arts Center Tu-Sa. 620 Market St (at Seventh Ave). 822.7161

70 Joshua Sears Building In 1891 Boston millionaire Joshua M. Sears built this two-story brick triangle in what was then the center of town to be the official bank of the Great Western Iron and Steel Works. The steel mill never produced so much as an ingot, and the bank failed without ever opening. The beautiful brick arches inside were covered up when the building's interior was divided into apartments in the 1940s. They were rediscovered by developer Lloyd Powell and his wife when they bought the place in 1982 and went at it with $800,000 and a trowel. The restoration won the Powells numerous awards, including *Metropolitan Home* magazine's "Home of the Year," and was featured on the "This Old House" TV show. ◆ 701 Market St (near Seventh Ave)

71 The Bucklin Home The Kirkland Land and Improvement Company built this wood-fram house (pictured below) in 1889, and in 1904 was bought by Harry Thompkins, who starte a successful shipyard at what is now **Carillon Point.** This house was nearly condemned after a fire in 1975, but the Bucklin family was allowed to buy it with the promise that they would restore it. Renovations began with beams and other lumber salvaged from—of all places—the old shipyard. It is now a private residence. ◆ 202 Fifth Ave W (between Second and Third Sts W)

72 Cafe Juanita ★★★$$ Back in the 1970s you couldn't get into this restaurant without either a reservation months in advance or a personal letter from the pope. But as the trendoids moved on, room opened up again for local guests, and owner Peter Dow could sit back a little and keep closer watch on his kitchen. Dow is a cautiou steward of his menu, rotating in some of his favorite specials without forgetting any tried-and-true successes. That means the *spiedin misti* (two skewers of lamb and Italian sausages, roasted with onions and green peppers) you order this week will probably always be on the menu. Dow also offers about 250 Italian wines, as well as three varieties produced under his own Cavatappi label: a Sauvignon blanc, a small amount of Cabernet Sauvignon, and a dark red, potent, and dry Maddalena which he makes himself from Nebbiolo grapes. ◆ Italian ◆ Daily dinn Reservations recommended. 9702 NE 120th Pl (near 93rd Ave NE). 823.1505

The Bucklin Home

Day Trips

CANADA

Vancouver

Fraser River

1

WASHINGTON

Strait of Georgia

Gabriola Island

Valdes Island

Thetis Island

Kuper Island

Galiano Island

Salt Spring Island

Mayne Island

N. Pender Island

Saturna Island

Boundary Bay

Bellingham Bay

Bellingham

542

Mt. Baker ▲
10,778 ft.

Mt. Baker
National Rec. Area

Waldron Island

Sucia Island

Lummi Island

5

to North Cascades
National Park

Sidney

Stuart Island

Sidney Island

Orcas Island

San Juan Island

Shaw Island

Blakely Island

Cypress Island

Samish Bay

20

Victoria

17

1

Lopez Island

Decatur Island

Anacortes

Burlington

Mt. Vernon

Deception Pass
State Park

Skagit Bay

Camano Island

Port Susan

Saratoga Passage

20

Juan de Fuca Strait

Vancouver Island

Dungeness National
Wildlife Refuge

Port Angeles

101

Port Townsend

20

Whidbey Island

Ferry

Everett

Mukilteo

Olympic National Park

Mt. Deception
7,788 ft. ▲

Mt. Constance
7,743 ft. ▲

▲ Mt. Olympus
7,965 ft.

104

Port Gamble

Puget Sound

2

Edmonds

Poulsbo

Grave of
Chief Sealth

3

Bainbridge Island

405

Lake Washington

Bellevue

Hood Canal

Bremerton

Seattle

90

Issaquah

Snoqualmie
Falls

101

16

Vashon Island

Renton

5

North Bend

Chester Morse Lake

18

3

Hartstene Island

Fox Island

Point Defiance
Park

Auburn

167

Lake Tapps

169

Shelton

Squaxin Island

McNeil Island

Tacoma

Puyallup

512

410

Anderson Island

8

Olympia

Fort Lewis
Military
Reserve

5

↓ to Portland

7

↓ to
Mt. St. Helens

Mt. Ranier
14,410 ft. ▲

20
10

40
20

Day Trips

After four or five days in Seattle, travelers may start to feel somewhat edgy, a little trapped, worried that there isn't anything more to do than revisit **Pike Place Market**, Pioneer Square, or the **Space Needle**. But nearby are volcanoes, vineyards, and villages . . . and that's just the beginning.

Within three hours from the city are rustic retreats in the **San Juan Islands**, ceremonial wine-grape crushings on the east side of **Lake Washington**, ski slopes, exotic summer gardens, and bird refuges. Architecture aficionados might want to head south for a look at Washington state's impressive capital complex at **Olympia**, while true urbanites could venture north into two of Canada's most interesting cities: **Victoria** is the modest but growing island-bound capital of British Columbia, providing a wealth of history in a cozy, shop-laden English atmosphere; and **Vancouver**, just across the **Strait of Georgia** from Victoria, is Canada's third-largest metropolis (after Montreal and Toronto). Rudyard Kipling, seduced by the Vancouver area's beauty, proclaimed in his *Letters of Travel* that "such a land is good for an energetic man . . . it is also not bad for the loafer."

And then there's **Mount St. Helens**, to the south of Seattle, which caught the world's attention when it violently blew its stack back in 1980. Although the state of Oregon tries to claim St. Helens as its own (it is physically closer to the city of Portland than to Seattle), the now-decimated peak remains one of Washington's prime draws.

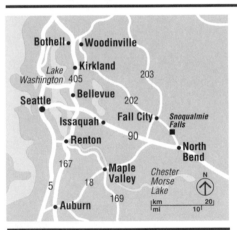

Eastside Wine Country

The greatest number of wineries are found in the suburbs east of Seattle. Begin at the **Paul Thomas Winery** (1717 136th Pl NE, Bellevue, 489.1569), launched on the reputation of its fruit wines but now best known for its production of Cabernet Sauvignons and Chardonnays. The winery was recently purchased by Associated Vintners in Woodinville, but it is still producing excellent wines at the **Bellevue** facility.

One of the Eastside's pioneer wineries, **Columbia,** has relocated from Bellevue to a quainter country location that includes picnic grounds (14030 NE 145th St, Woodinville, 488.2776). Wine maker David Lake is best known for his Cabernets and Merlots. There are daily wine tastings, and tours on weekends. Visitors can enjoy the patio and lawns, and purchase cheese and crackers in a small gift shop. Phone ahead to check on occasional concerts held on the premises.

Finally, drop by **Chateau Ste. Michelle** (14111 NE 145th St, Woodinville, 488.1133), just across the street from **Columbia** winery. Extensive grounds are open to picnickers, and classical concerts are held in an amphitheater during the warm months. If you have time, take a tour of the two-acre garden behind the grounds' historic **Stimson Mansion.** Timber magnate Frederick S. Stimson arrived in Seattle in 1889, bought 206 acres of prime agricultural land on the **Sammamish River,** and built **Hollywood Farm,** a state-of-the-art dairy and poultry ranch, anchored by the manse. Around 1910 he hired the famed Olmsted brothers to plan a garden, bordered by trees and shrubs, that would be filled with exotic plants. The formal results are still maintained today.

For a guide to Washington's wine-touring opportunities, check out *Northwest Wines* (1994; Sasquatch Press) co-authored by Paul Gregutt, wine columnist for the *Seattle Weekly*, and Jeff Prather, wine manager at **Ray's Boathouse** in Ballard.

Heading back to Seattle after a full day of tapping the grape, plan to take a detour from the Lake Washington floating bridges in favor of Highway 522 or Bothell Way, and stop for a sumptuous French dinner at **Gerard's Relais de Lyon** (17121 Bothell Way NE, Bothell, 485.7600). Owner/chef Gerard Parrat, a student and follower of famous French foodmeister Paul Bocuse, has been running this restaurant for almost 20 years. Parrat's cuisine remains firmly rooted in his Lyonnaise heritage. Presentation is exceedingly fancy (imagine a terrine with slivers of artichoke heart, squab breast, and rare foie gras embedded in aspic). Some offerings should not be missed (the lobster bisque, for instance). And the tangy Grand Marnier soufflé, from a Bocuse recipe, is especially popular. Reservations are essential.

nother excellent dining choice is **The Herbfarm** (2804 Issaquah-Fall City Rd, Fall City, 784.2222), bout 30 minutes east of Seattle. Chefs Ron mmerman and Jerry Traunfeld have created a staurant that provides an exceptional experience s well as excellent food. Meals begin with a lively ur of the grounds, with Zimmerman nipping off aves for you to rub and smell. After that sensual perience, you'll be far more aware of the flowers id herbs in what you taste; the legendary salads are good example. All the produce (except for lemons) id herbs used in the food preparation are grown re. Prix-fixe meals (six courses at lunch, nine at nner) are composed from fresh seasonal bounty id span the globe with their culinary influences— verything from Italian to Native American.

nfortunately, getting a reservation here is no easy sk. First, only 32 people can be accommodated one time. Second, there is just one seating per y (either lunch or dinner), and only on Friday, aturday, and Sunday. Third, the restaurant takes x months of advance bookings on two days each ar (a Wednesday in early April and a Wednesday mid-August; dates vary, so call ahead). About 25 ercent of the seating, however, is kept open until a eek before serving. So if you call at 1PM on a Friday check the following week's availability, you might t the jackpot. If not, you can stop by the farm store pen daily; closed in March) for herbs and other ourmet items to bring home.

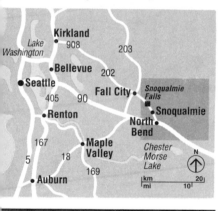

and of "Twin Peaks"

ng County's eastern cantons won international me when Washington native and filmmaker David nch chose to shoot his unsettlingly kinky TV ries, "Twin Peaks" (and later a prequel motion cture, *Twin Peaks: Fire Walk with Me*), in the small wns of **North Bend** and **Snoqualmie.** The series as noted for its tension-building background music slow jazz and finger snapping, and its population local characters, each weirder or lustier than the st. The mystery of young Laura Palmer's murder pt fans on the edge of their seats for two seasons d left those small Washington towns with a pularity founded on familiar exteriors and, as nch's FBI agent Dale Cooper would put it, amn fine cups of coffee."

gin your leap into "Lynchville" by taking Interstate from Bellevue to Exit 27. Follow the signs to oqualmie, then through the north end of town to

Snoqualmie Falls; or take Highways 908 and 202 from Kirkland to reach the falls by a more scenic route. This 270-foot cascade, a prominent background from "Twin Peaks," was renamed White Tail Falls for the show. It's *the* place to bring out-of-town guests. City folks and other tourists have been coming here to gawk since the late 19th century. A lookout point on a bluff to one side of the falls was improved and expanded not long ago, but crowds mount quickly on weekends, everybody equipped with cameras; arrive early if you hope to beat the stampede.

The Snoqualmie Indians have traditionally viewed this as a sacred site, and they've been struggling in recent years to maintain its natural appearance. The tribe has not had a happy relationship with Puget Power, the hydroelectric company that owns the land surrounding the falls and regulates how much water passes over its lip. Information panels at the overlook outline these additions and renovations, which include consideration for fisheries, wetlands, and even flood prevention; the Snoqualmie are mentioned only in relation to the discovery of the falls by whites. Ironically, Puget Power's buildings at the falls are historic landmarks, while the Snoqualmie have no legal means to protect the falls.

The world's first underground electric generator, built in 1898, lies 270 feet deep in a chamber excavated from solid basaltic rock behind the falls. From the lookout point, you can see the opening of the tailrace, a 450-foot-long tunnel where water diverted through the turbines rejoins the river at the base of the falls. A one-mile round-trip trail will take you down for a closer look and a faceful of spray.

Perched at the very edge of the gorge is **The Salish Lodge** (Hwy 202, 888.2556), known to Twin Peakers as the "Great Northern Hotel." Formerly the **Snoqualmie Falls Lodge,** the landmark was remodeled in the late 1980s. Although a country feel was retained, the place has lost its authentic weathered look. The **Salish Lodge Dining Room** is famous for its front-row view of the falls and its six-course country breakfast: a platter of fruit accompanied by the Eye Opener (fresh-squeezed orange juice blended with lime juice, honey, and egg, and topped with grated nutmeg), an assortment of bran and fruit muffins baked every half hour and served with honey butter, old-fashioned rolled oats with cream and brown sugar, and the main course of apple-pork sausage, smoked bacon, and a grilled ham steak with your choice of egg preparations, plus hash browns, and sourdough biscuits—buttressed by a stack of whole-wheat buttermilk flapjacks. Bring a change of belts. The wine list is also legendary. Sommelier Randy Austin says that at last count there were 725 labels available on the roster, including an 1882 Madeira Verdeljo ($250). Don't worry if you're not an expert oenophile; Austin has always been very helpful in educating the patrons about novel or arcane vintages to complement their meals.

Leaving the falls, backtrack through the town of Snoqualmie. Train buffs shouldn't miss a steam-train ride on the **Puget Sound and Snoqualmie Valley Railway** (746.4025), a 90-minute round-trip excursion between Snoqualmie and **North Bend** offered on weekends from April through October. The town of North Bend is sprinkled with Swiss chalet–style shops and restaurants and loomed over by **Mount Si**, a colossal peak that was featured ominously in a shot used for commercial breaks in the "Twin Peaks" series. With a sweeping view of the **Snoqualmie Valley** and a trailhead that starts just outside of town, Si is a popular hike; on weekends the 4.5-mile trail, though strenuous, is crowded with nature lovers. To get there, drive south on North Bend Way, turn left on Mount Si Road and continue for about 2.5 miles, watching for the trail sign. Just one caution: Keep track of the time—many people have spent miserable nights lost in these woods because they didn't allow enough time to hike back before dark. And the Haystack, a knob of bare rock at Si's top, is officially off limits. Views from there may be panoramic, but sudden sidewinds and updrafts can pick off even the most macho sight-seers like ripe fruit.

Finish your "Peaks" experience at the **Mar T Cafe** (137 North Bend Way, 888.1221), the show's pseudonymous "Double R Diner." Although the show is over, its popularity lives on here: A banner outside proclaims it "Home of Twin Peaks Pies," and paraphernalia like T-shirts, autographed photos, and a map that matches the fictitious names to the real places are all for sale. The large horseshoe counter ringed by shiny stools and the booths flanked by wood paneling are still the same as they were before fame came calling, and the ice-cream machine still hums like a diesel engine.

Bainbridge Island

Bainbridge has enjoyed some interesting history. In the late 19th century the island's southern end sported a couple of saloons, a giant mill that could cut 500,000 board feet over two 10-hour shifts, and the 75-room **Bainbridge Hotel.** (All have since disappeared.) In the early 20th century the island figured briefly into the well-publicized and often comic escape of Butch Cassidy cohort Harry Tracy from a maximum-security prison in Oregon. (Officials ultimately forced Tracy to kill himself.) Most of that colorful heritage is gone, leaving a fairly peaceful, still heavily wooded escape.

For many years, Bainbridge—about 35 minutes west of Seattle by ferry—was a haven for hippies and others whose supreme desire was to drop out of the public eye. But things change. Although threats to build a bridge across **Puget Sound** have come to naught, as Seattle grew, well-to-do residents who didn't fancy moving to one of the Eastside suburbs looked west instead.

The Bainbridge-bound ferry (464.6000) leaves from the Colman Dock/Pier 52 on the Seattle Waterfront. Ferries depart every 40 to 60 minutes from just after 6AM until slightly after 2AM; the last return trip leaves Bainbridge at about 1:15AM. Ferries dock at the **City of Bainbridge Island** (formerly named **Winslow**), home to a small Saturday farmer's market (held mid-spring through fall at **Winslow Green,** on the corner of Madison Avenue and Winslow Way), plus a couple of cafes and the small but interesting **Eagle Harbor Books** (157 Winslow Way, 842.5332).

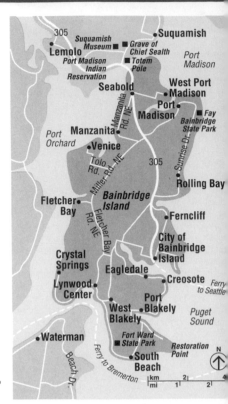

Stop in at the **Streamliner Diner** (397 Winslow Way, 842.8595), an island institution, and get on line. Breakfasts are legendary (just ask any of the people waiting for a table) and they're served all day. Try the omelettes, buttermilk waffles, or potatoes deluxe—a stir-fry of diced spuds, lots of onions, and fresh veggies, all beneath a generous layer of melted cheese.

Head west along Highway 305 and, in less than a mile, you'll come to the **Bainbridge Island Winery** (682 Hwy 305, 842.9463), the only estate winery in the Seattle area. Founded in 1981, it's only seven acres in size but has a growing reputation. Owners Gerard and Jo Ann Bentryn style the vintages in the German fashion—low in alcohol with some residual sweetness. The flagship wine is Müller-Thurgau, but Corbet Clark, in his book *American Wines of the Northwest,* also gives raves to the "surprising" Siegerrebe, "a cross of Gewürztraminer with Madeleine Angevine, itself an old French cross." The Bentryns also produce a popular strawberry wine. There's a picnic area, a wine-oriented antique shop, and a wine museum on the premises.

The 150 acres of **Bloedel Reserve** (7521 NE Dolphin Dr, 842.7631), about four miles farther west along Highway 305, were once the estate of a Canadian lumbering family. But since the 1980s, these woodlands and gardens have been open to the public from Wednesday through Sunday, with trails that give visitors a good look at exotic plant life imported from around the globe. Rhododendrons

...d azaleas are the most plentiful plantings, so spring the prime viewing season. Bring binoculars; birds ...joy a refuge here. Only 150 guests are allowed in ...ch day; make reservations early; admission charge.

...nally, cross the bridge onto the **Kitsap Peninsula** ... **Agate Pass** and turn left onto Sandy Pass Road to ...d the **Suquamish Museum** (15383 Sandy Hook ...d, 598.3311). This small museum recounts local ...story in a manner sensitive to the perspective ...f Puget Sound's Salish tribe. The life of Chief ...ealth is illuminated through both displays and ...hotographs. The museum is open daily from ...une through September; Friday-Saturday the ...st of the year; admission is charged.

...hief Sealth's burial site is nearby, next to **St. Peter's** ...atholic Mission Church in the Kitsap village of **...uquamish.** It's hard to miss the leader's tomb, ...hich is marked with a pair of long canoes ...ounted atop poles.

Whidbey Island

...anks to the US Supreme Court, Whidbey Island— ...50-mile snake of soil northwest of Seattle—is ...e longest island in the United States. (The court ...clared that challenger Long Island is a mere ...eninsula.) Unfortunately, the island's natural ...eauty and easygoing charm may soon be over-...n in the rush to attract tourists. More and ...ore amenities are being planned for Whidbey, ...ausing a local backlash from Seattleites who liked ...e island before it became popular. The time to ...e this place is now, before it's too late.

...hidbey is reached via a 20-minute ferry ride from ...e town of **Mukilteo,** 20 miles north of Seattle. ...rries leave every half-hour on Saturday and ...unday, from about 6AM until 1AM; the last return ...rry leaves Whidbey at about 12:30AM on Sunday. ...eekday service is more limited; call 464.6400 for ...hedules and information. The boat docks in the ...wn of **Clinton,** where motorists can pick up ...ighway 525.

...nce on Whidbey, follow the highway for three ...iles, then take the marked turn-off east to **Langley.** ...his tiny town maintains a distinctly quaint air; it ...ay be rivaled only by La Conner, Washington, in ...e number of new curio shops that sprout here ...nnually. Yet Langley seems especially susceptible ... the encroaching tourist industry: The town already ...as a glut in its number of high-priced but small-...ccupancy "boutique hotels," which sell themselves ... expansive views of **Saratoga Passage** and the **...ascade Mountains.** One of the most quietly ...xurious establishments is **Galitoire** (5444 S Coles ...d, 221.0548), a woodland escape surrounded by ...rdens and tall trees. Architect and innkeeper **...ahesh Massand** offers two sumptuous suites— ...e with a hot tub and private gym—and loves to ...rprise guests with gourmet canapes and ...ampagne in the afternoon.

...everal fine restaurants draw day-trippers from the ...ainland. Try the Middle Eastern **Cafe Langley** (113 ...rst St, 221.3090), renowned for its crab cakes ...d hummus. Or sample owner/chef Steve Nogal's

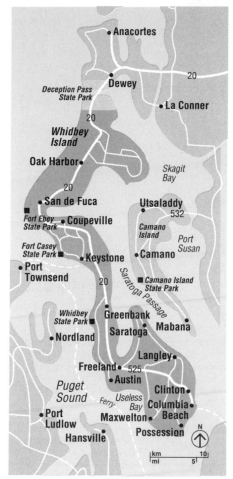

delectable five-course, prix-fixe weekend dinners at the **Inn at Langley** (400 First St, 221.3033), which concentrate on Northwest ingredients from vegetables to seafood. There's one seating a night, two nights a week, expanding to three nights weekly in the summer; reservations are taken three months in advance.

A visit to the **Meerkeek Rhododendron Gardens,** 15½ miles north of the ferry landing on Highway 525 to Resort Road (321.6682) is a must for spring visitors. There are 53 acres covered with some 2,000 varieties of Washington's official state flower in peak bloom from mid-April to mid-May. The gardens also feature wild flowers and summer perennials. Energetic types might want to head up-island for a walk around the gorge at **Deception Pass** (near Oak Harbor), with its 2,300 acres of forests and beaches. The gardens are open Wednesday through Sunday; admission charge.

Midway between those two attractions, three miles south of Coupeville on Admiralty Inlet, is **Fort Casey** (678.4519), decommissioned but still boasting its old gun mounts and some dramatic outlooks. It's open daily and is free.

195

Get a sense of history and stay a night or two at the **Fort Casey Inn** (1124 S Engle Rd, Coupeville, 678.8792). Children are welcome at this restored two-story, two-bedroom, Georgian Revival officers' quarters decorated with rag rugs, stenciling, and plenty of eagle motifs. Bikes are available free to guests. While in Coupeville visit the free **Island County Historical Museum** (Alexander and Front Sts, 678.3310), which is full of old photographs and Native American artifacts. The museum is open daily May through October; Saturday-Sunday in April. As the sun finally fades from the sky, stop by the **Captain Whidbey Inn** (2072 Wes Captain Whidbey Inn Rd, Coupeville, 678.4097, 800/366.4097).

This 1907 madrona log lodge (pictured above) was once most reachable by steamship from Seattle. Now you can wheel up here in just a few hours for dinner or drinks on a terrific deck overlooking **Penn Cove,** where some of this region's finest mussels are harvested.

There is a plethora of bed-and-breakfast establishments on the island, as well as a number of cottages for rent; contact the **Langley Chamber of Commerce** (221.6765) for more information.

San Juan Islands

There are 743 islands in the San Juan archipelago, but during high tide only about 170 of them are visible. Sixty of these are populated, most are privately owned (a few by single hermits), and the vast majority are unreachable except by private craft.

Kenmore Air (486.8400) offers scenic scheduled floatplane service from Seattle to the San Juans. But certainly the most relaxing means of travel to the four largest islands—**Lopez, Shaw, Orcas,** and **San Juan** (with an international spur on to Sidney, British Columbia)—is by ferry.

Washington State Ferries (464.6400) bound for the islands leave from the town of **Anacortes,** 78 miles north of Seattle (take Exit 230 from Interstate 5 and head 20 miles west to the terminal). During summer months there are 17 daily departures scheduled from Anacortes; fewer between Labor Day and Memorial Day. Return schedules vary per island. The wait for space on ferry car decks can be long, so bring reading material; folks have spent two or more hours in line during the summer tourist crush. But if you begin early (the first sailing of the day varies slightly each quarter, but is sometime around 6AM), you'll improve your chances of getting on when you want.

While at sea, the boats provide huge picture windows for ample viewing of madrona-forested hills and narrow beaches. Eagles, gulls, and other able aviators are frequently seen, as are small fishing craft. Weather here tends to be milder than in Seattle, as the islands snuggle into the "rain shadow" of the Olympic Mountains to the west. It takes approximately 1.5 hours to sail from Anacortes directly to **Friday Harbor,** on San Juan, the farthest you can go by ferry among these islands. But some visitors slow the journey's pace by getting off and on the boat periodically to tour the four principal isles.

The islands can be very crowded in the summer, so book accommodations early, preferably *weeks,* before your planned excursion. **Visitor Information Service** (468.3663) provides accommodations listings, and the **Washington Bed and Breakfast Guild** (800/647.2918) lists inns, farmhouses, and cottages run by charming and friendly innkeepers.

Flat, pastoral **Lopez** (about 45 minutes by ferry from Anacortes) provides the easiest bicycling on the islands, a 30-mile jaunt past sheep and cattle pastures that can be handled even by younger family members. One of the best ways to enjoy the island is to stay at the **Inn at Swift's Bay** (Port Stanley Rd, 468.3636). Robert Herrman and Christopher Brandmeir offer whatever amount of pampering or seclusion you might desire in their tasteful, comfortable mock Tudor home surrounded by perennial gardens. (They'll even pick you up at the ferry landing.) Five guest rooms are available in the inn, and there's also a romantic waterfront cabin for two. All guests have access to the hot tub down the garden path, and are provided with robes, flashlights, and flip-flops.

Ride down to the island's southwest corner and visit **Shark Reef Preserve** to observe seals barking and flopping about. Lopez village (known for its strong grapevine of information and liberal politics) barely makes it on the map. It boasts the small but interesting **Lopez Island Historical Museum** (Lopez Plaza, 468.2049) that is open Friday through Sunday from May through September (donation requested) and a bakery, **Holly B's** (Lopez Plaza, 468.2133).

All four islands can claim parks, but underpopulated **Shaw Island**—dominated by three orders of Catholic nuns (one member of which always comes down to meet the ferry)—offers very little else in the way of traveler amenities.

At 57 square miles, horseshoe-shaped **Orcas** (an hour and 20 minutes by ferry from Anacortes) is the largest of the islands. Generally hilly (okay for bike riding if you're in good shape), it's dominated by 2,409-foot **Mount Constitution,** on top of which is an old stone lookout that offers views of everything between Mount Rainier and Vancouver, BC. Drive up this peak or get a better feel for the island by huffing to it on foot through 4,934-acre **Moran State Park,** overlooking the island's eastern end.

The town of **Eastsound,** about 10 miles north of the ferry landing, is slowly being transformed into mini-Carmel, with bookstores, art galleries, and staurants. On Saturday, from April through ctober, local artisans and growers gather at a rmer's market on the grounds of the modest rcas Island Historical Museum (North Beach Rd, 76.4849). Also in Eastsound is **Bilbo's Festivo** Beach Rd and A St, 376.4728), a restaurant that rves food influenced by New Mexican, Mexican, d Spanish cooking styles in a setting of adobe alls and Navajo weavings. Mesquite-grilled dinners sirloin tips and of local fish are excellent, but so e the burritos. The best seating is in the courtyard, here you can enjoy the quiet of early evening, and here it's not unheard of for patrons to begin sing-ongs. **Christina's** (N Beach Rd and Horseshoe Way, 76.4904) is a more romantic restaurant, a walk-up llection of small rooms with a dining porch that erlooks the water. Offerings consist mostly of tisfying preparations of local seafood (including libut and oysters).

ke a little time to stroll the grounds of **Rosario esort** (Horseshoe Way, on the east side of Orcas, 6.2222), about 15 minutes from the ferry landing d three miles beyond Eastsound. A glistening ite mansion on the waterfront, it was built at the rn of the century by a former Seattle mayor and lionaire boat-builder Robert Moran, who left the y in 1904—after his doctor told him he had only six months to live. (As it turns out, Moran avoided the Reaper for another 37 years.) This resort is a wonderful place to hang out in good weather, inviting guests to drink buckets of margaritas by the pool and finish off lunch with a soothing afternoon massage. Meals in the dining room (including an almost-overwhelming Sunday brunch) are acceptable but not outstanding. Phone ahead for information on historical programs, including organ concerts and a history of the estate.

The most populated of the islands is **San Juan.** This was the site of a particularly bizarre border dispute, the comic Pig War of 1859, at a time when the British and the Americans shared an uneasy joint occupation of this island. The war was set off by an American farmer who shot and killed a pig that had been rooting in his garden. Turns out the porker belonged to the British Hudson's Bay Company. When the Brits sought to arrest the offending farmer, American infantry soldiers stepped in. Tempers and armaments escalated, until US President James Buchanan finally dispatched General Winfield Scott to negotiate a temporary truce. Joint occupation of the island continued until 1871, when none other than Kaiser Wilhelm I of Germany was asked to settle the border dispute. He drew the Canadian-US border to the west of the island, through **Haro Strait,** thereby ceding San Juan to the Americans. You can visit the national

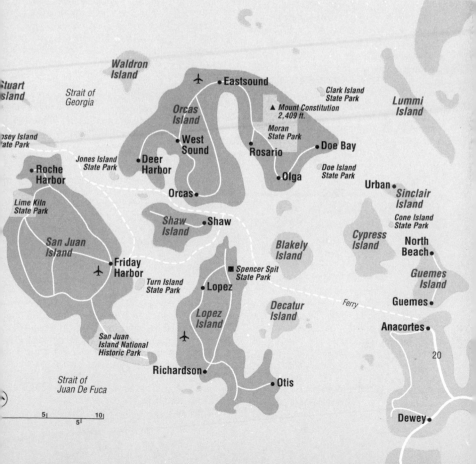

historic sites of **American Camp** and **British Camp.** To reach the former, follow Cattle Point Road about six miles from the town of Friday Harbor toward the island's southeast tip. The nattier British Camp is about 12 miles farther, located off West Valley Road.

Before or after taking in the old British installation, stop at **Lime Kiln State Park** (6158 Lighthouse Rd, 378.2044), which provides some of the best whale-watching opportunities in Washington state; posted signs will help you distinguish one species from another. (Premier viewing season is from late spring through early fall.) The **Friday Harbor Whale Museum** (62 First St, 378.4710) in town is a warehouselike structure stuffed with gray whale baleen, cetacean skeletons, and information about orcas and dolphins. The museum can also provide information about whale watching excursions. It's open daily; admission charge.

An unusual aspect of the San Juan Islands' beauty is that much of it is fairly new, reclaimed from previous devastation. As the 19th century became the 20th, the air here was muddied with noxious fumes from lime kilns operating on San Juan Island. **Roche Harbor,** on the north end of San Juan, once hosted some of the busiest kilns—not to mention a steam-belching railroad and lumberyards. Today the harbor's focal point is the **Hotel de Haro** (Tirte Memorial Dr, 378.2155) built in 1886 by John Stafford McMillin, a Tacoma lawyer and owner of the old Roche Harbor Lime and Cement Company here. McMillin built the 20-room hotel so his business clients (as well as a few other distinguished guests, including Teddy Roosevelt) might have a proper place to stay nearby. Worth visiting—if only for its Stephen Kingish oddity—is a mausoleum, tucked amid a stand of Douglas firs about a half-mile from the inn. The seven-pillared monument contains a round table and six chairs in its middle, each representing a member of McMillin's family. After a roam in the woods, stop on the hotel's deck, overlooking the harbor, for a cold beer and to watch great blue herons coast forlornly over the evergreens.

Victoria, British Columbia

Author Rudyard Kipling may have gone a bit overboard when he described this city on the southern tip of **Vancouver Island** in the early 20th century. "To realize Victoria," he wrote, "you must take all that the eye admires in Bournemouth, Torquay, the Isle of Wight, the Happy Valley at Hong Kong, the Doon, Sorrento, and Camp's Bay—add reminiscences of the Thousand Islands and arrange the whole around the Bay of Naples with some Himalayas for the background." But things are changing here. Rapidly. Finally shedding its reputation as a retirement camp to the world, Victoria has attracted some innovative shops and restaurants, and downtown sidewalks no longer roll up after 10PM.

To get there, you can extend your meandering journey through the San Juans via the **Washington State Ferries** (464.6400) to the town of **Sidney** on Vancouver Island, and then drive 40 miles north to Victoria. Direct service to Victoria from Seattle is available via seaplane from **Kenmore Air** (486.8400) which offers four scheduled flights daily; and by the **Victoria Clipper**'s (448.5000) passenger-only catamarans, which leave from Pier 69 on the Waterfront. There are two to four daily catamaran departures, with tour frequency highest from June through September. The trip lasts 2.5 hours. Board early for the best seats on the upper deck. Fares var according to the time of year. **Victoria Line Limited** a Canadian enterprise, operates the 190-car, 900-passenger *Royal Victorian* ferry from Seattle's Pier 48 from May through mid-September. The crossing time is 4.5 hours; there is one trip in each direction daily. For recorded information, call 800/668.1167; for reservations, call 625.1880 in Seattle, 604/480.5555 in Victoria.

A good starting point for your explorations is the wonderfully innovative **Royal British Columbia Museum** (675 Belleville St, 604/387.3701). Here dioramas record the extinction of woolly mammoth and the rise of Victorian storefronts; the area's Native American heritage is also well represented. The museum is open daily; there's an admission charge. Just across Government Street is the imposing Neo-Gothic **Parliament Building.** Free 25-30 minute tours are offered daily from May through Labor Day, and Monday through Friday the rest of the year; call 604/387.3046 for reservations. One block north is the 487-room **Empress Hotel** (7 Government St, 604/384.8111, 800/441.1414), opened in 1908 by the **Canadian Pacific Railway,** and host to such luminaries as Winston Churchill, John Wayne, and Richard Nixon (he and Pat honeymooned here). There was talk in the mid-196 of razing this grand dowager; instead, **Canadian Pacific** dumped $45 million into her restoration. Th money has paid off. A pavilion has been added to o side of the old entrance, leaving the original lobby for high tea every afternoon (reservations required, 604/384.8111). Several luxury attic rooms have be opened, offering magnificent perspectives over Inn Harbour. The hotel's elegant **Palm Court** and **Cryst: Ballroom** have been polished up, and a refurbishec conservatory at the hotel's back connects it with th **Victoria Conference Centre.**

Continue still farther north on Government Street to downtown's central shopping district. Here you will find **Sasquatch Indian Sweater Shop** (1233 Government St, 604/386.9033), which offers engulfing handmade sweaters; **Munro's Books** (1108 Government St, 604/382.2464), a 1909 ban! wonderfully transformed into the city's best and classiest bookstore; **Old Morris Tobacconist, Ltd.** (1116 Government St, 604/382.4811), with a floor to-ceiling humidor, along with a broad selection of pipes and related products; **Murchie's Tea and Coffee** (1110 Government St, 604/383.3112), redolent with the scents of buttery pastries and hot drinks; and the Dickensian treasure box of

oger's Chocolates and English Sweet Shop
913 Government St, 604/384.7021), full of
hocolate creams, almond brittle, and marzipan
ars. **Bastion Square,** on Wharf Street between
ates and Fort Streets, is home to many sidewalk
estaurants, a maritime museum, and what
s reportedly the location of Victoria's old gallows.

ast of downtown is **Craigdarroch Castle** (1050
oan Crescent, 604/592.5323), a spooky climb of
tone mounted above the city by coal tycoon Robert
unsmuir, who built this estate in the late 19th
entury after the discovery of coal deposits made him
he province's first millionaire. West of downtown,
ead for **Spinnaker's Brew Pub** (308 Catherine St,
04/386.2739) in the nearby **Esquimalt** community,
or a giant burger, a cold beer, and a soothing view
ack toward Victoria.

or a relaxed, pampered stay along the ocean, drive
ut to **Sooke Harbour House** (1528 Whiffen Spit Rd,
04/642.3421), about 45 minutes southwest of
ictoria in the town of **Sooke.** All 13 guest rooms
verlook the ocean, and most have a balcony or
errace. The meals served in the restaurant are
utstanding: dinner may include fresh seafood

caught by one of the owners, Sinclair Philip—an
expert diver, and will definitely include vegetables,
herbs, and edible flowers from the inn's
extensive gardens.

When the weather is good, Victoria dresses up in
nature's splendor with jewel-colored blossoms in its
many gardens—from pocket-size to large estates—
and in hanging baskets on nearly every street
downtown. Contact the **Travel Infocentre** (812 Wharf
St, 604/382.2127) for information on gardens at
Royal Roads, the **Royal BC Museum, Beacon Hill
Park, Government House, University Finnerty
Gardens,** and the **Gorge Waterway.** The most
famous spot is **Butchart Gardens,** 13 miles north of
Victoria in Brentwood (off Hwy 17, 604/652.4422),
where 50 acres of aggressively manicured property
are suffused with flowers and impressive deep rock
bays. If you do nothing else, be sure to pay a visit to
this place; the scents are splendid and the photo ops
abound. Light meals are available at the gardens'
entrance, and concerts are held here during the
summer months. There are special nighttime lighting
displays around Christmas. The gardens are open
daily; there's an admission charge.

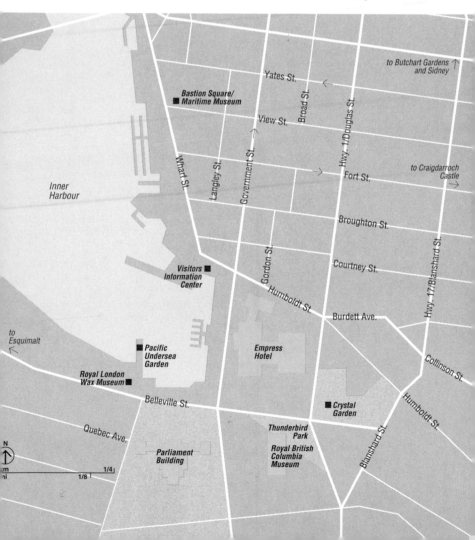

Vancouver, British Columbia

A little more than 200 years ago Captain George Vancouver sailed into nearby **Burrard Inlet** in 1792 to proclaim the area's beauty and claim it for England. Today Vancouver is a big city, with all the civic, cultural, and mercantile amenities (as well as the traffic). It's a cosmopolitan city too. Residents of Hong Kong, fleeing 1997 Chinese control of their island, are migrating here in droves, building what are called "monster houses" to hold the families that follow in their paths. Meanwhile, Seattle has extended its tourist-oriented grasp 250 miles north to Vancouver, opening more than 40 **Starbucks** outlets in the area. And at press time, plans were in the works to restore daily **Amtrak** service between Seattle and Vancouver.

Begin your explorations at **Stanley Park**, a great peninsular greensward northwest of downtown

(reached via Georgia Street), where there are swimming beaches, totem poles, and a zoo. Head downtown where all the establishments along **Robson Street** will attempt to drain away in an afternoon every dollar you've reserved for a week's worth of sight-seeing. On a sunny summer afternoon shoppers flock to the stretch between **Jervis** and **Granville Streets** to browse for linens and modernist lamps, or to circle vulturelike around the shoe stores. The culturally inclined will want to visit the **Vancouver Art Gallery** (750 Hornby St at Georgia St, 604/682.4668), a former courthouse designed by Canadian architect **Francis Rattenbury,** who is also responsible for the **Empress Hotel** and **Parliament Building** in Victoria. Then it's on to big-ticket department stores, such as **Eaton's,** within the **Pacific Centre** mall (701 Granville St, at Georgia St, 604/685.7112), where the background music is of plastic slapping confidently against countertops.

Granville Island Public Market (604/666.6477), an island and former warehouse district on the south

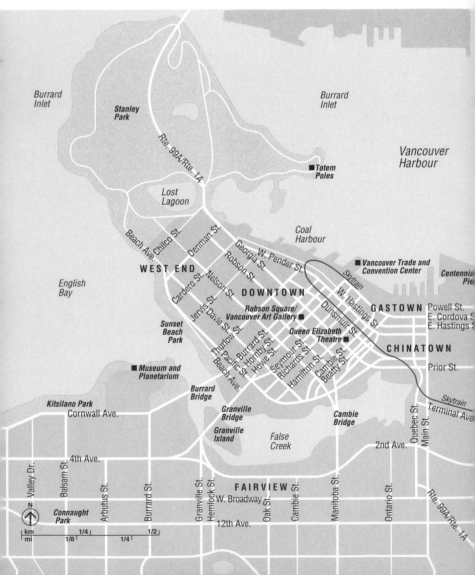

hore of **False Creek,** is thick with shops selling resh produce, Southwestern art, and the makings or beaded bracelets. Stop by the market area's **Granville Island Brewing Company** (604/687.27390) for excellent local craft beers, especially the Lord Granville Natural Pale Ale. If you visit on a Saturday or Sunday, arrive early or count on being engulfed by the masses who descend upon this place at any hint of sunshine.

More endearing—for its eclecticism and richness of architectural fenestration—is **Gastown**, on the opposite side of town. This area was once the center of Vancouver; then it was known as **Granville** (or **Luck-Lucky** to the local Indians) before an 1886 fire leveled much of it. Vancouver residents have reserved much of their heritage in this district. The huge brick-and-terra-cotta **Canadian Pacific Railway Station** (601 W Cordova St, between Granville and Seymour Sts, 604/682.2332) has been refurbished as a terminus for the **Sky Train** system that links downtown Vancouver with the community of **New Westminster.** Several turn-of-the-century edifices have been connected with a skylight to become **Sinclair Centre** (757 W Hastings St, between Howe and Granville Sts, 604/666.4438), a vast hive of card shops and art outlets. Others have been divided with ethnic restaurants and furniture outlets, leading some to say that Gastown has become too commercial.

Its opposite is **Chinatown,** just to the east, where gentrification has not shown its face. The area along **Pender** and **Hastings Streets** is thronged with humanity, particularly on weekend grocery shopping days. And, of course, there are plenty of restaurants to choose from.

Dining trends are tripping over one another here, but Italian restaurants remain especially popular. One of the local favorites is **Villa Del Lupo** (869 Hamilton St, between Georgia and Dunsmuir Sts, 604/688.7436), where chef Julio Gonzalez, along with partners Vince and Mike Piccolo, holds forth in an exceptional restaurant in an old house near the **Queen Elizabeth Theatre.** The menu focuses on Tuscan cuisine with a number of specials every night. For pasta, try the linguine with fresh Atlantic lobster. Service can be a tad slow but have a glass of *vino* and relax. At **Le Coq D'or** (3205 W Broadway at Truch St, 604/733.0035), owner Bruno Born has created an artsy French bistro, serving haute cuisine. Ask for lobster bisque with sherry and crème fraîche to begin, followed by veal medaillons with shiitake and morel mushrooms. Be sure to save room for the crème brûlée.

Olympia Capitol

In 1928 Governor Roland E. Hartley fumed over $7 million that had been spent to create a magnificent capitol complex for Washington state. Even on the day before state executives were to move into their new **Legislative Building** (Capitol Way, between 11th and 16th Aves, 586.8687), Hartley couldn't resist launching a few last darts at Washington's profligate lawmakers. "Today is an epochal day," he told reporters, "but it brings no joy to the heart of the taxpayer." Hartley worked himself into a bluster, the

newspaper drudges scribbling wildly. "May the new building be a deterrent, rather than an incentive, to future extravagance on the part of those in whose hands the business affairs of the state are entrusted." And he didn't stop there. After the complex's dedication, Hartley loaded some of the new capitol's "sumptuous furnishings"—including a few $47.50 spittoons—into an automobile and paraded them about the state to prove that his opponents in Olympia wouldn't hesitate to spend the taxpayers' hard-earned money. Of course, the governor neglected to mention that he had made sure his own office would be the most sumptuous in the building. Perched over **Budd Inlet,** at the southern tip of **Puget Sound,** Olympia shares the mediocrity of other small state capitols. But it's worth visiting, if only for the legislative campus and a couple of other sights.

Washingtonians first started talking about raising a permanent statehouse in 1892. The following year, a nationwide competition was launched to select an architect for the project. From 186 submissions, the commission chose **Ernest Flagg** of New York City, a young relative of Cornelius Vanderbilt and a graduate of the Ecole des Beaux-Arts in Paris. **Flagg** planned a compact, heavily ornamented structure with a short dome and Corinthian columns running the length of its entry facade. Unfortunately, income from government land grants fell short and construction on the building had to be halted soon after its foundations were laid. In 1901 the state made do with downtown Olympia's lordly old **Thurston County Courthouse** (now the **Board of Education Building**) as the temporary residence for Washington state government.

Forces didn't gear up to launch another capitol design competition until 1911. More money was available this go-around, but competition organizers insisted that **Flagg**'s foundation should be integrated into any new conception, probably as the base for one of several buildings on a government campus. **Flagg** naturally assumed that his original commission was still in effect; in the ensuing years, he'd enhanced his reputation by developing Manhattan's Singer Building and the Corcoran Art Gallery in Washington, DC. But the committee chose a couple of virtual unknowns: architects **Walter Wilder** and **Harry White.** Both had labored for a time with the famous New York firm of **McKim, Mead & White,** and in fact their plan for Washington's capitol owed an obvious debt to the work of that firm's late principal, **Stanford White,** who had created the Rhode Island capitol building in the early 1890s.

Wilder and **White**'s initial Roman Classical Revival design called for a **Legislative Building** surrounded by five office structures (one of which would replace the 1908 brick **Governor's Mansion**), as well as an arrangement of stairs and landings descending to Budd Inlet and a grand promenade stretching into downtown, with a new railroad station at its terminus. Budget limitations doomed some embellishments, but results were nonetheless impressive. Of Olympia, architecture historians Henry-Russell Hitchcock and William Seale wrote in their seminal work *Temples*

201

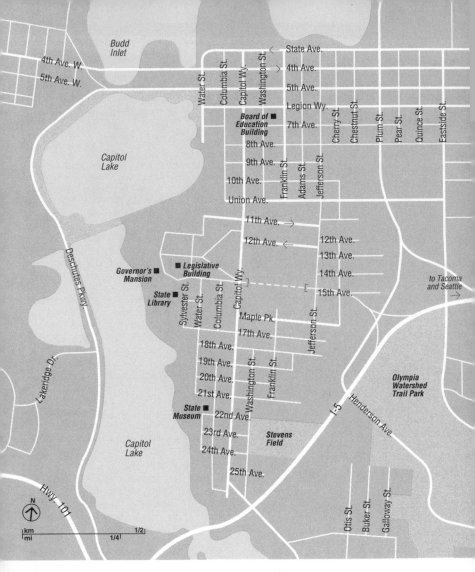

of Democracy: The State Capitols of the U.S.A., "the American renaissance in state capitol building reached its climax." At the time of its raising, the building's dome was the fourth tallest in the world—287 feet from the base—sliding into order behind those of St. Peter's of Rome (408 feet), St. Paul's Cathedral in London (319 feet), and the US Capitol (307 feet). A massive Tiffany chandelier was hung inside its Alaskan marble rotunda. Other components are less ostentatious. Stairs leading to the north-side main entrance offer an imposing approach but pass beneath a largely unadorned pediment. The building presents colonnades on all four elevations, but most are fairly plain-looking. **Wilder** and **White** concentrated much of their decoration along the roofline, giving it an anthemion cresting, and at the east and west ends of the building, where gables are fringed with dentilled cornices. A 1986 face-lift, directed by **Barnett Schorr Architects** of Seattle, scrubbed Mount St. Helens' ash from the dome's exterior. Polish and color—including 48 rosettes and false-gold flourishes on

column capitals—now brighten the rotunda's interior. Architecture and history enthusiasts should not miss an opportunity to visit. Free guided tours are offered daily.

A number of other structures on the eight-acre campus are also worth seeing: the **State Library Building** (16th and Water Sts, 753.5590), a more contemporary colonnaded edifice designed in 1959 by noted architect **Paul Thiry,** contains Northwest art by Mark Tobey and Kenneth Callahan, as well as a collection of published works by Northwest authors; the **Governor's Mansion** (Capitol Way and 15th St, 753.1488), a Georgian Revival–style relic, was designed in 1908 by **Ambrose J. Russell** and **Everett P. Babcock,** who created other manses and some churches around Puget Sound; and the Spanish-style **State Capitol Museum** (211 W 21st Ave, off Capitol Way, 753.2580), formerly the home of banker Clarence J. Lord, which now houses old logging photos, Native American baskets, and more. The museum is open Tuesday through Sunday; donation requested.

Not far away is the **Board of Education Building** Legion Way, between Franklin and Washington Sts, 753.6725), the former **Thurston County Courthouse** that was once home to Washington state's government. Architect **W.A. Ritchie,** armed with only a correspondent's education in architecture from the US Treasury Department, created this and other grand county courthouses in Spokane and Port Townsend. This imposing building blends massive stone archways nicely with rounded tower bases in a Romanesque Revival whole. There was originally a polygonal central tower on this structure, adding to its authoritative image, but that was destroyed by fire in 1928. A compatible west wing dates from 1905, when the courthouse began doubling as Olympia's City Hall. Restoration has made this a most inviting structure.

Mount St. Helens

Many mountains are taller than Mount St. Helens, with its summit 8,365 feet above sea level (it was 1,300 feet higher before its 1980 eruption), but the thrill of poking about what was very recently an active volcano can hardly be beat. Over the decade and a half since it last exploded, plants and wildlife have been returning to these slopes, and so have people—Mount St. Helens is now a national volcanic monument, attracting more than 600,000 people every year.

Begin your explorations with a stop at one or both of the two visitors' centers west of the mountain. Take Exit 49 off Interstate 5 and head about five miles east on Highway 504 to the **Silverdale Visitors' Center.** This center focuses on the area's history and geology, Native American legends, and events leading up to the eruption; there's also an interesting 22-minute video of the blast. A few miles farther along Highway 504 is the newer **Coldwater Visitors' Center,** which opened in 1993. It offers panoramic views of the crater and dome, and interactive exhibits that concentrate on the returning flora and fauna, as well as a bookstore, cafeteria, and gift shop.

For a good view of the blast's results (a crater two miles across and a half-mile deep), head to the northeast side of the mountain. You can pick up maps and get directions at the two visitors' centers (there are two additional information centers along the way) to guide you through the park. **Windy Ridge** (accessed via Forest Road 99) is about four miles north of Mount St. Helens and offers an unforgettable perspective. Park the car and climb a log-and-gravel path from there for still-better views of the mountain and what has become of **Spirit Lake,** once a popular vacation spot. It's so quiet up here it's hard to imagine that in 1980 this place echoed with a sound equivalent to 400 million tons of exploding TNT.

The mountain reopened to climbers in 1987; all must be registered, and steep fines are levied against hotdoggers. The peak season is from mid-May through October, when 110 climbers per day are allowed up to the crater's lip. Permits may be obtained in advance from the **Forest Service**

(Mount St. Helens National Monument, 42218 Northeast Yale Bridge Rd, Amboy, Washington 98601, 750.3900). Seventy spaces per day are filled in advance, but 40 additional spaces are available on what is essentially a first-come, first-served basis. Interested parties must put their names on a list at **Jack's Restaurant and Sporting Goods** (Rte 503, 23 miles east of Woodland and six miles from Cougar, 231.4276) the day before they hope to scale the mountain. At 6PM, the names for the next day are called until all 40 spaces are filled. (Unfortunately, each person can carry 12 people on a permit, so spaces go quickly.) During the off-season (mid-November to mid-May), climbers must still register at **Jack's,** but no advance permits are offered. Most climbers head up **Monitor Ridge** on the south face, a steep trek that may take seven to 10 hours round-trip. (Other routes are also available; ask the Forest Service for maps.) It's a dusty climb during most of the summer, after the snow has melted, so wear high boots to keep the ash out of your socks. Also, don't wear contact lenses—as the ash can get between them and your eyeballs—and bring plenty of water and energy food.

If you want to stay overnight (it's a four-hour round-trip drive on Interstate 5), consider a stay at the **Flying L Ranch** (25 Flying L La, Glenwood, 509/364.3488), a guest ranch popular with hikers, or the **Mio Amore Pensione** (Box 208, Trout Lake, 509/395.2264), a renovated farmhouse bed-and-breakfast.

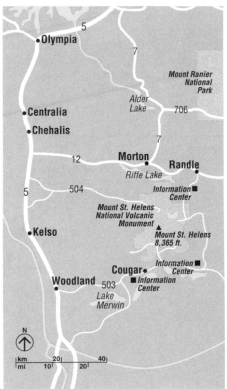

History

Archaeological evidence points to the existence of humans in western Washington as far back as 12,000 years ago. Native Americans living in this area were part of the Northwest Coast culture, which thrived from Oregon to southern Alaska. These clans were different than the great tribes found elsewhere in North America. In fact, they weren't organized as tribes at all, but instead gathered in small villages of family-size clans. Like the pioneers who would later invade the Pacific Northwest, the Native Americans who lived here were fiercely independent. Men became leaders not through any inheritance, but by dint of their abilities. They governed their fishing and gathering societies by example rather than might. Warfare was rare among these villages, and the land was bountiful, with plenty for all. What raids were made on other native groups may have had more to do with procuring slaves than territorial or clan rivalries.

Today's **King County** was populated by natives of the Coast Salish group. They averaged just under five-and-a-half feet in height, and the men had more facial hair than was common among North American Indians. Pressure boards were often applied in infancy to flatten their foreheads. They were fine woodworkers, if somewhat less given to ceremonial carving than their counterparts in what is now British Columbia, using mostly red cedar in their canoes, often-conical hats, and long, narrow houses. Their culture grew up around rivers, and each enclave had a slightly different subdialect (which would later frustrate whites trying to negotiate treaties). Storytelling was a rich tradition and provided an important historical record.

Bustling downtown Seattle was once land belonging to the Duwamish people. (The Suquamish, who were led in the mid-19th century by Chief Sealth, lived on the west side of **Puget Sound** and claimed all the islands between.) After King County's Indian War of 1855-56, which wasn't precipitated by the Duwamish but tainted them nonetheless, the Duwamish were forced onto reservation lands on the western shore of Puget Sound. But over the next decade they drifted back to their old village sites near Seattle and were employed as laborers. Government promises to award them their own reservation were not kept. Once one of the largest Native American groups on Puget Sound, numbering in the thousands, today there are only several hundred Duwamish still inhabiting King County.

1775— Spanish explorer Bruno Heceta sends a boat ashore south of today's **Cape Flattery,** a headland at the entrance to the **Strait of Juan de Fuca.** The crew is captured and killed by Native Americans.

1778— British Captain James Cook, on his third round-the-globe tour, discovers Cape Flattery; however, he plies north rather than east, so he misses Puget Sound completely.

M. BLUM

circa 786 — Sealth, son of Schweabe, chief of the Suquamish and Scholitza Indians, and a future chief himself, is born on **Blake Island,** in western Puget Sound.

790 — The Spanish establish the first white settlement at **Neah Bay,** on the northwest Washington coast.

Spanish explorer Manuel Quimper sails deep into the Strait of Juan de Fuca, encountering and naming some of the **San Juan Islands.**

792 — After circumnavigating **Vancouver Island** in southwestern British Columbia, English Captain George Vancouver and his second lieutenant, Peter Puget, launch two separate explorations of the "inland sea," which Vancouver names Puget Sound.

803 — President Thomas Jefferson dispatches Meriwether Lewis and William Clark west to the mouth of the **Columbia River,** which they reach in 1805. Other Yankees are encouraged to follow.

821 — The Florida Treaty transfers all rights to territory north of the 42nd parallel to the United States. Britain's Hudson's Bay Company (HBC), however, still claims sole rights to the **Oregon Territory,** especially property north of the Columbia River, including present-day Washington state.

845 — In defiance of HBC hegemony, Yankees begin spilling north across the Columbia River.

846 — Finally yielding to US pressure, Great Britain agrees to cede lands south of the 49th parallel (today's US-Canada border) to the Yankees.

850 — The Donation Land Law encourages settlement of America's western territories by awarding 320 acres to every white or "half-breed" who will occupy and farm the land for at least four consecutive years. Another 320 acres are given to any couple married by 1 December 1851.

851 — On 13 November, seven months after leaving Illinois, Seattle founder Arthur Denny and his party of 23 arrive at **Alki Point** aboard the ship *Exact.* Soon after, the families begin relocating to the east side of Elliott Bay for its thicker forests and deeper harbor.

852 — Pioneer Dr. David Swinton ("Doc") Maynard from Ohio arrives at Elliott Bay and befriends Chief Sealth. When he and other city founders decide that their settlement's informal moniker, **Duwamps,** is too inelegant, Maynard suggests "Seattle," a spin on the good chief's name that's easier to pronounce than the guttural Salish original.

Henry Yesler builds Seattle's first steam sawmill. Yesler's initial location is in **West Seattle,** but other pioneers convince him to build instead on Elliott Bay. The strip of land over which he drags his felled trees becomes known as "Skid Road."

1853 — President Millard Fillmore signs the act creating the **Washington Territory.**

1855 — Tensions between whites and Native Americans precipitate King County's so-called Indian War. The American battle sloop *Decatur,* sailing from Honolulu to protect Seattle settlers, rains cannonballs and grapeshot into forests beyond Third Avenue where invaders might be hiding. Natives retaliate by burning nearly every building in the county. After a final skirmish in March 1856, first Territorial Governor Isaac Stevens encourages punishment of warring Indians and the banishment of others to reservations.

1861 — Washington's **Territorial University** (which is later named the **University of Washington**) is built where downtown's **Four Seasons Olympic Hotel** now stands.

1863 — Seattle's first newspaper, the *Gazette,* rolls off its homemade presses. It will publish irregularly for the next three years.

1864 — Asa Mercer, a three-year Seattle resident and the **Territorial University's** first president, travels to New England, where he convinces 11 young women (remembered by history texts as the "Mercer Girls" and by television audiences as the inspiration for "Here Come the Brides") to return with him as wives for very lonely Seattle men. Appreciative bachelors thereafter elect Mercer as their territorial senator, without even expecting him to campaign.

1866 — Chief Sealth, who had somehow persuaded his people to stay out of the Indian War, dies at the Port Madison Reservation in Kitsap County.

1867 — Former San Franciscan Samuel Maxwell founds the *Weekly Intelligencer,* which becomes a daily in 1876 and merges with the failing *Post* five years later to form what is known today as the *Seattle Post-Intelligencer.*

1869 — The territorial legislature grants Seattle a city charter. City population: 1,107.

1870 — Seattle's first grade school is erected.

1872 — Representatives of the **Northern Pacific Railroad** visit Puget Sound to discuss the location of the railway's western terminus. To the shock of Seattleites, Tacoma is selected.

1878 — German immigrant Andrew Hemrich founds a small brewery in south Seattle. He calls his beer Rainier.

1879 — The city's first big fire destroys a number of wooden structures bordering the Waterfront, including **Yesler's Mill.**

1885 — Violence erupts when Seattleites hold an anti-Chinese congress and demand that local Asians leave western Washington. A similar declaration is made in Tacoma, which quickly puts its Chinese on trains headed for Portland. Seattle's Chinese don't depart so easily. After 197 of them are shipped to San Francisco, martial law is declared and US troops halt the forced exodus.

1889— In mid-summer the Great Seattle Fire destroys 30 city blocks in what is now the historical **Pioneer Square** area.

On 11 November Washington becomes the 42nd state of the Union.

1892— Reginald H. Thomson is appointed city engineer and begins a 20-year regrading program that will drastically change Seattle's topography.

1893— The first train traveling James J. Hill's new **Great Northern Railroad** line reaches Seattle from St. Paul, Minnesota. Hill goes on to create the country's first trade and passenger services, between Puget Sound and the Orient.

1896— Bombastic former Midwestern publisher Alden J. Blethen buys the ailing *Press-Times* newspaper and re-creates it as the *Seattle Daily Times.*

1897— The steamship *Portland* arrives in Seattle with a ton of gold from Alaska, beginning a well-publicized and profitable rush through this city of men bound for the Klondike.

1898— Hundreds of thousands of men are processed through a new 640-acre US Army base on **Magnolia Bluff,** bound for the Spanish-American War. The outpost is later named **Fort Lawton,** honoring a general killed in a Philippines skirmish.

1900— Illinois lumberman Frederick Weyerhaeuser, escaping diminishing timber reserves in the Midwest to land at Puget Sound, assembles a partnership to buy 900,000 forested acres in Washington and Oregon from the Northern Pacific Railroad. The Weyerhaeuser Company will dominate Northwest lumbering throughout the century.

Population of Seattle: 80,761—double what it was just 10 years before.

1907— **Pike Place Market** opens.

1908— William Boeing, the son of a wealthy Michigan timber baron, moves to Seattle after several years of running an independent timber operation in Grays Harbor in south Puget Sound.

1909— Seattle holds its first world's fair: the Alaska-Yukon-Pacific Exposition. After its close, the Olmsted Brothers, famed landscapers from Massachusetts, replan the fairgrounds as today's **University of Washington** campus.

1910— Washington's constitution is amended to give women the vote, about 10 years before most other states do so.

The US Congress authorizes construction of a ship canal linking **Lake Washington** with Puget Sound, and ground is broken within a year for the first lock.

Bill Boeing attends an air meet in California, where he becomes fascinated with the art of flying.

1914— As Europe comes to a boil with World War I, a barge loaded with dynamite for shipping to Russia explodes in Elliott Bay. Sabotage is suspected but never confirmed.

1916— Bill Boeing, along with navy officer G. Conrad Westervelt, founds an airplane enterprise on the **Duwamish River**—the beginnings of the Boeing Company.

In **Everett,** just north of Seattle, labor conflicts between members of the Industrial Workers of the World ("Wobblies") and lumber companies lead to the so-called Everett Massacre, during which at least seven men are killed and 31 others are wounded by rifle fire.

Washingtonians vote to make the sale and consumption of alcoholic beverages unlawful—four years before national Prohibition begins.

1917— In April, President Woodrow Wilson engages the United States in World War I. A month later, the **Lake Washington Ship Canal** opens and US Navy training craft begin docking off the **University of Washington** campus.

1918— The nation's influenza epidemic hits Seattle hard, killing 252 people out of every 100,000. Public assemblages are prohibited, and the local health department orders citizens to wear flu masks. The ban on congregation is lifted on 11 November, the day after the war's armistice is signed and a national holiday, so Seattleites can celebrate with each other.

1919— Three years after the Everett Massacre, Seattle hosts the nation's first general strike. Sixty thousand organized workers walk off their jobs in protest of the growing power of capitalists. The city lies tense and quiet for several days, until strikers agree to return to work. Unlike the protest in Everett, no blood is shed here.

1926— Bertha Landes is elected mayor of Seattle. She is the first woman to hold such an exalted post in a major US city.

1929— New York stock markets crash in late October. As with so many other trends since, it takes several months for the Great Depression to reach Seattle.

1931— Huge shantytowns spring up near the Waterfront to house Seattle's many unemployed, mostly men. Officials try to burn out these "Hoovervilles," but they always sprout anew.

1934— Longshoremen in Seattle, San Francisco, and elsewhere are idled for 98 days by the Pacific Coast waterfront strike. Strikebreakers are tossed into Elliott Bay or killed. Mayor Charles Smith fires his police chief for being too lenient with protesters, and orders a crowd of 2,000 strikers clubbed before the strike is settled.

940— The **Lacey V. Murrow Floating Bridge** opens on what is now I-90, connecting Seattle with its eastern suburbs.

941— After the bombing of Hawaii's Pearl Harbor, the United States enters World War II. Boeing Company, the **Puget Sound Naval Shipyard** in nearby Bremerton, and other area manufacturers kick into high gear to feed the war machine. The US Navy assumes control of Puget Sound shipping, and Seattle becomes a major Army transport center.

942— Fearful of spies and saboteurs, the Western Defense Command orders that Japanese people living in Seattle and elsewhere on the coast be interned. Asians from **Bainbridge Island** are the first ones sent to detainment camps in Idaho.

945— The atom-bombing of Hiroshima and Nagasaki ends the war with Japan. Victory celebrations are cooled, however, by news of peacetime economic declines, especially at Boeing, where annual sales drop from $600 million to $14 million.

949— The worst earthquake recorded in Seattle history (measuring 7.2 on the Richter scale) strikes in mid-April.

962— Seattle's second world's fair, the Century 21 Exposition, opens to six months of tremendous success.

963— Proposals to level **Pike Place Market** in favor of high-rise rookeries prompt an aggressive preservation campaign.

965— Efforts begin to revitalize **Pioneer Square,** the city's original—but deteriorating—downtown.

967— National unrest reaches Seattle when the **University of Washington**'s Black Student Union takes control of the university administration building.

Protests against the Vietnam War begin citywide.

Seattle advertising exec David Stern creates the now-ubiquitous Happy Face symbol.

968— The city launches its "Forward Thrust Program" for improvements that include a new domed stadium and parks, and street repairs. However, a plan to reduce traffic congestion by constructing light-rail train lines radiating from downtown into the suburbs fails at the voting booth.

City population: 587,000—seven times what it was at the turn of the century.

970— Boeing, suffering after demand for its jets fails to measure up to estimates, lays off 65,000 workers over the next two years—two-thirds of its work force. Unemployment in the city leaps 12 percent as a result. Despair grows and a billboard proclaims "Will the Last Person in Seattle Please Turn Out the Lights?"

1971— The Starbucks coffee company is founded. Its name comes from the java-dependent first mate in Herman Melville's novel, *Pequod.*

1974— A seven-acre historic district is created to save **Pike Place Market.**

1975— *Harper's* magazine names Seattle the country's most livable city.

1980— **Mount St. Helens** explodes a hundred miles south of Seattle, sprinkling King County with ash.

IBM execs meet with Bill Gates, a 25-year-old techie and co-inventor (with Paul Allen) of the computer language BASIC, who IBM hopes will help create the software needed for a first generation of personal computers.

1983— Citing financial woes, the *Seattle Post-Intelligencer* wins a joint-operating agreement with its rival, the *Seattle Times.*

The Washington Public Power Supply System (not-so-fondly nicknamed "Whoops") defaults on its $7-billion debt, ending hopes for cheap nuclear power in Washington and causing a tremendous ripple effect through Seattle financial circles.

1985— Aldus Corporation, an all-but-unknown Seattle computer software company, ships its first product, PageMaker, and creates a catchphrase to describe its operation: desktop publishing.

1986— Microsoft, Bill Gates's growing computer software company, offers its stock to the public. The value will go up 1,200 percent in just six years.

1989— Voters who are upset by a plague of new skyscrapers and construction-clogged streets in Seattle approve a cap on the height and bulk of downtown buildings.

Well-off Oregonians and Californians move to Seattle in hordes, creating a bizarre seller's market for real estate that drives local home shoppers out of town.

1990— The Lacey V. Murrow Floating Bridge sinks into Lake Washington.

1992— Race rioting in Los Angeles spills over into laid-back Seattle, where vandals and arsonists control city streets for most of a week.

After 60 years, **Longacres** horse track is shut down; Boeing plans to raze it in favor of a flight-training center.

1993— Boeing announces production cutbacks and massive layoffs, causing a tidal wave of doubt over Seattle's fiscal future.

1994— **Nirvana** rocker Kurt Cobain is found dead of a gunshot wound, an apparent suicide, at his home in Seattle.

Index

A

Index

Index

Restaurants

Only restaurants with star ratings are listed below and at right. All restaurants are listed alphabetically in the main (preceding) index. Always call in advance to ensure a restaurant has not closed, changed its hours, or booked its tables for a private party. The restaurant price ratings are based on the average cost of an entrée for one person excluding tax and tip.

★★★★ An Extraordinary Experience
★★★ Excellent
★★ Very Good
★ Good
$$$$ Big Bucks ($35 and up)
$$$ Expensive ($25-$35)
$$ Reasonable (10-$25)
$ The Price Is Right (less than $10)

Index

Hotels

The hotels listed below and at right are grouped according to their price ratings; they are also listed in the main index. The hotel price ratings reflect the base price of a standard room for two people for one night during the peak season.

$$$$ Big Bucks ($180 and up)

$$$ Expensive ($120-$180)

$$ Reasonable ($80-$120)

$ The Price Is Right (less than $80)

$$$$

$$$

Credits

Writer/
Researcher
Loralee Wenger

Writers and Researchers
(Previous Edition)

Heather Doran
 Barbieri
John Doerper
Matthew Fleagle
Nick Gallo
David George Gordon

David Hooper
J. Kingston Pierce
Jodi Pintler Pierce
Giselle Smith
Charles Smyth
Adam Woog

ACCESS®PRESS

Editorial Director
Lois Spritzer

Managing Editor
Laura L. Brengelman

Senior Editor
Beth Schlau

Associate Editors
Kathryn Clark
Kathleen Kent

Contributing Editor
Susan Cutter Snyder

Map Editor
Karen Decker

Manager of Design and
Production
Cherylonda Fitzgerald

Designers
Michael Blum
Carrē Furukawa
Claudia Goulette

Map Designers
Michael Blum
Patricia Keelin

Manager, Electronic
Publishing
John R. Day

Cover Design
Carl Purcell

Special Thanks
Jim Andrews
Jerry Stanton
Ron Warren

Smith Tower

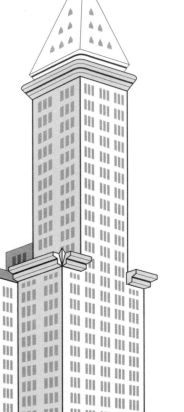

M. BLUM

PRINTED IN HONG KONG

ACCESS®
The Neighborhood Guide

Other Destinations:

- Boston
- Cape Cod, Martha's Vineyard & Nantucket
- Caribbean
- Chicago
- Florence/Venice/Milan
- Hawaii
- Las Vegas
- London
- Los Angeles
- Mexico
- Miami/S. Florida

- Montreal & Quebec City
- New York Restaurant
- Orlando/Central Florida
- Paris
- Rome
- San Francisco
- San Francisco Restaurant
- Santa Fe/Taos/Albuquerque
- Seattle
- Ski Country Eastern US
- Ski Country Western US
- Wine Country France

Pack lightly and carry the best travel guides going: ACCESS®. Arranged by neighborhood and featuring color-coded entries, ACCESS® guides are designed to help you explore—not to leave you standing on the corner thumbing madly through an index. Whether you are visiting Philadelphia or Paris, you'll need a sturdy pair of walking shoes and plenty of ACCESS®.

HarperReference
A Division of HarperCollinsPublishers